Treating Child and Adolescent Mental Illness

A Norton Professional Book

Treating Child and Adolescent Mental Illness

A Practical, All-in-One Guide

Jess P. Shatkin, MD, MPH

W. W. Norton & Company

New York • London

Copyright © 2009 by Jess P. Shatkin

All rights reserved
Printed in the United States of America
First Edition

For information about permission to reproduce selections from this book, write to Permissions, W. W. Norton & Company, Inc., 500 Fifth Avenue, New York, NY 10110

For information about special discounts for bulk purchases, please contact W. W. Norton Special Sales at specialsales@wwnorton.com or 800-233-4830

Manufacturing by Quebecor-World-Fairfield Graphics
Book design by Bytheway Publishing Services
Production manager: Leeann Graham

Library of Congress Cataloging-in-Publication Data

Shatkin, Jess P.
   Treating child & adolescent mental illness : a practical, all-in-one guide / Jess P. Shatkin. — 1st ed.
       p. ; cm.
   Includes bibliographical references and index.
   ISBN 978-0-393-70545-4 (hardcover)
   1. Child psychopathology.   2. Adolescent psychopathology.   3. Child psychopathology—Treatment.   I. Title.   II. Title: Treating child and adolescent mental illness.
   [DNLM: 1. Mental Disorders—psychology.   2. Mental Disorders—therapy.
3. Adolescent Psychology.   4. Adolescent.   5. Child Psychology.   6. Child.
WS 350 S533t 2009]
   RJ499.S4896   2009
   618.92'89—dc22   2009018468

ISBN: 978-0-393-70545-4

W. W. Norton & Company, Inc., 500 Fifth Avenue, New York, N.Y. 10110
www.wwnorton.com
W. W. Norton & Company Ltd., Castle House, 75/76 Wells Street, London W1T 3QT

1 2 3 4 5 6 7 8 9 0

For my mother, Joyce, who showed me the wonder of childhood; and for my father, Eugene, whose dinner table stories about his patients kept me on the edge of my seat.

Contents

Acknowledgments

Upon completion of my residency in general psychiatry and my fellowship in child and adolescent psychiatry at the UCLA Neuropsychiatric Institute, I found myself in central Arkansas providing care to both children and adults as a National Health Service Corps scholar. I had sought out this opportunity while still a medical student, signing on to work as a physician in a federally designated Health Professional Shortage Area in exchange for educational loan support—a decision driven by both idealistic and financial considerations. Once away from the safe confines of the university and the big city, I immediately had two realizations. First, although I was equipped to provide a wide range of patient care, I was still really a novice in the field of child, adolescent, and family mental health. Second, most of the mental health care for youth in our country is provided by individuals not specifically trained to do this work.

As I began seeing children and families at the Western Arkansas Counseling and Guidance Center in Fort Smith, I felt the need to codify my knowledge. I reviewed my notes from residency. I reached for other sources as well and read avidly. I started teaching family practice residents in Fort Smith at the local community hospital. I met with a group of therapists at my clinic each week and learned a great deal from them as we reviewed our cases together. I also met regularly with primary care practitioners in and around Fort Smith and found that they felt poorly equipped to treat child and adolescent mental illness, even though they were often called upon to do so.

After completing my service in Arkansas, I moved to Pittsburgh and took my first academic position as an assistant professor at the Western Psychiatric Institute and Clinic at the University of Pittsburgh. Now 2 years into my career, I felt more knowledgeable, and for the next 3 years I continued to expand both my clinical experience and teaching. The book you have before you began in Pittsburgh with the lectures and seminars that I gave to the general psychiatry residents, developmental-behavioral pediatric fellows, child and adolescent psychiatry fellows, and psychotherapists whom I supervised and taught in my role as Medical Director of the Center for Children and Families. In 2005, I moved to New York University, where I took a newly created position as Director of Education and Training. I have continued to see patients and teach about child and adolescent mental health to trainees, medical students, psychotherapists, and undergraduate and graduate students.

The first I need to thank are my former teachers from UCLA. Although they are far too numerous to name them all, Mark DeAntonio, David Feinberg, Fred Frankel, James McCracken, Caroly Pataki, James Spar, and Michael Strober deserve special mention for training me and even now continuing to share their wise counsel and friendship with me. At the University of Pittsburgh, I worked alongside Boris Birmaher, David Brent, David Kupfer, Martin Lubetsky, Ken Nash, Harold Pincus, and Neal Ryan, each of whom generously mentored me. At the New York University Child Study Center and Bellevue Hospital Center, where I currently work, there are too many to thank, but I am particularly indebted to Lori Evans and Matthew Cruger for educating me on the finer points of behavioral therapies and neuropsychological testing. Surely, few child and adolescent psychiatrists are so fortunate as to count among their friends and colleagues such a star-studded cast of characters.

I must also thank the many therapists, primary care practitioners, general psychiatry residents, pediatric residents, family medicine residents, child and adolescent psychiatry fellows, and undergraduate and graduate students who have participated in my seminars on psychopathology and evidence-based treatment over the past decade. They have taught me, challenged me, and helped me to sharpen my teaching, contributing immeasurably to this book, although I alone bear the fault of any shortcomings. I would also like to thank the children, adolescents, parents, and teachers who have shared their stories with me and allowed me a privileged glimpse into their lives.

There are a number of individuals who have directly supported this project. Harold S. Koplewicz, founder and director of the NYU Child Study Center, who brought me to NYU and whose mentorship and encouragement is enormously appreciated, was instrumental in starting me on this book. Completing all of the research and references was a monumental task, and I was helped immensely by Zoe Scott, Nadia Addasi, and Elana Bloomfield, whose assistance was simply outstanding.

Regis Scott demonstrated remarkable patience as she designed (and countless times redesigned!) the graphics for this book. Kalma Mitchell deserves special mention for her expert transcription of the first draft and her undying support for my efforts. At W. W. Norton, I would like to thank my editor, Andrea Costella, who believed in this project and was kind, patient, encouraging, and at her desk every single time I called, and Kristen Holt-Browning, who thoughtfully guided me through every step of the editing process.

Four individuals who represent the target audience of this text have given generously of their time by reading each chapter and providing me with comments, critique, and areas for further consideration. My best friend, Charles J. Mayer, MD, MPH, a family practitioner in Seattle, Washington, with whom I took an oath in fifth grade that we both would one day become physicians; my best friend-in-law, Mira Renchner-Kelly, LCSW, a psychotherapist in Mt. Kisco, New York; my colleague and friend, Rahil Jummani, MD, a child and adolescent psychiatrist at NYU; and my father, Eugene P. Shatkin, MD, a pediatrician and child and adolescent psychiatrist in Novato, California. My goal in writing this book has been to translate the core essential knowledge of this wonderful and vibrant field, and the absolute material that a high functioning clinician must understand (as I have learned it myself), into a digestible and useful format. These four individuals have helped me considerably with this task.

Finally, and most importantly, I wish to thank my wife, Alice Jankell, our daughter Parker Tillie, and our son Julian, who constantly distracted me with games, theater, swimming, piano practice, wrestling, reading, movies, baseball, gymnastics, chess, tall tales, and all manner of shenanigans, and without whom I would have completed this book far sooner. May it always be so.

Preface

Emerging evidence continues to point to an increase in the prevalence of mental health problems among children, adolescents, and young adults. Whether this increase is due to better diagnosis, an actual increase in prevalence, or both is unknown, but half of all lifetime cases of mental illness are now recognized to begin by age 14 and three-quarters by age 24 (Kessler et al., 2005a). Despite effective treatments, however, there are typically long delays, sometimes decades, between when individuals first experience clinically significant symptoms and when they first seek and receive treatment.

Severe, disabling depression affects approximately 17% of adolescents and young adults nationally, while anxiety in its many forms results in significant impairment in approximately 13% of children and adolescents (Fleming and Offord, 1990; Kashani, Sherman, Parker, & Reid, 1990; Kessler and Walters, 1998; Shaffer et al., 1996). Other mental illnesses, such as attention-deficit/hyperactivity disorder (ADHD, with a prevalence of 3–7%) and bipolar mood disorder (with a prevalence of over 1%), affect smaller numbers but are ubiquitous among children, adolescents, and young adults, causing an untold amount of suffering and lost productivity (Lewinsohn, Klein, & Seeley, 1995). Despite the fact that federal government spending on antidrug measures has increased over tenfold in the last 15 years, over 50% of high school seniors have experimented with an illicit drug, 23% have used an illicit drug within the past 30 days, and over 30% have been drunk within the past 30 days (Johnston, O'Malley, Bachman, & Schulenberg, 2005). Suicide, the most feared and tragic outcome of mental illness, is the third most common cause of death among adolescents and young adults, preceded only by accidents and homicide (Anderson and Smith, 2005).

In addition to simply documenting the epidemiology of mental illness and engaging in treatment, the field of child and adolescent psychiatry is currently making major strides into uncovering the etiology of some of the illnesses affecting our youth. Through basic scientific research and clinical investigation, our understanding of the neurobiological basis of mental illness has grown immensely over the past three decades. Putative genes have been identified for Tourette's syndrome, ADHD, and many syndromes resulting in mental retardation, and the advances in neuroimaging have allowed us to better understand many of the neural networks involved in ADHD, schizophrenia, autism, obsessive-compulsive disorder, and dyslexia (Abelson et al., 2005). As our understanding grows, so will our ability to target treatments for these illnesses. Concurrent with the research advances, the growth in evidence-based treatments, including medications and psychotherapies, has already advanced our ability to treat specific symptoms, such as psychosis, mania, tics, anxiety, hyperactivity, and depression, allowing many individuals to lead healthy, happy, and productive lives.

Mental health practitioners who treat children and adolescents—including social workers, psychologists, educational specialists, and psychiatrists—are in short supply. The United States' Federal Bureau of Health Professions has named child and adolescent psychiatry the most underserved of all medical subspecialties. The current workforce consists of approximately 6,300 child and adolescents psychiatrists, whereas the need has been estimated to be over 30,000 (Kim, 2003; Thomas and Holzer, 2006). Child and adolescent psychiatrists are not alone, however, as the national need for child and adolescent social workers, educational specialists, and psychologists is equally as great.

The disparity in service delivery is also notable. While one in three Caucasian children receive the mental health care they need, the same is true for only one in five African American children and only one in seven Latino children nationwide. Many have advocated that we provide mental health care to our children by establishing clinics in public schools. Such clinics have repeatedly demonstrated themselves to be effective in accessing youth, yet fewer than 10% of our 80,000 public schools provide comprehensive mental health services at this time (U.S. Department of Health and Human Services, 1999).

In the face of service demands that overwhelm our ability to provide care for the many children and families in need, we face a potentially crippling trifecta—first, children represent an underserved and disenfranchised group with no voice of their own when it comes to policy and organizational decision making; second, although our society has taken great strides, there remains significant stigma attached to those with mental illness and to families with a child who is ill; and finally, within the medical establishment itself, psychiatry (and particularly child psychiatry) suffers an undeserved reputation as an ineffectual and weak discipline couched within soft science. This book represents an effort at addressing these concerns and is aimed at an audience of first-line treatment providers.

Few texts currently exist that explain the core scientific knowledge and clinical application of this knowledge for an audience of primary-care practitioners and psychotherapists. While the requirements for training child and adolescent psychiatrists are formally circumscribed by the Accreditation Council for Graduate Medical Education, the fact is that the vast majority of child and adolescent mental health services worldwide are provided by primary-care physicians, psychologists, and all manner of therapists, ranging from master's-level social workers to marriage and family therapists (Accreditation Council for Graduate Medical Education, 2007). Nearly 85% of all psychotropic medications prescribed to children in the United States, including stimulants, antipsychotics, antidepressants, anxiolytics, and mood stabilizers, for example, are written by primary-care practitioners, yet these individuals generally receive virtually no formal training in child and adolescent mental health (Goodwin, Gould, Blanco, & Olfson, 2001). Understandably, most primary-care physicians and therapists do not feel comfortable treating child and adolescent mental illness, but given the paucity of trained specialists, they have little choice.

Consequently, this text has been written as a comprehensive but user-friendly guide for those practitioners who provide the vast majority of child mental health care but who have the least amount of training. This book describes the basics of child and adolescent psychopathology and the treatments that have been shown to work, including medications, psychotherapies, and psychosocial interventions. I am hopeful that it will have great value for a variety of health care practitioners, including pediatricians, family practitioners, nurse practitioners, general psychiatrists, psychologists, occupational therapists, speech and language therapists, social workers, and marriage and family therapists, who all too often find themselves confronted with a mentally ill child who they feel ill equipped to help. This book also provides the core clinical knowledge necessary for entry-level child and adolescent psychiatry residents and psychology interns, and as such I am also hopeful that it will serve as a useful primer for these trainees as well. In addition, this book will have utility as a reference for schoolteachers, school counselors, and concerned parents. Finally, there are a host of undergraduate and graduate courses in child and adolescent psychopathology at colleges and universities nationwide for which this book could serve as a core text. Perhaps most important, my greatest wish for this book is that it be a "call to arms" of sorts, encouraging those who work with, care for, and treat mentally ill children and adolescents to utilize the material within these pages to advocate for more research, earlier screening, and better treatment of our children.

A Note About Clinical Studies

Throughout this book, numerous treatment studies will be referenced. In order to properly interpret these studies, it is important for the reader to have a grasp of various types of methodologies employed in clinical investigations.

Randomized, double-blind, placebo-controlled trials are the gold standard or best type of clinical intervention study, regardless of whether it is a medication, psychotherapy, or community intervention that is being investigated. In these studies participants are randomly assigned to treatment groups. In one group the subjects receive an active treatment, for example, a medication under study. In the other group the subjects receive a placebo or sham treatment. Neither the subject nor the practitioner dispensing the treatment is aware of which treatment is being given, thus the "double-blind" component. There are numerous other types of studies that can be performed, but none provides us with data as reliable as the randomized, double-blind, placebo-controlled trial.

Sometimes a single randomized controlled study does not provide adequate information about a treatment, and the best answer to the study question can be found by combining the results of numerous trials. Systematic reviews report the results from many studies. A meta-analysis combines many randomized controlled trials and reanalyzes the data by putting it into summary form. Meta-analyses are limited in their utility by the "worst" or most limited study among the group, but the results from such pooled analyses often remain very useful.

When it is impossible, unethical, or too expensive to employ a blinded approach, we sometimes engage in treatment studies in an open-label fashion, such that both the subjects and the practitioner know which treatment is being delivered. Open-label studies do not employ a placebo, and therefore it is impossible to determine how many subjects improve simply because they are taking a medication or receiving a therapy, regardless of its effect. Still, open-label studies are often utilized for medications and treatments that are new to the market and provide useful results for the later construction of more detailed and sophisticated studies.

Randomized controlled trials are expensive and take a great deal of time and effort. Consequently, researchers often use observational studies in which groups of people are followed or observed over time. Observational studies may take many forms, including case-control studies, cohort studies, chart reviews, and case reports. In a case-control study, two groups of individuals are viewed retrospectively to determine what caused the disorder or illness. The "cases" are those who have a certain disorder or illness under study, whereas the "controls" are an otherwise similar group who do not have the disorder or illness. By contrast, cohort studies follow a group of individuals prospectively who experienced a similar exposure or share a common characteristic. They are followed over time to substantiate or refute an association between a given exposure or characteristic and a health outcome. Chart reviews and case reports similarly describe the experiences of individuals who have received certain treatments, but these analyses are highly subjective and open to numerous types of bias. Thus, while observational studies are often quicker to complete and are certainly less expensive, their results are generally not highly reliable.

Many studies will be discussed throughout this book. While our greatest power comes from multicenter randomized, double-blind, placebo-controlled trials, we have relatively few of these studies among children and adolescents. Consequently, we must often draw inferences from among the remaining open-label studies and observational data that are available to us, in addition to our clinical experience and evidence from studies of adults.

Treating Child and Adolescent Mental Illness

1

Introduction

The life of a child and adolescent psychiatrist is thrilling. We have the honor of working with children, adolescents, and their families who struggle with difficulties related to their emotions, behavior, and cognition. Yet we are a relatively new group of physicians in a new field. Our professional organization, the American Academy of Child and Adolescent Psychiatry, has been in existence for just over 50 years, and our numbers are still very small. Given the paucity of child and adolescent psychiatrists and psychologists, there is an enormous need for other medical professionals such as pediatricians, social workers, general psychiatrists, and psychologists not trained directly to work with children, along with all manner of physicians, including family practitioners and internists, to help address the mental health needs of children and adolescents.

HISTORY

Prior to the 17th century, children were not generally considered deserving of basic human rights. Recognizing and demarcating childhood itself as a separate and necessary period of time to be cherished and during which time children are nourished, encouraged, supported, and allowed to move through innate developmental phases appears to be a result of social changes emanating from the Victorian Age. Between the 17th and 18th centuries, it is estimated that up to 70% of children died before reaching five years of age. In fact, it was not until the mid-1800s in Western societies that all children were presumed to have the right to some level of education and access to health care. This currently unimaginable situation becomes somewhat understandable when we recognize that because the child mortality rate was remarkably high until 200 years ago, families often did not emotionally invest fully in a child until he had lived past his fifth year, by which point many key developmental milestones had been passed.

Although mental illness was described in adults prior to the 18th century, professional and medical texts rarely discussed children's mental health problems before then. At this time essentially all recognized etiologies for disordered behavior in children were based upon religious explanations and, perhaps to a lesser degree, magic. The separation between medicine, science, religion, and magic was virtually nonexistent, and mental health practitioners, psychiatrists who were sometimes known as "alienists" because the insane were thought to be estranged or alienated from their normal faculties, had very few tools by which to understand, diagnose, and treat mental illness.

Up until the mid-1800s, the predominant theory utilized to explain most health problems was humoral in nature. Humoral theories were based upon the tradition of Galen, a second-century Greek physician who had suggested that disease occurred due to an excess in the production of any one of the four body "humors." As Galen defined them, the humors were blood, yellow bile, black bile, and phlegm. It was believed that the physiological imbalances that resulted from an excess in the production of one of these humors should be treated by nonspecific therapies, such as bleeding, purging, or vomiting.

In Europe the emergence of a social conscience and the effort to treat children with humane care and to provide social protection began to take root following industrialization. Industrialization brought modern thinking but also humanism, and social services became a new consideration. This change likely occurred due to the fact that as cities grew more quickly than their infrastructures could tolerate, injustice and the discrepancy between rich and poor became much more evident. The English philosopher and physician John Locke (1632–1704) advocated for individual rights, asserting that children deserved to be cared for sensitively and raised with affection. Locke's ideas contrasted with the prevailing harsh and frequently indifferent childrearing culture of his time. He also suggested that children are born as a tabula rasa, or a blank slate without preformed mental content or innate ideas, upon which the environment plays a major role in the development of the personality. Without kindness and care, Locke proposed that children would suffer emotional damage. His ideas, drawn in part from numerous philosophers and probably originating in some form with Aristotle, later became a key tenant of psychoanalytic theory.

Jean-Marc Itard (1775–1838) is probably the first physician who documented his efforts to help a special needs child. Victor of Aveyron was found in the French countryside at 11 or 12 years of age, having lived abandoned and alone since the age of 2 or 3. Victor could not speak, was inattentive, and was insensitive to many essential sensations, including temperature. Despite Itard's attempts to socialize Victor, the child was never able to fully rejoin society. Nonetheless, this well-publicized case of an exceptionally deprived child and the subsequent efforts to understand and heal his emotional and cognitive impairments placed an emphasis where heretofore one had not been noted in society.

At the same time, Philippe Pinel (1745–1826), known as the father of French psychiatry, discarded the long-held notion that mental illness was due to possession by demons and began to classify his observations of the mentally ill. He developed the concept of "moral treatment," the idea that the mentally ill should be provided psychosocially humane care and that an emphasis upon moral discipline should accompany all treatment interventions. Pinel also made some of the first efforts into what we now consider to be psychotherapy. He worked solely with adults, but along with American Benjamin Rush (1745–1813), who was a physician, educator, writer, and humanitarian, an increasing recognition of the unique difficulties of the mentally ill began to be appreciated.

Benjamin Rush, who lived and practiced in Philadelphia and whose picture adorns the seal of the American Psychiatric Association, advocated for the abolition of slavery and signed the Constitution of the United States of America. His practice was aimed at providing care for the poor, and his greatest contributions to medical science were the reforms he instituted in the care of the mentally ill during his 30 years as a senior physician at the Pennsylvania Hospital. He was known as a compassionate physician, who replaced routine reliance on archaic procedures with more careful clinical observation and study. The year before he died he published *Medical Inquiries and Observations upon the Diseases of the Mind*, the first American textbook on psychiatry.

Also in America, Dorothea Dix (1802–1887) became an important teacher and social reformer for the treatment of the mentally ill. She established over two dozen benevolent mental hospitals for the treatment of mentally ill and disabled children and adolescents, who had previously been kept in asylums, and in some cases cellars and cages. Although she did not contribute to our understanding of the nature of mental illness, she was a pioneer in addressing the inequities of care.

As infectious disease became increasingly treatable, physicians accepted the idea of a biological basis of disease, illness, and mental illness. Although the mental effects of some physical illnesses came to be recognized by the late 1800s, for example, syphilis and Huntington's disease, still little could be done for afflicted individuals. The first efforts at explaining mental illness from a biological vantage point focused on identifying a physical cause within the patient, and often resulted in blaming the individual for the illness. Consequently, attitudes toward the mentally ill and their treatment shifted yet again to contempt, fear, and negativity. During the late 19th and early 20th centuries, emerging ideas of public health and medicine—such as eugenics, sterilization, and institutionalization—were at times paradoxically used against the mentally ill, to prevent the "insane" from interacting with the rest of society (Mash and Wolfe, 2005).

PSYCHOANALYTIC THEORY

By this time, most mental health practitioners had become discouraged by their inability to treat mental illness in children. Although Sigmund Freud (1856–1939) believed that the origin of mental illness was largely biological, he also believed in the importance of experience in the shaping of psychopathology, and he was the first to imbue mental disorders with meaning by bridging them to childhood experiences. Although currently psychoanalysis does not inspire great faith in the majority of psychiatrists and psychologists, and most do not view psychoanalysis as a "hopeful" movement, in its time psychoanalysis and its theory gave true hope to a small and exhausted field that felt its work was, more often than not, futile. A working theory had been advanced that relied upon psychotherapy as an innovative treatment and suggested that patients could improve, see relief from symptoms, and maybe even be cured of mental illness.

While Freud's theories rested upon the drive to develop and reach sexual maturity, other psychoanalytically oriented theories soon followed. Erik Erikson (1902–1994), for example, imagined a developmental theory that emphasized psychosocial development throughout the entire life cycle. Jean Piaget (1896–1980) developed a theory based upon cognitive development. Others postulated theories that relied upon a genetically determined capacity for the development of patterns or systems of behavior in which a child acts on the environment from the very beginning of his or her life. The clinical implication of these structural theories is that some kind of reorganization within the child is required in order to grow and develop, such as the resolution of an intrapsychic conflict or an alteration of the family homeostasis. The implication is also that without having achieved a certain developmental milestone at a certain time of life, a child will not develop properly and can, therefore, develop mental illness.

Sigmund Freud's drive theory, the most well known of the psychological development theories, suggested that aggressive and sexual drives are the primary motivating forces in our quest for pleasure. In Freud's theory the end goal of development is sexual maturity. He identified five stages beginning in infancy and ending at puberty (see Table 1.1). Jean Piaget identified four stages with the end goal of development being cognitive maturity or adultlike thinking, which would start at infancy and conclude somewhere between about 11 and 16 years of age (see Table 1.2). Erik Erikson's theory comprised eight stages where "normal" development hinged upon successfully traversing eight dichotomies beginning at birth and ending in old age. Perhaps most important, Erikson's model of development was the first to suggest that life is an ongoing process and that one is not fully "developed" simply because he has reached puberty, is able to think abstractly, or can effectively separate from his parents (see Table 1.3).

Table 1.1. Freud's Drive Theory

■ Freud postulated that aggressive and sexual "drives" are the primary motivating forces in our quest for pleasure and that the end goal of development is sexual maturity. Freud defined five stages on the developmental pathway to sexual maturity:

1. Oral Phase (Infancy, birth to 18 months)
   Infants strive to obtain pleasure and relief from discomfort through the most immediate means possible. The greatest source of pleasure is the mouth.
2. Anal phase (a.k.a. Sadistic Phase, 18–36 months)
   As infants develop, they acquire anal sphincter control. A sense of autonomy emerges and the infants derive pleasure from controlling their bowels.
3. Phallic-Oedipal Phase (3–6 years)
   Children work through the Oedipus complex. They have conflicting feelings about their sexual desires and fear of punishment for these feelings. Children will often repress these desires and identify with the same-sex parent instead. The greatest source of pleasure is the genitals.
4. Latency Phase (6–12 years)
   During the elementary school years, defense mechanisms, which bar from consciousness certain unacceptable impulses, are strengthened. The libido is transferred from parents to friends, and children enjoy being with members of the same sex.
5. Puberty and Adolescence
   Adolescents struggle to control sexual and aggressive urges, to separate from their families, to develop sexual relationships, and to achieve a sense of identity. Development is considered complete.

Table 1.2. Piaget's Cognitive Development Theory

■   Piaget identified four major stages of cognitive development:

1. Sensorimotor Stage (birth to 2 years)
   Infants' knowledge of the world is limited to their sensory perceptions and motor activities. Behaviors are limited to simple motor responses to sensory stimuli.
2. Preoperational Stage (2–7 years)
   Children develop language, although they do not yet understand concrete logic. They also become adept at using symbols while playing and pretending.
3. Concrete Operational Stage (7 years to adolescence)
   Children begin to think logically about concrete events but have difficulty understanding abstract concepts.
4. Formal Operational Stage (adolescence)
   Adolescents acquire the ability to think about abstract concepts.

Table 1.3. Erikson's Psychosocial Theory

■   A psychoanalytic theory comprising eight stages, where "normal" development hinges upon successfully traversing dichotomies at each of these eight stages:

1. Basic Trust vs. Mistrust (Birth to 1 year)
   Infants develop the ability to trust based upon the consistency of their caregivers. If trust develops successfully, they acquire confidence and security. Unsuccessful completion of this stage can result in an inability to trust.
2. Autonomy vs. Shame and Doubt (1–3 years)
   Children begin to assert their independence. If encouraged, children become more confident in their ability to survive in the world. If overly controlled, children may doubt their own abilities.
3. Initiative vs. Guilt (3–5 years)
   Children assert themselves more frequently and develop a sense of initiative. If criticized, they develop a sense of guilt.
4. Industry vs. Inferiority (6–11 years)
   Children begin to develop a sense of pride in their accomplishments. If encouraged, they will become industrious. If restricted, children begin to doubt their own abilities.
5. Identity vs. Role Diffusion (11 years–end of adolescnece)
   Adolescents become more independent and begin to form their own identities.
6. Intimacy vs. Isolation (21–40 years)
   Young adults explore long-term relationships with individuals outside of their families. Avoiding intimacy can lead to isolation and loneliness.
7. Generativity vs. Stagnation (40–65 years)
   Middle-aged adults have established careers and settled down within relationships. If they have not achieved these objectives, they may become stagnant.
8. Integrity vs. Despair (over 65 years)
   Elderly adults reflect on their accomplishments and derive integrity from a successful life. If they perceive their lives as unproductive, the result is despair.

Margaret Mahler (1897–1985) did not develop a new theory. Rather, she systematically observed and detailed the unfolding of object relations in children and infants (see Table 1.4). Object relations represents a more modern adaptation of psychoanalytic theory that places less emphasis on the drives of aggression and sexuality as motivational forces and more emphasis on human relationships as the primary motivational force in life. In other words, object relations theory suggests that people seek relationships rather than pleasure (e.g., Freud). Mahler identified six stages leading to the development of normal object relations, beginning at birth and ending somewhere around 5 years of age.

Although most of the psychoanalytic or child development theories were focused on understanding adults, both Anna Freud (1895–1982) and Melanie Klein (1882–1960) were particularly important in applying analytic theories to children. The work of Anna Freud and Melanie Klein led to the development of the field of child psychoanalysis and a recognition of the importance of nonverbal communication such as play and drawing in understanding children.

Table 1.4. Mahler's Observations on Separation and Individuation

- Mahler's intent was not to add new theory but to systematically observe and detail the unfolding of object relations in children and infants.
- Six stages of development lead to normal object relations, predicated upon a recognition of "separateness":

1. Normal Autism (birth to 2 months)
   Infants are detached and self-absorbed. (Mahler eventually abandoned this phase as research in child development disproved the existence of a normally "autistic" phase.)
2. Symbiosis (2–5 months)
   Infants are aware of their mother, but there is no sense of individuality.
3. Differentiation (5–10 months)
   Infants differentiate between themselves and their mothers. They demonstrate increased alertness and interest in the outside world.
4. Practicing Sub-Phase (10–18 months)
   As infants begin to crawl, they explore actively and become more distant from their mothers.
5. Rapprochement (18–24 months)
   Children desire to share their discoveries with their mothers and experience conflicting feelings about staying with their mothers or being more independent.
6. Object Constancy (2–5 years)
   Children understand that they have separate identities from their mothers. As a result, they internalize the representations that they have formed of their mothers. Deficiencies in positive internalization may lead to low self-esteem in adulthood.

BEHAVIORAL PSYCHOLOGY

The first evidence-based psychotherapies in mental health were rooted in behavioral theory and the early investigations of Ivan Pavlov (1849–1936), John B. Watson (1878–1958), and B. F. Skinner (1904–90), whose research first described behavioral conditioning. While psychoanalysis sought to resolve unconscious conflicts, behavioral therapy aimed to shape behavior and improve individual adaptation (Mash and Wolfe, 2005). As the evidence supporting behavioral theory grew, the psychotherapeutic treatments applied in the early 20th century, such as psychoanalysis, became increasingly questioned. In fact, sparse data was generated during this time, other than case reports, which demonstrated the efficacy of psychodynamic treatment interventions in the care of both individuals and groups (e.g., children within group homes and orphanages). In addition, psychoanalytic approaches were acknowledged even by the primary theorists themselves to be most often of little utility for children with developmental disabilities and mental retardation, the very areas where behavioral theorists first demonstrated significant strides.

Throughout the past four decades, research supporting the utility of behavioral therapies has continued to mount, leading to the increased acceptance of behavioral treatments for all manner of difficulties, including anxiety, depression, substance abuse, personality disorders, and disruptive behavior. Since the 1970s, the use of behavioral methods in the treatment of children and adolescents has become and remained more the norm than the exception. Behavioral treatments currently in vogue, such as cognitive behavior therapy (CBT), parent management training (PMT), interpersonal therapy (IPT), dialectical behavior therapy (DBT), applied behavior analysis (ABA), motivational interviewing (MI), and habit reversal training (HRT), will be described in detail throughout this text.

RISK AND RESILIENCE

As we begin to think more about psychopathology, we must consider the multitude of problems that can occur during childhood and interfere with normal child development. We must constantly ask ourselves: *What is normal? What is abnormal? When does an emotional issue or behavioral disturbance become a definable pathology? Which pathologies require clinical treatment and when? Which problems might children simply grow out of? Why do some children struggle more than others with the same symptoms or diagnosis? What accounts for the waxing and waning of symptoms over time? How can one help a child affected by psychopathology to become normal?* These are the core questions addressed in this book.

We speak frequently of risk factors in health care, and mental health is no different. A risk factor is defined typically as a variable (e.g., being physically abused as a child, growing up in poverty, etc.) that increases the likelihood of a negative outcome (e.g., psychopathology, disability, etc.). Epidemiological studies over the past 50 years have clarified a number of primary risk factors for child psychopathology, including poverty, inconsistent and deficient caregiving, parental mental illness, death of a parent, breakup of the family, homelessness, community disasters, early pregnancy, and neonatal complications. These risk factors are particularly damning in the absence of compensatory strengths and resources on the part of the child, family, and social environment. It is remarkable, however, how some children who have numerous risk factors and numerous psychiatric diagnoses seem to be in some way resilient and can traverse the pitfalls of their illness with success. A resilience factor, then, is a variable that decreases the likelihood of a negative outcome, despite being at risk for psychopathology. Resilience factors are much more difficult to categorize and may change over time depending upon the child and the environment. They may typically include self-confidence, flexibility in one's approach to problem-solving, intelligence, coping skills, and emotional support from trusted family members and friends. Individual, family, and social factors all have an impact on the development of a child's resilience.

Although children are faring better today than in the past, still nearly one in five children lives in poverty in the United States and one in six in Canada (Statistics Canada, 2006; U.S. Bureau of the Census, 2005). One-third of youth in the United States experience poverty at some point during their childhood, which is of great concern, given that low income is correlated with many other difficulties that impact mental health, including lower salaries, decreased educational achievement, poor access to health care, inadequate nutrition, a single-parent home, limited resources, and an increased likelihood of exposure to violence. Clearly, poverty takes a tremendous toll on children. Low socioeconomic status confers nearly three times the rate of conduct disorder, two times the rate of chronic illness, and more than twice as many school problems, hyperactivity, and emotional disorders as compared to children who are not poor. Furthermore, the worse the poverty, the greater the incidence of childhood violence, which increases three times in girls and five times in boys over standard rates for those who grow up in poverty (Brooks-Gunn & Duncan, 1997; Mash & Wolfe, 2005; McLoyd, 1998; Ross, Shillington, & Lockhead, 1994; Tremblay, Pihl, Vitaro, & Dobkin, 1994).

Another unfortunate but ubiquitous feature of childhood is abuse. Nearly 1 million substantiated cases of child abuse and neglect occur annually in the United States and approximately 60,000 in Canada. Over one-third of children 10–16 years of age in the United States, or 6 million of our youth, are physically or sexually assaulted during these years by family or others they know. Unquestionably, abuse and trauma in their many forms (physical, sexual, and emotional) interfere with normal child development and predispose children and adolescents to psychopathology (Mash & Wolfe, 2005; Trocmé & Wolfe, 2001; U.S. Department of Health and Human Services, 2003).

GENDER, RACE, AND CULTURE

Boys and girls commonly express psychopathology in different ways. Virtually all neurodevelopmental disorders—such as mental retardation syndromes, autistic spectrum disorders, Tourette's syndome, and ADHD—are more common in boys than in girls for reasons that remain elusive. Some of the differences we see between boys and girls may have to do with the established definitions of these disorders. For example, while boys may demonstrate overtly aggressive behavior, such as fighting and property damage, girls may demonstrate aggression in more covert means, such as gossiping or spreading rumors. Consequently, girls may less commonly receive a diagnosis of conduct disorder or oppositional defiant disorder in part, at least, because the infractions made by boys are much more easily witnessed. In general, girls tend to internalize their distress, resulting more often in difficulties with anxiety, depression, somatization, eating disorders, and emotional withdrawal. Boys, in contrast, tend to demonstrate more externalizing problems, such as aggression, hyperactivity, and delinquency. Figure 1.1, which shows internalizing and externalizing behavior scores from the Child Behavior Checklist (a standardized rating scale of children's behavior), demonstrates that the developmental trajectories of boys and girls differ substantially. At a very early age boys and girls have roughly the same rate of internalizing troubles, but as they age, females show a greater preponderance. By contrast, the externalizing disorders are more common in males at a younger age, but as the children reach late teen years the proportion of males and females begins to equalize (Bongers, Koot, van der Ende, & Verhulst, 2003).

Understanding and employing resilience is key to preventing and tempering child mental illness. Some resilience factors are shared by the sexes and include positive same-gender role models and emotional support. Resilient girls are generally raised within households where risk-taking

Figure 1.1. Male and female differences in the expression of externalizing and internalizing behaviors. Measures of externalizing disorders on the Child Behavior Checklist are greater for boys than girls at a young age. By adolescence, the differences between the genders diminish. Internalizing problems, on the other hand, occur in roughly the same number of boys and girls at a young age, but by adolescence girls tend to demonstrate more internalizing problems than boys.
Adapted from Bongers et al. (2003).

and independence are encouraged. These girls also have significant emotional support from a primary female caregiver, such as a mother, older sister, or grandmother. Resilient boys, similarly, are generally raised with a positive male role model, such as a father, older brother, or grandfather. In contrast to girls, however, boys appear to benefit more clearly from significant structure and rules within the home, along with being encouraged to express their emotions (Werner, 1995).

There are other differences between males and females that emerge as early as infancy. It has been generally reported that men use far fewer words per day on average than women and that beginning in the teen years females may receive a larger neurochemical (e.g., dopamine) "rush" from talking and gossiping than males. By 8 weeks in utero, testosterone produced by the testes in males begins to lead to enlargement of the amygdala, where aggressive and fear-driven behaviors are believed to be housed. Male babies also generally show more interest in objects, while female babies show more interest in faces. In fact, female babies increase their visual interest in faces by 400% within the first 3 months of life, whereas males demonstrate virtually no change within this time period. In addition, girls' brains typically mature about 20% faster than boys' until the mid-teen years, which may explain why girls frequently tend to develop language quicker, toilet train earlier, and adjust their behavior to societal expectations and norms more rapidly (Brizendine, 2006).

Race and culture also have an impact on the development of child psychopathology. Minorities are overrepresented in many disorders such as substance use, delinquency, and teen suicide (Mash & Wolfe, 2005). These differences, however, are largely a result of coexisting conditions more commonly encountered by racial minorities, such as poverty, limited access to care, and the quality of care received by most minority groups. Consequently, once socioeconomic status, age, gender, and referral status are controlled for, few differences remain in the rate of psychological disorders among children of different races (Boney-McCoy & Finkelhor, 1995).

As noted, the barriers to receiving and accessing care are greater among racial minorities. We know, for example, that children without insurance receive less medical attention and that African American children with ADHD are less likely to receive stimulants than Caucasian children. The reasons for these discrepancies are not exactly clear, though there is no doubt that poor children and those from ethnic minorities reap far fewer benefits from society. To compound the problem, racial and ethnic minorities have historically been neglected in studies of child psychopathology, and most research has not been based upon diverse populations. Thus, our understanding of risk and resilience factors, epidemiology, course of illness, and treatment strategies for child and adolescent mental illness is largely limited to the dominant, Caucasian population (Centers for Disease Control, 2001; Children's Defense Fund, 2002).

ADOLESCENCE

Adolescence, the period between childhood and adulthood, is the physically healthiest time of life. The improvements in strength, speed, reaction time, reasoning, and immune function, as well as increased resistance to the extremes of heat, cold, hunger, dehydration, and most types of injury, are truly phenomenal. Ironically, however, the overall morbidity and mortality rates increase by 200% between late childhood/early adolescence (10–14 years of age) and later adolescence (15–19 years of age). The primary reasons for this paradox (e.g., the increases in mortality and morbidity seen in adolescence) are the changes seen in behavior, cognition, and emotion that take place during these years.

The three most common causes of death in adolescence are accidents, homicide, and suicide (see Table 1.5). In addition, sickness or morbidity due to proper psychopathology increases greatly during this time. Depression, for example, increases from a prevalence of around 4% in school-age children to around 15% among adolescents. Rates of substance abuse, eating disorders, anxiety disorders, and psychotic disorders as well all rise greatly during the teen years and lead to major increases in morbidity, approaching or reaching adult levels in some

Table 1.5. Leading Causes of Death in 15–19 year-olds

— UNITED STATES, 2001 —	
Cause	# of Deaths
Accidents	6646
Homicide	1899
Suicide	1611
Cancer	732 ⎫
Heart disease	347 ⎪
Congenital anomalies	255 ⎪
Chronic lower respiratory disease	74 ⎬ 1599
Stroke	68 ⎪
Influenza and pneumonia	66 ⎪
Blood poisoning	57 ⎭

Source: Anderson and Smith (2003).

cases. However, it is the sensation-seeking and risk-taking behavior that is of greatest concern during adolescence. Imagine, for example, Romeo and Juliet. They were only 14 years of age and had known each other for only four days, yet they each committed suicide because they felt they could not live without each other. This type of erratic and emotionally charged behavior is characteristic of adolescents (Anderson & Smith, 2003).

Why adolescents demonstrate such an increase in risk-taking behavior is not entirely clear. A Darwinian or evolutionary argument would posit that in order to become successful and to survive as one approaches adulthood, one must become more of a risk-taker, sensation seeker, and adventurer when striking out on one's own. In current society there is also peer pressure, which has an influence, and there is, of course, the growth and development of the brain itself.

We recognize now that cognitive development (that is, planning, reasoning, problem-solving, logic, and organization) correlates more strongly with age and experience than with sexual and physical maturation. While early theorists postulated that child development is complete by the time of sexual maturity (e.g., Freud) or abstract cognition (e.g., Piaget), neuroscience now tells us otherwise. We currently believe that while motor tracks are fully mature by 15 to 16 years of age, cognitive tracks may not be fully developed until one's mid-20s, and social and emotional nerve tracks may not fully mature until the mid-30s (Keverne, 2004; Larson et al., 2007; Levin & Hanten, 2005; Yakovlev & Lecours, 1967). Consider these findings for a moment—if correct, they clearly help to explain why adolescents are so physically capable and can be such wonderful athletes, while also clarifying why they make such impulsive decisions and are extremely swayed by their emotions.

The prefrontal cortex, the newest part of the brain and that which more than any other cerebral structure makes us truly "human," acts to inhibit impulsive and motivational drives. Yet this structure is still somewhat immature in adolescence. Thus, when dopamine increases in the nucleus accumbens (secondary to drug abuse or sexual activity) and a pleasure response occurs in the limbic system, an adolescent may have little ability to inhibit the motivation to continually seek out such pleasurable activities. Likewise, the degree of frontal lobe control needed to inhibit hyperactivity, sit still, and study instead of being distracted by anxiety, or take cognitive control of depressive thoughts, may be more than most adolescents can manage. Other factors also potently influence the adolescent brain, including the onslaught of new hormones, many of which are not understood and have not yet been characterized. The normative pruning of serotonin circuits in the adolescent brain may also lead to an increase in impulsivity, and common maladaptive behaviors of adolescence, such as a decrease in sleep and an increase in the use of caffeine and other substances, undoubtedly contribute to the impairments in judgment that we commonly see during these years.

PSYCHIATRIC DIAGNOSIS

Tolstoy opens *Anna Karenina* (1877) with the statement: "Happy families are all alike; every unhappy family is unhappy in its own way." While literate and wonderfully thoughtful, from a psychiatrist's point of view, Tolstoy's statement is in error. In contrast to Tolstoy, who believes that happiness is all the same but that unhappiness is always unique, a psychiatrist accepts a great range of "normal" or "happy." In other words, there are many ways to feel good, many ways to be successful, and many satisfactory ways to experience one's emotions, behavior, and cognition. However, unhappiness or mental illness increasingly can be traced to specific causes or etiologies and most often expresses itself in characteristic patterns depending upon the illness. For example, the symptoms of depression are reproducible in patient after patient and include difficulties with sleep, appetite, energy level, concentration, mood, pleasure-seeking behavior, hopelessness or guilt, slowed or agitated thinking or behavior, and suicidal thoughts. Virtually every individual who appears clinically depressed presents with a constellation of these symptoms. The same holds true for most psychiatric diagnoses, including anxiety, ADHD, schizophrenia, dementia, and so forth. While the causes of these illnesses have heretofore remained largely hidden, research into disease etiology is also increasingly demonstrating that these illnesses are perhaps more alike than they are dissimilar.

In defining a psychological disorder we must look for a pattern of behavioral, cognitive, emotional, and physical symptoms demonstrated by an individual that result in some level of disability, a risk of suffering further harm, or distress. In the words of psychiatry, there must be an associated "functional impairment"; that is, a diagnosis is not valid, regardless of symptoms, without impairment or difficulty in achieving one's milestones or maintaining success in work, school, or relationships.

If an internist believes a patient may have diabetes, the physician takes a complete medical history and then requests a few simple blood tests that can clarify the problem based upon abnormal levels of blood glucose. However, the field of mental health has no such reliable biological tests to determine the presence, severity, or treatment response for mental illness. Consequently, we have had to develop a diagnostic system or nosology to help clinicians recognize the existence and severity of mental illness.

The most commonly employed diagnostic code book in the field of mental health is the *Diagnostic and Statistical Manual of Mental Disorders* (*DSM*) of the American Psychiatric Association. We are currently using the fourth edition of this manual, which was published in 1994. Having gone through four editions to date, with a fifth planned for the next decade, we are consistently refining our understanding of the key symptoms that indicate various mental diagnoses. The *DSM* is a vital guidebook that aids us in the diagnosis of mental illness based upon symptoms. Still, being able to list important symptoms has not further clarified the etiology or our understanding of the origin of mental illness.

The *DSM* is phenomenological in that it builds diagnoses upon symptoms or phenomena, and a certain number of symptoms are required in order to meet diagnostic criteria. For example, the *DSM-IV* lists nine symptoms of depression, which include: (a) depressed or irritable mood; (b) anhedonia; (c) suicidal thoughts; (d) impairment in sleep; (e) psychomotor agitation or retardation; (f) change in appetite; (g) difficulty concentrating; (h) guilt or hopelessness; and (i) a decrease in energy. While many individuals, perhaps the majority, may experience one or two of these symptoms on any given day, the *DSM* requires that five of nine of these symptoms be present for at least a 2-week period in order to establish a diagnosis of depression. Five of nine is not a magical combination of symptoms—it is simply the point at which significant impairment generally appears to result. It is therefore the number of symptoms selected as the diagnostic set point.

While extremely useful in helping us to understand or categorize which individuals suffer from which problems, it is important to remember that the diagnoses in the *DSM* are symptom-driven and may be the result of biological, psychological, and social factors, many of which may be very difficult to ascertain. Throughout this book, we will refer to the *DSM* for diagnoses repeatedly, but we will not reprint them here per se, as they are easily found in the *DSM*. This text, rather, will focus on providing the clinician with a brief understanding of the clinical presentation, etiology, epidemiology, and natural history of each disorder, followed by an explanation of *how* to ascertain the diagnosis. This text comprises not simply symptom checklists, as in the case of the *DSM*, but a more thorough understanding of how to determine the presence of symptoms within affected individuals and the evidence-based treatments (including medication, psychotherapy, and psychosocial interventions) that can be utilized to treat each disorder.

Understanding the history of the *DSM* is instructive for the student of psychopathology. The first edition of the *DSM*, the *DSM-I*, was published in 1952 (American Psychiatric Association, 1952). This slender volume considered all disorders that did not have a clearly defined cause to be "reactions" or psychologically charged responses to some emotional trauma. There were three primary categories of reaction: (a) schizophrenic reactions; (b) antisocial reactions; and (c) psychoneurotic reactions, which included the anxiety reaction, dissociative reaction, conversion reaction, phobic reaction, obsessive-compulsive reaction, and depressive reaction. The *DSM-I* was well couched within the predominant psychoanalytic theories of the day and upon Freud's emphasis of the importance of mastering anxieties generated by characteristic conflicts at particular stages of psychosexual development. The authors of the *DSM-I* agreed that psychopathology was due to the failure of resolving these conflicts, and consequently it was implied, if not absolutely stated, that anxiety lay at the core of all psychiatric diagnoses.

The *DSM-II* was published in 1968 and provided, for the first time, signs and symptoms of the disorders themselves, although no formal diagnostic criteria were described. In 1973, during the sixth reprinting of the *DSM-II*, homosexuality was finally removed as a mental disorder. Heretofore, homosexuality had been a catchall category for all "sexually deviant" behaviors referenced in the *DSM*.

Clear diagnostic criteria for the disorders were first published in the *DSM-III* in 1980. This version of the *DSM* demonstrated better interrater reliability, indicating that different examiners were, for the first time, highly likely to arrive at the same diagnosis for the same patient when using these diagnostic parameters. The *DSM-III* was also a landmark for child and adolescent mental health by including a group of disorders "usually first present in infancy, childhood, or adolescence," including reactive attachment disorder, separation anxiety disorder, overanxious disorder, and avoidant disorder. In addition, adult anxiety diagnoses were now permitted to be applied to children and adolescents.

The most fundamental changes to the *DSM* occurred in 1987 with the publication of the *DSM-III-R* (revised). While both the *DSM-III* and *DSM-III-R* were criticized by some researchers, particularly because of the inclusion of childhood diagnoses due to incomplete evidence of their validity at that time, the *DSM-III-R* moved the pendulum still further away from psychiatry's psychoanalytic history by taking an entirely atheoretical approach to the diagnosis of psychiatric illness and eliminating altogether the term *neurosis* from the lexicon. The *DSM-IV* (our current incarnation) of 1994 largely provided a refinement of the nosology. At this time the *DSM* remains a necessary and highly useful tool to the practitioner, which allows clinicians to agree on patient diagnoses, the ultimate goal of which, of course, is to determine the best treatment for each patient.

2

Attention-Deficit/Hyperactivity Disorder

Attention-deficit/hyperactivity disorder (ADHD) is the most commonly diagnosed childhood behavioral disorder. Over the past two decades, our ability to diagnose and effectively treat ADHD has improved significantly, and we are now able to help children who would have otherwise long suffered without assistance. Children affected by ADHD more often than not suffer coexisting conditions, such as learning disorders and behavioral difficulties, that are equally if not more disruptive to their healthy development.

CLINICAL PRESENTATION

Throughout the first half of the past century, ADHD was thought to be the result of developmental problems in utero, and the diagnosis given to extremely hyperactive and impulsive children was *minimal brain damage*. As studies of affected children grew, it was realized that these children were not technically brain damaged and that the concept of minimal brain damage, therefore, was in error. From approximately 1950 to 1970, those children with severe hyperactivity and impulsivity were, rather, considered to suffer from a purely hyperkinetic or hyperactivity syndrome. The *DSM-II* (American Psychiatric Association, 1968) recognized a diagnosis similar to what we now view as ADHD for the first time and labeled it within the psychiatric lexicon as the *hyperkinetic reaction of childhood*.

During the 1970s, over 200 peer-reviewed publications brought to the forefront a frequently co-occurring symptom of those children who suffered impairing hyperactivity and impulsivity, namely inattention. Based upon this wealth of new scientific data, the entire concept of the disorder was reconsidered from one of hyperactivity to one of inattention by the time the *DSM-III* was published (American Psychiatric Association, 1980). The new diagnosis, "Attention Deficit Disorder (with or without symptoms of hyperactivity)," reflected this change. Attention deficit now became the cornerstone or sine qua non of the diagnosis itself. As researchers learned more during the following decade that these three symptoms were most commonly intertwined and present in some combined fashion, with the publication of the *DSM-III-R* (revised) (American Psychiatric Association, 1987), attention deficit disorder (ADD) was once again renamed; this time as ADHD with a series of mixed criteria. The diagnosis was now based upon the presence of at least 8 of 14 symptoms, which could constitute a variety or intermingling of difficulties including hyperactivity, impulsivity, and inattention. With the publication of the *DSM-IV* (American Psychiatric Association, 1994), our current psychiatric diagnostic codebook, the diagnosis became "ADHD (primarily inattentive type, hyperactive/impulsive type, or combined type)." As our understanding of the disorder has grown, then, so has our ability to diagnose it more accurately, which is reflected in each successive version of the *DSM* (Barkley, 1998).

Children diagnosed with ADHD can present clinically in myriad ways. The most easily recognizable children are remarkably physically active and almost always viewed by others as disruptive and extremely impulsive. Many of these children are falsely believed to be willfully dismissive of others' needs and desires, and as a result they are increasingly ostracized as they age. Preschool children are particularly forgiving of their peers' idiosyncrasies, but with age children become less forgiving, especially when one of them is always moving too quickly from topic to topic, rarely able to stay focused in a school or extracurricular activity, and distracting for others to be around. As a result, we commonly see affected children who are untreated by school-age years struggling with their self-esteem, for other children simply do not want to learn and play with them. Such social isolation, however, only compounds the feelings that these children already have about themselves as they indeed wonder why they cannot focus, stay seated, and control their impulses like their peers.

Another type of child affected by ADHD is simply inattentive but not generally hyperactive or impulsive. This child typically does better with peers but will also soon be filled with self-doubt as to why he cannot stay focused like his friends, be attentive on the ball field, and complete his schoolwork in the allotted time. As parents and teachers make fruitless but genuine efforts to help this child with his schoolwork (often employing tutors at home and special assistance at school), they become increasingly frustrated with his apparent lack of drive and determination. None of this dissatisfaction goes unnoticed by the child who begins to view himself as an academic failure, incapable of succeeding in school and often with friends. After years of disappointment, akin to the child affected by hyperactivity and impulsivity, he is likely to lose faith in himself, undermine his own academic and social progress, and despair for his future.

ETIOLOGY

The etiology of ADHD is not clear, but research increasingly points to the cause of the disorder as neurological with limited environmental influence. Numerous brain structures have been implicated in some fashion, including the dorsal lateral prefrontal cortex, the dorsal anterior cingulate cortex, the striatum, and the parietal cortex. Imaging studies have demonstrated that the caudate nucleus and globus pallidus (striatum), which contain a high density of dopamine receptors, are smaller in children affected by ADHD than in control groups. This research has also demonstrated that children with ADHD have smaller posterior brain regions (e.g., the occipital lobes), particularly in areas that coordinate the activities of multiple brain regions, such as the rostrum and splenium of the corpus callosum and the cerebellar vermis. Furthermore, we are now convinced that children with ADHD have smaller brain volumes in virtually all regions. Total cerebral volume, including cortical white and gray matter, is smaller by about 3%, and cerebellar volume is smaller by about 3.5%. These volumetric abnormalities persist with age, except those found within the caudate nucleus. There appear to be no gender differences, and the volumetric findings correlate with the severity of ADHD symptoms. Importantly, children who are unmedicated for ADHD show roughly the same differences in brain volume abnormalities as compared to those children who have been medicated or treated for ADHD, suggesting that the medication itself is not responsible for these changes (Castellanos et al., 2002).

Research has also begun to demonstrate that children suffering from ADHD have decreased cortical thickening in the anterior cingulate cortex, a key region involved in cognitive control (Makris et al., 2007). Some studies have found that children with a worse clinical outcome have a thinner left medial prefrontal cortex at baseline than those children with a better outcome (Shaw et al., 2006). Taken as a whole, these studies increasingly point to neurological abnormalities in children diagnosed with ADHD.

Another potential cause of ADHD lies within the genetic code, and there are a number of genes that have been found to date to be associated with the disorder. Rare mutations in the human thyroid receptor beta

gene on chromosome three have resulted in symptoms suggestive of
ADHD and are found in those with a general resistance to thyroid hormone (Hauser et al., 1993). The dopamine transporter gene on chromosome five has also been implicated as a possible genetic cause of ADHD
(Gill, Daly, Heron, Hawi, & Fitzgerald, 1997). When the dopamine presynaptic transporter (DAT), which is coded by chromosome five, is somewhat overly active and reabsorbs too much dopamine, the postsynaptic
neuron cannot be fed adequate amounts of the neurotransmitter, which
may result in an inability to maintain focus and attention (see Figure 2.1).
Lastly, the dopamine receptor D4 gene on chromosome eleven and the dopamine receptor D5 gene on chromosome four have also been implicated,
such that malfunction of these genes on the postsynaptic receptor does not
allow transmission of dopamine (Swanson et al., 1998) (see Figure 2.2).
Malfunction at chromosome five, eleven, or four and the resulting impairments at the dopamine transporter gene, D4 or D5 receptors would support the dopamine hypothesis of ADHD; that is, essentially that somehow a
deficiency of dopamine leads to the clinical findings of ADHD.

ADHD is a familial illness. Family studies have repeatedly demonstrated that a sibling's risk of having the disorder is two to five times
greater than the general population risk. The parents are also at risk, and
there is a three to five times increased likelihood that if a child is affected,
a parent is also affected. Twin studies have shown that ADHD is highly
genetically bound. Monozygotes (identical twins) have about an 80% risk

Figure 2.1.   Significance of DAT dysfunction.

Figure 2.2.   Significance of DRD4 or DRD5 dysfunction.

of suffering ADHD if the identical sibling is affected. ADHD is more tightly genetically bound among monozygotes than breast cancer, asthma, and schizophrenia (Faraone, 2000; Hemminki & Mutanen, 2001; Palmer et al., 2001).

Finally, there are a number of potential nongenetic causes of ADHD that are also likely to be neurobiological in nature. Children born of low birth weight, for example, are more likely to suffer ADHD symptoms as they age. The same is true for children who have suffered traumatic brain injury, experienced excessive perinatal stress, whose mothers smoked during pregnancy, and who faced severe early deprivation. The precise reasons for these findings are not clear, yet it appears to be more than simply a correlation. Rather, it is likely that infants and children who face such circumstances suffer subsequent developmental and neurobiological damage resulting in symptoms of inattention, hyperactivity, and impulsivity (Nigg & Casey, 2005).

EPIDEMIOLOGY

Approximately 1 in 20, or 5% of children worldwide, are affected by ADHD. International research has demonstrated that between 3% and 7% of schoolchildren are affected, although in some studies the percent of affected children is far greater (Goldman, Genel, Bezman, & Slanetz, 1998).

As with virtually all neurobehavioral disorders of childhood, males are more commonly affected than are females. In the past when ADHD was viewed largely as a disorder of hyperactivity and impulsivity, the vast majority of patients diagnosed were male. Our current understanding of ADHD, however, as not only a hyperkinetic disorder, but also a disorder of inattention, has led us to study females more carefully. We now understand that the likelihood of boys and girls being affected is much less discrepant than we had previously thought, such that we now believe males are probably affected only about twice as often as females. Girls typically but not always show less hyperactivity, exhibit fewer conduct problems and externalizing behaviors, and are more often to be "politely inattentive" and not as overtly disruptive as boys.

Over 80% of children with ADHD demonstrate some sort of psychopathology as adults. Over half and perhaps as many as two-thirds continue to struggle with ADHD, but other impairments, such as mood, anxiety, and learning disorders, commonly persist or develop (Cantwell, 1996). Furthermore, adults with ADHD face more problems maintaining employment, an increase in sexual and reproductive risks, an increase in motor vehicle accidents and traffic violations, an increase in substance abuse, and a higher accident rate than those not affected by ADHD (Barkley, Murphy, & Kwasnik, 1996; Biederman, Wilens, Mick, Faraone, & Spencer, 1998; Biederman, Petty, et al., 2008). This increase in risk translates into higher associated medical costs and more outpatient medical care, inpatient hospitalizations, and emergency room visits for those with ADHD (Leibson, Katusic, Barbaresi, Ransom, & O'Brien, 2001).

Parents commonly ask about the risk of substance abuse among children who are treated for ADHD with stimulants. After much investigation, we now recognize that individuals with ADHD have a greater risk of substance abuse than the general population. However, the data clearly show that adolescents with ADHD who have been treated with stimulants have, in fact, lower rates of substance abuse than untreated adolescents who suffer ADHD (Wilens et al., 2008).

Primary-care practitioners are increasingly called upon by patients to treat ADHD. ADHD-related outpatient visits to primary-care practitioners increased from 1.6 million to 4.2 million between 1990 and 1993, along with an increase in the use of stimulant medications to treat the disorder (Swanson, Lerner, & Williams, 1995). Between 1991 and 2000 the annual production of methylphenidate rose by 740% in the United States. Production of amphetamine increased 25 times during this same time period (Diller, 2002).

Although we find ADHD present within every culture studied, still the United States uses the vast majority of stimulants. In the year 2000

America utilized 80% of the world's stimulants, with most other industrialized countries using about 10% the amount the United States uses (Diller, 2002). Canada uses stimulants at about 50% of the U.S. rate. Hawaii has the lowest per capita use of methylphenidate by a factor of about five. High stimulant utilization areas are found mostly in the eastern United States near college campuses and clinics that specialize in the diagnosis and treatment of ADHD (U.S. Drug Enforcement Agency, 2000). In 2004 approximately 2.5 million children in the United States ages 4 to 17 years took medication for ADHD, and sales of medications used to treat ADHD rose to 3.1 billion dollars in 2004 from 759 million in the year 2000 (Food and Drug Administration, 2006; Scheffler, Hinshaw, Modrek, & Levine, 2007).

Concurrent with an increase in the diagnosis and treatment of ADHD in children, adults have also been recognized to suffer from ADHD. The use of medications in adults increased 90% between 2002 and 2005, and the use of medications to treat ADHD in adults age 20–44 rose 19% in 2005 alone. That same year an estimated 1.7 million adults age 20–64 years and 3.3 million children under 19 took a medication for ADHD (Okie, 2006).

With all of the increase in treatment, we would be remiss if we did not ask ourselves why the diagnosis has appeared to occur more frequently in recent years. There are numerous possible explanations. Perhaps the most evident reason is that physicians and allied professionals are much better at recognizing ADHD today than we were in the past. Increasingly, not only child and adolescent psychiatrists, but also neurologists, pediatricians, and primary-care practitioners, including primary-care physicians, nurse practitioners, and physicians' assistants, are being trained in the identification and treatment of ADHD.

Many wonder whether an increase in scholastic demands also accounts for some of the growth we have witnessed in the diagnosis and treatment of ADHD. This suspicion is impossible to fully substantiate, but many argue convincingly that the increased reliance on standardized testing within our schools and the consequent increase in focus required of students to perform on standardized exams has led to increasing parental anxiety about school performance and a greater likelihood that they will have their children evaluated for ADHD. As a result of the No Child Left Behind federal legislation, schools and teachers are also under increasing pressure for their students to perform well on standardized tests in order to maintain necessary funding. Parent and teacher pressure along with a visit to a physician for an evaluation will not, in and of themselves, result in a diagnosis of ADHD, but we must also not forget the recent changes to our health care system (e.g., the influence of managed care), which have left physicians and therapists with less time to complete an evaluation and to arrive at a proper diagnosis. In addition, the availability of an increasing number of medications for the treatment of ADHD and the influence of the pharmaceutical industry on physicians have, no doubt, fostered an increase in the treatment of this disorder.

Finally, the 1991 amendments to the Individuals with Disability Education Act (IDEA) may have also inadvertently supported an increase in the diagnosis and treatment of ADHD by establishing the category of other health impaired (OHI). The OHI categorization now allows children with ADHD to receive special education services, whereas heretofore only children with a recognized learning disorder were given such supports. Consequently, a child with ADHD who is suffering academically can now also receive special assistance at school. While entirely justifiable and reasonable, the addition of OHI to the IDEA may have encouraged some parents and teachers to identify children more readily who may have been left to struggle in silence in the not too distant past.

CLINICAL COURSE

The first symptom of ADHD most often reported is hyperactivity. In some cases mothers report that even in utero the child was active and kicking from nearly the moment of conception. More commonly, however, parents note a gradual onset of symptoms during the primary years. Often by 2, 3, or 4 years of age, parents will report that their children appeared very active and constantly "on the go." As the children age and are able to make more choices for themselves, impulsivity is more easily spotted. As children age into their teen years, hyperactivity and impulsivity diminish in most cases. By mid-adolescence and into adulthood, it is much less common to experience proper hyperactivity, although some degree may remain and be described now as a sense of internal restlessness. Inattention, for those who are affected by this type alone or by combined type ADHD, commonly persists to some degree well into adulthood, but often diminishes at least somewhat over time.

The natural history of ADHD is understood in general terms to follow the "rule of thirds," such that approximately one-third of children demonstrate significant symptom resolution and are not terribly bothered in adulthood; about one-third of children continue to experience inattention into adulthood; and about one-third of children continue to experience symptoms in all domains (hyperactivity, impulsivity, and inattention) and to suffer other related difficulties, such as oppositional defiance, severe conduct-disordered behavior, excessively poor academic achievement, substance abuse, and perhaps even some antisocial traits as adults. Although one-third of children appear to generally outgrow their ADHD, the majority of children affected by ADHD appear to maintain the diagnosis into adulthood, with the strongest predictor of a poor prognosis being prepubertal aggression (Cantwell, 1996).

Studies of specific age-related changes in children with ADHD indicate that preschool children, ages 3 to 5 years, are often identified as having hyperactive and impulsive symptoms. By school age, 6 to 12 years, children are often noted to suffer from a combination of symptoms (or inattentive symptoms alone in the case of inattentive type only). By adolescence, 13–18 years, youths complain of inattention often with some restlessness, while adults often complain of inattention with periodic impulsivity.

DIAGNOSIS

Given the high prevalence of ADHD, it is not uncommon to mistake the combined symptoms of hyperactivity, inattention, and impulsivity for another disorder. However, many other possible explanations for the disorder (a.k.a., the "differential diagnosis") exist, including mood and psychotic disorders, anxiety disorders, learning disorders, mental retardation and borderline intellectual functioning, oppositional defiant and conduct disorders, pervasive developmental delay (e.g., autism and Asperger's), substance use disorders, and various personality disorders. Symptoms of hypervigilance and impulsivity are also sometimes found among children who have been physically or sexually abused or subject to excessively harsh parenting. Finally, there are a number of general medical illnesses that can also result in a clinical picture that appears to be something like ADHD, including seizure disorders, chronic otitis media, hyperthyroidism, sleep apnea, various drug-induced inattentional syndromes, head injury, hepatic illness, toxic exposures, and narcolepsy.

The *DSM-IV* diagnostic criteria for ADHD include two general symptom categories: (a) inattention; and (b) hyperactivity and impulsivity. The *DSM-IV* demands that six of nine symptoms in either or both domains be present in order to meet diagnostic criteria. These symptoms are listed in Table 2.1. The *DSM* also demands that a series of so-called functional criteria be met in order to qualify for the diagnosis—the symptoms must have persisted for at least 6 months; at least some symptoms must have existed before 7 years of age; there must be impairment in two or more settings (e.g., home, school, church, ball field, etc.); and there must be social, academic, or occupational impairment (American Psychiatric Association, 2000).

Table 2.1. Diagnostic Symptoms of ADHD*

Inattentive symptoms	Hyperactive/impulsive symptoms
Makes careless mistake in homework or gives poor attention to detail	Is often fidgety
Has difficulty maintaining attention in tasks or play	Has difficulty staying seated
Does not listen when spoken to directly	Runs or climbs excessively at inappropriate times
Has difficulty following instructions	Has difficulty engaging in leisure activities quietly
Is poorly organized	Is hyperactive or appears driven as if by a motor
Avoids tasks requiring sustained mental effort	Talks excessively
Loses items necessary for tasks and activities	Blurts out responses or answers to questions before the questions have been fully asked
Is easily distractible	Has difficulty awaiting turn
Is forgetful in daily activities	Interrupts or intrudes upon others

Adapted from *DSM-IV* (American Psychiatric Association, 2000).

Many parents ask about having their child "tested" for ADHD. As yet, there is no single test to identify ADHD. Assessing *DSM-IV* symptoms to determine the degree of impairment is, at this time, the most useful measure of ADHD. The clinician must be careful, however, because ADHD should never be diagnosed in a one-to-one setting. Many, perhaps most, children affected by ADHD are able to focus and contain their behavior when the attention is focused solely on them, such as during a school tutorial, during a visit with a physician or therapist, or while playing video games. During these moments, all attention is focused entirely on the child who is getting feedback to every statement, movement, and nuance. Rather, it is during shared or group activities, or when a child must wait his turn, that the symptoms of ADHD are most clearly evident. Consequently, the observations of not only the clinician, but also the parents, grandparents, or other caregivers, schoolteachers, coaches, Sunday school teacher, and so forth are vital in establishing a diagnosis.

Although there is no "test" to establish the diagnosis of ADHD, neuropsychological testing is often useful in measuring symptom severity. As would be expected, most children with ADHD have significant impairments in executive functioning, including their ability to maintain attentional vigilance, utilize working memory effectively, plan, organize, and inhibit impulsive responses. Neuropsychological testing of children with ADHD typically identifies impaired spatial working memory, ability with mazes and planning, stop-task response suppression, and naming speed. Perhaps the most popular neuropsychological tests for ADHD are the continuous performance tasks. These instruments require a child to stay focused on a computerized task, such as pressing the space bar each time a certain letter or number appears on the screen, while varying the pace of the stimuli and adding in purposeful distractions. The tests, which include the Test of Variables of Attention (TOVA), the Conners' Continuous Performance Test (CPT), and the Intermediate Visual and Auditory Continuous Performance Test (IVA), are sometimes useful for monitoring symptoms and the changes that occur over time and with treatment (Nigg et al., 2005). However useful they may sometimes be, it is important to recognize that neuropsychological tests have not been found to be reliable diagnostic tools for ADHD.

The diagnosis of ADHD is multifactorial and relies upon a thorough clinical interview, collateral interviews with individuals who see the child in numerous settings, an early age of onset of at least some symptoms, and symptoms in more than one setting. The clinical interview should include a diagnostic assessment of the primary complaint and a review of other possible explanations for the observed symptoms. More specifically, the clinician should assess not only inattention, hyperactivity, and impulsivity, but also general behavior (including oppositional and conduct difficulties), mood, anxiety, psychosis, trauma, vocal and motor tics, and substance abuse. A full medical history, including a detailed developmental, family, educational, and social history, should also be assessed.

Because children are often not the best historians and almost universally have trouble describing their symptoms of ADHD and other mental disorders (at least until adolescence), various objective rating scales have been designed for use by parents, teachers, and other collateral informants to help identify symptoms. Some of the better-known rating scales for ADHD include the SNAP (Swanson, Nolan, and Pelham) for parents and teachers, the Connors Scales for teachers, parents, and affected adults, the ADHD Rating Scale (ADHD-RS), the Vanderbilt ADHD Rating Scales for parents and teachers, and the SKAMP (Swanson, Kotkin, Agler M.-Flynn, and Pelham) for teachers. These rating scales are readily available as freeware or for purchase on the Internet.

Some individual practitioners will engage in a treatment trial with medication in order to establish or confirm the diagnosis. This approach is not advised as the risk of adverse effects is not insignificant. Furthermore, many individuals, perhaps most, without ADHD will show some degree of improvement in their attention and focus, along with a decrease in impulsivity and general activity level, when treated with a stimulant medication. When an individual is affected by ADHD, however, the degree of improvement with treatment is remarkable and much greater than that typically seen by individuals who are unaffected. Although reliable indicators are not available, commonly children with ADHD will show a greater than 50% improvement according to parent report in their symptoms of inattention, hyperactivity, and impulsivity, whereas individuals unaffected by ADHD may show only small increases of 10–15% improvement in their ability to focus and pay attention.

Other practitioners will employ a placebo trial before initiating treatment with a stimulant. While placebo responses in many areas of medicine are high, they are moderate in ADHD (approximately 30%) but not sustained, thereby only further prolonging the effort at establishing a proper diagnosis (Sandler, Glesne, & Geller, 2008). Consequently, this method is also not recommended.

Approximately two-thirds of children with ADHD present with one or more coexisting or comorbid Axis I disorders (Biederman et al., 1996; Spencer, Biederman, & Wilens, 2000). The percentage of children comorbid with another diagnosis varies greatly by study, but there is no denying that comorbidities remain a major concern for most children with ADHD. Anxiety disorders, behavioral disorders, mood disorders, tics, and learning disorders are extremely common comorbidities among children with ADHD.

TREATMENT

Treatment for ADHD typically involves three primary considerations: (a) medication; (b) behavioral therapy; and (c) educational support. The Multimodal Treatment Assessment (MTA) study of 1999, as well as numerous other studies, demonstrated clearly that medication is the most effective and reliable treatment for children suffering from the core symptoms of ADHD (MTA Cooperative Group, 1999). Behavioral treatments, by contrast, have never demonstrated the efficacy that medications have for the primary symptom domains of ADHD (e.g., inattention, hyperactivity, and impulsivity). Behavioral treatments have, however, proven to be of great utility for commonly related impairments that beset children with ADHD, such as oppositional behavior and defiance. The MTA study also found that more frequent and higher dosing of stimulant medication, along with increased physician contact, leads to better treatment response and improved outcomes for children affected by ADHD.

Stimulants remain the most effective and most commonly employed treatment for ADHD. Although not entirely elucidated, the mechanism of action appears to involve the reuptake inhibition of dopamine and, to a

Figure 2.3. Probable mechanism of action of methylphenidate. Methylphenidate blocks the reuptake of dopamine into the presynaptic neuron, thereby increasing the amount of dopamine within the synapse that is free to interact with the postsynaptic neuron.

lesser extent, norepinephrine (see Figure 2.3). In addition, stimulants cause an increase in the release of presynaptic norepinephrine and dopamine. Some stimulants are also mild inhibitors of monoamine oxidase (MAO), an enzyme which breaks down norepinephrine and dopamine, thereby leaving more active neurochemical in the synapse for a longer period of time. Amphetamine, but not methylphenidate, also promotes passive diffusion of norepinephrine and dopamine into the synaptic cleft and promotes the release of norepinephrine from cytoplasmic pools (Wilens & Spencer, 1998).

The response rate to stimulants is remarkably high and far greater than with most psychiatric medications. Regardless of the stimulant selected, typically 70% of children and adolescents with ADHD will respond favorably to the first medication trial (Spencer et al., 1996). If the first stimulant attempt is not effective, the second stimulant trial will usually pick up an additional 10–15% of individuals such that 85% of those affected by ADHD will show statistically significant symptom improvement by the time they have tried two stimulants (Elia, Borcherding, Rapoport, & Keysor, 1991). This degree of efficacy is rarely found with treatments in any medical discipline. As implied, there is no significant difference in response rates when looking at large populations of youth treated with amphetamine, methylphenidate, or any of their derivatives, and numerous studies have demonstrated efficacy for these treatments in preschool children, school-age children, adolescents, and adults (Arnold, 2000).

Historically, children and adults with ADHD were treated with immediate release medications that were dosed numerous times throughout the day to maintain effect. The first long-acting stimulant medications for the treatment of ADHD were designed to result in a steady blood level of stimulant throughout the day. These medications, however, such as Ritalin SR and Metadate ER, were found to be ineffective for many patients. We now realize that maintaining a steady blood level of a stimulant throughout the day does not effectively treat ADHD beyond a few hours for most individuals due to tachyphylaxis or the fact that the body's response to stimulants diminishes rapidly. Consequently, the blood level of a stimulant must be steadily increased throughout the day in order to maintain a continued response. Over the past decade, numerous long-acting medications have been developed that take advantage of our increasing knowledge of how these medications must be dosed (Swanson et al., 2003).

It is important to note that this method of treatment does not result in addiction or any habit-forming effect of the medication. Rather, due to the fact that all individuals respond to the benefits of stimulants for only about as long as the half-life of the drug (presumably because of tachyphylaxis), another dose of the medication must be delivered approximately every half-life in order to maintain clinical response. (See the Appendix for a thorough discussion of psychopharmacology, including drug half-lives). As the half-life of methylphenidate is about 2½ to 4 hours and the half-life of amphetamine is about 4–6 hours, these medications must be dosed at those intervals if a sustained clinical response is to be achieved. The newer long-acting medications, such as Concerta, Adderall-XR, Focalin-XR, Metadate-CD, Ritalin-LA, Vyvanse, and Daytrana, take advantage of our understanding of tachyphylaxis, and by various mechanisms they increase the blood level of stimulant throughout the day, mirroring the effects of dosing an immediate release medication numerous times throughout the day, thereby resulting in continual efficacy (see Figure 2.4).

Although doses vary considerably, the average dose of methylphenidate in the United States is typically about 30 mg per day and that of amphetamine about 20 mg per day. Body weight was historically utilized to determine the most effective dose for a given patient. Approximately 1 mg/kg per day for methylphenidate and 0.6 mg/kg per day for amphetamine

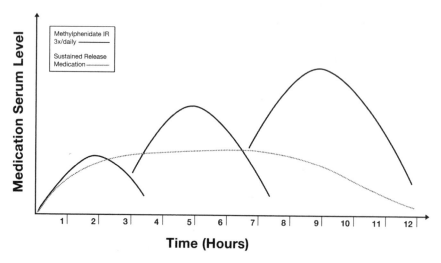

Figure 2.4. Tachyphylaxis and stimulant dosing. As can be seen in figure 2.4, the use of a sustained-release medication (or one that maintains a steady blood level of stimulant throughout the day) does not result in an increase in blood levels and therefore is not effective after the first few hours of treatment. In contrast, repeated dosing of immediate-release medications does lead to increasing blood levels throughout the day and is the model for the newer and successful long-acting stimulant medications.

were the generally accepted values. However, we now realize that weight-based dosing is rarely accurate as children, adolescents, and adults may require far lower or far higher doses, depending upon idiosyncratic features that have yet to be elucidated (Rapport & Denney, 1997). Consequently, we currently dose these medications to clinical response, lowering the dose or changing the medication if side effects develop.

In many cases children do not adequately benefit from stimulants because they are not properly dosed for a sufficient period of time. Compounding this problem is the fact that many practitioners are not comfortable prescribing stimulants and will therefore provide only a low dose, which will not generally result in notable benefit. For these reasons practitioners are now often advised to follow a forced dosage titration when starting a stimulant medication in a child diagnosed with ADHD. A forced dosage titration takes place over a relatively short period of time and relies upon increasing the dose every week or two until clinical benefit is achieved. For a child taking immediate-release methylphenidate, the practitioner may begin the dose at 5 mg three times a day for the first week, advance the dose to 10 mg three times a day for the second week, and advance the dose still further to 15 mg three times a day for the third week. A more conservative approach may involve dosing at 5 mg, then 7.5 mg, then 10 mg weekly. As long as rating scales are utilized during this period of time by the parents and teachers and side effects are well monitored by the family, the practitioner will typically know within 3 weeks if methylphenidate is helpful for this child.

Utilizing a long-acting methylphenidate product for the same child, Concerta, for example, the practitioner may prescribe 18-mg tablets in the morning for the first week, 36-mg tablets in the morning for the second week, and 54-mg tablets in the morning for the third week. If at any point side effects are encountered, the family is instructed to call the practitioner, stop the medication, and seek clarification as to how to proceed. For a child prescribed Adderall-XR, a long-acting amphetamine, a dose of 10 mg per day may be utilized for the first week, 20 mg for the second week, and 30 mg for the third week. Again, if impairing side effects are encountered, the family should contact the practitioner and clarify whether or not to continue.

The starting stimulant dosage and weekly increases are determined by the practitioner's clinical experience and perception of symptom severity. Although we do not rely upon weight-based dosing any longer, sometimes practitioners will initiate treatment with some consideration of the child's weight. For example, a practitioner may start a child of 25 kg on a forced dosage titration of Concerta of 18 mg for the first week, 27 mg for the second week, and 36 mg for the third week; while a child of 50 kg may be dosed at 18 mg for the first week, 36 mg for the second week, and 54 mg for the third week. Although an imprecise science, as long as the child's caregivers understand the potential side effects of treatment, dosage increases in this fashion result in the most rapid assessment of medication efficacy.

Side effects of stimulants are common but rarely significant and insurmountable. The four most common difficulties are nausea, headache, insomnia, and a decrease in appetite. Other less frequent side effects include the unmasking of motor and vocal tics, anxiety, hypertension, tachycardia, diaphoresis (sweating), tremors, and even psychosis. Insomnia and appetite suppression are generally the most distressing side effects for patients and can be so bothersome that the medication dose may need to be decreased or the medication itself changed. On some occasions, additional medication may be necessary to address these side effects. Relative contraindications to the use of stimulants include hypertension, symptomatic cardiovascular disease, glaucoma, hyperthyroidism, severe Tourette's syndrome, significant drug abuse, and psychosis. Depending upon the nature and severity of these difficulties, the practitioner may decide to treat with stimulants or alternative medications (see below).

There have been increasing popular concerns about the cardiac safety of stimulants, and a number of patient advocacy groups and physicians have suggested that caution is demanded of those prescribing stimulants (Biederman, Spencer, Wilens, Prince, & Faraone, 2006). This issue has been explored in great detail by the American Academy of Pediatrics (AAP) and the American Heart Association (AHA), and it has been clearly determined that children with heart conditions have a higher incidence of ADHD than the general population (Vetter et al., 2008). Current recommendations endorsed by these leading medical specialty organizations include the following: First, it is advised that all children who are diagnosed with ADHD be carefully evaluated for heart conditions prior to treatment. Second, the most important features of this assessment are a patient and family cardiovascular history along with a physical examination focused on cardiovascular risk factors. Acquiring an electrocardiogram (ECG) or echocardiogram is not mandatory or advised for all patients. However, it is recognized that obtaining an ECG or echocardiogram is reasonable if risk factors are identified, including a history of chest pain, dizziness, syncope (fainting), exercise intolerance, shortness of breath, or a family history of sudden cardiac death. Finally, treatment of patients with ADHD should not be withheld because an ECG is not performed unless further cardiac investigations are indicated. It is important to note that medications that treat ADHD have not been shown to cause heart conditions, nor have they been demonstrated to cause sudden cardiac death. However, stimulant medications that treat ADHD almost always result in modest increases in heart rate and blood pressure. While these side effects are not usually considered dangerous, blood pressure, heart rate, and cardiovascular symptoms should be monitored regularly in patients treated for ADHD (see Table 2.2).

The standard of care for treatment with stimulants includes the measurement of vital signs (e.g., blood pressure and heart rate), as well as a cardiac exam and a full family history. As previously discussed, the identification of cardiac concerns suggests the need for an ECG and a pediatric cardiology referral for possible echocardiogram prior to treatment. During treatment, height and weight measurements should be performed annually at a minimum and compared to published norms for age. If height for age decreases by more than one standard deviation while on treatment with stimulants, referral to a pediatric endocrinologist to evaluate possible growth hormone deficiency or hypothyroidism should be considered. Blood pressure and heart rate should be evaluated at least twice annually and any time prior and subsequent to a dosage increase. If the patient's medical history is unremarkable, laboratory and neurological testing are not indicated. Psychological and neuropsychological testing

Table 2.2.   Cardiac Safety in Children and Adolescents Treated for ADHD

- The American Heart Association (AHA) released a statement on April 21, 2008, regarding the cardiovascular evaluation and monitoring of children receiving drugs for the treatment of ADHD. As a result of language in the news release and the statement as published, there have been conflicting interpretations of the recommendations regarding the use of an electrocardiogram (ECG) in assessing children with ADHD who may need treatment with medications. A joint advisory by the American Academy of Pediatrics (AAP) and the AHA clarified these remarks on May 16, 2008.
- The scientific statement included a review of data that show children with heart conditions have a higher incidence of ADHD.
- Because certain heart conditions in children may be difficult (even, in some cases, impossible) to detect, the AAP and AHA feel that it is prudent to carefully assess children for heart conditions who need to receive treatment with drugs for ADHD.
- Obtaining a patient and family health history and doing a physical exam focused on cardiovascular disease risk factors (Class I recommendations in the statement) are recommended by the AAP and AHA for assessing patients before treatment with drugs for ADHD.
- **Acquiring an ECG is a Class IIa recommendation. This means that *it is reasonable* for a physician *to consider* obtaining an ECG as part of the evaluation of children being considered for stimulant drug therapy, but this should be at the physician's judgment, and it is *not mandatory* to obtain one.**
- Treatment of a patient with ADHD should not be withheld because an ECG is not done. The child's physician is the best person to make the assessment about whether there is a need for an ECG.
- Medications that treat ADHD have not been shown to cause heart conditions nor have they been demonstrated to cause sudden cardiac death. However, some of these medications can increase or decrease heart rate and blood pressure. While these side effects are not usually considered dangerous, they should be monitored in children with heart conditions as the physician feels necessary.

Accessed on January 27, 2009, at http://americanheart.mediaroom.com/index.php?s=43&item=398.

are not mandatory and should be performed only if the patient's history suggests general low cognitive ability or low achievement in language or mathematics relative to the patient's intellectual functioning (AACAP Work Group on Stimulant Medications, 2002).

There are numerous pros and cons to the use of stimulants for the treatment of ADHD. As previously noted, stimulants are highly effective and have been utilized successfully for many years. However, their use results in a limited duration of action, and there are sometimes significant side effects and occasional contraindications. Consequently, a variety of other medications have been developed for the treatment of ADHD.

Many children, perhaps over half of those who initiate treatment with a stimulant, may develop a transient motor tic (e.g., a repetitive, rhythmic motor movement, such as eye blinking or nose wrinkling) (Borcherding,

Keysor, Rapoport, Elia, & Amass, 1990; Tannock, Schachar, & Logan, 1995). Most tics diminish with time and are not a cause for great concern by the child or family (see Chapter 8). At this time it is not clear that stimulants cause tics, although they may "unmask" them or make them more evident. The comorbidity or co-occurrence of tics in individuals with ADHD, whether or not they have been treated with stimulants, is quite high and generally noted at between 10% and 15%. Historically, it was believed that stimulants caused motor and vocal tics. We now realize that stimulants actually improve tics in many cases, so our understanding is not quite as simplistic as it once was (Gadow, Sverd, Sprafkin, Nolan, & Ezor, 1995).

For children who develop tics while taking stimulants, a slight decrease in the stimulant dose or a discontinuation or change of stimulant is often effective. At other times we are able to use habit reversal therapy, a behavioral therapy targeted directly at tics (see Chapter 8). If the tics are adequately severe, we may consider other medications, such as atomoxetine (Strattera) for the treatment of ADHD, which may be less likely to cause tics, or alpha-2 agonists, such as clonidine (Catapres) or guanfacine (Tenex), or even antipsychotic medications. The mechanism of action of alpha-2 agonists is much less clear but may involve decreasing activity in the locus coeruleus noradrenergic cell bodies to improve attentional arousal and cognitive processes (Pliszka, McCracken, & Maas, 1996). Although frequently employed in children and adolescents, alpha-2 agonists are not FDA approved for the treatment of ADHD; their sole FDA indication is for hypertension in adults.

More commonly, alpha-2 agonists have been utilized to decrease residual hyperactivity, impulsivity, and aggression, and to treat insomnia and treatment-emergent motor and vocal tics. Doses of clonidine (Catapres) have typically been 0.1–0.3 mg per day and 1–3 mg per day for guanfacine (Tenex), although these dosages are sometimes doubled. A routine physical examination and the assessment of vital signs should be performed prior to initiation of treatment. Contraindications to the use of alpha-2 agonists include coronary artery disease and impaired liver and renal function. Side effects most commonly include rebound hypertension and tachycardia, hypotension, sedation, dizziness, constipation, headache, and fatigue. When initiating treatment with an alpha-2 agonist, we generally begin with late afternoon or evening dosing and titrate toward the morning. With a child successfully utilizing a stimulant for the treatment of ADHD but who is suffering insomnia or late-afternoon rebound hyperactivity, we may begin with 0.05 mg (½ tablet) of clonidine (Catapres), or 0.5 mg (½ tablet) of guanfacine (Tenex), an hour before bedtime. This treatment may allow the child to relax, become less agitated and aggressive, and sleep better through the night. If the child continues to have afternoon difficulties after 3 or 4 days of this evening dose, we may add another dose of the same amount around 3:00 or 4:00 in the afternoon when he comes home from school. Should disruptivity, aggression, agitation, or tics persist, we may add yet a third dose toward the morning after 3 or 4 more days. If the initial dose is not sufficient, we may increase the dose to a full tablet, 0.1 mg of clonidine or 1.0 mg of guanfacine, in the evening, afternoon, and morning, using the same dosage titration.

Monitoring blood pressure is important, but the use of ECGs is not routinely necessary unless there is suspicion of cardiac concern or impairment. Alpha-2 agonists have been shown to effectively reduce hyperactivity and impulsivity, both with and without methylphenidate; and in more recent studies they have even been found to improve inattention, although to a much lesser extent than stimulants (Biederman, Melmed, et al., 2008; Sallee et al., 2008; Tourette's Syndrome Study Group, 2002). For the treatment of ADHD, however, the clinical efficacy of alpha-2 agonists compared to stimulants is much less profound.

Combining a stimulant with an alpha-2 agonist is a common and effective strategy for children with ADHD who also struggle with behavioral rebound in the afternoon, motor or vocal tics, comorbid aggression, or insomnia (Hazel & Stuart, 2003). A small number of physicians remain hesitant to prescribe these medications in conjunction with each other because of four reported deaths of children who were prescribed both methylphenidate and clonidine. In each of these cases, however, there were extenuating circumstances that better accounted for the cause of death, such as an overdose of medication, an unrelated surgery, a history of syncope, and preexisting damage to the heart valves. At this time the Food and Drug Administration (FDA) places no limitations on the combined use of these medications and posts no advisories against their conjoint use. In addition, neither the American Academy of Pediatrics nor the American Academy of Child and Adolescent Psychiatry advises against their combined use nor recommends routine ECG monitoring, presuming there is no cardiac history (AACAP Workgroup on Stimulant Medications, 2002).

Atomoxetine (Strattera) is another FDA-approved medication for the treatment of ADHD that works by a novel mechanism. Atomoxetine is a norepinephrine and dopamine reuptake inhibitor at the presynaptic neuron in the prefrontal cortex. Because atomoxetine does not have any effect on dopamine in the limbic system or striatum, the medication is typically associated with a lower risk of motor and vocal tics and has no abuse potential. Other advantages to atomoxetine include its 24-hour duration of action and the fact that it is not classified as a Schedule II medication by the Drug Enforcement Agency (DEA). As a result, atomoxetine prescriptions can be called in to pharmacies, and refills can be given on prescriptions. Unfortunately, however, it is quite clear to most practitioners that treatment of ADHD with atomoxetine does not result in as robust a response as with stimulants. This clinical observation has now been confirmed in a series of studies as well (Gibson, Bettinger, Patel, & Crismon, 2006; Mano, Tom-Revzon, Bukstein, & Crismon, 2007). Side effects of atomoxetine most commonly include a decrease in appetite, dizziness, stomachache, sedation, and mild changes to blood pressure and heart rate. There have been three reports of liver toxicity, each of which resolved when the medication was discontinued (Bangs et al., 2008), and some adults suffer anticholinergic side effects, such as dry mouth, constipation, urinary retention, and sexual dysfunction, such as decreased libido, erectile disturbance, and anorgasmia. Finally, atomoxetine has been serendipitously found to be effective in the treatment of enuresis or bed-wetting (see Chapter 15).

The dosage of atomoxetine is entirely weight based. Typical starting dosages are between 0.5 and 1.0 mg/kg/day for up to 1–2 weeks; thereafter, the dose can generally be increased to 1.2–1.8 mg/kg/day, which is therapeutic for most individuals. Not infrequently, a higher dosage is administered, up to 2 or even 3 mg/kg/day; although studies have not demonstrated any increase in efficacy beyond 1.8 mg/kg/day. For children and adolescents who suffer excessive side effects due to stimulants but who require the efficacy of a stimulant, a common strategy is to combine a therapeutic dose of atomoxetine along with a lower dose of stimulant. Together, these medications sometimes result in therapeutic benefit with a decrease in side effects as compared to a higher dose of the stimulant alone.

There are a number of other treatments that have historically been utilized for the treatment of ADHD and are sometimes still employed for children who have severe symptoms that are not adequately treated with stimulants and/or alpha-2 agonists. These medications are also used for the small number of children who cannot tolerate the side effects of stimulants and alpha-2 agonists.

The tricyclic antidepressants, particularly desipramine (Norpramin, Pertofrane), have been successfully employed for the treatment of ADHD. However, their use must be weighed carefully against the cardiac risk of treating a child with a tricyclic antidepressant due to the possible cardiac arrhythmia that can ensue with their use. Because of their cardiotoxicity, these medications should only be prescribed by an experienced practitioner and must be employed along with routine cardiac monitoring, including ECGs (see Chapter 10).

Bupropion (Wellbutrin) has been demonstrated to be effective in some studies, but the findings have been inconsistent (Conners et al., 1996; Daviss et al., 2001). This medication is not approved for the treatment of ADHD by the FDA, indicating that the data supporting this treatment is not as yet adequately impressive. Furthermore, practicing clinicians rarely find bupropion to be of great use for the treatment of ADHD. Bupropion may be more of a consideration for a child suffering from comorbid depression and for whom the practitioner cannot entirely ascribe the inattention and lack of focus to ADHD but rather to some combination of ADHD and major depression. However, bupropion has little data to support its use as an antidepressant for children and adolescents as well (see Chapter 10). Another antidepressant, venlafaxine (Effexor) has some contradictory open- label data, suggesting that it may have some utility for the treatment of ADHD, but it is rarely employed by physicians (Findling, Greenhill, et al., 2007).

A novel medication for the treatment of narcolepsy and excessive daytime sedation associated with sleep apnea and shift work sleep disorder, modafinil (Provigil) has also shown variable efficacy in the treatment of ADHD. Three recent randomized, double-blind, placebo-controlled trials at dosages of generally more than 300 mg per day have, however, yielded positive results (Biederman & Pliszka, 2008). Side effects to modafinil are relatively infrequent and include insomnia, headache, and decreased appetite, along with an extremely rare risk of severe dermatologic disorders, such as Stevens-Johnson syndrome.

Two new stimulant formulations have recently arrived on the market. Lisdexamfetamine (Vyvanse) is an amphetamine pro-drug stimulant, which has a 12-hour duration of treatment. Because this medication is a "pro-drug," it is not metabolized to an active stimulant until it is digested. In patients with a history of drug abuse, the treatment has been shown to be less pleasurable and therefore may have utility among those at risk of drug abuse who require treatment for ADHD. Additionally, the methylphenidate patch (Daytrana), which is worn for 9 hours a day, demonstrates 12-hour efficacy for the treatment of ADHD.

As previously noted, behavioral treatments for the core symptoms of ADHD are not generally effective. Various psychotherapies, including cognitive behavior therapy, parent management training, and social skills training have not demonstrated consistent efficacy. These treatments are often effective, however, for a variety of common comorbidities including oppositional defiant disorder and conduct disorder.

Organizational skills training represents a new approach to the behavioral treatment of ADHD. Organizational skills training involves the application of a manualized treatment, which is flexibly applied to individual needs and incorporates meetings with the child and the parents, consultation with teachers, and a focus on practical routines that children can repeatedly employ. Behavioral modification techniques, including rewards and reinforcement, are used to motivate change. Particular areas of focus typically include tracking assignments, organization of the settings in which children study and work, materials management (e.g., collection, storage, and transfer of their schoolwork), time management and scheduling, setting priorities, and planning for both short- and long-term projects. While these treatments are useful for some children, studies have not yet demonstrated their efficacy in the treatment of ADHD (Langberg, Epstein, & Graham, 2008).

A variety of educational aids, including individual educational plans (IEPs) and various accommodations (e.g., 504 plans), are also often helpful for children with ADHD. These learning supports will be discussed in greater detail Chapter 4.

3

Disruptive Behavior Disorders

While identifying disruptive behavior in children is simple, parents and teachers often have a much more difficult time deciding whether the observed behavior is "normal," typical, or socially acceptable. All children become angry and misbehave at times, but it is how they express their anger and manage their feelings that is important. In the words of Aristotle: "Anyone can become angry, that is easy . . . but to become angry with the right person, at the right time, for the right purpose, and in the right way . . . this is not easy."

CLINICAL PRESENTATION

What constitutes normal childhood behavior? This question is routinely asked by all parents and teachers. As is evident from even the most elementary of observations, the range of normalcy or what we might consider "typical" is quite large, particularly when it comes to disruptive behavior. "Normal" or "typical" children are often oppositional and defiant. There is not a single child who has reached his second birthday, who is gaining command of the language, who has not uttered the word "no" dozens upon dozens of times. "Normal" children have tantrums. "Normal" children are periodically mean-spirited in word, deed, and action. "Normal" children occasionally lie and cheat and are sometimes purposefully annoying. Most important, however, "normal" children generally grow out of these behaviors, and most children grow up to be responsible adults, even those who have suffered terrible misfortune growing up or who have been plagued by major psychiatric illnesses.

Consequently, any child who will meet diagnostic criteria for a disruptive behavior disorder, such as *oppositional defiant disorder* or *conduct disorder*, will suffer a degree of impairment that is quite profound and far beyond that which "normal" children experience. These affected children will not only occasionally lie or cheat and demonstrate disruptive, agitated, oppositional, and defiant behavior, but they will demonstrate these behaviors on a regular basis often without regard for the rights and concerns of others. These children will suffer impairments in all aspects of their lives, with family at home, with friends, and with teachers and other adults. Even without direct treatment, most children who are disruptive at a young age will become "civilized" with time, show major improvements, and will not meet criteria for a disruptive behavior disorder as they age. For a significant minority of children, however, their behaviors will worsen, and they will become increasingly isolated from peers, family, and society.

ETIOLOGY

There are numerous biological, psychological, and social factors that are likely to contribute to the development of oppositional defiant disorder and conduct disorder in children and adolescents (Burke, Loeber, & Birmaher, 2002).

Biological

From the moment of conception, children are vulnerable to factors that may influence the later development of disruptive behavior, and potential links have been demonstrated between parental substance abuse, pregnancy and birth problems, and maternal smoking. What is not clear at this time, however, is whether these associations are due to an actual biological exposure in utero, or simply due to being raised in a chaotic and disruptive environment.

A variety of neurophysiological and neuroanatomical findings have been identified in children, adolescents, and adults with a history of disruptive behavior disorders. Decreased frontal lobe glucose metabolism, for example, has been repeatedly shown to be connected with violent behavior. In addition, frontal lobe brain damage is associated with aggression and orbitofrontal damage with impulsive aggression. Furthermore, it has been suggested that amygdala malfunction is associated with problems interpreting social cues, such as facial expression, and that suppressing negative emotion may hinge in part on a connection between the amygdala and the prefrontal cortex, such that if either is damaged, the individual may become considerably more impulsive and aggressive.

Neurotransmitters have also been associated with the development of disruptive behavior in children and adolescents. Low levels of 5-hydroxy-indoleacetic acid (5-HIAA), a serotonin metabolite, in the cerebrospinal fluid have been correlated with current and future aggression; yet higher serotonin blood levels have been found in boys with childhood-onset as opposed to adolescent-onset conduct disorder and are correlated with violence in adolescence. The meaning of these findings is not clear but may suggest that a lower turnover of serotonin, or perhaps being a slower utilizer of serotonin, in the central nervous system is associated with disruptive behavior and aggression. Finally, low salivary cortisol levels are correlated with oppositional defiant disorder, while testosterone, interestingly, has only variably been associated with aggression.

The autonomic nervous system, which generally functions without our being aware but can be influenced by our purposeful behavior, exerts influence on such functions as heart rate, blood pressure, respiratory rate, and galvanic skin response. Severely disruptive children and adolescents have been repeatedly found to demonstrate altered autonomic nervous system function. For example, boys with oppositional defiant disorder generally maintain a lower heart rate at baseline but a higher heart rate when exposed to experimentally induced frustration. In addition, a lower galvanic skin response has been found in disruptive boys and a higher skin conductance has been noted among boys who do not engage in violent behavior.

Finally, there are a variety of neurotoxins that may possibly induce oppositional or agitated behavior in children, such as lead, which is a preventable risk factor. High levels of lead in children have been associated with increased aggression and higher delinquency scores on standardized rating scales. There remain a variety of other potential neurotoxins, such as organophosphate pesticides; food additives, including antibiotics and hormones; and other chemicals that are newly present in our food supply and environment. We have little understanding of their impact on a growing fetus and young child. Although there is no data to suggest that these factors are as yet impacting children's behavior, we must remain vigilant as to this possibility (Burke et al., 2002).

Psychological

Research into child development has generally supported the notion that children are born with certain temperaments. In the original studies of temperament, nine characteristics were indentified, including activity level, regularity, initial reaction, adaptability, intensity, mood, distractibility, persistence and attention span, and sensitivity. Taken together, the unique combination of these nine characteristics results in a child who is described as "easy," "difficult," or "slow to warm up" (Thomas, Chess, & Birch, 1968). Some mothers will say that they knew their child was aggressive from the time they were pregnant because the child was kicking excessively in the womb or came out crying from day one. Others will report that their child was always calm and easy to be with. Regardless of how it is labeled, an infant with a difficult temperament, or one who expresses a great deal of negative emotion, has a willful and impulsive way of responding, and is relatively inflexible, is more likely to be disruptive later in childhood (Sanson & Prior, 1999).

Another area of developmental psychology research, attachment theory, has also been investigated as a possible etiology of disruptive behavior. Attachment theory suggests that infants must establish secure relationships with adult caregivers in order to promote normal social and emotional development (Siegel, 1999). The research in attachment has, however, to date been equivocal, with no clarity as to whether or not children with attachment disorders have a greater risk of developing disruptive behavior.

Evidence of neuropsychological impairment has been found among some young children with severely disruptive behavior, but testing, while attractive in theory, has not yet been able to clearly parse out psychosocial factors from neuropsychological deficits as the etiological agent. While specific neuropsychological tests have consistently demonstrated that low intelligence is a possible predictor of disruptive behavior, most studies looking at the IQ and its contribution to the development of oppositional defiant and conduct disorder have not controlled well for children with ADHD, which itself greatly increases the likelihood of disruptive behaviors. Finally, although disruptive behavior in boys is a risk factor for the subsequent development of reading problems, in girls the opposite appears true; that is, early struggles with reading are predictive of later behavioral problems.

Behavioral inhibition, which can be viewed as the tendency to show fear and avoidance in unfamiliar situations, is a research construct that can be demonstrated in children using a variety of rating scales and techniques. Those children who are behaviorally inhibited or shy tend to demonstrate a decreased risk of later delinquency. This effect may be related to anxiety, which has been shown to temper physical aggression even in boys who are already disruptive. In contrast, research findings also point to the fact that socially withdrawn boys or those who do not relate well to peers, not due to behavioral inhibition or shyness, have a greater risk of delinquency.

Another important psychological research construct is that of social cognition or the degree to which individuals are able to understand the behaviors and intentions of others around them. We sometimes informally refer to this factor as one's social or emotional IQ. Boys with disruptive behavior disorders tend to focus more on concrete and outward qualities of individuals and are self-centered in their description of peers; that is, they do not demonstrate an understanding of the other person's point of view. Boys with disruptive behavior disorders and boys with ADHD also commonly have problems understanding social cues and what others mean by their body language, eye contact, and general expressions. In addition, boys with disruptive behavior disorders tend to respond aggressively to problems. In research studies, these boys are more likely to misinterpret an awkward glance from a peer as an aggressive message. Furthermore, both boys and girls who suffer from conduct disorder demonstrate less empathy, an important finding considering that empathy is known to mediate and decrease aggressive behavior. Finally, early physical maturation is associated with increased behavior problems in girls but not in boys. The reasons for this finding are unclear, but they are consistent (Burke et al., 2002).

Social

There are a number of psychosocial factors that also may contribute to the development of oppositional defiant disorder and conduct disorder, perhaps the most impressive of which is parenting. Poor management of a child's behavior is related to an increase in disruptive behavior, while positive parenting may, in fact, be protective. Parental psychopathology or major mental illness in the parents, however, is probably even more predictive of the development of disruptive behavior disorders in children than is bad parenting. Aspects of bad parenting associated with disruptive behavior include poor monitoring of children's activities and behaviors, harsh and inconsistent or punitive discipline, differential treatment of siblings, and coercion. While severe and abusive physical punishment is strongly related, mild physical punishment is less so but still correlated with the development of disruptive behavior in children.

Assortative mating is another psychosocial risk factor for the development of disruptive behavior disorders. Female delinquents are more likely to have intimate relationships with male delinquents than vice versa. Consequently, females with a history of disruptive and agitated behavior are more likely to have a child who is the product of two offenders than are males with a history of disruptive behavior. The increased risk to the off-spring, although not easily quantifiable, is likely to be significant for both genetic and environmental reasons.

Both physical and sexual abuse have been demonstrated to signifi-cantly increase the risk of conduct disorder. Furthermore, some data suggest that abused children have trouble with social processing and demonstrate hostile attribution biases, encoding errors, and positive evaluations of ag-gression (Dodge, Pettit, Bates, & Valente, 1995). These findings indicate that abused children may not understand social interaction in the same way as other children do and may misinterpret social cues as aggressive when not, in fact, intended to be so. As would be expected, sexually abused boys are less likely than sexually abused girls to suffer internalizing prob-lems but are equally or more likely than girls to reveal conduct or exter-nalizing problems.

Peers also directly and indirectly contribute to the development of oppositional defiant disorder and conduct disorder. For example, adoles-cents spend approximately one-third of their time talking with peers ver-sus less than 10% of their time talking with adults (Spear, 2000). As such, the peer group becomes highly important and influential in the life of an adolescent. While normal peers generally reject those with conduct dis-order, simultaneously they often inadvertently reinforce the behavior by compliance and passivity. Association with like-minded deviant peers tends to concretize the behavior and social role of youth with conduct disorder. Chronically maltreated children are more aggressive and more commonly rejected by peers as early as grammar school. Aggressive girls appear to be more commonly rejected by peers, as aggressive boys are sometimes feared and looked up to by the general student population.

Finally, disruptive behavior in children is associated with growing up in poor and disadvantaged neighborhoods. A variety of factors ap-pear to be important and predictive of later violence, including the in-creased availability of drugs, community disorganization, neighborhood adults involved in crime, poverty, and exposure to violence and racial prejudice (Burke et al., 2002).

EPIDEMIOLOGY

The epidemiology of disruptive behavior disorders varies a great deal de-pending upon the study, where it was completed, and how many children were involved (Loeber, Burke, Lahey, Winters, & Zera, 2000). Rates of op-positional defiant disorder vary somewhere between 2% and 16%, but we generally accept that about 5% of children suffer oppositional defiant disorder prior to teenage years. The rate tends to decrease with age, and there is a great deal of diagnostic stability for both males and females, particularly when the expression is more severe. As previously noted, oppositional defiant disorder is more common among children from lower socioeconomic strata.

The rates of conduct disorder vary from 1% to 10% in epidemiological studies. Among children and adolescents diagnosed with conduct disorder, there is, of course, significant crossover with those first diagnosed with oppositional defiant disorder. In contrast to oppositional defiant disorder, the frequency of conduct disorder increases with age, and there is a great deal of diagnostic stability, depending on the study, ranging between 44% and 88% at 3–4 years post–initial diagnosis (Lahey et al., 1995; Offord et al., 1992).

CLINICAL COURSE

Gender differences do not typically emerge until after 6 years of age in children with oppositional defiant disorder. From about 7 years of age until puberty, the disorder is more prevalent in males. After puberty, the male-to-female ratio equalizes. In general, symptoms of oppositional defiant disorder are evident by 8 years of age. Typically, symptoms emerge gradually over months or years, first at home with parents and other adults with whom the child is familiar. Over time symptoms generalize to include other adults, such as teachers and coaches, and other settings in the child's life, such as school and camp.

Oppositional defiant disorder itself can be relatively benign, and even without formal treatment most children traverse the disorder naturally, growing out of it as they age. About 30–40% of individuals, however, will go on to develop conduct disorder and about the same percentage of individuals with conduct disorder, 30–40%, will go on to develop antisocial personality disorder. Earlier age at onset typically predicts a worse prognosis and greater likelihood of progression to conduct disorder and antisocial personality disorder (Steiner, Remsing, & the AACAP Work Group on Quality Issues, 2007).

The clinical course of conduct disorder is considerably more severe. Oppositional defiant disorder is a common, but not necessary, precursor, and less severe behaviors tend to emerge first, such as lying, shoplifting, and fighting. Onset of conduct disorder is rare after 16 years of age. In some cases the behaviors are adaptive or even protective. For example, in threatening, impoverished, or high-crime neighborhoods, children may join gangs in order to find some protection, solace, and a supportive

Early Childhood   **Middle Childhood**   **Late Childhood and Adolescence**

Figure 3.1.   A developmental progression for antisocial behavior. This theoretical model of delinquency suggests that inadequate parental management in early childhood inadvertently supports the development of child behavior problems. By middle childhood, poorly behaved children are rejected by their peers and suffer academic failure, which leads these children to commit to deviant peer groups and furthers the likelihood of delinquency. Adapted from Patterson, DeBarshe, & Ramsey (1989).

peer group. A diagnosis in this environment may not be appropriate. In the majority of children the disorder remits by adulthood, but as previously noted, a substantial proportion (30–40%) will go on to develop antisocial personality disorder.

While a theoretical model of delinquency has not been satisfactorily designed, some of the key factors in the development of delinquency include an early childhood characterized by poor parental monitoring and inconsistent or harsh parenting, along with a general lack of discipline. Those children who are vulnerable may then go on to develop conduct problems. In middle childhood, conduct-disordered children are often rejected by normal peers and suffer academic difficulties, perhaps because of a comorbid learning disorder or perhaps because the child himself has simply not been taught how to discipline himself and properly learn. With repeated academic and social failures, the child may then become committed to a deviant peer group and by late childhood or early adolescence is engaging regularly in delinquent behaviors (see Figure 3.1).

DIAGNOSIS

The differential diagnosis for disruptive behavior disorders includes ADHD, mood disorders, adjustment disorders, and anxiety disorders. According to the *DSM-IV*, the criteria for oppositional defiant disorder require that

Table 3.1. Diagnostic Symptoms of Oppositional Defiant Disorder*

1. Often loses temper
2. Often argumentative
3. Often defiant
4. Often angry
5. Often blames others
6. Often purposefully annoys others
7. Often touchy or easily upset
8. Often spiteful or vindictive

Adapted from *DSM-IV* (American Psychiatric Association, 2000).

four of eight symptoms be present for at least 6 months and that each of these symptoms be present "often" (American Psychiatric Association, 2000). This pattern of negativistic, hostile, and defiant behavior includes frequently losing one's temper, arguing with adults, actively defying or refusing to comply with rules, deliberately annoying others, blaming others for one's own mistakes or behavior, being touchy or easily annoyed by others, being angry and resentful, and being spiteful or vindictive (see Table 3.1). While almost all children will at times experience some of these symptoms, the *DSM* relies upon the key word *often* to indicate that occasional difficulty is not adequate for a diagnosis.

Many children who meet diagnostic criteria for oppositional defiant disorder suffer low self-esteem; alternatively, others, as if by a defense mechanism, demonstrate an inflated self-esteem. Mood lability, low frustration tolerance, cursing, and the early use of alcohol and drugs are other commonly associated symptoms of children diagnosed with oppositional defiant disorder. The most common Axis I comorbidities include ADHD, learning disorders, and communication or speech disorders. Approximately 50% of children with ADHD also suffer oppositional defiant disorder or conduct disorder, while 70% of children with oppositional defiant disorder or conduct disorder suffer ADHD.

The diagnosis of conduct disorder is predicated upon three or more symptoms that have been present within the past 12 months from four general categories; at least one symptom must have been present within the past 6 months in order to qualify for the diagnosis. Conduct disorder represents a more severe form of behavioral disruption because its diagnosis demands that the individual have a repeated pattern of behavior that ignores or violates the basic rights of others or major age-appropriate societal norms. The four primary categories are aggression to people and

Table 3.2.   Diagnostic Symptoms of Conduct Disorder*

Aggression
  (1) frequently bullies or threatens others
  (2) frequently starts physical fights
  (3) has used a weapon that can cause serious physical harm to others
  (4) has a history of physical cruelty to people
  (5) has a history of physical cruelty to animals
  (6) has stolen from a victim
  (7) has forced someone into a sexual act

Property Destruction
  (8) has deliberately started a fire
  (9) has deliberately destroyed property

Stealing and Dishonesty
  (10) has broken into someone's house, building, or car
  (11) often lies to obtain something or to avoid obligations
  (12) has stolen things without confronting a victim

Violating Rules
  (13) often stays out at night against parent's wishes, beginning before age 13
  (14) has run away from home overnight at least twice
  (15) has often been truant from school, beginning before age 13

Adapted from *DSM-IV* (American Psychiatric Association, 2000).

animals, destruction of property, deceitfulness or theft, and serious violation of rules (see Table 3.2).

Based upon the child's age at onset of the disorder, two subtypes of conduct disorder have been recognized. They differ in their presenting symptoms, developmental course, prognosis, and gender. The childhood onset or "unsocialized" type typically requires at least one criterion to be met before age 10. These individuals are usually male, frequently aggressive, often demonstrate disturbed peer relations, often first suffered oppositional defiant disorder, may have concurrent ADHD, and are most likely to have persistent conduct disorder and later develop antisocial personality disorder. The second subtype is adolescent in onset or the so-called socialized type. These youths demonstrate an absence of conduct disorder symptoms prior to age 10 and are more likely to have normal peer relationships, less likely to display aggressive behaviors, and less likely to suffer persistent conduct disorder and later develop *antisocial personality disorder*. While still more commonly male than female, the preponderance of males is far greater in the childhood onset type.

Children diagnosed with conduct disorder face an increase in accident rates and generally lower self-esteem (although, as with oppositional defiant disorder, the self-esteem of these children is occasionally defensively inflated). In addition, conduct disorder is often associated with early sexual contact, the development of sexually transmitted diseases and pregnancy, and an increase in alcohol, drug use, and risk-taking behavior. These children sometimes attend alternative schools and live in foster placement, and they attempt and complete suicide at a higher rate than other youth. The most common Axis I comorbidities include ADHD, learning disorders, communication or speech and language disorders, anxiety disorders, mood disorders, and substance use disorders. The best predictor of a later diagnosis of conduct disorder in a young child is cruelty to others and weapon use. Below the age of 13, cruelty, running away, and breaking and entering are also highly predictive of later conduct disorder.

For a sizeable number of children, depression leads to conduct disorder. Depending upon the study, children with depression are between three and nine times more likely to be diagnosed with a disruptive behavior disorder (Angold & Costello, 1993).

Rating scales for the identification and classification of disruptive behavior disorders are not well established. The Swanson, Nolan, and Pelham (SNAP) Scale and the Connors Scale, both of which are used for diagnosing ADHD, include a number of disruptive behavior measures, as do most ADHD rating scales. Other instruments, such as the Disruptive Behavior Disorder Rating Scale, can be helpful in identifying the symptoms but also typically include many symptom questions for ADHD, given the high comorbidity between ADHD and the disruptive behavior disorders. Many of these scales are available as freeware and can be found on the Internet.

TREATMENT

Before addressing the treatment of oppositional defiant disorder and conduct disorder, it is worthwhile considering protective factors. Unfortunately, our research in this area is not strong and does not provide clear guidance (Stouthamer-Loeber, Loeber, Wei, Farrington, & Wikström, 2002). All agree that controlling for risk factors is probably the most effective step toward prevention. There is some evidence, however, that programs for preschool children, such as Head Start, may decrease later delinquency and oppositional defiant disorder and conduct disorder (Connor, 2002). Other early intervention programs have some supporting data as well. These programs sometimes address the children directly, teaching improved interpersonal problem solving skills and helping them to regulate their emotions (Conduct Problems Prevention Research Group,

1992); or focus on the parents and teachers, helping them to strengthen the children's social support, improve parenting practices, and provide key proficiencies for children, such as anger management and social skills (Webster-Stratton & Reid, 2003). In general terms, relationships and mentoring appear to be at least somewhat protective against the development of oppositional defiant disorder, characterized by good relations with at least one parent, good peer relations, and consistent and attentive parental monitoring.

In addition to prevention strategies, it is important to remember that comorbidities are more commonly the rule than the exception with highly disruptive children. Therefore, addressing any coexisting conditions is absolutely necessary in order to see any sustained improvement. The most common concurrent diagnoses, including ADHD, anxiety and mood disorders, learning disorders, and communication disorders, must be identified and treated. The clinician should look closely for these problems even when they are not initially reported by the patient and family and have not previously been a focus of treatment.

Behavioral Parenting

By and large, treatment strategies aimed directly at affected children, such as psychotherapy, have not clearly demonstrated their utility regardless of the type (e.g., supportive, psychodynamic, play, cognitive behavior, etc.). To be fair, the effects and benefits of individual psychotherapy are difficult to measure, and many therapists continue to engage in psychodynamic approaches, whereby the child or adolescent builds an attachment to a therapist as the basis of behavior change. This therapeutic approach is nonspecific and almost always includes the parents in some fashion or other, as parents typically have their own conflicts and anxieties, which lead to poor parenting practices. There are, however, a number of short-term, evidence-based therapies designed specifically for parents and disruptive children.

Parent management training (PMT) is a very well established treatment that has demonstrated major and sustained reductions in the disruptive behavior of children ages 2 through 12 years (Kazdin, 1997, 2005). For younger children (ages 2 through 6 years) whose symptoms are exceptionally severe, *parent-child interaction training* (PCIT) has also shown great utility (Herschell, Calzada, Eyberg, & McNeil, 2002). Both PMT and PCIT rely upon basically the same behavioral modification principles, are highly therapist directed, and have a strong evidence base supporting their use. Both treatments are time limited, requiring generally somewhere between 4 and 20 weeks to teach to parents. Parent training approaches are so effective that even teaching this material to parents by means of a video in the absence of a therapist has been shown to result in significant and sustained efficacy (Bradley et al., 2003; Montgomery, Bjornstad, & Dennis, 2006).

Although most PMT techniques are timeworn, straightforward, and incorporate much of what effective parents have been doing for years, for many parents such an approach is not intuitive. Virtually all children, whether diagnosed with a disruptive behavior disorder or not, demonstrate immense improvements in behavior after their parents have received PMT. The training is designed to help parents increase the behaviors they like and decrease the behaviors they dislike. Typically, the major topic areas covered include: Effective Commands, Tactful Praise, Ignoring, Scheduling, Behavioral Reward Programs, Limit Setting, Punishments and Time-Out. The emphasis in PMT is always on positive reinforcement for which an unlimited number of strategies can be devised. Punishments are relatively few in number and are employed sparingly, as they quickly lose their power to change children's behavior if overutilized.

Two similar treatments, *collaborative problem solving* (CPS) and *problem solving skills training* (PSST), address children's cognitive distortions and teach them new ways of managing social situations. While early research into CPS suggests it to be at least as effective as PMT (Greenberg, Siemicki, Dorfman, et al., 2004), it is still a relatively new treatment and has not been largely replicated; and while PSST has been shown to be effective in altering children's cognitive perceptions, it is understood that altering cognition is not always a reliable means of improving behavior (Kazdin, 2003).

Psychosocial Interventions

Although often employed for youths with severely disruptive behavior, studies of foster care generally show only mild improvements in the behavior of children and adolescents who are placed within a foster home (Reddy & Pfeiffer, 1997). Programs designed to reduce bullying at school, however, have strong empirical support, particularly when they address campus awareness, teach children and parents about the effects of bullying, employ a program of assertive monitoring of school behaviors, and intervene with specific individuals (Spivak & Prothrow-Stith, 2001).

Perhaps the most effective treatment for both children and adolescents who are severely disruptive is *multisystemic therapy* (MST). MST is an intensive family and community-based behavioral intervention designed to address and treat the problems in every setting, including home and school, mitigating multiple risk factors simultaneously. MST adopts an integrated approach that commonly utilizes aspects of PMT, PSST, and marital and family therapy, along with other interventions targeted at substance abuse, bullying, classroom social skills, improving communication between teachers and parents, special education services, and legal services. MST has been shown effective in reducing antisocial behavior for as long as 5 years posttreatment and appears to be cost-effective in the long run by decreasing recidivism and persistent overutilization of psychiatric and social services (Henggeler & Lee, 2003).

Medication Treatment

There are a number of psychopharmacological interventions that have been utilized for many years, and new strategies are being applied regularly. However, it should be noted that the FDA has not yet "approved" any medication for the treatment of oppositional defiant disorder or conduct disorder. While sometimes useful, medications for the treatment of disruptive behavior should be considered adjunctive or palliative but not curative. Behavioral, family, school, and community-based interventions, as specified above, should be the main focus of treatment (Pappadopulos et al., 2003; Schur et al., 2003).

Antipsychotics are increasingly utilized for the treatment of disruptive behavior in children and adolescents (Olfson, Blanco, Liu, Moreno, & Laje, 2006). In the United States the estimated number of office-based visits by children and adolescents that included antipsychotic treatment increased from approximately 201,000 in 1993 to 1,224,000 in 2002. From 2000 to 2002 the number of visits that included antipsychotic treatment was significantly higher for males than for females and for white non-Hispanic youth than for youth of other racial or ethnic groups. Overall, roughly 9% of mental health visits and 18% of visits to psychiatrists included antipsychotic treatment. Antipsychotics were most commonly used for diagnoses of disruptive behavior disorders (38%), mood disorders (32%), pervasive developmental disorders or mental retardation (17%), and psychotic disorders (14%).

Although haloperidol (Haldol), molindone (Moban), chlorpromazine (Thorazine), and thioridazine (Mellaril) have been employed for many years, the data supporting their use is scant, and the side effects are often significant though rarely permanent (Campbell, Cohen, & Small, 1982; Campbell et al., 1985; Greenhill, Solomon, Pleak, & Ambrosini, 1985; Platt, Campbell, Green, Perry, & Cohen, 1981) (see Chapter 12 for a thorough discussion of the side effects of antipsychotic medications).

In recent years risperidone (Risperdal) has demonstrated efficacy in identical 6-week multicenter randomized, double-blind, placebo-controlled trials that followed identical protocols and incorporated 163 boys ages 5 to 12 years with oppositional defiant disorder or conduct disorder and subaverage intelligence (e.g., IQs ranging from 36 to 84) with or without ADHD. These individuals demonstrated a decline in aggression by an average of 56% versus children who were given placebo and demonstrated a 22% decrease in aggressive behaviors (LeBlanc et al., 2005). Large-scale reviews of pilot, open-label, and larger clinical trials of over 800 children and adolescents with oppositional defiant disorder, conduct disorder, or disruptive behavior disorder NOS who were treated with risperidone at doses of 0.02 to 0.06 mg per kilogram per day found target symptom improvement compared with placebo and baseline functioning within 1 to 4 weeks of treatment (Pandina, Aman, & Findling, 2006).

Much less data is available to support the use of quetiapine (Seroquel), olanzapine (Zyprexa), and aripiprazole (Abilify) in the treatment of disruptive behavior disorders. Although many clinicians find these medications effective at times, the scientific data supporting their use is minimal and based upon open-label trials, chart reviews, pilot studies, and case reports (Findling, Reed, et al., 2006, 2007; Handen & Hardan, 2006; Masi et al., 2006).

The mood stabilizers, including lithium (Lithobid, Eskalith), divalproex sodium (Depakote), and carbamazepine (Tegretol), have also been employed for the treatment of disruptive behavior in children. Two randomized controlled trials compared lithium with placebo and found that at therapeutic doses lithium was efficacious and safe for the short-term treatment of aggressive inpatient children and adolescents with conduct disorder. Other studies as well have found lithium to be efficacious in the treatment of behavior disorders in children. One small randomized, double-blind, controlled study (Donovan et al., 2000), one randomized but open-label trial (Steiner, Petersen, Saxena, Ford, & Matthews, 2003), and one small open-label trial (Saxena, Howe, Simeonova, Steiner, & Chang, 2006) have demonstrated divalproex sodium to be effective for the treatment of aggression and explosive temper associated with oppositional defiant disorder and conduct disorder. It is likely, however, that divalproex sodium and carbamazepine are more likely to be effective for disruptive behavior among children and adolescents who are at risk for the development of a major mood disorder such as *bipolar disorder.*

Small randomized controlled trials have also demonstrated that clonidine (Catapres) may be useful for aggressive behavior in children with ADHD and comorbid oppositional defiant disorder and conduct disorder (Connor, Barkley, & Davis, 2000; Hazell & Stuart, 2003). In a meta-analysis of 11 double-blind randomized controlled studies from 1980 to 1999, clonidine demonstrated a moderate effect size (0.58) on symptoms of ADHD comorbid with conduct disorder, developmental delay, and motor tics (Connor, Fletcher, & Swanson, 1999). A number of other medications, such as beta-blockers, benzodiazepines, buspirone (Buspar), and naltrexone (Revia, Vivitrol), have been demonstrated to be useful as adjunct agents in case series and case reports, but there is little impressive data to suggest their regular use for this population of children (Riddle et al., 1999).

Based upon the currently available data and clinical experience, a reasonable treatment approach for a child or adolescent with severely disruptive behavior first requires a clear psychiatric diagnosis. In addition, all coexisting Axis I disorders should be identified and aggressively treated. Addressing concurrent problems, such as ADHD, depression, anxiety, and learning disorders, often considerably alleviates many of the disruptive behaviors. If direct treatment of the disruptive behaviors is necessary, all appropriate behavioral modification efforts, particularly those aimed at the parents, are clearly the first line of attack. If medications are to be employed, starting modestly, for example, with an alpha-2 agonist, would be a reasonable but not mandatory first step. If the behavior does not respond, the practitioner should revisit the diagnosis and make certain that other disorders are not unaddressed. If further medication efforts are necessary, then antipsychotics and mood stabilizers can be considered, but the practitioner and family must carefully weigh the considerable side effects of these medications. When absolutely necessary, the use of antipsychotics and mood stabilizers should be viewed as a short-term treatment effort to be employed while behavioral efforts are ongoing. Medications for disruptive behavior disorders are, at their best, treatments and not cures.

4

Learning Disorders

Learning disorders affect about 5% of American youth but are more commonly diagnosed among those with comorbid psychiatric disorders. New etiological research documents the neurobiological underpinnings of learning disorders with increasing clarity. These findings have direct relevance to novel treatment interventions. In addition, changes in government policy over the last 30 years have provided educational support and accommodations to children who struggle with learning disorders, helping to maximize their academic success.

CLINICAL PRESENTATION

Given the variety of ways in which learning disorders can present, they often go unrecognized (Cohen et al., 1993). Fear of humiliation due to learning troubles may present as school refusal, somatic symptoms, or even oppositional defiant disorder. About half of children with a learning disorder also have a comorbid psychiatric disorder, such as ADHD, a speech and language disorder, or an anxiety or mood disorder. Even children who do not meet diagnostic criteria for another Axis I disorder frequently suffer demoralization, depression, low self-esteem, and deficits in social skills (Kauffman, 1997; Kavale & Forness, 1995). Children with learning disorders typically have a long history of poor academic achievement and may have more difficulty than their peers in understanding others' moods, particularly in ambiguous situations (Bryan, 1991). The school dropout rate for children with learning disorders is twice that of students without such disabilities and in some samples reaches nearly 50% (Blackorby & Wagner, 1996).

ETIOLOGY

Beginning in utero, the human brain grows actively by cell division. Cell migration occurs as developing neurons travel to preprogrammed areas where they will ultimately reside. In most cases, cell migration proceeds in expected ways. Alterations in cell migration, however, have been seen in the brains of adult dyslexics. Autopsies have shown that the planum temporale and Wernicke's area, parts of the brain believed to be important for understanding and interpreting speech and written language, are less organized and less well ordered. In fact, the neurons in these areas appear to be scattered, less dense in formation, and somewhat haphazardly assigned. The cause of this disorganization is not known, but presumably both prenatal and postnatal cell migration could account for these changes (Galaburda, Sherman, Rosen, Aboitiz, & Geschwind, 1985).

Other studies have suggested that there is a reversal or reduction in the normal leftward asymmetry of the planum temporale in dyslexia, but this finding has been disputed (Heiervang et al., 2000). Problems with phonological processing, awareness of the sound and structure of words, along with a disruption in the white matter connections between posterior and frontal brain regions have been repeatedly found among those with dyslexia (Temple, 2002). Differences in brain activation have also been shown to occur in those suffering from dyslexia. Positron emission tomography (PET) scans have demonstrated altered activation in brain areas important for reading, which is associated with changes in the density of white and gray matter for those with dyslexia versus nonimpaired readers (Silani et al., 2005).

Effective readers rely on posterior regions of the brain (e.g., the temporal and parietal lobes and the angular gyrus), which are involved in automatic word recognition and reading. Those without dyslexia can read most common words without even paying much attention to their meanings, allowing the brain to multitask. Studies of regional brain blood flow among dyslexic adults, however, demonstrate that dyslexics overuse the frontal areas of the brain and are unable to tap into the automatic fluent recognition of words in the posterior regions. Dyslexics appear to sound out the words they read each and every time they see them, as if they have never seen them before. This sounding-out approach is precisely what happens for all readers when they are confronted with new written words or similar stimuli. In this case, the frontal lobes of the brain are recruited to break down the word into phonemes or specific sounds and pieces in order to consciously read the word. Common words do not call upon the frontal lobes to any great degree for most readers in the absence of dyslexia. The conscious and considerable effort that individuals with dyslexia must employ to read each and every word causes an increase in blood flow noted on fMRI (functional magnetic resonance imaging) to the oral/motor speech areas and the frontal lobes, the site of executive function, organization, and planning (Shaywitz et al., 1998).

Because of the poor connectivity between the frontal lobes and posterior regions of the brain among those with dyslexia, the frontal lobes themselves may also be developmentally impaired in areas important for reading. Studies in remediation have demonstrated that with additional support and training children can improve their reading abilities and functionality. Early but not widely replicated studies also suggest that with remediation there is a subsequent alteration in blood flow, as measured by fMRI, such that blood flow increases to the temporoparietal region, which is key for reading fluency, and away from the frontal lobes, which is overused among those with dyslexia (Temple et al., 2003).

EPIDEMIOLOGY

The prevalence of learning disorders ranges greatly in studies from 2% to 10%. This range has largely to do with the fact that there are few population-based epidemiologic studies that have applied strict diagnostic criteria. Among the studies that have been completed, inconsistencies in the ages of children evaluated and the populations selected for study (e.g., clinically referred as opposed to a more general population of children) have contributed to the varying range in prevalence.

We generally accept that approximately 5% of children in the United States suffer from a learning disorder. Boys are more commonly diagnosed than girls, although as with ADHD and other externalizing disorders (e.g., oppositional defiant disorder and conduct disorder), boys are more likely to be identified because they are more often disruptive and therefore more easily noticed by teachers (Beitchman & Young, 1997). Approximately 50% of children who receive special services at public schools throughout the country are learning disordered.

Reading disorder, or dyslexia, is essentially the sine qua non of learning disorders. That is, reading disorder is the most common form of learning disorders, and it is relatively rare to find an individual who suffers a mathematics or writing disorder in the absence of reading disorder.

Sixty to 80% of those who suffer from reading disorder are male, and the prevalence is estimated at 4% of school-age children in the United States. Reading disorder aggregates in families such that 35–40% of those with reading disorder have a first-degree relative who is also affected (Beitchman, Cantwell, Forness, Kavale, & Kauffman, 1998).

Mathematics disorder makes up the vast bulk of the remaining children who suffer a learning disorder. The prevalence is roughly 1% of school-age children in the United States. Mathematics disorder frequently co-occurs with reading disorder. *Disorder of written expression,* or *writing disorder,* is much more difficult to categorize and diagnose because standardized tests have not to date demonstrated themselves to be particularly useful. It is uncommon to find a child with a disorder of written expression who is not also suffering from dyslexia.

CLINICAL COURSE

As previously noted, the course of learning disorders is commonly severe. Although estimates vary from 25% to 97%, a large percentage of juvenile delinquents and incarcerated adults suffer from learning disorders (Grigorenko, 2006). Although learning disorders do not result in incarceration directly, they do account for a great deal of lost school and work time and, as previously described, are commonly associated with other Axis I disorders, in addition to an increase in lowered self-esteem, poor social functioning, and an increase in school dropout.

DIAGNOSIS

There are a variety of ways in which learning disorders are identified. Traditionally, a learning disorder is diagnosed when an individual's achievement on individually administered standardized tests in reading, math, or written expression is substantially below that expected for age, schooling, and level of measured intelligence. The phrase "substantially below" is usually defined as a discrepancy of more than two standard deviations between one's performance on an achievement test, for example in reading or math, and one's score on an IQ test. This discrepancy of two standard deviations demonstrates a clear difference between one's given ability (IQ) and one's demonstrated functioning (achievement). In many cases, learning disorders are defined not strictly by IQ and achievement test scores, but rather by correlation with one's expected level of functioning, given the age of the child or grade level in school. Because we now understand the typical patterns in performance among children with learning disorders, however, problems can often be identified by neuropsychological testing even if the discrepancy between grade, age, or IQ and academic functioning or achievement is not readily evident. A child who struggles with reading, for example, regardless of whether she meets standardized testing criteria, will typically show characteristic problems with phonological coding and rapid word retrieval, a pattern indicative of a reading disorder.

Reading disorder, or dyslexia, is characterized by distortions, substitutions, or omissions in reading. Both oral and silent reading are typically slow with frequent comprehension errors. Reading disorder is thought to arise from a left hemisphere deficit, or defect, in the planum temporale, which, as previously noted, has been found to be lacking in expected asymmetry. More disorganized and smaller cell bodies have also been noted in the visual magnocellular system. These changes typically persist into adolescence and adulthood if not effectively remediated. Even though we can now visualize some discreet brain changes among those with reading disorder, such means are not useful for diagnosis, which still rests upon clinical observation. The best predictors of adult reading levels are believed to be an individual's general intelligence and initial severity of the reading disorder.

Mathematics disorder usually becomes apparent by the second or third grade, as mathematics principles become increasingly important at school. Many skills may be effected, including linguistic skills, which are important for understanding mathematical terms, operations, concepts, and decoding; perceptual skills, which are important for recognizing and reading numerical symbols, mathematical signs, and grouping objects; attentional skills, which are necessary for writing numbers and figures correctly, remembering to "carry" numbers, and minding operational signs; and mathematical skills, which involve following steps, counting objects, and learning multiplication tables (American Psychiatric Association, 2000). Mathematics disorder is associated with a pattern of deficits in neurocognitive and adaptive functions generally attributed to the right hemisphere, which include spatial recognition and visuoperceptual/ simultaneous information processing. When concurrent problems in social and emotional functioning accompany problems with general mathematical abilities, this characteristic cluster of symptomatology is referred to as a *nonverbal learning disorder* (NVLD).

NVLD generally persists into adulthood and may worsen over time. Those with NVLD face an increased risk for internalizing disorders, such as anxiety and depression, along with social and emotional difficulties. The abnormal language characteristics, such as poor prosody and pragmatic use of language, coupled with a good vocabulary and the pronounced social difficulties that these children evidence, have led to questions about a connection between Asperger's disorder, schizoid personality disorder, and mathematics disorder. (For more information on NVLD, see Chapter 7.)

Disorders of written expression comprise the third category of learning disorders. Their prevalence, as previously reported, is unknown, and they are difficult to diagnose because standardized tests are not particularly useful. Generally, disorders of written expression involve a combination of difficulties with composing written text, such as grammar and punctuation errors, poor paragraph organization, multiple spelling errors, and poor handwriting.

There is a great overlap between Axis I disorders and learning disorders. Those diagnoses most commonly comorbid or co-occurring with learning disorders including conduct disorder, oppositional defiant disorder, ADHD, anxiety, and depression.

Educational Testing

In order to understand the utility of the IQ score, one must understand the distribution of IQ within the general population. Intelligence tests, along with virtually all commonly utilized educational and achievement tests, are scored on a standard scale, such that a score of 100 points is the defined "normal" or average. The typical standard deviation is 15 points. Plotted on a curve, then, the grid looks something like a bell where the precise center is at 100 and 50% of the population is captured between a score of 90 and 109 (see Figure 4.1).

IQ tests correlate with and predict school achievement, and as such they are a good measure of academic intelligence. IQ tests are relatively stable, and their stability increases with age; but they are not unchanging. Heredity and environment influence IQ scores, and no test is free from cultural influences. Some questions on IQ tests rely upon knowledge of facts and recognition of material that individuals must have been exposed to in order to perform well.

Scores on IQ tests are descriptive but not explanatory. The IQ score tells us where an individual does well and where he struggles, but not why he struggles. The IQ also fails to measure many factors that are important to individual success and happiness, such as creativity, perseverance, discipline, and one's social ability. In summary, IQ tests are very useful for measuring academic intelligence and predicting school achievement, but they otherwise have little utility.

There are numerous tests of intelligence available today, all of which do essentially the same thing and typically score children on the same scale.

Figure 4.1. IQ score distribution. The IQ score distribution follows a typical bell-shaped curve where the vast majority of individuals in the population lie within the normal range between 85 and 115. Approximately 16% of the population falls to the left of the normal range, indicating below average IQ, and 16% falls to the right, indicating above average IQ.

The most commonly utilized scales are the Wechsler scales and include the Wechsler Preschool and Primary Scale of Intelligence (WPPSI, now in its third edition) for children 2.6–7.3 years of age; the Wechsler Intelligence Scale for Children (WISC, now in its fourth edition) for children 6–16.11 years of age; and the Wechsler Adult Intelligence Scale (WAIS, now in its third edition) for individuals 16–89 years of age. Other commonly utilized scales include the Stanford-Binet Intelligence Scale, which is commonly employed for individuals whose intelligence is thought to reside at the upper and lower ends of the IQ scale; the Kaufman Assessment Battery for Children, and the Woodcock-Johnson Tests of Cognitive Ability.

The WISC recently entered its fourth edition. Previously, the WISC-III gave summary scores for verbal IQ, performance IQ, and full-scale IQ. The WISC-IV provides a more comprehensive understanding of one's academic potential by providing summary scores or indices in verbal comprehension, perceptual reasoning, working memory, and processing speed. The WISC-IV also adds a number of new domains to IQ testing such as word reasoning, matrix reasoning, letter-number sequencing, and symbol search and cancellation. In contrast to the WISC-III, the WISC-IV has been normed on typical or normal student populations as well as students receiving special education services, such as those affected by ADHD, learning disorders, mental retardation, and so forth.

In addition to the standard IQ tests, there are a number of special-purpose educational tests that address particular populations. The Gessell Developmental Scales and the Denver Developmental Screening Test are designed for infants and toddlers; the Vineland Adaptive Behavior Scale and American Association on Mental Retardation (AAMR) Adaptive Behavior Scale are both designed to determine the degree to which individuals with mental retardation are able to function independently within society; and the Hiskey Nebraska Test of Learning Aptitude is designed for the hearing impaired, while the Liter International Performance Scale is designed for those with limited reading abilities.

A variety of tests are commonly employed to evaluate academic achievement or abilities within a specific domain, such as reading, writing, and arithmetic. Some achievement tests are administered to large groups of students in public school systems in an effort to monitor not only individual progress, but also how well the schools are teaching the students. Those instruments most commonly utilized are the Stanford Achievement Tests (Stanford 9), the California Achievement Tests (CAT), and the Iowa Tests of Basic Skills. There are also a number of individually administered achievement tests, which are most commonly used along with an IQ test in order to determine a potential learning disorder. The most common individually administered achievement tests are the Wide Range Achievement Tests (WRAT-III), the Wechsler Individual Achievement Tests (WIAT), and the Woodcock-Johnson Psychoeducational Battery, Revised (WJ-R).

Neuropsychological testing is performed in an effort to understand the behavioral expression of brain dysfunction and is utilized to aid in the diagnosis and treatment planning of patients. There are a number of general standard neuropsychological test batteries utilized in children such as the Halstead Reitan, the Luria-Nebraska, and the NEPSY. These tests comprise a broad range of components that measure all manner of functioning, including general motor function, visual motor integration, perceptual ability, language, memory, and various executive functions.

A number of specialized component neuropsychological tests exist as well. Those that specifically measure motor function include the Purdue Pegboard and the Dynamometer Grip Strength Test. The Reitan-Klove Sensory-Perceptual Examination, an element of the Halstead Reitan, is commonly utilized to measure sensory perception on various sides of the body. The Bender Gestalt and Developmental Test of Visual Motor Integration are both designed to measure visual-motor integration.

Common tests of expressive and receptive language, as well as phonology, include the Peabody Picture Vocabulary Test and the Boston Naming Test; and tests of short-term, long-term, verbal, and visual memory and memory storage include the Wide Range Assessment of Memory and Learning (WRAML) and the Buschke Selective Reminding Test. Finally, the tests of executive functioning, or those that directly measure frontal lobe activity involved in organization, attention, and planning, include the Stroop-Color Word Test, the Wisconsin Card Sort, Trail Making Test, Continuous Performance Test, and the Tower of London.

Projective testing is yet another category of neuropsychological testing occasionally employed with children in whom we are concerned about the presence of a thought disorder or perceptual disturbance, such as psychosis. Projective tests present the examinee with vague or ambiguous stimuli, such as drawings, written or visual scenarios, or sentences with various words left out that the patient must complete. In theory, these tests demand that the patient "project" his or her unconscious thoughts, feelings, perceptions, and emotions onto the scenario presented, revealing something about the patient that she is unable or unwilling to speak about. For example, a child is presented with a vague drawing of a scene and asked to describe what is happening. Children will give various responses to this type of stimulation, and it is often difficult to score these tests. However, a great deal of useful clinical information can be gleaned from this exercise, such as a child's perception of himself and others, a sense of his internal emotional state, and a sense of his values. Various commonly utilized projective tests include the Rorschach, Human Figure Drawing Test, Kinetic Family Drawing, Thematic Aperception Test (TAT), and the Sentence Completion Test.

TREATMENT

No medications have been demonstrated to be useful specifically for learning disorders. Many children with learning disorders, as previously described, suffer from comorbid Axis I disorders, particularly ADHD. For those with ADHD, the use of stimulants is often helpful in improving attention and memory with subsequent benefits in academic achievement. However, stimulants are not advised or recommended for the general population who simply would like to stay awake to study throughout the night or to get "an edge" in studying for exams or writing papers. Stimulant medications should only be given to those with an established diagnosis of ADHD. These medications can have significant side effects and are readily abusable.

One recent small Italian study of the use of gingko biloba demonstrated benefit for a small group of children with learning disorders (Donfrancesco & Ferrante, 2007). The postulated theory of action is an increase in brain blood flow.

Other treatment avenues for learning disorders have included the use of tutors and various learning specialists. There are a number of specific methods to help children suffering from dyslexia to gain strategies in reading, such as the decoding of words. Specific proprietary methodologies include those sponsored by Lindamood-Bell, Orton Gillingham, and Preventing Academic Failure. Fast Forward is a computer-based program designed to help children blend speech sounds in an effort to speed the normal process of phonological manipulation. Although each method undoubtedly has its merits, head-to-head studies have not been completed, and therefore we do not know if one is more beneficial than another.

A variety of accommodations and modifications are provided for by federal law and are often of great benefit for children with learning disorders. The Rehabilitation Act of 1973 (Public Law 93-112) protects those with disabilities from discrimination (physical, mental, and emotional) in federally funded programs, which include public schools. This law established the 504 Plan, which demands that students receive "reasonable accommodation" for their disabilities. An "accommodation" allows a student to complete the same assignments or tests as other students but with changes in timing, formatting, setting, scheduling, response and/or presentation (as indicated for each child). A "modification" is an adjustment to an assignment or test that changes the standard or the way in which the test or assignment measures a student's learning.

Typical 504 accommodations and modifications include providing students with alternative books that are easier to read but that teach similar concepts; providing audiotapes of textbooks and/or chapter summaries; giving shorter assignments focused on mastering only the key concepts; substituting alternatives for written assignments, such as clay models, posters, or collections; and providing a computer for written work or a word processor, such as an Alpha Smart. In addition, alternative seating; using both oral and printed directions; providing visual aids; providing time for transitions between activities; allowing additional time for tasks, such as homework, without a penalty; using worksheets that require minimal handwriting; reading test questions aloud; grading spelling separately from content; and allowing the use of a calculator for math are also commonly utilized accommodations and modifications.

A law of even greater importance for children with learning disabilities was passed in 1975. Public Law 94-142, the Education of All Handicapped Children Act (later renamed the Individuals with Disability Education

Act, IDEA), which established the IEP or individual educational plan, guarantees a free and appropriate education to each child with a disability in every state and locality across the country and requires schools to provide a customized educational environment for learning-disabled children. In 1991 the Individuals with Disability Education Act Amendments and Reauthorization added the category of "other health impaired," which extended the purview of the law to include children with physical and emotional illnesses, such as ADHD and anxiety disorders, whose academic work suffered as a result of their primary illness.

The process of receiving learning support is standardized throughout the country. In order to obtain an evaluation for a possible IEP, a parent simply needs to write a letter to the school district requesting an evaluation of his or her child's learning. A typical IEP request letter is modeled in Figure 4.2. Generally, a parent requests an IEP, although this request may also be initiated by a concerned teacher, school principal, or psychologist with the approval of the parent. Once the referral is made, the child is evaluated. The testing utilized will vary depending upon the difficulties the child appears to face and may include some combination of IQ and achievement testing, additional language or academic testing, as well as neuropsychological and projective testing. After the testing is completed and analyzed, a meeting is held with concerned personnel from the school along with the parents. If an IEP is deemed necessary, a formal document is written, services are provided, and an annual follow-up meeting to assess progress is held each year. Children receiving IEP services are typically reevaluated every 3 years. The timing of the IEP process is described in Table 4.1.

The process of receiving support through 504 services is generally less formal. Many teachers, in fact, will automatically provide learning accommodations and modifications, particularly for younger children, before even consulting the parents. It is important, however, for parents to understand these changes in their child's learning environment and to have them formally written down. Otherwise, these supports may not accompany their child through different grades and schools.

The content of a typical IEP will include the child's current performance and functioning, the annual goals for the child, any special education and related services, participation with nondisabled children, participation in state and district testing, dates and places of services, transitional services, and how progress will be measured. Members of the student's IEP team will include the student (as appropriate), the regular education teachers, any special education teachers or providers, a school system representative, the parents, and an individual who can evaluate and interpret the test results, such as a school psychologist. Representatives

DATE

(Principal's name)
(Child's school)
(School address)
(City, State, Zip Code)

Re: Child's name & date of birth

Dear *(Principal's name)*:

I am writing to request an assessment for special education for *(child's name)*, a student in the *(child's grade)* grade at *(child's school)* School. *(Child's name)* lives at *(child's address)*, which is within the *(school district name)* School District. I am *(child's name)*'s *(your relationship to child)*.

I believe my child has a *(name of learning disability if known)* disability impacting his ability to learn in school. *(Describe child's educational performance, including grades, behavior, and disciplinary history, if any. Include reports of primary-care physicians, psychiatrists, psychologists, social workers, teachers, or therapists, if any. Explain why you believe these behaviors result from a learning disability.)* Because of his learning disability, I believe *(child's name)* would benefit from special education services. *(Explain which services the child needs if known.)*

Additionally, I am requesting that the *(school district name)* School District evaluate *(child's name)* for any program modifications or services for which he is eligible under Section 504 of the Rehabilitation Act and the Americans with Disabilities Act.

Thank you for consideration of my request. I look forward to hearing from you within the next 15 days.

Sincerely,

(Your signature/your full name)

cc: School District Superintendent

Figure 4.2.   Sample IEP request letter.

Table 4.1. Timing of the IEP Process

1. 15 working days from request to school response.
2. 10 workweeks to complete testing and evaluation.
3. 10 working days to meet with the parents and IEP team upon completion of testing.
4. 10 working days for the parents to respond to the IEP meeting.
5. If the parents are unsatisfied, they can try and reach agreement with the school.
6. Parents can then request mediation.
7. Parents can then request due process.
8. Parents can write a letter of complaint to the State Department of Education.

from various service agencies from which the student may require support (e.g., foster care) and those who have special knowledge of the child or special expertise in an area of the child's difficulties (e.g., a physician or therapist) may also be invited to the meeting.

Children with IEPs may require a variety of related services, depending upon the severity of their impairments. Those listed under the IDEA and commonly indicated include audiology services, counseling services, early identification and assessment of disabilities, medical services, occupational therapy, orientation and mobility services, parent counseling and training, physical therapy, psychological services, recreation, rehabilitation counseling services, school health services, social work services in school, speech and language pathology services, and transportation. Special factors to consider include the child's behavior, proficiency in English, blindness or visual impairment, any special communication needs, and those who may be deaf or hearing impaired.

5

Speech and Language Disorders

Over 50% of children diagnosed with a speech and language disorder are believed to suffer social, emotional, and/or behavioral problems (Prizant & Meyer, 1993). Communication deficits are perhaps most common among those with *autism spectrum disorders,* but approximately one-third of children referred to psychiatric clinics for the treatment of conduct disorder and other behavioral problems have associated speech and language difficulties. In addition, more than two-thirds of children with ADHD have language problems (Giddan, 1991), and children with communication disorders are more likely to experience maltreatment and abuse (Knutson & Sullivan, 1993).

CLINICAL PRESENTATION

The presentation of speech and language disorders varies greatly depending upon the precise difficulty. The *communication disorder* diagnostic categories identified by the *DSM-IV* include *expressive language disorder, mixed receptive-expressive language disorder, phonological disorder, stuttering,* and *communication disorder not otherwise specified* (American Psychiatric Association, 2000). While there is much overlap and similarity between these conditions, each disorder has its unique characteristics.

Expressive language disorder is characterized by a variety of features, all of which impact a child's ability to articulate thoughts into speech. Typical problems include a paucity of speech, a restricted vocabulary, problems learning new words, difficulty with word finding, vocabulary mistakes, problems with phraseology, little variety in sentence structure, and odd ordering of words. Children with these problems are also typically slow to develop language in general and have a limited grasp of grammar. Intelligence and language comprehension are usually unaffected.

Many of the impairments are quite similar for children with *mixed receptive-expressive language disorder*. Yet in this case the difficulties include not only the expression of language, but also the understanding of words and sentences or specific types of words and their context. The range of pathology is quite variable. While some children may only have trouble with certain types of terminology or complicated sentences, others may struggle with basic vocabulary and experience deficits in auditory processing, such that they are unable to differentiate sounds, build associations between sounds and symbols (e.g., letters), or are unable to remember and classify language. Many children with mixed receptive-expressive language disorder also have trouble maintaining a conversation and following commands and may appear as if they are inattentive or confused when spoken to. Given that children must first develop receptive language before they can begin to speak or develop expressive language, an unadulterated receptive language disorder in children, similar to Wernicke's aphasia in adults, is never diagnosed.

Phonological disorder is defined as impairment in the ability to use expected speech sounds appropriate for age. These children's speech is characterized by misarticulation such that, for example, the "s" is pronounced with a lisp. Alternatively, certain sounds may be omitted from words such that, for example, "place" is pronounced as "pace," lacking the "l." Other children may incorrectly substitute one sound for another, such that, for example, "car" is pronounced as "dar." Phonological disorder cannot be attributed solely to deficits or abnormalities in intelligence, hearing, or the structure and physiology of speech mechanisms. For some affected children, the substitutions and misarticulations may be idiosyncratic or atypical, such that certain sounds are oversimplified, avoided, reversed, or misordered. In other cases the phonological errors follow a prescriptive pattern. Phonological disorder is the most prevalent type of speech and language disorder, accounting for up to 80% of clinical speech referrals (Edwards, 1984).

Stuttering is characterized by impairment in speech fluency or frequent repetitions or prolongations of various sounds, syllables, or words. Other interruptions in speech, such as sound blocking, hesitations, or tense pauses, may also be present. Typically, the words will begin with fragmentation of syllables or words followed by repetition of single sounds or syllables, prolongations, or forceful articulation. Stuttering is generally more severe when there is pressure to communicate, high stress, or anxiety, such as when interviewing for a job or giving a report at school, and is often absent during reading aloud, singing, or speaking with inanimate objects or pets. Stuttering is not to be confused with normal speech repetitions, which occasionally occur when children repeat whole words or phrases (e.g., *"I need I need to go to the bathroom"*) or speak in incomplete sentences or only with interjections or parenthetical remarks.

Although often unaware of the problem at onset, children who stutter eventually may try to decrease the problem by changing the rate of their speech, avoiding certain situations (e.g., speaking in public), or not using troublesome words or sounds. Stuttering is sometimes accompanied by motor tics, eye blinking, tremors, or other body movements. Untreated children may eventually complain of social troubles because of the anxiety, shame, and frustration they feel secondary to the embarrassment of stuttering.

ETIOLOGY

Both expressive language disorder and mixed receptive-expressive language disorder can be acquired or developmental in nature (American Psychiatric Association, 2000). In the acquired type, problems develop after a period of normal development, typically as a result of a neurological or medical complication, such as encephalitis, traumatic brain injury, brain irradiation, or damage from tumors or seizures. Focal lesions generally affect language in children if they are unilateral to the left side of the brain. Children younger than 10 years of age often recover completely from aphasias. Prenatal exposure to drugs and alcohol, or parental behavior disorders such as abuse and neglect, are also associated with the development of language disorders in children. Developmental language disorders are not associated with a known postnatal neurological insult or physical insult and persist from the earliest of ages.

The developmental type of both expressive language disorder and mixed receptive-expressive language disorder is more likely to occur in families where a first-degree relative is affected or where there are other family members with a speech and language or learning disorder. The acquired type does not aggregate in families. Some types of phonological disorder are more common in families, as is the case with stuttering.

As previously noted, anxiety and stress have been shown to aggravate stuttering but do not play a role in the disorder's etiology. Those who stutter show laryngeal behavior that is different from typical speakers, even during fluent speech (Conture et al., 1984). Based upon family and twin studies, there is significant evidence of a possible genetic linkage as the risk of stuttering among first-degree relatives is more than three times the general population risk. Among men who have a history of stuttering, approximately 10% of their daughters and 20% of their sons will stutter. Theoretical causes include biological vulnerability, environmental demands and expectations, and temperamental characteristics of the speaker.

Medications—such as tricyclic antidepressants, monoamine oxidase inhibitors, and phenothiazines—have also been reported to cause stuttering (Brady, 1991). PET (positron emission tomography) studies indicate left hemisphere dysfunction with compensatory right hemisphere responses in some cases of stuttering, such that motor regions involved in speech production are more active in stutterers.

EPIDEMIOLOGY

The prevalence of speech and language disorders varies by type (American Psychiatric Association, 2000). Expressive language disorders are more common in males than females. Language delays are noted in about 10–15% of children under 3 years of age. The frequency of expressive language disorder among school-age children ranges from about 3% to 7%. The developmental type is more common than the acquired type. The developmental type of mixed receptive-expressive language disorder is also more prevalent among males and is estimated to occur in up to 5% of preschool children and 3% of school-age children. Still, it is considerably less common than expressive language disorder, as expected.

Phonological disorder affects the largest number of children, although in most cases its impact is mild. Only about 2% of school-age children 6–7 years of age experience moderate to severe difficulties. The prevalence of phonological disorder among preschool children ranges from 3% to 15%. Prevalence drops to about 0.5% by 17 years of age.

Stuttering is about three times more common in males than females and affects approximately 1% of prepubertal children. By adolescence, the prevalence drops below 1%.

CLINICAL COURSE

The clinical course of speech and language disorders varies by diagnosis. Most speech problems are evident by 3 or 4 years of age. If a child's speech is significantly delayed beyond that point, one must seriously consider other diagnoses that could result in a delay in speech, such as an autistic spectrum disorder or mental retardation.

Expressive language disorder is typically noted by age 3, although milder forms may not be evident until adolescence, when language demands become more complex. Those affected by the developmental type typically attain relatively normal language capabilities by late adolescence, although slight difficulties may endure, sometimes even into adulthood. Those affected by the acquired type vary greatly in speech and language impairment and improvement depending upon the nature and site of the insult.

Mixed receptive-expressive language disorder is typically evident by age 4, and although full recovery is common, the prognosis is generally worse than for those diagnosed with expressive language disorder. Many children, although not as many as with expressive language disorder, ultimately develop normal language abilities. Most children with the developmental type improve substantially, but a minority continue to have difficulties that persist into adulthood. As with expressive language disorder, course and prognosis among those with the acquired type will vary depending upon the nature and site of the insult. Children affected by more severe forms of mixed receptive-expressive language disorder are more likely to suffer comorbid learning disorders (American Psychiatric Association, 2000).

Most cases of *phonological disorder* are identified by the time a child enters preschool or kindergarten, when his speech is found to be unintelligible to teachers and other children. However, children as young as age 3 are sometimes diagnosed if the speech is incomprehensible even to family members. The clinical course is variable and dependent upon the etiology and degree of impairment. A significant number of children who are afflicted require special services throughout their elementary school years. Most children whose phonological disorder is not due to a medical condition show spontaneous resolution by age 6 (American Psychiatric Association, 2000), but up to 75% of children with delayed speech development in preschool years may suffer an associated language disorder later in life (Shriberg & Kwiatkowski, 1988).

Stuttering generally begins around 5 years of age and almost always before age 10. The onset is typically slow, occurring over many months, often starting with long words or the beginnings of sentences and only becoming evident over time. The disorder tends to wax and wane in frequency and severity. As the child ages and becomes increasingly aware of the problem, he may develop means for avoiding the use of certain difficult words, phrases, and emotional responses that tend to elicit the stuttering. Somewhere between 20% and 80% of individuals who stutter recover by late adolescence (American Psychiatric Association, 2000).

DIAGNOSIS

If a speech and language disorder is suspected, other syndromes or causes of communication difficulties should be ruled out, particularly problems understanding language, which are the least evident and most difficult to identify. These disorders include hearing impairments (sometimes secondary to a history of chronic ear infections), mental retardation, autism spectrum disorder, and any organic causes of speech and language problems, such as cleft palate, apraxia, cerebral palsy, or an acquired aphasia. In addition, psychiatric comorbidities, which can complicate learning and speech, such as ADHD, learning disorders, and anxiety disorders, should be ruled out.

Speech and language disorders are typically identified through careful speech and language testing and occasionally neuropsychological testing. Diagnostic instruments include individually administered standardized examinations that test nonverbal intelligence, receptive language skills, and expressive language skills. In the case of expressive language disorder, the nonverbal intelligence and receptive skills are significantly better than the expressive skills. In the case of mixed receptive-expressive language disorder, standardized tests typically show nonverbal intelligence to be significantly higher than both expression and comprehension of language.

Phonological disorder is often identified without excessive neurological or speech and language testing and is determined by a child's inability to use expected speech sounds appropriate for age. Errors in creating, using, depicting, and organizing sounds, along with sound replacements or exclusions, are clear indicators. Speech and language testing remains useful and often necessary for these children, however, as other language impairments are often present and will not be identified without a thorough evaluation.

Stuttering is also often evident under clinical observation alone. As previously described, stuttering is characterized by problems with speech fluency or frequent repetitions or prolongation of sounds, syllables, or words. In order for *DSM-IV* criteria to apply to any of the communication disorders, difficulties with speech and language must interfere with academic or occupational achievement or with social communication (American Psychiatric Association, 2000).

TREATMENT

There is a great deal of overlap among the treatments for most speech and language disorders that affect children and adolescents. The choice of treatment is best determined by a certified speech and language therapist, who may recommend individual treatments and/or small group therapy. Children commonly receive both types of treatment with varying frequency. A complete psychiatric evaluation is generally also advised to rule out common comorbidities, such as learning disorders and ADHD, along with any possible medical or neurological causes for the impairments. *Social skills training* and *parent management training* are also sometimes helpful for both the child and parent, respectively, for associated educational, social, and behavioral problems.

The behavioral approach to the treatment of speech and language disorders varies by practitioner. Some use behavioral modification approaches while others use more child-centered approaches, such as *indirect language stimulation*. With this method, the parent and therapist use "self talk," describing each thing they are doing out loud and in detail, such as "I hold the key. I unlock the door. I get inside the car." Other indirect language stimulation techniques include parallel talk, where the adult describes out loud what the child is doing; description, where the adult uses labeling and explanatory phrases to identify and describe the child's experiences (e.g., "that dog is a Chihuahua," or "that car is long and blue"); and expansion, where the adult repeats the child's words but with proper enunciation and grammar.

Another commonly employed technique is *whole language instruction*, which was initially applied to children with reading disorder. Because readers tend to grasp the whole meanings of words and children tend to speak words in their entirety, not broken down into their parts, it was reasoned that children should be taught to read by the same mechanism; that is, by whole words, not by reading words in their component parts. Speech therapists apply this intervention by creating a rich communicative environment that leads to incidental learning. Numerous play opportunities and focused stimulation are employed to elicit language targets.

By and large, those specific speech and language therapies that have been tested demonstrate efficacy (Enderby & Emerson, 1996). Still, few treatments have been tested, and major problems remain regarding the terminology and classification of speech and language disorders among children. Additionally, most children do better over time regardless of intervention, and most speech and language disorders appear to spontaneously resolve by early school age. Further scientific efforts must be put into identifying those affected children whose impairments will not improve independently and are in need of more intensive intervention.

Psychopharmacological interventions are not routinely effective or helpful in the treatment of speech and language disorders. More commonly, medications and psychotherapy are used to treat the psychiatric comorbidities that may be interfering with the child's ability to function and use language effectively. For example, some stutterers who have been treated for anxiety related to speaking have shown an improvement in symptoms (Van Riper, 1973), but treating anxiety per se has not typically been found effective.

6

Mental Retardation

The unattractive term *mental retardation* has long been applied to individuals with both intellectual impairments and behavioral delays and continues to be used as a descriptive clinical diagnosis to this day. While most causes of mental retardation remain elusive, we can now categorize the cognitive deficits that individuals face and identify risk factors and certain behavioral characteristics that are typical of affected individuals. In recent years, we have also become better at distinguishing mental retardation from the commonly comorbid psychiatric conditions that these individuals often face.

CLINICAL PRESENTATION

The clinical presentation of mental retardation is as varied as is the number of causes. Over 500 etiologies of mental retardation have been identified to date, but still we are unable to identify an organic cause in the vast majority of cases (Dykens, Hodapp, & Finucane, 2000; King, State, Shah, Davanzo, & Dykens, 1997). Skills and impairments suffered by children and adults with mental retardation often correlate to their IQs, but problems with adaptive functioning, such as communication, self care, and social skills, are also always evident. Among those affected by certain well-defined or "classic" mental retardation syndromes, such as *Down syndrome* or *fragile X syndrome*, we observe a typical profile of impairments. As we learn more about the etiology of each syndrome of mental retardation, we become better able to predict the impairments that affected individuals will suffer.

The more severely affected the child, the earlier in life mental retardation is generally diagnosed. For the vast majority of children, however, the impairments are considered "mild," and therefore are often not immediately evident. Consequently, those children who are not identified on the basis of speech, cognitive, or motor delays early in life may not be recognized until they enter preschool or even kindergarten, when it becomes clear that they cannot keep up with their peers.

ETIOLOGY

The three most common causes of mental retardation are, in order, Down syndrome, fragile X syndrome, and *fetal alcohol syndrome* (King et al., 1997). Together, these three disorders account for 30% of all identified cases of mental retardation (Batshaw, 1993). Of the hundreds of known causes of mental retardation, well over 150 have been related to the X, or female, chromosome to date (Ropers & Hamel, 2005). Fragile X accounts for 40% of all X-linked syndromes and is the most common inherited cause of mental retardation.

Although we are aware of hundreds of mental retardation syndromes, still no clear etiology or explanation for the clinical symptoms observed is found in about three-quarters of those affected by mild mental retardation and about one-third of those affected by severe mental retardation (McLaren & Bryson, 1987). The specific etiologies that have been identified are more commonly observed among the most severe, yet rare, syndromes. Although intelligence as measured by IQ appears to be somewhat heritable such that somewhere between 45% and 80% of the variability seen in IQ scores is due to genetic factors (Russell & Tanguay, 1996), no evident and reliable familial pattern of inheritance of mental retardation has been established. Certain specific illnesses, however, that result in mental retardation are heritable. Tay-Sachs and phenylketonuria (PKU), for example, are autosomal recessive genetic disorders that lead to inborn errors of metabolism that cause mental retardation. A variety of single-gene aberrations following strict Mendelian inheritance with variable manifestations, such as tuberous sclerosis, have also been demonstrated to result in mental retardation, as can hereditary chromosomal aberrations, such as fragile X.

Mental retardation can also result from early problems during embryonic development. Chromosomal changes as seen in Down syndrome, for example, or prenatal damage due to toxins such as maternal alcohol ingestion or infections during the prenatal period can cause mental retardation. Environmental deprivation during the neonatal period, characterized by inadequate social, emotional, and linguistic nurturance, can also predispose a child to mental retardation. While such severe environmental deprivation is not typical, we clearly recognize that there are critical developmental periods during which time key brain structures are established. In the same way that patching the eye of a newborn monkey for the first months of life will result in permanent blindness in that eye because of the lack of visual stimulation necessary for neuronal growth, we believe that a lack of social, emotional, and cognitive stimulation can result in similar brain damage in children.

A variety of problems can occur during pregnancy and the perinatal period that also can predispose a child to mental retardation or act as a causal agent, including fetal malnutrition, prematurity, hypoxia, viral and bacterial infections, and trauma. Numerous medical conditions acquired during infancy or childhood can also cause mental retardation. Examples include neonatal infections, trauma, and lead or other heavy-metal poisoning. Finally, the majority of children diagnosed with autistic disorder suffer from mental retardation, and it is not clear how these disorders are bound and which, if either, causes the other (American Psychiatric Association, 2000).

EPIDEMIOLOGY

The prevalence of mental retardation is about 1% worldwide and typically ranges from 1% to 3% in developed countries. The prevalence of mental retardation due to biological factors is similar among children of all socioeconomic classes. However, certain etiologic factors are linked to lower socioeconomic strata, such as lead poisoning and premature birth. Children born to a family at the lower end of the socioeconomic spectrum, then, are more likely to suffer mental retardation.

Mental retardation is more common among males where the ratio is approximately 1.5 to 1, male to female. As previously described, in those cases without a specifically identified organic or biological cause, the mental retardation is usually milder.

CLINICAL COURSE

The course of mental retardation varies depending upon the etiology and level of impairment. Children diagnosed with *mild mental retardation*, previously referred to as "educable," comprise the largest number of those with mental retardation, approximately 85% of all cases. Generally speaking, these children develop social skills and language capabilities by 5 years of age, suffering minimal sensory and motor impairments, and are often indistinguishable from typical children until elementary school. By adolescence, these youths can develop academic skills equivalent to the sixth-grade level. By adulthood, they are usually able to support themselves, and many lead independent lives. In fact, the diagnosis may not hold throughout one's entire life, as adaptive functioning may improve adequately so that diagnostic criteria are no longer met in adulthood (King et al., 1997). Others require more social and vocational support, along with assistance and supervision, particularly at times of high stress (American Psychiatric Association, 2000).

Children diagnosed with *moderate mental retardation*, previously referred to as "trainable," comprise about 10% of those with mental retardation. Most of these children develop the ability to communicate by speech and other means as youngsters. They generally benefit greatly from social and vocational training and, with some supervision, are able to manage their own personal care. Peer relations suffer, particularly by adolescence, as they struggle with social skills and convention. Academically, they are unlikely to surpass the second-grade level. As adults, they often do well in supervised venues within the community, performing unskilled or semiskilled work (American Psychiatric Association, 2000).

Children diagnosed with *severe mental retardation* comprise about 3–4% of those with mental retardation. These children struggle with communication but may eventually learn to speak and engage in simple self care. They often benefit from basic education, such as learning the alphabet and how to count, and can be taught to recognize important "survival" words and objects, such as stop signs. They require a great deal of supervision as adults but can often learn to perform some simple duties. Most of these individuals remain with their families or in group homes unless they suffer from a comorbid medical condition that demands specialized care (American Psychiatric Association, 2000).

The most severely affected children are those with *profound mental retardation*, who comprise 1–2% of the total population of those with mental retardation. Most of these individuals suffer from a recognized neurological or medical condition that accounts for their symptoms and have severe impairments in sensory and motor function. Extensive supervision, training, and a highly structured environment are required for the development of maximum speech, motor, and self-care capacities (American Psychiatric Association, 2000).

Individuals with mental retardation present with a broad variety of personalities, behaviors, and temperaments. As expected, those who struggle more with communication skills may tend to evidence more disruptive, impulsive, and aggressive behaviors. The prevalence of comorbid Axis I disorders is estimated to be three to four times that of the general population. A review of representative studies found a prevalence of Axis I disorders among mentally retarded persons ranging from 27% to 71% (Bregman, 1991), yet the presentation and symptoms of the disorders appear to be much the same, such that ADHD, depression, and anxiety look the same in an individual who is mentally retarded as they do in an individual who is not (American Psychiatric Association, 2000). Similarly, individuals with mental retardation and comorbid Axis I disorders are generally thought to respond to medications in much the same way as those without mental retardation, although, as we shall see, there is very little data to support this assertion.

DIAGNOSIS

According to the *DSM-IV*, the diagnosis of mental retardation demands impairment in IQ as well as adaptive functioning (e.g., how well the individual functions in his/her daily life). The IQ score of 70 or below must be determined by an accepted test of intelligence, such as the Wechsler, Stanford-Binet, Woodcock-Johnson, or Kaufman. (See Chapter 4, "Learning Disorders," for a detailed description of these tests.) Impairments in adaptive functioning are generally measured using either the AAMR (American Association of Mental Retardation) or Vineland Adaptive Behavior Scale. The Vineland and AAMR are designed to assess how well individuals cope within the social environment, manage typical life demands, and meet the standards of independence expected of their age. These tests should always be administered by a qualified neuropsychologist.

The *DSM-IV* defines the severity of mental retardation (mild, moderate, severe, and profound) by the individual's IQ score, but, as previously described, adaptive functioning is a core component and must be considered as well. According to the *DSM-IV*, mild mental retardation corresponds to an IQ of 50–55 to approximately 70. Moderate mental retardation corresponds to an IQ of 35–40 to 50–55. Severe mental retardation corresponds to an IQ of 20–25 to 35–40, and profound mental retardation corresponds to an IQ of less than 20–25. These numbers are given in ranges for two reasons: (a) Each IQ test has a certain standard error, which recognizes that an individual's IQ score may be slightly different, although not profoundly different, on any given day depending on how the person is feeling, how rested the person is, and so forth; and (b) these numbers must leave room to take into account an individual's level of adaptive functioning, such that even if the IQ is a bit lower, for example, one's adaptive functioning may be high enough place him or her in a less impaired category of mental retardation and vice versa (American Psychiatric Association, 2000).

Borderline intellectual functioning is yet another category described within the *DSM-IV* but is not considered a proper diagnosis. This descriptor is applied to an individual whose IQ lies somewhere between 71 and 84 but does not have any particular or stereotyped challenges with adaptive functioning.

The most commonly comorbid conditions or coexisting Axis I disorders among those with mental retardation include ADHD, mood disorders (both depression and bipolar disorder), pervasive developmental disorders such as autism spectrum disorders, stereotypic movement disorders, and various mental disorders secondary to general medical conditions.

There are a variety of specific mental retardation syndromes that bear discussion given their prevalence, their classic behavioral presentations, and the genetic lessons that they so clearly illustrate; these include Down syndrome, fragile X syndrome, fetal alcohol syndrome, Prader-Willi syndrome, Angelman's syndrome, and Williams syndrome.

Down Syndrome

As previously described, Down syndrome is the most common cause of mental retardation and the most common chromosomal abnormality that leads to mental retardation. Occurring in approximately 1.2 per 1,000 births, Down syndrome is due to the nondisjunction or inadequate separation of chromosome 21 during early embryonic cell division. These individuals have relative strengths in their visual processing (versus auditory processing) and their social functioning. Relative weaknesses include language expression and pronunciation. Most individuals with Down syndrome are well engaged socially, require very little psychiatric care, and, in fact, are generally recognized to suffer less severe psychopathology than other developmentally delayed groups (State, King, & Dykens, 1997). Unfortunately, given coexisting problems that result from nondisjunction of chromosome 21, by 40 years of age affected individuals nearly always demonstrate postmortem neuronal defects that are indistinguishable from Alzheimer's disease and contribute to deteriorating cognitive function early in life.

A recent population-based survey of social and health care records of children with Down syndrome found that females had better cognitive abilities and speech production as compared to males and that males had more behavioral troubles. ADHD symptoms were often seen in childhood across gender, and depression was diagnosed more often in adults with mild to moderate intellectual impairment than among those with more severe intellectual impairment. Autistic behavior was more common in those with major intellectual impairment, and, as previously noted, the elderly commonly demonstrated declines in adaptive behavior that are consistent with a diagnosis of Alzheimer's disease (Määttä, Tervo-Määttä, Taanila, Kaski, & Iivanainen, 2006).

In addition to the social, emotional, and psychiatric features, there are a variety of physical features that are well recognized and occur in most cases of Down syndrome, including a flattened face, straight hair, small ears, and protrusion of the tongue. In addition, these individuals commonly have a single crease on their fifth finger, are hypotonic, and have slanted palpebral fissures or eyelid openings (Jones, 1997).

Fragile X Syndrome

Fragile X syndrome is, again, the most common inherited cause of mental retardation, affecting approximately 1 in 4,000 males. Fragile X syndrome is due to a trinucleotide repeat of DNA, a group of over 200 trinucleotides of the CGG base pairs on the FMR-1 gene found at the X chromosome, region Q27.3. Some degree of CGG repeat is normal, and only as the base pairs expand past 50 repeats, in some cases reaching over 3,000 repeats, does the syndrome express itself. Fragile X syndrome illustrates two genetic principles: (a) *dynamic mutation*, meaning that more mutations occur with successive generations; and (b) *anticipation*, meaning that the severity of the disorder increases with successive generations. General problems include mental retardation, mild connective tissue dysplasia, and macro-orchidism. Only about half of females with the full mutation have IQs in the borderline or mild mentally retarded range versus over 95% of males, as males do not have another X chromosome to compensate for the damage to their single X chromosome (Garber, Visootsak, & Warren, 2008).

Fragile X syndrome increases the risk for ADHD and social phobia. In addition, somewhere between 10% and 25% of individuals with fragile X may meet criteria for autistic disorder or show significant autistic-like symptoms, although numbers as high as 60% have been reported (Dykens et al., 2000). Individuals with fragile X syndrome suffer increasing deficits in adaptive and cognitive functioning with age, with a predictable decrease in IQ beginning around puberty. Their relative strengths include verbal long-term memory while their relative weaknesses are in areas of short-term memory, visual-motor integration, sequential processing, mathematics, and attention (State et al., 1997).

The characteristic physical signs of fragile X syndrome include macrocephaly, prognathism (enlarged and protruding chin), thickening of the nasal bridge, large ears, dental crowding, and epicanthal folds (a skin fold from the upper eyelid that covers the inner or medial corner of the eye). Features occasionally noted include nystagmus (slow rhythmic eye movements in one direction and saccade-like quick movements in the other direction), strabismus (a wandering eye), epilepsy, hypotonia, flat feet, and mitral valve prolapse, among others (Jones, 1997).

Fetal Alcohol Syndrome

Fetal alcohol syndrome has an incidence of 0.5–2 cases per 1,000 births and is the most preventable environmental cause of mental retardation. The precise amount of alcohol required to induce the full syndrome is unclear, but we do know that even 7 to 14 alcoholic beverages per week results in growth deficits, an increase in disruptive behavior, and neurocognitive problems, such as difficulties with math, language, and memory. Visual-spatial ability, attention, and processing speed may also be impaired. Binge drinking (more than 5 drinks at a time) and drinking more than 7 drinks per week are both known to put children at significantly higher risk for the full syndrome (U.S. Surgeon General, 2005).

Given that alcohol is a known and potent teratogen, complete abstinence prior to conception and during pregnancy makes the most sense. From a public health perspective, no amount of alcohol consumption during pregnancy can be considered safe. Certainly drinking alcohol during the first few weeks after conception seems to carry no clear risk as it takes about two weeks for the fertilized egg to implant in the uterine wall, and during this time the egg is feeding off of its own yolk supply, which is not dependent on maternal blood. However, by week 3 following conception, as the egg embeds into the uterine wall, the source of nutrition comes directly from the mother, and alcohol use in moderate to large amounts will now have a direct impact on the developing fetus.

The full syndrome is characterized by mental retardation (average IQ of 63), fine motor difficulties, irritability, joint abnormalities, and heart murmur with ventricular septal defect. The characteristic facial features include macrocephaly, shortened palpebral fissures, bilateral ptosis (drooping of the upper eyelid), thin upper lip, small mandible, flattened nasal bridge, smooth philtrum, and protruding ears. Other problems may include cleft lip with or without cleft palate; central nervous system deformities such as meningomyelocele and hydrocephalus; neck deformities such as mild webbing; cervical vertebrae and rib abnormalities; cardiac deformities such as the tetralogy of Fallot and coarctation of the aorta; and hypoplastic labia majora and strawberry hemangiomas (Jones, 1997).

Prader-Willi Syndrome

Prader-Willi syndrome results from a deletion in the long arm of chromosome 15 between sections 11 and 13 (15Q11-13) and has a prevalence of about 1 case in 15,000 births. Sixty to 80% of the affected individuals have a microscopic deletion on paternal chromosome 15. The remaining cases of Prader-Willi syndrome have two copies of the maternal chromosome with no paternal chromosome, resulting in *uniparental disomy*. That is, these individuals have a section of chromosome that is only from the mother and not from the father, thus uniparental.

In contrast to fragile X syndrome, where we observe a deterioration of cognitive performance and adaptability with age, there is relative stability in the adaptive functioning of those affected by Prader-Willi syndrome during adolescence and early adulthood (King et al., 1997). Their relative strengths include expressive vocabulary, long-term memory, visual spatial integration, and visual memory. It has been noted that many children with Prader-Willi syndrome have an unusual interest in jigsaw puzzles. Their relative weaknesses are in areas that include sequential processing and visual and motor short-term memory (State et al., 1997).

Behaviorally, these children commonly suffer temper tantrums, emotional lability, and mood symptoms. They are also known to be particular anxious, as evidenced by frequent skin picking and obsessive compulsive symptoms. Over 50% of those affected, in fact, are diagnosed with obsessive-compulsive disorder, and one of the most common expressions is compulsive overeating and the hoarding of food (State et al., 1997).

Children born with Prader-Willi syndrome suffer from infantile hypotonia, hyperphasia (e.g., an expansive appetite), morbid obesity, small hands and feet, and mild mental retardation in two-thirds of those affected, moderate in one-third. These children typically have a notably almond-shaped cranium, small genitalia, and often scoliosis, osteoporosis, high pain tolerance, and temperature instability (Jones, 1997).

Angelman Syndrome

Chromosomally similar to Prader-Willi, yet vastly different in expression, is Angelman syndrome. These children suffer from severe mental retardation and are commonly plagued by seizures and a lack of speech but episodes of laughter. Ataxia, along with jerky arm movements and paroxysms of laughter in the absence of speech, has led to those with Angelman syndrome being described in the literature as "happy puppets." As with Prader-Willi syndrome, these children suffer from an error in chromosome 15Q11-13. However, in the case of Angelman syndrome, all identified cases of deletion are traced to the mother's chromosome 15. Angelman syndrome and Prader-Willi syndrome, then, illustrate the genetic concept of *genomic imprinting* or the fact that the parent of origin of the deletion at the same locus impacts the phenotype or expression of the disorder. Consequently, while deletion of paternal 15Q11-13 results in Prader-Willi syndrome, deletion of maternal 15Q11-13 results in Angelman syndrome (Jones, 1997).

Williams Syndrome

Williams syndrome has received a great deal of attention from researchers in recent years because even though it is extremely rare, those affected show unique strengths and weaknesses. While always resulting in global mild to moderate retardation, these individuals often show great strength in linguistic functioning. Their relative strengths include a remarkable facility for recognizing facial features, increased interest and talent in music, and a loquacious, pseudomature "cocktail party speech," which allows them to speak fluidly and easily. Relative weaknesses include an increased risk for ADHD and high rates of anxiety, fears, and phobias. Physically, these individuals suffer from cardiovascular anomalies, protruding lips, infantile hypercalcemia, hoarse voice, renal anomalies, and growth deficiency. Affected individuals typically show major impairments in visual-spatial abilities. Williams syndrome is due to the deletion of the elastin gene 7Q11.23 (Dykens et al., 2000; Jones, 1997; State et al., 1997).

TREATMENT

There are no specific therapies or medications for mental retardation. Treatments are typically symptom specific and include pharmacological interventions, behavioral therapies, and psycho-education for the family, teachers, and other caregivers. Treatments tend to focus on social support, parent training, social skills training, and engaging the patient in the community to the greatest degree possible. Much effort is placed into managing the living situation of the patient and helping him or her find a meaningful life filled with valued activities. Addressing the individual needs of the child is paramount in establishing a robust treatment plan.

While no medications have specifically been designed or identified to treat mental retardation, nor to address specific symptoms associated with mental retardation, medications are commonly employed for many of the comorbidities and behavioral disturbances that children and adults with mental retardation face, such as agitation, aggression, irritability, and self-injurious behavior. Rates of psychotropic medication use vary from study to study but are commonly 15–40% in institutions and 20–30% in community settings, excluding anticonvulsants, which are commonly employed for comorbid seizure disorders that plague so many children with mental retardation (Singh, Ellis, & Wechsler, 1997).

Stimulants

ADHD is the most widely diagnosed psychiatric disorder among children and adolescents with mental retardation. This finding is not surprising, given the fact that ADHD is the most common behavioral disorder in childhood. Prevalence rates are estimated at 8–16% (Emerson, 2003; Stromme & Diseth, 2000). At least 20 randomized, double-blind, placebo-controlled trials have been published involving the use of methylphenidate (Ritalin) with individuals with mental retardation. Positive response rates range from 45% to 65% in these studies (Aman, Collier-Crespin, & Lindsay, 2000), notably lower than the rates found within the non-mentally retarded population, which approach 80% (Greenhill et al., 2001). As expected, positive response to medication is predicted by a higher IQ (greater than 50) and higher scores at baseline on parent/teacher ratings of activity and inattention (Handen & Gilchrist, 2006). Given the global neurological deficits that many children with mental retardation face, these individuals may be more susceptible to side effects from stimulants. Still, we have limited data on the use of nonstimulant alternatives with this population, and therefore stimulants remain the preferred treatment for ADHD.

Antidepressants

Antidepressants have commonly been employed in the treatment of children with mental retardation who suffer from depressive mood disorders, anxiety, self-injurious behavior, and stereotypic movement disorders. Antidepressants include both the selective serotonin reuptake inhibitors (SSRIs), such as fluoxetine, sertraline, paroxetine, and citalopram, and the tricyclic antidepressants, such as clomipramine. Among 15 published case reports and four prospective open-label trials involving children and adults with mental retardation and/or autistic spectrum disorders, decreases in self-injurious behavior, irritability, or depressive symptoms were noted for most patients treated with fluoxetine (Prozac), except in two studies (Aman, Arnold, & Armstrong, 1999). However, among the negative studies, fluoxetine led to increased aggression, agitation, and hypomanic behavior for a number of individuals.

There are no studies of sertraline (Zoloft) for the treatment of children with mental retardation. Luiselli, Blew, and Thibadeau (2001) noted a case of one adult with severe mental retardation who showed improvement in self-injurious behavior with sertraline. In addition, among adults with mental retardation and autism spectrum disorders, sertraline has been found to reduce self-injurious behavior and aggression (Hellings, Kelley, Gabrielli, Kilgore, & Shah, 1996). Similarly, there are no studies of fluvoxamine (Luvox) for the treatment of mental retardation and any of its comorbidities for children and adolescents. One open-label study of 60 adults with mental retardation who were treated with 200–300 mg per day of fluvoxamine reported a significant reduction in aggression after 3 weeks of treatment (La Malfa, Bertelli, & Conte, 2001). No significant side effects were reported.

Paroxetine (Paxil) has been studied in small numbers of adults and children with mental retardation for the treatment of self-injurious behavior, aggression, and depression. By and large, these open-label, retrospective, and case studies demonstrated brief, time-limited effects or benefits for only a small number of individuals (Handen & Gilchrist, 2006). In a 9-week depression study of seven adolescents, four no longer met criteria for depression posttreatment with paroxetine at dosages of 20–40 mg per day (Masi, Marcheschi, & Pfanner, 1997). Side effects varied in these trials, but in some cases individuals discontinued treatment because of an increase in agitation, aggression, and hypomanic behavior.

Other antidepressant studies in adults have been conducted with both clomipramine (Anafranil) and citalopram (Celexa). Six of 10 patients treated with clomipramine in a double-blind, placebo-controlled fashion demonstrated reductions in the intensity and frequency of hyperactivity, irritability, and stereotyped behaviors (Lewis, Bodfish, Powell, & Golden, 1995). In a subsequent study by the same group, clomipramine led to a 50% or greater reduction in the intensity of self-injurious behavior as compared to placebo (Lewis, Bodfish, Powell, Parker, & Golden, 1996). In the second study one patient suffered seizure and another tachycardia and agitation. A more recent retrospective review of 38 institutionalized mentally retarded adults found reductions in aggression, self-injurious behavior, depression, and disruptive behavior among those treated with

SSRIs or clomipramine (Janowsky et al., 2005). Finally, citalopram was studied in 20 mentally retarded adults at dosages of 20–60 mg per day in an open-label fashion. Sixty percent of patients demonstrated moderate to marked improvement in depression for one year (Verhoeven, Veendrik-Meekes, Jacobs, van den Berg, & Tuinier, 2001).

Antipsychotics

Antipsychotics or neuroleptics are commonly employed in the treatment of those with mental retardation. The first generation or so-called typical antipsychotic medications have a long history of use among the mentally retarded for disorders other than psychosis, such as hyperactivity, antisocial behavior, stereotypies, self-injurious behavior, and aggression (Handen & Gilchrist, 2006). The second generation or atypical antipsychotics are now being increasingly prescribed to this population in the hope that they cause fewer side effects, which is particularly important given the likely increased vulnerability of these individuals to medication side effects.

Among the atypical antipsychotics, clozapine (Clozaril) has demonstrated efficacy in the treatment of resistant psychosis among individuals with mental retardation (Antochi, Stavrakaki, & Emery, 2003). However, the side effect profile of clozapine can be so egregious and difficult to manage (e.g., agranulocytosis, excessive weight gain, seizures, and Type II diabetes) that we rarely employ this medication unless absolutely necessary.

Risperidone (Risperdal), another atypical antipsychotic, has been found effective in managing aggression, irritability, and self-injurious and repetitive behaviors in both children and adults with mental retardation in numerous studies (Aman et al., 1999; Handen & Gilchrist, 2006). Aman, De Smedt, Derivan, Lyons, and Findling (2002) demonstrated a beneficial response in 53.8% of children (versus 7.9% on placebo), 5–12 years of age, in a large multicenter double-blind, placebo-controlled trial. Differences among those on active medication were evident within the first week of this 6-week study. Snyder et al. (2002) also found risperidone better than placebo for the treatment of disruptive behaviors in a randomized controlled trial of children with mental retardation. Zarcone et al. (2001) found reductions in self-injurious behavior, aggression, property destruction, and stereotypies in 20 children and adults treated with risperdone. Finally, Gagiano, Read, Thorpe, Eerdekens, and Van Hove (2005) found significant benefit for mentally retarded adults treated with risperidone vs. placebo in a randomized controlled trial, 52.8% vs. 31.3%. As with clozapine, all atypical antipsychotic medications can cause significant side effects that must be monitored closely, including weight gain, sedation, extrapyramidal side effects and movement disorders, prolactin elevation, and liver damage. (See Chapter 12 for a thorough discussion of the side effects and monitoring of antipsychotic medications.)

Olanzapine (Zyprexa), another atypical antipsychotic, has been utilized somewhat less in the treatment of these children, perhaps because of the excessive weight gain commonly associated with this medication. While no placebo-controlled studies of olanzapine exist in this population, a number of chart reviews and open-label trials of adolescents and adults with mental retardation suggest that it is often useful in decreasing aggression, irritability, and self-injurious behavior (Handen & Gilchrist, 2006). Of great concern is the fact that olanzapine, probably more so than the other atypicals, has a great propensity to induce significant weight gain, which can result in insulin resistance and Type II diabetes, among other side effects that are common to all atypical antipsychotics.

Little data is available on quetiapine (Seroquel), another atypical antipsychotic. Quetiapine has been reported to quiet hyperactivity, inattention, and conduct problems among children and adolescents with mental retardation in a retrospective chart review, but no other published data is available (Handen & Gilchrist, 2006). One small open-label study on the use of aripiprazole (Abilify) has been published, which demonstrates significant utility for the treatment of aggression, hyperactivity, impulsivity, and self-injurious behaviors (Valicenti-McDermott & Demb, 2006). No published data on the use of ziprasidone (Geodon) exist as yet.

Mood Stabilizers

Mood stabilizers, such as lithium and the anticonvulsants divalproex sodium (Depakote), carbamazepine (Tegretol), topiramate (Topamax), and lamotrigine (Lamictal), have also been employed in the treatment of those with mental retardation. Lithium is typically indicated for the treatment of bipolar disorder but has been shown effective for mood lability, aggression, and disruptive behavior among the mentally retarded in numerous studies (Antochi et al., 2003). Furthermore, lithium has demonstrated benefit for the treatment of self-injurious behavior in at least two double-blind, placebo-controlled studies (Craft et al., 1987; Tyrer, Walsh, Edwards, Berney, & Stephens, 1984). Given the low therapeutic index and high potential toxicity of lithium, along with this population's increased vulnerability to medication side effects, however, lithium requires close monitoring and is rarely utilized.

Divalproex sodium has been sometimes employed for the treatment of self-injurious behavior and aggression in mentally retarded children and adults with demonstrated efficacy (Antochi et al., 2003). A review of 17 reports of 164 patients treated with divalproex sodium for aggressive and violent behaviors found a composite response rate of 77% (Lindenmayer & Kotsaftis, 2000). While there may be benefit for some patients with mental retardation, the side effects of divalproex sodium are not insignificant and can include liver failure, pancreatitis, thrombocytopenia, birth defects, and possibly polycystic ovary syndrome, in addition to milder side effects, such as weight gain, sedation, alopecia, and tremor. Consequently, this medication must be utilized with great care.

Other anticonvulsants, such as carbemazepine and lamotrigine, have no supporting data for their use in children with mental retardation. Studies of carbemazepine in adults with mental retardation are weakly supported (Aman et al., 2000). Finally, a retrospective open-label study of topiramate in children with severe mental retardation found that 74% of the sample of 22 demonstrated improvement (Janowsky, Kraus, Barnhill, Elamir, & Davis, 2003).

Other Treatments

Numerous other medications, such as propranolol, buspirone (Buspar), clonidine (Catapres), and naltrexone, have been employed for the treatment of aggressive, anxious, disruptive, and self-injurious behavior among those with mental retardation. The data supporting these medications, which include open-label, retrospective, and case studies but no randomized controlled trials, yield contradictory results. Virtually no data exist on the use of antihistamines and sedative-hypnotics, which may lead to confusion in some patients.

Although there is little data, electroconvulsive therapy (ECT) has been used in the mentally retarded and developmentally delayed population subsequent to failed behavioral and pharmacological interventions. Kessler's 2004 review of 16 successful case reports between 1968 and 2001 demonstrates a potential role for ECT, particularly given that none of these individuals suffered significant side effects or further cognitive deterioration.

7

Autism Spectrum Disorders

Autism spectrum disorders (ASD) are characterized by severe impairment in several areas of development, including reciprocal social interaction, verbal and nonverbal communication, and the normal range of behaviors, interests, and activities. These disorders are generally observed within the first few years of life and are often associated with mental retardation and an assorted group of medical conditions, such as chromosomal abnormalities, congenital infections, and structural abnormalities of the central nervous system. The *DSM-IV* describes five disorders under the rubric of *pervasive developmental disorders*; these include *autistic disorder, Asperger's disorder, Rett's disorder, childhood disintegrative disorder,* and *pervasive developmental disorder not otherwise specified (NOS)* (American Psychiatric Association, 2000). The inclusion of Asperger's disorder as a *DSM-IV* diagnosis was controversial in 1994 when the most recent edition of the *DSM* (version IV) was published. The initial intention of the *DSM* committee was to make Asperger's disorder a research criterion or tentative diagnosis, but due to outcry from parents, clinicians, activist groups, and a number of research scientists, Asperger's was ultimately included as a separate and independent diagnostic category (Klin, Volkmar, & Sparrow, 2000). The degree to which Asperger's is truly different from high-functioning autism, if at all, has yet to be clarified.

Given the infrequency of Rett's disorder and childhood disintegrative disorder and the fact that these are generally treated by neurologists, these two disorders will not be covered in this chapter. We will focus, instead, on the ASDs—those illnesses that present psychiatrically and have clear social, emotional, and cognitive manifestations and outcomes.

Throughout this chapter, the term *ASD* will be used to refer to all children within the autism spectrum. However, specific reference will also be made to the most severe form of the disorder, autistic disorder, and Asperger's disorder, a higher-functioning form.

CLINICAL PRESENTATION

Before we understood that autism is a unique problem of its own, autistic children were often thought to be schizophrenic. Therefore, much of the early research and data on autistic children is muddied by diagnostic uncertainty. Case examples and histories of children with schizophrenia and severe mental illness, such as psychotic depression and bipolar disorder prior to the 1940s and 1950s, are, consequently, very difficult to take at diagnostic face value.

In 1943 Leo Kanner of the Johns Hopkins Medical Center described 11 cases of what he termed *early infantile autism*, noting the ways in which this presentation was distinctive from psychosis and schizophrenia. Kanner's unfortunate choice of the word *autism* was meant to convey the unusual egocentric quality of these children, following upon Bleuler's description of schizophrenia. Paul Eugen Bleuler was a Swiss psychiatrist who, in 1912, defined the four "As" of schizophrenia. Bleuler noted that schizophrenics are ambivalent, display a flattened affect, speak with loose associations, and are autistic, a term he coined to describe the self-centered nature of these individuals. He derived the word from the Greek terms *autos* or "self" and the suffix *ismos* or "action or state." Kanner's use of the term *autism* to describe these individuals inadvertently contributed to the ongoing confusion between autism and schizophrenia. Many of Kanner's original observations have persisted over time. However, his speculations about certain aspects of the illness, for example, that these children generally have normal intelligence, that there is a lack of association with other medical conditions, and that poor parenting and education could result in an autistic syndrome, have been proven incorrect.

Coincidentally, Asperger's disorder was defined at about the same time that Kanner was making his observations on autism. In Austria in 1944, Hans Asperger proposed a novel diagnostic concept, which he termed *autistic psychopathy*, based upon his observations of four children. Ironically, he borrowed the same term from Bleuler that Kanner did, and his understanding of these children, too, resembled Kanner's concept in many ways. Neither Asperger nor Kanner was aware of the other, however, and so these two diagnostic constructs grew in parallel. In 1981 Lorna

Wing in England coined the term *Asperger's* to describe a group of children who had numerous autistic symptoms but who did not meet full criteria for autistic disorder. She also was hoping to avoid the use of the word *psychopathy* and to separate this group of children from the general grouping of autistic children. To date, Asperger's syndrome has been better described in the European literature, and in the United States these children have generally been diagnosed with high-functioning autism.

There are a number of historical myths about autism that many practitioners still rely upon. For example, we have been led to believe that children with autism never make eye contact, show affection, or smile; that inside a child with autism is a normal child or a genius waiting to emerge; that children with autism do not speak, but they could if they wanted to; that children with autism never relate well to peers and adults and do not want friends; that children with autism are manipulative and selfish; that autism is an emotional disorder; and that autism can be outgrown, or that progress means a child is not autistic. These myths have been perpetuated because, like most stereotypes, there is some truth to these statements for some individuals. However, we have now come to understand that the diversity of clinical presentations among autistic children is quite broad and encompasses children with a wide range of impairments. Although a small number of these children may be gifted in remarkable ways, the so-called "idiot savants" as they were previously described and as most notably displayed in the film *Rain Man*, the vast majority of autistic individuals display no such special skills.

Autistic disorder is the best studied and most severe of the pervasive developmental disorders. The diagnosis formally entered the psychiatric diagnostic lexicon in 1980 with the publication of the *DSM-III*. Better definitions have been hindered by continuity with other disorders, the broad range of syndrome expression, changes in syndrome expression with age, a high frequency of autistic-like symptoms in those with mental retardation, and the relative infrequency of this disorder. In most cases there is no period of unequivocally normal development, although in many cases, perhaps as high as 20%, parents report normal development for the first year or two of life, followed by a sudden onset of symptoms.

ETIOLOGY

We now know that autism is a biological disorder with multiple etiologies. Clearly there is no single cause, nor is there a single cure. As yet, no biological marker or single test can establish a diagnosis of autism. There is no evidence of parenting defects or emotionally induced autism.

The so-called "refrigerator mother" theory, a psychoanalytic paradigm from the 1950s and '60s that proposed autism to be the result of frigid and withholding mothers, is now discredited. Currently, the view is that some factor or factors act through one or more mechanisms to produce a final common pathway of central nervous system insult that results in the behavioral syndrome of autism.

Research into the causes of ASD presently abounds and focuses on a number of unique areas. Genome abnormalities, mechanisms underlying the expression of genes during brain development, structural and functional abnormalities in the brain, as well as behavioral expressions of ASD are all active areas of current inquiry.

Genetics

Numerous candidate genes have been proposed as possible areas for investigation. The fragile X gene, FXR1, for example, has been studied extensively, given that approximately 10–25% of children with fragile X syndrome demonstrate significant autistic symptoms (Dykens et al., 2000). The same is true of chromosome 15, due to the recognition that many children with Angelman's syndrome and Prader-Willi syndrome demonstrate autistic-like symptoms. Chromosome 17 (region Q11-21) and chromosome 22 (Shank 3 gene) have also been suggested. Because genes are essentially the blueprints of life, the hope that a single gene or series of inherited genes will lead to a clear etiology of ASD is very attractive yet too simplistic an approach, as genes are likely to be only one component of what ultimately accounts for ASD.

The suggestion that ASD may be due to random and spontaneous errors in DNA replication rather than directly inherited genes has recently become somewhat popular. *Copy number variations*, or errors that involve the addition or loss of large DNA sequences that occur during replication, may be responsible. DNA variations are often benign. Genes are constantly being duplicated as cells in the body are repaired and replaced. Redundancy and natural rejection of imperfect duplications protect the body from genetic errors that can result during this process. However, genetic mistakes may also result in disease. Though copy number variations have been known about for some time, they have more recently been suggested as a possible etiology for a wide variety of disorders, including ASD. This theory is particularly provocative, given that perhaps as many as 90% of ASD cases appear to be sporadic and show no clear familial pattern or inherited pathway (Sebat et al., 2007).

Mirror Neurons

Another attractive etiological theory of ASD involves mirror neurons. In monkeys mirror neurons are found in the inferior frontal gyrus and inferior parietal lobe. These neurons become active when monkeys watch someone perform a task. A similar system is theorized to exist in the human brain where these neurons are thought to be important for understanding the actions of others and for learning new skills by imitation. This proposed mirror system may also contribute to our *theory of mind*, a theoretical construct that allows us to empathize and understand others' beliefs, desires, and intentions and is generally impaired in those with ASD. Electroencephalogram studies have now demonstrated less activity compared to controls, presumably due to decreased mirror neuron activity, in the inferior frontal gyrus (specifically the pars opercularis) in children and adults with ASD (Oberman et al., 2005).

Amygdala

The amygdala, or "almond," (so named because of its physical appearance in the brain), has many important roles, including fear conditioning, memory consolidation, and the generation of emotional responses. The amygdala has long been suspected to be a source of some concern in ASD, and there are a variety of findings related to the amygdala that at present time appear to be somewhat contradictory. Recent neuroimaging studies have demonstrated fewer neurons in the amygdala among those diagnosed with ASD. However, prior amygdala research found larger structures among children with autism (Schumann et al., 2004), and larger right amygdala volume has been associated with more severe social and communication impairments in autistic 3- and 4-year-olds, which is predictive of a more severe clinical course and outcome (Munson et al., 2006). In addition, early postmortem evaluation studies of adult autistic brains reported higher cell density in the amygdala (Rapin & Katzman, 1998). Consequently, the role and importance of the amygdala is not clear at this time, but it does appear to be altered in some way in autism. More recent theories suggest that social fear in autism may cause an early rapid increase in amygdala growth, which over time leads to a toxic response that results in the death of amygdala cells and structural shrinking (Nacewicz et al., 2006).

Other studies have revealed that individuals with ASD who have smaller amygdalae have more difficulty identifying facial expressions and spend the least amount of time looking at the eyes relative to other, less emotionally salient parts of the face. Similar results in terms of gaze fixation and brain response to human faces have been noted among well siblings of people with ASD (Dalton et al., 2005). Additional data supporting the importance of amygdala volume has been put forth by Dalton et al. (2007) who found that individuals with ASD and small amygdalae spent 40% more time than those with larger amygdalae identifying and labeling facial expressions. They also found that those individuals with the largest amygdalae spent about four times longer looking at the eyes than those with the smallest. In addition, those with small amygdalae reported more nonverbal social impairment as children.

Basal Ganglia

Another area of the brain that has received some attention is the basal ganglia. The basal ganglia represents a variety of structures including the globus pallidus, thalamus, putamen, and caudate nucleus. Evolutionarily speaking, the basal ganglia is a very old part of the brain and among other things is involved in regulating and managing body movement. Furthermore, the basal ganglia, most particularly the caudate nucleus, is known to be an important structure that is very active among those who engage in repeated behaviors, such as obsessive thinking and compulsive behavior, as in obsessive-compulsive disorder (OCD), or repetitive motor and vocal tics, as in Tourette's disorder (Baxter et al., 1988; Bloch, Leckman, Zhu, & Peterson, 2005). Among his original 11 cases, Kanner described "an anxiously obsessive desire for the preservation of sameness" (Kanner, 1965). This "sameness" has come to be described in modern parlance as the stereotyped ritualistic and perseverative motor behaviors, interests, and activities in which children with ASD engage. Given the staunch demand for routine and repetition, some have wondered about a possible phenomenological similarity between ASD, OCD, and Tourette's syndrome.

Whereas individuals with Tourette's or OCD feel compelled to engage in what they recognize to be distasteful ritualistic behaviors or to obsess upon certain subject matters, individuals with ASD typically experience passion about their particular interests or behaviors and express a desire to engage in repetitive activities. In the language of psychoanalysis, we would describe the desire for sameness among those with ASD as *ego-syntonic* or in sync with the needs of the ego, whereas individuals with OCD and Tourette's syndrome find their repetitive behaviors and thoughts to be *ego-dystonic* or at odds with their ego or self-image. In other words, those with OCD and Tourette's syndrome feel compelled to worry or behave as they do but do not desire to be engaged in these activities. While the caudate nucleus and other structures within the basal ganglia have been implicated in all three disorders based upon imaging studies, both structural and functional abnormalities in this area have been demonstrated among those with ASD; and, in fact, larger caudate nucleus volumes have been correlated to an increase in repetitive behaviors among these children (Hollander, Anagnostou, Chaplin, Esposito, et al., 2005; Sears et al., 1999).

Visual Tracking

The data available on visual tracking is fascinating and highly illustrative of some of the social and emotional challenges that individuals with ASD face. It has long been known that autistic individuals have trouble with facial recognition, and studies over the past decade have looked carefully at the eye movements of individuals with ASD when presented with faces (Dawson et al., 2002). In virtually all cases, individuals with ASD do not follow the most salient features when studying faces or watching other individuals. Whereas a person without autism would typically watch the eyes for the greatest amount of information, a person with autism may wander in his gaze to the mouth where there is movement or to the shoulder or to the clothes to gather information from other sources (Klin, Jones, Schultz, Volkmar, & Cohen, 2002).

Observations of visual tracking correspond nicely to data obtained from studying the fusiform gyrus, which lies under the temporal lobe. For a number of years, we have known that the fusiform gyrus has a special role in facial recognition. In nonautistic individuals the *fusiform facial area* becomes very active when looking at faces. In autistic individuals this area only seems to become active when looking at faces they recognize very well, such as their mothers and fathers. A more recent debate in the scientific literature has centered on whether the fusiform gyrus is only a facial recognition area or whether it is a general recognition area for things that people enjoy or like (Gauthier, Skudlarski, Gore, & Anderson, 2000). Regardless, it does appear that for experts in a certain subject area, and perhaps for an autistic child who is passionate about trains, for example, the area is stimulated when the child sees trains in the same way that the area is stimulated or excited when the child sees the face of his mother or father.

Most information, as previously noted, obtained from personal interaction comes from watching the eyes of the individual with whom one is speaking. As already noted, however, those with ASD have a great deal of difficulty with visual tracking. The most impaired individuals seem to look haphazardly at everything and anything in the field of vision and appear highly disorganized. Moderately impaired individuals appear to look at objects within a room, and the higher-functioning individuals tend to look at the mouths where there is movement. Thus, the vast majority of individuals with ASD, when engaged in a personal conversation, do not gather information from the eyes (Klin et al., 2002).

By 6 months of age, most individuals are better at recognizing faces when they are presented right side up as opposed to upside down. This *facial inversion effect*, as it is known, appears never to be achieved by many with ASD or, at the least, to be seriously impaired (Bookheimer, Ting Wang, Scott, Sigman, & Dapretto, 2008). Consequently, these individuals tend to recognize faces equally poorly, be they right side up or upside down. Imaging studies of the *fusiform facial area* indicate that among individuals with ASD the area is less stimulated, less active, and receives less blood than a typical or normal individual when interacting with others and observing faces of others (Schultz et al., 2000). In nonautistic children the fusiform gyrus is activated in response to any human face. In autistic children this activation is normal only when shown pictures of their mothers but diminished when shown pictures of strangers (Sterling et al., 2008). It is suggested that autistic individuals, therefore, may be trained to learn better facial recognition skills, thereby improving their social skills.

Brain Size

For many years it was believed that the brains of autistic individuals were larger than those of nonautistic individuals. However, recent work has demonstrated that at birth children with autism have slightly smaller heads but then show sudden and excessive growth within the first 2 years of life (Courchesne, 2004). Brain structures growing at the most deviant rate are those that are vital for cognitive, social, emotional, and language functioning, and include cerebral, cerebellar, and limbic areas. The increase in brain size appears to be due to an increase in the quantity of gray matter (Petropoulos et al., 2006). Although the implications of this alternate growth pattern have yet to be elucidated, a delay in neuronal development and maturation or specification of brain tissue in children with autism has been suggested. By adolescence, brain size typically normalizes, but by then the damage has been done.

Vaccines

In 1998 Wakefield et al. published a highly controversial report in which they suggested that childhood vaccinations might be the cause of autistic disorder, particularly in those children with comorbid gastrointestinal sensitivities. The measles, mumps, and rubella (MMR) vaccine came under particular scrutiny in large part because of thimerosal, a mercury-containing preservative used in the vaccine. Although an appealing theory, subsequent analyses in Europe and the United States have shown that the number of cases of ASD has continued to grow regardless of vaccine exposure (Schechter and Grether, 2008; Stehr-Green, Tull, Stellfeld, Mortenson, & Simpson, 2003). Even with the subsequent removal of thimerosal, ASD rates have remained on the rise. Honda, Shimizu, and Rutter (2005) found that even though the MMR vaccine has essentially not been used in Yokohama, Japan, since 1992, the number of cases of ASD has continued to grow. A large retrospective cohort study of all children born in Denmark between 1991and 1998, over half a million children, found no correlation between the administration of the MMR vaccine and ASD (Madsen et al., 2002). Finally, a 2004 report by the Institute of Medicine confirmed, based upon all of the available data, that there was no connection between MMR and ASD (Institute of Medicine of the National Academies, 2004).

Most recently, a population study from southern England demonstrated the same finding (Baird et al., 2008). This study looked not at behavioral symptoms of ASD, but at blood samples for the presence of persistent measles infection or an abnormal immune response. The authors suggested that if the MMR vaccine or one of its component parts was causing autism, we would expect to see a significant antibody response among those children who have autism. The results of the blood sample analysis showed there was no difference in circulating measles virus or antibody levels between those children who developed ASD and those who did not. In summary, then, it is quite clear that vaccines are not a cause of ASD. Wakefield's original report was based upon 12 cases. Even though most of his coauthors subsequently retracted their support and disavowed the findings, concern over the possible connection between autism and MMR has led many parents to withhold the MMR and other vaccines from their children.

Diet

Another popular theory is that autism is caused by diet and nutrition. This theory suggests that some children with ASD will show symptom improvement when gluten, which is found in wheat products, or casein, found in dairy products, is removed from their diet. The hypothesis is that these two proteins are difficult for these children to digest and that the undigested metabolites of these proteins "leak" through the gut (ergo the "leaky gut" hypothesis of autism) and into the blood circulation where they have an opioid-like effect on the central nervous system. The leaky gut theory hypothesizes that vaccines like MMR or proteins like gluten damage the gut, causing an increase in various peptides, such as casein, to flow into the bloodstream and central nervous system, where they can then lead to deleterious effects on brain opioid receptors resulting in autistic symptoms (Hunter, O'Hare, Herron, Fisher, & Jones, 2003). Opioids can be tested for in the urine, and some individuals with ASD and self-injurious behavior have, in fact, been found in a few small studies to have higher levels of opioids in their urine (Sher, 1997). These data have been recently refuted, however, with more sophisticated screening techniques (Cass et al., 2008). Still, the theory is particularly attractive when considering autistic children who suffer from self-injurious behavior, as these children appear to be relatively immune to self-induced pain. One potential flaw with this theory is that naltrexone, an opioid-blocking agent, has not been proven to be particularly helpful for those individuals with autism who suffer self-injurious behavior.

Few studies of diet to date have been conducted in children with ASD, and the current evidence supporting such diets is of poor quality (Millward, Ferriter, Calver, & Connell-Jones, 2008). Among eight recognized studies of gluten-free and casein-free diets among children with ASD (six of which were open, one of which used a single-blind approach, and one of which used a double-blind approach with no placebo and included only 15 children), all open and single-blinded studies reported improvement when casein and gluten were removed from the children's diet (Christison & Ivany, 2006). The double-blind study demonstrated no group effect, although some parents reported improvement in their children's disruptive behaviors when they followed the diet (Elder et al., 2006). The possibility that these proteins, casein and gluten, or other dietary factors, may improve or worsen ASD is certainly possible, but larger randomized, double-blind, placebo-controlled trials are needed in order to ascertain any true benefit.

EPIDEMIOLOGY

Autism is ubiquitous and occurs all over the world. The incidence ranges considerably depending upon the study, but conservative estimates from the 1980s and '90s typically reported autistic disorder to occur at a rate of about 5 per 10,000 in the general population (American Psychiatric

Association, 2000). Being a relatively new diagnosis not initially intended for inclusion in the *DSM-IV*, the prevalence rates of Asperger's have gone largely uncharacterized. With the development of improved diagnostic measures, however, and the recognition of the broad "spectrum" of disorders subsumed under the umbrella term of *autism* or ASD, we now recognize that many more children are affected than had previously been thought. In 2007 the Centers for Disease Control (CDC) published the largest epidemiological study to date on the prevalence of ASD in the United States. Their estimates were based upon survey data of 407,578 children 8 years of age from 2002 in 14 states. They reported a prevalence of ASD ranging from 3.3 per 1,000 children in Alabama to 10.6 in New Jersey with most sites ranging from 5.2 to 7.6. The overall average nationwide was 6.6 per 1,000 or 1 in every 152 children across all sites.

Many individuals wonder if the increase in the prevalence of ASD represents a true increase in cases or whether we are simply seeing some diagnosis switching between those children who were previously diagnosed with attention-deficit/hyperactivity disorder (ADHD), learning disorders, mental retardation, or other psychiatric impairments and who are now being diagnosed with ASD. While we currently do not have a clear answer to this question, national data do not show decreases in the prevalence of mental retardation and speech and language disorders concurrent with the increases in ASD diagnoses, suggesting that these disorders do not account for any diagnostic reclassification or shifting (Newschaffer, Falb, & Gurney, 2005).

As with virtually all neurodevelopmental disorders, males are more commonly affected than females. The male-to-female ratio of ASD varied between 3.4:1 to 6.5:1 in the 2007 CDC study. Generally speaking, the male-to-female ratio is accepted to be about 4.3:1 (Newschaffer et al., 2007). According to the *DSM-IV*, Asperger's disorder is diagnosed about five times more commonly in males (American Psychiatric Association, 2000). Familiar patterns are now well established yet still only account for a relatively small number of cases. Twin studies show a 60–96% concordance for identical twins with autistic disorder versus a 5–24% concordance for fraternal, or nonidentical, twins, but these percentages run even higher when one looks at the full range of ASD symptoms and cognitive impairment (Bailey et al., 1995; Ritvo, Freeman, Mason-Brothers, Mo, & Ritvo, 1985; Rutter, 2000; Steffenburg et al., 1989). Studies also suggest that each subsequent child born into a family with one autistic child has between a 2–14% chance of having an ASD or a risk of about 3–22 times that of the general population (Newschaffer et al., 2007; Sumi, Taniai, Miyachi, & Tanemura, 2006).

CLINICAL COURSE

The prognosis and course of autistic disorder is highly dependent upon the level of functioning at any given time. By school age, autistic children can be divided into three general groups. Those who are low functioning have a verbal and nonverbal IQ of less than 70. These children are considered mentally retarded and comprise about 50% of affected children. The second group includes those who are mid-functioning and whose nonverbal IQ is greater than 70 but whose verbal IQ is less than 70. These children will meet criteria for a diagnosis of either mental retardation or borderline intellectual functioning, depending upon their full-scale IQ score. Mid-functioning individuals comprise about 25% of affected children. The third group is high functioning and includes those whose verbal and nonverbal IQs are greater than 70, who are not mentally retarded, and who comprise about 25% of affected children (Howlin, Goode, Hutton, & Rutter, 2004).

Many children with autistic disorder will show improvement by adolescence, which predicts a better adult outcome. Their activity level or hyperactivity tends to decrease, their behavior becomes more manageable, and their self-help skills improve. Communication continues to develop and becomes more robust. Although the IQ usually remains stable, these individuals often become more social and more adept at using social skills as they age. A large percentage, perhaps as many as 35% of children, will develop seizures of all types as they age (Deykin & MacMahon, 1979; Olsson, Steffenburg, & Gillberg, 1988; Parmeggiani et al., 2007).

Because the *DSM* has historically forbidden numerous other diagnoses, such as ADHD, in the presence of autistic disorder, investigators have not always looked for these disorders among affected individuals. Although we have only recently begun to identify comorbid psychiatric disorders among those with ASD, we now realize that over 70% of individuals are likely to suffer a co-occurring diagnosis. The most common diagnoses identified include anxiety, ADHD, and disruptive behavior disorders (Simonoff et al., 2008).

There are a number of other illnesses commonly associated with autistic disorder and frequently found in association. These illnesses include, most notably, mental retardation, the most common coexisting disorder, which affects somewhere between 50% and 75% of those with autistic disorder. Fragile X is likely the most common cause of mental retardation among those with autistic disorder, accounting for perhaps as many as 15–25% of cases (Dykens et al., 2000). Down syndrome is also not uncommon. Other associated illnesses include epilepsy, various developmental syndromes such as Turner's, tuberous sclerosis, and metabolic disorders such as phenylketonuria.

Few prognostic indicators are recognized for autistic disorder. Those predictors known to be related to outcome are IQ and communication skills by age 6 (Gillberg & Steffenberg, 1987; Newschaffer et al., 2007). Among those factors not known to be related to outcome are family history of neuropsychiatric disorders, adequacy of parenting, and the family environment or atmosphere.

As expected, the natural history of Asperger's disorder is somewhat different from autistic disorder. Asperger's is also a lifelong disorder, yet the improvements among those with Asperger's may be more significant than among those with autistic disorder. By adolescence some individuals may learn to apply explicit verbal rules or routines in stressful social situations, which help them to negotiate difficult interactions and minimize their anxiety. Children and adolescents with Asperger's disorder will commonly establish relationships with older individuals because these friendships are often more comfortable for them, as adults tend to be more understanding and permissive of odd or idiosyncratic behavior. Given these individuals' difficulties with managing social conventions, establishing peer relations is quite difficult.

Asperger's has a better prognosis than autistic disorder (Szatmari et al., 2000). As with autistic disorder, the best predictors of improved outcome are intellectual level and communicative speech (Klin et al., 2000). Adults are often capable of gainful employment and self-sufficiency. As with autistic disorder, there is an increased frequency of Asperger's disorder among first-degree relatives, and an increased risk of autistic disorder and general social problems are also suspected (American Psychiatric Association, 2000).

The *phenotype* or expression of autistic disorder is reliable. Younger children often express little outward interest in establishing relationships. As they age, they may develop greater social interests, but they still generally lack an understanding of the social conventions required for successful friendships and intimate relationships. Those more severely affected are often unable to demonstrate an understanding of the needs and interests of others and cannot identify important emotions, such as happiness, sadness, distress, and anger, even among those closest to them.

Communication among those with autistic disorder, including not only speech, but also body language and other nonverbal forms of interaction, is characterized by delays and sometimes a complete lack of functional ability. When speech is present, individuals often demonstrate atypical intonation or prosody. The grammatical and syntactical structures of speech are often delayed, and these individuals may repeat stereotyped phrases, jingles, and commercials that they have overheard elsewhere. Comprehension, too, is often delayed, and imaginative play involving language is often absent or markedly impaired. Perhaps of greatest impact are the weaknesses in the pragmatic and social use of language, such as the inability to understand humor and irony.

The behavioral phenotype of autistic disorder is characterized by stereotyped behaviors, interests, and activities. Nonfunctional routines and rituals, an "insistence on sameness" as described by Kanner, obsession with certain odd interests and activities, strange motor mannerisms, and a fixation on parts of objects further characterize these individuals (American Psychiatric Association, 2000).

The phenotypic expression of Asperger's disorder is similar to that of autistic disorder but less severe. While individuals demonstrate odd social and emotional functioning, their communication is typically better, although not normal. In addition, the stereotyped behaviors, interests, and activities seen in autistic disorder are often seen as more "quirky," idiosyncratic, or odd among those with Asperger's disorder; in contrast to autistic disorder, where those symptoms are almost always severely impairing.

DIAGNOSIS

The assessment of a child with suspected ASD must be broad ranging and incorporate virtually all aspects of the child's life and functioning. Motor skills, including both gross and fine motor, should be evaluated, along with verbal and nonverbal communication. The emotional assessment of a child with possible ASD should include a review of social skills, as well as family attachments, friendships, self-concept, and mood. Academic and cognitive ability must be explored with standardized measures, and a behavioral and family assessment should also be completed.

ASD are clinically identified long after they begin, with some studies reporting as long as 80 months from the first symptoms noted by parents to the first diagnosis by a clinician (Oslejskova, Kontrová, Foralová, Dusek, & Némethová, 2007). Even when brought to the attention of a clinician, the diagnosis commonly still takes over a year to establish (Wiggins, Baio, & Rice, 2006).

At this time there remains no good measure of how "autistic" someone is. Although we frequently employ a variety of rating scales to help us clarify the degree of symptomatology (see below), we remain unable to determine how biologically or neurologically impaired by autism one individual is as compared to another. Typically, we measure the severity of autism in part by the level of intellectual functioning or IQ and communication skills. Among those with severe intellectual impairment or mental retardation, the relationship between cognitive abilities and adaptive functioning, as determined by a Vineland or AAMR inventory (see Chapter 4), is vital and often a useful starting point for determining clinical interventions.

Autism is typically a retrospective diagnosis for which the developmental history is essential. There are no reliable measures by which to diagnose the illness before onset of symptoms. Because the natural course of ASD is generally toward improvement, we may misdiagnose affected adolescents and adults if we do not obtain an adequate history. One of the greatest hallmarks of the diagnosis is an inconsistency in development, which results in regressions, spurts, delays, and greater variation than would be expected in transition from one developmental stage to the next.

It is important to remember that there are numerous developmental oddities that typical or normal children who are not autistic do experience. These normal behaviors include spinning, toe-walking, enjoying the effect of strobe lighting, having odd or rigid food preferences, and disliking labels and seams in their clothing. The difference between typical or normal children and autistic children is that normal children generally grow out of these oddities. Thus, the emphasis upon developmental delay in the diagnosis of ASD is warranted.

Among children with autistic disorder, there are two types of onset generally reported. In the greatest number of cases, symptoms are present in the first year of life. Many of these children will fail to initiate baby games with parents at 4–6 months, such as peek-a-boo or giggling and other interactions. These children may not communicate common emotions well, such as hunger and pain, and parents may wonder why their children do not shout out for them and do not seem to connect with them. In another series of cases, perhaps as many as 20%, development is apparently normal until approximately 12–24 months of age, when symptoms appear. It is unclear as to whether or not the symptom onset is actually sudden in these 20% of cases, or if these parents simply do not know the signs of normal development, consequently not recognizing their child's impairments until nearly 2 years of age when their delays become much more pronounced and obvious. A common referral from such a family notes, "He began to speak and then stopped."

Medical Evaluation

Each child with a suspected diagnosis of autism must be medically evaluated. This evaluation will vary depending upon the child and his needs but should start with a full medical history. At a minimum, each child should also receive a complete physical examination, including auditory and visual screening, a speech and language evaluation, and an occupational and physical therapy evaluation. Growth milestones, such as head circumference, should be followed, and neuropsychological testing should be completed, particularly IQ and achievement testing. The utility of neuroimaging, such as a magnetic resonance imaging or computed tomography scan, and electroencephalogram (EEG) is less clear. With an adequate index of suspicion, the physician may order an EEG to rule out a seizure disorder, including Landau-Kleffner syndrome (acquired epileptic aphasia), and neuroimaging to rule out tuberous sclerosis and various leukodystrophies, which may result in autistic-like symptoms.

The laboratory assessment of a child with suspected ASD will also depend upon the individual clinical presentation. Without any clear indication, laboratory analyses are often not necessary. When employed, specific testing may include cytogenic and molecular screening for the fragile X DNA probe and DNA for MECP-II for Rett's syndrome. A karyotype or general chromosomal analysis is rarely done, but specific chromosomal testing for Di George or velocardial facial (VCF) syndrome (22Q11), Williams syndrome (7Q11.23), and Prader-Willi syndrome and Angelman's syndrome (15Q11-13) will sometimes be considered if signs or symptoms suggestive of these disorders are present. Fluorescence in situ hybridization (FISH) is a specific tool that is sometimes used to identify the presence or absence of particular DNA sequences on suspected chromosomes, such as 15Q11-13. Finally, laboratory assessment may also include obtaining ASO (antistreptolysin O) titers and anti-DNase B, which could indicate a recent streptococcal infection and the pediatric autoimmune neuropsychiatric disorders associated with strep (PANDAS) syndrome (see Chapter 8), and metabolic screening of a 24-hour urine for uric acid, calcium and phosphorus, magnesium, homovanillic acid, and creatinine. Various purine and calcium disorders, lactic acidosis, phenylketonuria, and infectious causes, such as herpes or cytomegalovirus (CMV), may be identified through these processes.

DSM-IV Diagnostic Criteria

The signs and symptoms of ASD often depend upon chronological and mental age. The diagnostic criteria of autistic disorder have been established by the American Psychiatric Association and are found in the *DSM-IV*. The diagnosis requires six symptoms from among the three primary domains of impairment: (a) social and emotional functioning; (b) communication; and (c) restricted behaviors, activities, and interests. The social challenges that children with ASD suffer are characterized by difficulties with establishing and managing peer relationships, demonstrating empathy and emotional interchange with others, sharing or engaging in shared experiences, and using nonverbal behaviors to promote social interaction, such as body language and eye contact. Communication impairments may include a delay in the development of language itself, an inability to sustain or initiate a conversation, stereotyped or repetitive use of language, and a lack of creative and make-believe play. Stereotyped or repetitive behaviors, interests, and activities are characterized by a preoccupation with a particular interest, behavior, or activity to the exclusion of others, inflexible adherence to nonfunctional rules, rituals, or routines, repetitive motor movements or mannerisms, or a preoccupation with parts of objects (see Table 7.1). The *DSM-IV* requires that a total of at least six impairments be noted, with at least two from category one and at least one from category two and category three. Finally, the *DSM* requires that at least some symptoms be present by 3 years of age.

The difference between Asperger's disorder and autistic disorder has been a source of debate in recent years. Some suggest that Asperger's disorder is simply a variant of ASD or a higher-functioning form of autistic disorder. Researchers recognize that the diagnosis of Asperger's disorder, as represented in both the *DSM-IV* and International Classification of Diseases (ICD-10), is tentative (World Health Organization, 1993). However, clinicians have adopted the diagnosis more readily and employ it often in an effort to characterize their patients and help them obtain needed services.

Table 7.1.   Diagnostic Symptoms of Autistic Disorder*

A. Social and Emotional Functioning
   a. Difficulty establishing and managing peer relationships
   b. Little ability to experience and demonstrate empathy and emotional exchange with others
   c. Trouble sharing or engaging in shared experience
   d. Poor use of nonverbal behaviors to promote social interaction
B. Communication
   a. Delay in, or complete lack of, language development
   b. Inability to sustain or initiate a conversation
   c. Stereotyped or repetitive use of language
   d. Lack of creative and make-believe play
C. Restricted Behaviors, Activities, and Interests
   a. Preoccupation with a particular interest, behavior, or activity to the exclusion of others
   b. Inflexible adherence to nonfunctional rules, rituals, and routines
   c. Repetitive motor movements or mannerisms
   d. Preoccupation with parts of objects

Adapted from *DSM-IV* (American Psychiatric Association, 2000).

Asperger's Disorder

The *DSM-IV* diagnostic criteria for Asperger's are identical to those for autistic disorder with the exception of impairments in communication, which are absent from the diagnosis of Asperger's. Consequently, Asperger's looks to be simply autistic disorder without the communication deficits. Yet perhaps one of the most obvious facets of the presentation of an individual with Asperger's disorder is, in fact, the severe deficits in the social and pragmatic use of language in spite of relative strengths in formal language domains (Klin et al., 2000). In large part due to the lack of available research, communication impairments in Asperger's disorder have not as yet been described in the current diagnostic nosology of either the *DSM-IV* or ICD-10. However, it is clear that individuals with Asperger's disorder have major difficulties with using language socially, as evidenced by their often verbose and egocentric speech about their particular areas of interest, which may appear to outsiders as a monologue; lack of socially reciprocal speech or failure to invite others into the conversation; and often monotone speech with little inflection and normal alteration in prosody. In addition to the evident language impairments, these individuals generally demonstrate difficulties in nonverbal areas, such as visual motor skills, which also cause them social difficulty. Consequently, while early speech development, such as vocabulary and rote memorization, is often not noted to be a problem, major troubles in the pragmatic and conversational use of language become evident with maturation (Volkmar & Klin, 2000).

Another frequent area of impairment among those with Asperger's disorder is motor function, most commonly described as clumsiness and awkwardness. Although not a core diagnostic feature for either the *DSM-IV* or ICD-10, motor impairments are described as an associated feature in each classification system. Even Asperger himself in his initial case descriptions noted that his subjects had delayed motor skills and were somewhat uncoordinated. While the difficulties are generally mild, they are likely to contribute to peer rejection, particularly for males for whom athletic ability as a child is a cornerstone of social acceptance.

Individuals with Asperger's are often interested in establishing friendships and intimate relationships but simply do not know how to do so. They often approach peers in peculiar ways, by telling about a particular interest or passion in a one-sided and pedantic fashion, for example, which is virtually guaranteed to annoy others. Furthermore, the concrete interpersonal style of those with Asperger's disorder makes it difficult for them to assess the emotional states of others, impairs their understanding of social cause and effect, limits their appreciation of humor and irony, and leads to misinterpretations of others' behaviors and intentions. Repeated social failures can lead to clinical depression and anxiety, which are not uncommonly seen in individuals with Asperger's disorder (Volkmar & Klin, 2000).

Since Asperger's disorder is a relatively new diagnostic concept, it is presumed that impaired individuals who would currently receive a diagnosis of Asperger's disorder were previously, and are likely to be still, diagnosed with alternative disorders. Affected adults seeing a general psychiatrist, for example, may be diagnosed with a schizoid personality disorder, due to their lack of close relationships, emotional detachment, odd communication style, and rigid thoughts and behavior. Those individuals seeing a learning specialist may be diagnosed with a nonverbal learning disorder because of their impaired tactile perception, psychomotor coordination, visual-spatial organization, and nonverbal problem solving, while maintaining rote verbal abilities. Those seeing a neurologist may be diagnosed with a so-called developmental learning disability of the right hemisphere, and those seeing a speech pathologist may be diagnosed with a semantic-pragmatic disorder because their speech is sufficient in appearance (grammar and sound) but damaged in content and use (effective communication) (Volkmar & Klin, 2000).

Asperger's disorder is often not evident until school age, when academic and social demands first become apparent. Affected individuals may feel victimized and socially isolated with age, as they feel further removed from peers. Although mental retardation is typically not observed, ADHD is often a first diagnosis, given the frequent hyperactivity and inattention that many of these children tend to display. In addition, Tourette's syndrome and obsessive-compulsive disorder may be more common among these individuals. Certainly, anxiety and mood disorders, as previously noted, are common with age as individuals develop an increased self-awareness of their poor social insight and abilities and become repeatedly frustrated in their attempts to establish satisfactory social relationships.

Because of the disproportionate reliance upon language as means of relating socially, gathering information, and relieving anxiety, individuals with Asperger's disorder are limited in their learning strategies. Facts gathered through rote memorization may be learned relatively easily, but higher-level concepts are much more difficult, such as what is meant by the concept of "number," "more or less," "greater than and less than," "fraction," and so forth.

Most individuals with Asperger's disorder will experience significant nonverbal learning problems, but the converse is not always the case. The primary assets among individuals with nonverbal learning disorders are proficiency in rote verbal skills and in some simple motor and psychomotor skills. The primary deficits include bilateral tactile perceptual problems; bilateral psychomotor coordination deficiencies; visual perceptual organizational deficiencies; poor adaptation to novel and otherwise complex situations; deficits in nonverbal problem solving, concept formation, and hypothesis testing; a distorted sense of time; much verbosity in a repetitive and straightforward manner; relative deficiencies in mechanical arithmetic, as compared to proficiencies in reading, word recognition, and spelling; and significant deficits in social perception, judgment, and interaction, while maintaining well-developed verbal capabilities. These deficits can and should be determined by routine neuropsychological testing.

The diagnosis of pervasive developmental disorder NOS is essentially a catchall for those individuals who demonstrate some ASD impairments but who do not meet specific criteria for autistic or Asperger's disorder.

Rating Scales

Rating scales are often employed to aid in the assessment of symptoms of those with ASD. Some of the available scales include the Gilliam Autism Rating Scale (GARS), the Gilliam Asperger's Disorder Scale (GADS), the Child Autism Rating Scale (CARS), the Social Communication Questionnaire (SCQ), the Social Responsiveness Scale (SRS), and the Autism-Spectrum Quotient. Each of these scales has its weaknesses, but each can also be effectively utilized by the practitioner in an effort to aid in the clinical diagnosis and treatment response. The current "gold standards" of evaluation are the Autism Diagnostic Observation Schedule (ADOS), a clinical survey performed directly with the child by a trained examiner, and the Autism Diagnostic Interview (ADI), a survey of the parent(s) of the child. At present time the ADOS and ADI are the best validated rating scales. While not designed to identify Asperger's disorder per se, each of these scales does give a cutoff score for both autistic disorder and ASD.

In addition to the diagnostic rating scales, there are a number of brief screening tools that should be utilized by primary care providers to identify early signs of ASD. The Checklist for Autism in Toddlers (CHAT) and the Modified Checklist for Autism in Toddlers (M-CHAT) are tools designed to assist primary care providers in identifying the early signs of autism (Baron-Cohen, Allen, & Gillberg, 1992; Baron-Cohen et al., 1996; Robins, Fein, Barton, & Green, 2001). The CHAT is a five-item checklist for primary-care practitioners and a nine-item checklist of questions for parents that is recommended at the 18-month pediatric evaluation (see Table 7.2).

Table 7.2.   Checklist for Autism in Toddlers (CHAT)

Observations by primary care practitioner:
1. Look for sustained eye contact.
2. Get child's attention; then point out an interesting object in the room. The typical child should look to where the physician points.
3. Ask the child to point out something in the room (e.g., "show me the light"). The absence of pointing by 18 months is a cardinal sign of ASD.
4. Show the child a doll and a cup and ask, "Can you give the baby some juice?" An autistic child will have difficulty engaging in pretend play.
5. Ask the child to build a tower of three blocks. (The purpose of this task is to assess social interaction).

Children who fail items 2, 3, & 4 are at risk of ASD and warrant further evaluation.

Questions for parents:
1. Does your child enjoy being swung or bounced on your knee?
2. Does your child take interest in other children?
3. Does your child like climbing on things such as stairs?
4. Does your child play peek-a-boo or hide-and-seek?
5. Does your child ever pretend?
6. Does your child ever use his index finger to point to or ask for something?
7. Does your child ever use your index finger to point and indicate an interest in something?
8. Can your child play appropriately with small toys without just mouthing, fiddling, or dropping them?
9. Does your child ever bring objects to you to show you something?

Children who fail items 5 and 7 are at risk of ASD and warrant further evaluation.

The M-CHAT (see Table 7.3) is a more detailed but better-validated screening tool for toddlers between the ages of 16 months and 30 months of age to assess risks for ASD. The M-CHAT is quick to administer and can be employed as part of a well child checkup. Because the goal of the M-CHAT is to identify as many cases as possible, the instrument is very sensitive and has a high false-positive rate, meaning that not all children who appear to be at risk for ASD will actually meet diagnostic criteria when further evaluated.

Finally, the American Academy of Neurology has enumerated five early warning signs of ASD (Filipek et al., 2000). A child's inability to reach any of these developmental milestones is suggestive of the need for an evaluation to rule out ASD:

• No babbling by 12 months.
• No gesturing, pointing, or waving good-bye by 12 months.

Table 7.3. Modified Checklist for Autism in Toddlers (M-CHAT)

Instructions: Please fill out the following about how your child usually is. Please try to answer every question. If the behavior is rare (e.g., you've seen it once or twice), please answer as if the child does not do it.

1. Does your child enjoy being swung, bounced on your knee, etc.?	Yes No
2. Does your child take an interest in other children?	Yes No
3. Does your child like climbing on things, such as up stairs?	Yes No
4. Does your child enjoy playing peek-a-boo/hide-and-seek?	Yes No
5. Does your child ever pretend, for example, to talk on the phone or take care of a doll or pretend other things?	Yes No
6. Does your child ever use his/her index finger to point, to ask for something?	Yes No
7. Does your child ever use his/her index finger to point, to indicate interest in something?	Yes No
8. Can your child play properly with small toys (e.g., cars or blocks) without just mouthing, fiddling, or dropping them?	Yes No
9. Does your child ever bring objects over to you (parent) to show you something?	Yes No
10. Does your child look you in the eye for more than a second or two?	Yes No
11. Does your child ever seem oversensitive to noise (e.g., plugging ears)?	Yes No
12. Does your child smile in response to your face or your smile?	Yes No
13. Does your child imitate you (e.g., you make a face—will your child imitate it?)?	Yes No
14. Does your child respond to his/her name when you call?	Yes No
15. If you point at a toy across the room, does your child look at it?	Yes No
16. Does your child walk?	Yes No
17. Does your child look at things you are looking at?	Yes No
18. Does your child make unusual finger movements near his/her face?	Yes No
19. Does your child try to attract your attention to his/her own activity?	Yes No
20. Have you ever wondered if your child is deaf?	Yes No
21. Does your child understand what people say?	Yes No
22. Does your child sometimes stare at nothing or wander with no purpose?	Yes No
23. Does your child look at your face to check your reaction when faced with something unfamiliar?	Yes No

A child fails the M-CHAT when two or more critical items are failed or when any three items are failed. Yes/No answers convert to pass/fail responses. The "critical" items are numbers: 2, 7, 9, 13, 14, and 15. Among typically developing children, the answers to all questions above should be "yes," except for numbers 11, 18, 20, and 22.

© 1999 Diana Robins, Deborah Fein, & Marianne Barton, http://www.firstsigns.org/downloads/ m-chat.PDF. Accessed April 5, 2009.

- No single words spoken by 16 months.
- No two words spoken together spontaneously by 24 months that are not echolaliac.
- Any loss of previously acquired language or social skills at any time.

TREATMENT

The first step in the treatment of ASD is to identify and address all co-morbid Axis I disorders, which commonly include ADHD but may also include anxiety, depression, and even psychosis. Coexisting psychiatric conditions are highly common in ASD, with some studies finding over 70% of affected individuals demonstrating one or more additional diagnosis (Simonoff et al., 2008). The same medications utilized for the treatment of these disorders in typical or normal individuals are utilized in the treatment of those with ASD.

The treatment of ASD must be comprehensive and involve all aspects of the patient's life. We increasingly recognize that early intervention is vitally important for the best outcome (Rogers, 1996). Individuals who are diagnosed and treated early will have improved chances of living a satisfying and productive life and are likely to show the greatest amount of symptom improvement with age (Paul, 2008). Family and caretaker psycho-education is another linchpin of early intervention. Academic support, speech and language therapy, and occupational and physical therapy as indicated are all standard but nonspecific measures commonly employed in the treatment and support of children with ASD. Although many treatments exist for children with ASD, the two best-established treatments at this time are *applied behavior analysis* (ABA) and medication (Foxx, 2008).

ABA is the bedrock of effective treatment for ASD. ABA is the umbrella term for a variety of behavioral modification therapies, including *discreet trials training* and the *Lovaas method*. In comparison to the many other treatments available for children with ASD, the data supporting ABA is overwhelming (Foxx, 2008). ABA focuses on teaching small, measurable units of behavior in a systematic manner. Problematic target behaviors are chosen, antecedents are identified, and corrective behaviors are then taught. Typically, the patient is given a stimulus, such as a question or an activity that must be completed, along with a hint or cue, if necessary, as to what the correct response should be. If the patient responds correctly, he or she is rewarded with something simple, such as praise, a small candy, or a "high five." All other responses are ignored or corrected in a neutral fashion. As the patient's responses become more reliable and accurate, the cues become withdrawn until the individual is responding independently. It is through this type of behavioral shaping that ABA is typically employed. ABA therapy is not simply discreet trial training, however, as an ABA therapist or program utilizes a comprehensive series of interventions aimed at every setting and every possible moment in order to shape the behavior of a child.

Although the data supporting ABA is far superior to that supporting other treatments, there are a number of other therapies that have some supporting data for the treatment of ASD. The *picture exchange communication system* (PECS), for example, utilizes symbols to teach communication strategies to those with ASD and severe language deficits. PECS has been shown effective for children and adults in initiating interaction and in communicating in the classroom when used regularly, but studies have yet to demonstrate the maintenance and generalization of gains to venues outside of the classroom once formal intervention has ceased (Howlin, Gordon, Pasco, Wade, & Charman, 2007).

While lacking a firm evidence base, social skills training appears to hold promise and should be utilized to teach social norms and expectations and to improve empathy (Laugeson, Frankel, Mogil, & Dillon, 2008). Many forms of social skills instruction are available, including social stories, video modeling, social problem solving, pivotal response training, scripting procedures, priming and prompting procedures, self-monitoring, and computer-based interventions (Bellini & Peters, 2008). Another social skill lacking in many children with ASD is "joint attention," the ability to share focus with another individual. Joint attention skills correlate with communication and social skill development and may provide an avenue for building such skills among those with ASD (Jones, 2008). Imitation is sometimes used to strengthen joint attention. Studies have shown that children with ASD who are imitated show greater social engagement for longer periods of time (Tiegerman & Primavera, 1981). Furthermore, therapeutic activities focused on adults following the lead of an ASD child and imitating their behaviors have led to increases in joint attention and more active social participation by affected children (Stephens, 2008).

TEACHH or the treatment and education of autistic and related communication handicapped children comprises a series of nonspecific and highly individualized methodologies designed to help the child with ASD to communicate and develop autonomy. Educational means are utilized, along with basic behavior modification methodologies, such as scheduling, establishing clear expectations, and reorganizing the physical environment, to promote success. The results of studies evaluating TEACHH vary greatly because of the highly individualistic means of the interventions, but some studies have been favorable (Ospina et al., 2008).

Although scattered and inconsistent data exist on many other therapies, those that are most effective clearly employ a behavioral approach. While some therapies, such as *Greenspan's floortime*, emanate from a staunch theoretical perspective, others, such as alternative diets or secretin therapy, are generally vague in their rationale. Regardless, it must be emphasized again that the most effective therapeutic treatments for children with ASD are behavioral in nature. In addition to educational and psychotherapeutic treatments, however, medications have also proven themselves useful.

Although few randomized, double-blind, placebo-controlled trials exist, virtually all psychiatric medications have been tried for the treatment of ASD. The antipsychotic risperidone (Risperdal) alone, however, has demonstrated efficacy in the treatment of ASD and has been approved by the Food and Drug Administration for children and adolescents 5–16 years of age. Risperidone helps to decrease the irritability that many of these children suffer, along with other behavioral problems such as aggression, deliberate self-injury, and temper tantrums (McCracken et al., 2002; Shea et al., 2004). Risperidone has also shown efficacy in small numbers of preschool children, as young as age 2 years, in separate randomized, double-blind, placebo-controlled studies (Luby et al., 2006; Nagaraj, Singhi, & Malhi, 2006).

The dosage of risperidone will vary by practitioner, but typically the lowest dose of 0.25 mg is applied once daily, usually in the evening to start, because of the common sedative side effect that follows. Over time, the dosage may be increased and may reach as high as 2–4 mg per day. Risperidone is also available as a liquid of 1 mg per cc, and smaller doses can be given in that fashion, particularly for children who cannot swallow a tablet.

The side effects of risperidone, as with all antipsychotic medications, can be significant and may include weight gain, insulin resistance, liver function abnormalities, elevations in cholesterol, hyperprolactinemia, hypersalivation, movement disorders, and sedation. Long-term studies of antipsychotic side effects are hard to come by, but a recent review of over 800 children who were treated with risperidone for disruptive behavior disorders found that weight increases stabilized after 6 months and that initial increases in prolactin often came down to normal limits within about 3 months (Pandina et al., 2006).

Other antipsychotic medications have also shown benefit in open-label trials and case studies. Although scant data is available, small numbers of children and adolescents with ASD have benefited from treatment with olanzapine (Zyprexa), ziprasidone (Geodon), quetiapine (Seroquel), and aripiprazole (Abilify) for the treatment of irritability, anxiety, hyperactivity, and aggression (Kemner, Willemsen-Swinkels, deJonge et al., 2002; Posey, Stigler, Erickson, & McDougle, 2008). In general, then, the use of antipsychotics is common but not always recommended because of side effects. Prior to using such intensive medications, a full trial of behavioral therapy should be employed.

A more typical psychopharmacological treatment approach for a child with ASD will include addressing the Axis I comorbidities, such as ADHD. Although the *DSM-IV* prohibits a diagnosis of ADHD in the presence of a Pervasive Developmental Disorder, such as Autistic disorder or Asperger's disorder, some clinicians see these disorders as separate entities and will treat them as such. Others believe that the inattention, hyperactivity, and impulsivity of children with ASD are different from that typically seen in children with ADHD, and that these symptoms are a part of the ASD, as opposed to comorbid ADHD. Furthermore, stimulants are sometimes agitating for children with ASD. For these reasons, it may be wise to start treatment of these symptoms with an alpha-2 agonist, such as guanfacine (Tenex) or clonidine (Catapres), followed by atomoxetine (Strattera) and then a stimulant if necessary. One small placebo-controlled trial (Frankhauser et al., 1992), one retrospective chart review (Posey et al., 2004), and extensive clinical experience with children with ASD have shown that alpha-2 agonists, such as clonidine and guanfacine, are effective for the treatment of hyperactivity, inattention, and motor tics in children and adolescents with ASD (see Chapter 2 for a complete discussion of these medications for the treatment of ADHD).

Antidepressant medications are also sometimes used for comorbid anxiety and depression or simply to help decrease agitation and perseveration among those with ASD. Results for fluvoxamine (Luvox) have been mixed with some double-blind, placebo-controlled trials in both children and adults showing benefit for symptoms of repetitive thoughts and behavior (McDougle et al., 1996; McDougle, Kresch, & Posey, 2000) and at least one open-label study showing no benefit (Martin, Koenig, Anderson, & Scahill, 2003). The only other placebo-controlled, double-blind study of an antidepressant for the treatment of ASD in children involves fluoxetine (Prozac), which was found to be beneficial for the treatment of repetitive behaviors (Hollander, Phillips, Chaplin, Zagursky et al., 2005). Among open-label studies, sertraline (Zoloft) was found to be helpful in adjusting to transitions for children with ASD (Steingard, Zimnitzky, DeMaso, Bauman, & Bucci, 1997), and fluoxetine was noted to be helpful in decreasing some of the core symptoms of autism (DeLong, Ritch, & Burch, 2002). The remaining studies are few in number and comprise mostly case reports and retrospective chart reviews, which provide little guidance in the treatment of children and adolescents with ASD (Posey, Erickson, Stigler, & McDougle, 2006).

ASD are extremely perplexing and devastating for the families of affected children. As our understanding of ASD grows, so will our ability to provide effective treatments. In the meantime, however, families will understandably often grasp at anything within their reach to help their children. Although testimonials supporting virtually all therapies can be found, with the exception of those treatments described above there is little else at this time that a clinician can offer a family with confidence. Some alternative treatments, such as chelation therapy, have even proven themselves deadly (Baxter & Krenzelok, 2008). Other unproven methods, such as holding therapy, dietary and vitamin regimens, anti-yeast therapy, porcine secretin hormone, brushing therapies, and Higashi daily life therapy, among others, may someday demonstrate utility, but at this time they are viewed through a scientific lens as being benign at best. At the end of the day, parents and practitioners must make their own judgments about how to help children affected by ASD.

In 2006 the U.S. federal government passed the Combating Autism Act, Public Law 109-416, which authorized $945 million over 5 years for research, screening, intervention, and education of ASD and developmental disabilities. Major areas of study supported by this law at the National Institutes of Mental Health include identifying the subtypes of autism and various effective treatments. Federal support, along with continued scientific inquiry, will hopefully result in better evidence to guide our treatment interventions in the coming years.

8

Tourette's and Tic Disorders

The history of Tourette's disorder is fascinating and a study in how our understanding of behavioral disorders has changed over time. The first case of what is now known as Tourette's was reported by a French physician, Itard, in 1825. He described the case of the Marquise de Dampierre, a woman of notability and great importance. The marquise suffered motor tics, coprolalia (uncontrollable offensive speech), and echolalia (repeating the words of others) from the age of 7 years. Itard wrote,

> In the midst of a conversation that interests her extremely, all of a sudden, without being able to prevent it, she interrupts what she is saying or what she is listening to with bizarre shouts and with words that are even more extraordinary and which make a deplorable contrast with her intellect and her distinguished manners. These words are for the most part gross swear words and obscene epithets and, something that is no less embarrassing for her than for the listeners, an extremely crude expression of a judgment or of an unfavorable opinion of someone in the group (1825, p. 405)

The more she herself was troubled by her own words, explained Itard, "the more she is tormented by the fear that she will utter them, and this preoccupation is precisely what puts them at the tip of her tongue where she can no longer control it" (Kushner, 1995). Itard was describing the sense of premonitory urge that often precedes the expression of a tic in just the same way as we understand it today.

In 1885, George Gilles de la Tourette described nine cases of the syndrome that now carries his name. One of his cases was the Marquise de Dampierre, who by then was in her 80s. Throughout much of the 20th century, Tourette's disorder was believed to be of psychogenic origin.

More recent research, however, has resulted in a return to Tourette's original impression of the disorder as a nonprogressive hereditary neurological condition. This final point is illustrative of many recognized psychiatric conditions, which as little as 40 years ago were believed to be entirely psychogenic in origin, but in their original descriptions and case studies were thought to be neurological, genetic, or somehow physical in nature.

CLINICAL PRESENTATION

A *tic* is defined as a sudden, rapid, repetitive, involuntary, nonrhythmic and stereotyped motor movement or vocalization (American Psychiatric Association, 2000). Tics may be simple, thereby implicating only a few muscles or simple sounds, or complex, in which case they involve multiple groups of muscles resulting in more fluid and larger movements that may include words and sentences. Both motor and vocal tics can be simple or complex. A *simple motor tic* is very brief, generally lasting fewer than several hundred milliseconds. Examples include blinking the eyes, jerking the head, sucking the lips, opening the mouth, wrinkling the nose, shrugging the shoulders, and contorting the face. Some simple motor tics are more difficult to observe, such as crunching the toes.

A *complex motor tic* lasts longer than a simple motor tic, typically seconds or even longer; examples include crouching, jumping, touching, pulling at clothes, skipping, sticking out the tongue, gesturing with the hands, tensing muscle groups, repeatedly smelling things, pounding the chest, holding the body in an unusual position, and retracing one's steps or weaving while walking. Both *copropraxia* (sudden, uncontrollable offensive gestures made in a tic-like fashion, such as "flipping someone off" or grabbing one's genitals) and *echopraxia* (an involuntary mirroring of another's movements) are considered complex motor tics.

Vocal tics can also be simple or complex. Simple vocal tics are typically brief sounds that are without meaning and not related to the situation at hand. These may include snorting, barking, honking, coughing, spitting, sniffing, grunting, laughing, and perhaps most commonly, throat clearing. Complex vocal tics are clearly language based; examples include making unusual changes in volume or pitch, stuttering, and blurting out words or phrases.

There are a number of so-called *lalias*, all of which are considered complex vocal tics. *Palilalia* is the repeating of one's own sounds or words; *echolalia* is the repeating of other's sounds or words; and *coprolalia* is the involuntary utterance of a socially objectionable word or phrase and may include cussing, blasphemy, or racial slurs. Although coprolalia is perhaps the most recognizable of the vocal tics, it is found in fewer than 10% of individuals who suffer from tic disorders.

Tourette's disorder typically begins with a simple motor tic on the face, such as blinking. The tics persist and generalize to other parts of the body, waxing and waning over time. Eventually explosive vocalizations, such as throat clearing, hiccupping, or uttering nonsense or intelligible words, ensue.

Most affected individuals report that their tics are irresistible but that they can suppress them at times. Children, particularly at onset, are sometimes oblivious to their tics, but with age they become only too aware of their symptoms, in large part due to the responses of others. Many individuals who suffer from tics and Tourette's describe a premonitory urge or an increasing tension or physical feeling that is relieved when the tic bursts forth. One patient notes, "I guess it's sort of an aching feeling in a limb or a body area, or else in my throat if it proceeds a vocalization. If I don't relieve it, it either drives me crazy or begins to hurt (or both)—in that way it's both mental and physical." Another patient reports, "A need to tic is an intense feeling that unless I tic or twitch I feel as if I'm going to burst. Unless I can physically tic, all of my mental thoughts center on ticking until I am able to let it out. It's a terrible urge that needs to be satisfied" (Leckman, Walker, & Cohen, 1993).

Individuals affected by Tourette's and tic disorders may feel the need to perform a tic repeatedly or in a specific way until it has been done "just right" and feels as if it is no longer necessary to repeat it. Tics often occur in short groupings and may be separated by minutes or hours without tics. Tics generally disappear during sleep and during intense sexual arousal, and they often change in severity over the course of the day. Commonly, they also change in location and intensity, coming and going with time. Tics also fluctuate in their rate of recurrence and in how much they disrupt one's life. Affected individuals are often better at suppressing tics when in public than when they are alone. In fact, tics are quite common when an individual is relaxed, such as when listening to music or watching television, and less frequent when an individual is engaged in directed purposeful activity, such as reading. Tics are also commonly aggravated by stress, such as school and work pressures.

ETIOLOGY

As yet, no clear etiology for tics and Tourette's disorder has been elucidated. Current research implicates numerous factors, including certain brain structures and the circuits that interconnect these structures, neurotransmitters, perinatal insults and infections, and immune response, all of which are likely to contribute to the ultimate expression of the disorders. Although the brains of those affected by tics and Tourette's are grossly normal, certain morphological abnormalities have been found in magnetic resonance imaging (MRI) studies of those with Tourette's; these include a loss or reversal of normal asymmetries of the putamen and lenticular nucleus; variation in corpus callosum morphology among males; decreases in the density and number of GABAergic neurons in the basal ganglia; and decreases in the volume of the caudate nucleus (Faridi and Suchowersky, 2003; Kalanithi et al., 2005; Peterson et al., 2003).

Single photon emission tomography (SPET) studies have found hypoperfusion in the basal ganglia bilaterally, anterior cingulate cortex, left dorsolateral prefrontal cortex, and the orbital and anterior medial regions of the frontal and temporal lobes. Similarly, positron emission tomography (PET) studies have shown decreased metabolic activity in the prefrontal cortices and the striatum, implying abnormal interconnections between these areas. Functional magnetic resonance imaging (fMRI) studies have found an increase in the activation of the supplemental motor cortex, which may suggest an alteration of motor pathway organization among affected individuals. Such fMRI studies have also revealed variable brain activity when affected individuals try to suppress a tic, resulting in a bilateral decrease in globus pallidus and putamen activation, or when they allow a tic, resulting in abnormal signals in the primary motor and speech (e.g., Broca's) areas, along with striatal activity (Faridi & Suchowersky, 2003).

Neuotransmitters also appear to have a role in Tourette's disorder. The clearest evidence of this association rests upon the fact that dopamine blockade suppresses tics, and dopamine-releasing drugs tend to exacerbate them. Other data also suggests the importance of dopamine in tics. For example, Tourette's patients have been found to release more dopamine in response to amphetamine than normal controls, and increased innervation of dopamine neurons has been found in the striatum of affected individuals (Swain, Scahill, Lombroso, King, & Leckman, 2007).

Tourette's disorder has also been tied to a variety of perinatal insults and environmental factors. Perinatal hypoxia is associated with an increased risk of developing Tourette's, as is prenatal maternal smoking. Individuals with Tourette's also report higher levels of psychosocial stress and have higher levels of corticotrophin-releasing factor (CRF) in the cerebrospinal fluid than normal controls (Swain et al., 2007).

Yet another possible cause of Tourette's disorder is infection with group A beta-hemolytic streptococci (GABHS). Known in the scientific parlance now as PANDAS (pediatric autoimmune neuropsychiatric disorders associated with strep), this proposed infectious etiology of Tourette's disorder and obsessive-compulsive disorder (OCD) in all likelihood accounts for a relatively small number of cases. The theory suggests that GABHS infection in a select group of individuals may induce neuron damage and an autoimmune response, leading to the production of auto-antibodies that attack certain nerves in the brain, which result in the characteristic tics of Tourette's along with obsessive thinking and compulsive behavior. Evidence for this association is based upon the fact that rats demonstrate an increase in total and daily oral stereotypies when their brains (e.g., striatum) are infused with sera from patients with Tourette's disorder containing high levels of GABHS antibodies. In contrast, those rats injected with sera from normal controls and Tourette's patients with low levels of antibodies demonstrate no such changes in behavior (Swedo et al., 1998; Yeh et al., 2006).

Children affected by PANDAS typically experience the rapid onset of symptoms following a GABHS infection, such as strep throat. Symptoms may include not only Tourette's, but also symptoms of obsessive-compulsive disorder. The autoimmune response triggered by strep causes the production of auto-antibodies that attack the host, specifically, it appears, the basal ganglia, which is highly important in managing body movement and behavior. This same process is known to cause rheumatic fever when these auto-antibodies attack the mitral valve, arthritis when these auto-antibodies attack joints, and abnormal movements when these auto-antibodies attack the basal ganglia, resulting in Sydenham's chorea or St. Vitus' dance.

Finally, tics and Tourette's disorder are known to have a genetic basis. Family studies have found that Tourette's syndrome is inherited and that first-degree relatives of a proband or affected individual are at increased risk (Faridi & Suchowersky, 2003). Chronic and transient tics are also found at increased rates among first-degree relatives, suggesting alternate expressions of Tourette's (Faridi & Suchowersky, 2003). Twin studies have found a much higher concordance rate among monozygotic (identical) twins (up to 53%) than among dizygotic (nonidentical) twins (up to 8%) (Price, Kidd, Cohen, Pauls, & Leckman, 1985). If chronic motor tics are included in the count, monozygotic twin pairs are nearly 90% concordant, and dizygotic twin pairs are nearly 30% concordant (Leckman & Cohen, 1996). Although tic disorders are not passed consistently and reliably from generation to generation, an autosomal dominant pattern of inheritance with variable penetrance has been indicated by studies to date, suggesting that other factors, such as *genomic imprinting*, may be at play (see Chapter 6). Regardless, family members of an affected individual are clearly at significant risk (Faridi & Suchowersky, 2003).

Abelson et al. (2005) recently identified a chromosome 13 inversion in a patient with Tourette's disorder. The gene *SLITRK1* is suggested to be responsible for the expression of Tourette's in the identified patient and other unrelated individuals. With rare exceptions such as *SLITRK1*, however, Tourette's disorder is most often likely to be due to multiple genes (Swain et al., 2007).

EPIDEMIOLOGY

Tics and Tourette's disorder have been found in all racial and ethnic groups studied. Due to misdiagnosis, underreporting, and the fact that most data have emanated from clinical samples, the precise prevalence is unknown. While motor tics are quite routinely observed, certainly Tourette's is an uncommon phenomenon. One large study of over 28,000 Israeli Army recruits, aged 16–17 years, identified an overall rate of 4.3 per 10,000, slightly higher in males (4.9) than females (3.1) (Apter et al., 1993). A Swedish screening study of 11-year-old children that utilized both a survey and a physical examination reported a 1.1% incidence among boys and a 0.5% incidence among girls (Kadesjö & Gillberg, 2000). By contrast, a lifetime prevalence of Tourette's disorder of 0.39% was found in a population study that utilized structured diagnostic interviews from 1975 to 1992 in upstate New York (Peterson, Pine, Cohen, & Brook, 2001). This same study identified a nearly 18% prevalence of tics in early childhood, which fell to 2–3% by adolescence. Zohar et al.'s (1999) review of population studies reported rates of Tourette's disorder ranging from 0.05% to 0.1% among children. Finally, the *DSM-IV* reports the prevalence at 5–30 per 10,000 in children and 1–2 per 10,000 in adults, reflecting the diminishing impact of Tourette's disorder with age (American Psychiatric Association, 2000).

CLINICAL COURSE

About 20–25% of children will develop a *transient tic disorder* at some time before age 18 years (Pringsheim et al., 2003). In order to meet *DSM-IV* diagnostic criteria, these tics must occur often throughout most days for at least a month but for less than 1 year (American Psychiatric Association, 2000). Eye blinking, snout reflex, throat clicking or clearing, sniffing, and a facial grimace are perhaps the most common expressions, which are likely to wax and wane, exacerbate with stress, and then dissipate over time. Tics usually begin between 3 and 8 years of age.

Tourette's disorder generally starts with a simple motor tic and then later generalizes to both motor and vocal tics. Tics may begin as early as

2 years of age but typically start between 6 and 7 years. A prepubertal exacerbation is common with Tourette's, as is a postpubertal attenuation, followed by stabilization of symptoms in adulthood (Faridi & Suchowersky, 2003). Once considered a lifelong disorder, one retrospective cohort study has demonstrated that approximately 50% of patients were asymptomatic by 18 years of age (Leckman et al., 1998). Tourette's symptoms typically stabilize in adulthood with up to 65% of patients showing no changes in symptoms over 5 years (de Groot, Bornstein, Spetie, & Burriss, 1994).

DIAGNOSIS

The diagnosis of Tourette's disorder rests upon the presence of persistent motor and vocal tics. By *DSM-IV* criteria the tics must be present numerous times per day on most days for at least 1 year in the absence of a 3-month or more tic-free period (American Psychiatric Association, 2000). Tics rarely begin after the age of 18 years, and the *DSM* relies upon this criterion as well for the diagnosis of Tourette's disorder.

The differential diagnosis of Tourette's disorder is broad and includes a variety of movement disorders, infectious etiologies, perinatal insults, trauma, toxins, medications, and drug abuse. By establishing the required time criteria for the diagnosis (e.g., both motor and vocal tics for at least 1 year), one can rule out a diagnosis of transient tic disorder (American Psychiatric Association, 2000). Other disorders, such as Huntington's disease, Lesch-Nyhan syndrome, Sydenham's chorea, and multiple sclerosis, commonly result in movement disorders that can be mistaken for Tourette's disorder. Congenital central nervous system conditions and various birth defects can also result in tics and should be considered. A complete birth and developmental history will assist the clinician in assessing these variables. In addition to GABHS, as described above, postviral encephalitis, HIV infection, and Lyme disease can cause both motor and vocal tics. Head trauma and seizure disorders must also be considered, and the onset of tics should be measured against any known history of injury. Toxins, such as carbon monoxide and gasoline, prescription medications, such as antipsychotics, L-dopa, stimulants, and lamotrigine, and drugs of abuse, such as amphetamine and opiate withdrawal, can also cause tics and should be ruled out.

Genetic disorders, such as Hallervorden-Spatz disease, Wilson's disease, hyperekplexias, Rett's syndrome, and neuroacanthocytosis, can result in tics, as can various chromosomal abnormalities, such as XYY, XXY, and fragile X syndrome. Finally, both children and adults diagnosed with autism spectrum disorders (ASD) often demonstrate repetitive and stereotyped movements (Faridi & Suchowersky, 2003). In extreme cases these actions may include hand flapping, head wagging, body rocking, odd posturing, and spinning, but in less affected individuals these movements may simply include blinking, sticking out the tongue, or other repetitive motor movements that may be misinterpreted as a tic. To distinguish between ASD and true tics or Tourette's as the cause, the clinician should remember that tics have an involuntary quality and occur in bouts, whereas autistic stereotypies appear self-soothing and intentional (American Psychiatric Association, 2000).

Comorbidities are more commonly the rule than the exception when it comes to both tics and Tourette's disorder, with nearly 95% of children with moderate Tourette's and 100% of those with severe Tourette's qualifying for another psychiatric diagnosis (Coffey et al., 2000). Somewhere between 50% and 90% of clinically referred children and adolescents with Tourette's disorder carry a cormorbid diagnosis of attention-deficit/hyperactivity disorder (ADHD), oppositional defiant disorder, or conduct disorder (Leckman, 2003). Comorbid ADHD is also commonly associated with aggression, low frustration tolerance, explosive behavior, and noncompliance (Swain et al., 2007). Similar clinically derived samples show a high co-occurrence of ADHD and Tourette's disorder, ranging between 8% and 80% (Towbin & Riddle, 1993), and ADHD and discreet tic disorders, ranging between 8% and 34% (Biederman et al., 1996; Spencer, Biederman, & Wilens, 1999). Regardless of the precise frequency, it is apparent that ADHD and Tourette's syndrome frequently co-occur in those patients who seek medical attention. ADHD also occurs at an increased rate in the families of patients with Tourette's disorder, suggesting a shared group of genes (Faridi & Suchowersky, 2003).

OCD is also strongly associated with Tourette's disorder, with as many as 60% of clinically referred children and adolescents demonstrating significant symptoms or full diagnostic criteria (Schapiro, 2002). In the opposite direction, up to 7% of referred children with OCD have comorbid Tourette's disorder and 20% have comorbid tics (Coffey & Park, 1997). Some data suggest a difference in the nature of the obsessions and compulsions in Tourette's patients with comorbid OCD as opposed to pure OCD patients. Tourette's patients tend to have more obsessions focused on symmetry and doing things until they are "just right," along with more aggressive and sexual obsessions (Faridi & Suchowersky, 2003). In addition, these individuals may have an earlier age of onset, be more commonly male, and be less responsive to treatment with selective serotonin reuptake inhibitors (SSRIs) (American Psychiatric Association, 2000). Furthermore, individuals affected by comorbid Tourette's and

OCD may engage in more touching and counting behaviors, whereas OCD patients without Tourette's report more contamination obsessions, washing compulsions, and hoarding (American Psychiatric Association, 2000; Faridi & Suchowersky, 2003).

A number of other comorbidities have also been reported among those with Tourette's disorder. As with any disorder where the impairment is entirely apparent to others, those affected may suffer any number of psychosocial difficulties. Symptoms of anxiety (especially phobias and separation anxiety) and depression may be due to the stress and public humiliation that individuals with Tourette's often feel or perhaps due to some shared genetic roots between anxiety disorders and Tourette's (Swain et al., 2007). Impairments in peer relations and social skills have also been reported (Bawden, Stokes, Camfield, Camfield, & Salisbury, 1998; Carter et al., 2000). As many as one-third of children with Tourette's and ADHD may be diagnosed with a learning disorder, although this finding may rest more upon the ADHD than the Tourette's (Faridi & Suchowersky, 2003). Finally, migraine headaches are also up to four times more common among those with Tourette's disorder (Swain et al., 2007).

There are a number of rating scales available for assessing tics, including the Tourette Syndrome Global Scale (TSGS), the Yale Global Tic Severity Scale (YGTSS), and the Tourette Disorder Scale (TODS). These simple tracking devices are useful for determining the nature and severity of tics and for following them over time. Probably the most commonly utilized scale is the YGTSS, which allows the clinician and family to rate tic symptoms upon a Likert scale from "not at all" to "almost always" present.

TREATMENT

At the outset, education and support of the child, his peers, family, and school are vital. Because tics and Tourette's cause the child to stand out, everyone in his circle of family and friends should be taught about the disorder. Not infrequently, parents will come into the child's school and instruct the teachers and other children about the disorder, which often results in great success. The Tourette Syndrome Association (http://www.tsa-usa.org/) has many online resources, including instructional material and videos that families can use to educate themselves, teachers, and the child's peers. Although not a direct treatment for the tics themselves, supportive counseling and family therapy are also often helpful for the child and family, respectively, in dealing with the stress of the disorder, enhancing coping skills, and supporting self-esteem and adjustment at school.

Diet, exercise, and other lifestyle changes may be helpful, as well, by decreasing overall stress, which may lessen the tics.

Given the overwhelming prevalence of comorbid psychiatric disorders, their treatment must also be one of the clinician's first considerations. The treatment of ADHD, OCD, and other coexisting disorders often leads to improvement in the tics as well (Swain et al., 2007). OCD should be treated with cognitive behavior therapy (CBT), along with an SSRI antidepressant (e.g., fluoxetine, sertraline, fluvoxamine, paroxetine, citalopram, or escitalopram) or clomipramine if indicated (see Chapter 9). Because some children with OCD and comorbid Tourette's disorder do not seem to respond as well to SSRIs as do those children with OCD who do not have Tourette's, augmenting the treatment with an antipsychotic medication, which appears to enhance the effect of the SSRI, is often useful and not uncommon (Bloch et al., 2006).

Historically, there was great concern that stimulants would "unmask" tics or cause them to deteriorate. Psychiatrists were hesitant to prescribe stimulants for the treatment of ADHD in an individual suffering from a tic or Tourette's disorder given anecdotal reports of worsening. However, numerous recent studies, including double-blind, placebo-controlled trials, have found that stimulants do not cause a significant worsening of tics among these patients (Erenberg, 2005; Kurlan, 2003). These same studies have also demonstrated that ADHD responds equally well to stimulants among those who have tics and Tourette's. While no statistically significant group effects have been demonstrated, there is no doubt that some individuals will at least acutely experience an increase in the severity of their tics when they are treated with a stimulant. However, because of the natural waxing and waning of tics, which can be coincident with medication changes, the practitioner must not rush to judgment that a certain medication either relieved or worsened the tic symptoms. Rather, a thoughtful and measured approach to medication changes will serve the patient best by giving each treatment an adequate trial before labeling it beneficial or detrimental.

Although no medications have been approved by the Food and Drug Administration for the treatment of tics, pharmacological treatments are frequently employed and very often helpful. The older antipsychotic medications—haloperidol (Haldol) and pimozide (Orap)—have been approved by the FDA for treatment of Tourette's, and along with risperidone (Risperdal) have the best evidence of efficacy, with numerous randomized, double-blind, placebo-controlled trials supporting their use (Swain, 2007). While their mechanism of action in the treatment of tics and Tourette's is not known, it is thought that dopamine receptor blockade of the basal ganglia is foremost in their beneficial effects. Although adequate long-term safety studies have not been performed and would likely prove them to be equally troublesome, albeit in different ways, risperidone is now more commonly employed than haloperidol given its relative ease of use. Prior to treatment with an antipsychotic, the practitioner should consider the safety guidelines laid out in Chapter 12 and collect adequate baseline patient data. If starting with risperidone, an initial dosage of 0.25 mg per day would be typical, perhaps given in divided doses. In the aforementioned studies, dosages of risperidone have ranged between 1.0–3.5 mg per day. Pimozide is now used less frequently, given its greater likelihood of causing cardiac disturbance via extending the QTc rhythm (Zemrak & Kenna, 2008).

Other antipsychotic medications have also shown promise in the treatment of tics and Tourette's. In one small double-blind, placebo-controlled trial, ziprasidone (Geodon) demonstrated efficacy (Sallee et al., 2000). Because of its novel mechanism of action as a mixed dopamine agonist/antagonist, there is also a great deal of interest in aripiprazole (Abilify), which has proven beneficial for the treatment of tics and Tourette's in case studies and open label trials (Seo, Sung, Sea, & Bai, 2008; Davies, Stern, Agrawal, Robertson, 2006). Finally, olanzapine (Zyprexa) and quetiapine (Seroquel), two additional antipsychotics, have also demonstrated efficacy in open-label trials, chart reviews, and case reports for the treatment of tics and Tourette's (Copur, Arpaci, Demir, & Narin, 2007; McCracken, Suddath, Chang, Thakur, & Piacentini, 2008; Mukaddes, & Abali, 2003; Stephens, Bassel, & Sandor, 2004; Van den Eynde, Naudts, De Saedeleer, van Heeringen, & Audenaert, 2005).

More benign and commonly utilized first treatments are the alpha-2 agonists, clonidine (Catapres) and guanfacine (Tenex). These medications are generally prescribed for hypertension, where they act centrally in the brain by decreasing norepinephrine tone. They are thought to resolve tics by essentially the same mechanism of action at dosages of 1–2 mg two to three times a day for guanfacine or 0.1–0.2 mg two to four times a day for clonidine. When starting an alpha-2 agonist, it is wise to begin dosing in the evening, such as 0.05 mg of clonidine or 0.5 mg of guanfacine about an hour before bedtime. If well tolerated and necessary after 3–4 days, adding another pill about 4 to 6 hours prior to the first, and later a third tablet in the morning by the same titration, is common practice. When discontinuing clonidine or guanfacine, the taper should be done in the same way and with the same pacing but in reverse order (see Chapter 2).

A number of other medications have been employed for the treatment of tics and Tourette's, some of which have reasonable data to support their use. Desipramine, a tricyclic antidepressant, for example, has been shown in a double-blind, placebo-controlled study to reduce symptoms of ADHD by 42% and tics by 30% from baseline (Spencer et al., 2002). Practitioners are advised, however, to proceed cautiously with tricyclic antidepressants when treating children and adolescents, given their potential for cardiac toxicity (see Chapter 10). Pergolide (Permax), a dopamine agonist that is used in the treatment of Parkinson's disease, has also been shown in double-blind studies to be moderately effective but has been removed from the U.S. market because of its potential to cause cardiac valvular disease (Gilbert, Sethuraman, Sine, Peters, & Sallee, 2000; Gilbert et al., 2003). Pramipexole (Mirapex), another dopamine agonist used in the treatment of Parkinson's and restless legs syndrome, is currently under study as a possible treatment for Tourette's. Numerous other medications, including flunarizine, naloxone, opiates, delta-9-tetrahydrocannabinol, baclofen, nicotine, L-dopa, odansetron, metaclopromide, topiramate, levetiracetam, donepezil, selegiline, and benzodiazepines, have supporting data from small open-label trials and case studies but would generally only be attempted after failure of numerous other treatments with more supporting data (Faridi & Suchowersky, 2003; Swain et al., 2007).

Should a child present in the context of a recent strep throat infection with a case of rapid-onset tics, Tourette's, and/or obsessive-compulsive symptoms suggestive of PANDAS, the child should receive a throat culture. Blood work for ASO (antistreptolysin O) titer and anti-DNase B should also be performed. If the index of suspicion remains high, a full course of antibiotics should be employed, such as penicillin VK, at therapeutic dosages for 10–14 days. Should symptoms continue, immunomodulatory therapies, such as intravenous immunoglobulin and therapeutic plasma exchange, have both proven useful in a placebo-controlled trial (Swedo, Garvey, Snider, Hamilton, & Leonard, 2001). However, at present time these treatments should only be performed within the context of a research trial or by an experienced clinician.

While often effective, medications should only be attempted for the treatment of tics and Tourette's disorder after other treatments have failed because of their potential to cause side effects. Mild difficulties are unlikely to require medication, as many affected individuals can hide their tics or do well without any major disruption in their lives. If education, relaxation, and supportive therapies are not adequately effective, a trial of a more specific therapy is indicated prior to the use of medication.

Behavioral therapies in general have not resulted in remarkable benefits for most patients (King, Scahill, Findley, & Cohen, 1999). However, in recent years a more precise treatment for tics has emerged that has supporting data from case studies and randomized trials (Swain et al., 2007). Habit reversal training (HRT) is a behavioral treatment designed to treat repetitive behavior disorders, such as tics, nail biting, trichotillomania, skin picking, and thumb sucking. HRT relies upon five aspects: (a) awareness training; (b) competing response training; (c) contingency management; (d) relaxation training; and (e) generalization training. In the treatment of tics and Tourette's, these five components are designed to increase the awareness of one's tics and then to allow for the development of a competing response that the individual will perform instead of the tic. For example, when the patient feels the urge to tic, instead of shouting out, he will learn to stomp his foot lightly, or squeeze his hand into a fist, and so forth. These competing responses are more socially acceptable and less disruptive. In order for HRT to be effective, the patient must have a premonitory urge or a sensation of some sort that occurs prior to the tic. When applicable, HRT is an acceptable and durable treatment for tics that has been found effective in controlled trials (Piacentini & Chang, 2006).

9

Anxiety Disorders

All children experience anxiety. Thus, while approximately 10–20% of children and adolescents suffer from a diagnosable anxiety disorder, many more children, in fact, experience significant anxiety that does not technically meet diagnostic criteria (Walkup et al., 2008). For example, studies have found that approximately 40% of grade-school children have fears of separation from their parents; 40% of children ages 6 to 12 years have seven or more specific fears that trouble them; 30% of children worry about their competence and require considerable and regular reassurance; and 20% of grade-school children are afraid of heights, shy in new situations, or anxious about public speaking and social acceptance (Bell-Dolan, Last, & Strauss, 1990). Girls typically report more anxiety and stress than boys, although this finding may be an artifact of social expectations, as boys are encouraged to be "tough" and not to share their worries. Thankfully, children outgrow most of their worries as they age and mature.

As most of us recognize, some anxiety is useful and even necessary in order to motivate us to action. In 1908, Yerkes and Dodson proposed the curve seen in Figure 9.1 to explain the relationship between the level of arousal or stress and performance. As described by Yerkes and Dodson, one's performance typically increases as one's arousal, anxiety, or stress increases up to a certain optimal level. At some point, however, when the level of arousal or anxiety gets too high, one's performance becomes impaired. Research as well as practical experience suggests that the Yerkes-Dodson correlation does exist, but the reasons for the relationship have yet to be elucidated (Anderson, 2000; Anderson, Revelle, & Lynch, 1989; Broadhurst, 1957; Duffy, 1957).

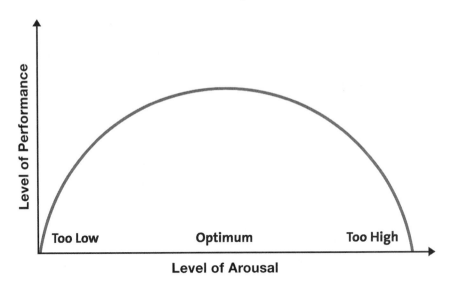

Figure 9.1. Yerkes-Dodson correlation. As proposed by Yerkes-Dodson, performance improves at an optimal level of arousal. Both minimal and maximal arousal result in impaired performance. Adapted from Yerkes & Dodson (1908).

A number of questions help us to distinguish normal or typical from pathological anxiety in children and adolescents. We must first wonder about the object of worry. Is this issue something a child this age should be worrying about? Secondly, we must ask ourselves whether the degree of distress is reasonable or realistic given the child's developmental stage. We then look at the degree of impairment. Is the anxiety interfering with the child's life on a daily basis? How is the child's social, academic, and family functioning affected by the anxiety? Finally, we want to know about the child's coping skills. Is the child still bothered even when the stressor is not present? Does the child worry about future occurrences, and is the anxiety present across multiple settings?

Given that fear and worry are normative experiences, the clinician must be able to distinguish developmentally normal from abnormal fears and worries. Infants, for example, are commonly fearful of loud noises, surprises, and strangers. Toddlers may be fearful of imaginary creatures or monsters, darkness, and separation from their parents and siblings. While some degree of worry is normal, those children with high levels of anxiety early in life are more likely to continue to suffer from anxiety as they age. Children who are confident and eager to explore novel situations at 5 years of age are less likely to manifest anxiety in later childhood and adolescence, yet children who are passive, shy, or fearful, and avoid new situations at the same age, are more likely to exhibit anxiety later in life (Caspi, Henry, McGee, Moffitt, & Silva, 1995). In general, younger children tend to report more normative anxiety symptoms than do older children.

School-age children often worry about injury and natural events and disasters, such as storms, lightning, earthquakes, and volcanoes. These children may also interpret ambiguous or vague situations in a negative way and underestimate their own competency or ability to handle themselves in such situations. For example, they may misread another's facial expression or view a remark made by a peer as a criticism, which only acts to reinforce their anxiety. These children are not being paranoid in a psychotic sense, but they are likely to experience *attribution bias*, an error in cognition based upon incomplete evidence and their own high anxiety, which causes them to be more suspicious of others' intentions.

As children age their anxiety often tends to diminish, but in some cases the anxiety simply finds a new expression (Last, Perrin, Hersen, & Kazdin, 1996). While separation anxiety diminishes in frequency, for example, panic disorder tends to increase with age (Ollendick, 1998). By adolescence, normative fears tend to mirror those of adults more closely and are typically related to school, social capabilities, and issues of physical and mental health.

CLINICAL PRESENTATION

Young children commonly have difficulty recognizing and describing their emotions. It is no surprise, then, that preschool and school-age children suffering from an anxiety disorder often present with physical or somatic symptoms, such as headache, stomachache, and nausea. Adolescents are much better at identifying their feelings but still may present, as may younger children, with oppositionality or disruptive behavior when feeling anxious. Although there is much crossover among the anxiety disorders, there are some differences in how children with different disorders present.

Separation Anxiety

Children suffering from separation anxiety experience excessive fear when separated from home or primary attachment figures. The anxiety can be quite severe and commonly occurs not only during separation, but also in anticipation of separation. Children typically worry about their own safety and health or that of their parents. Symptoms may include bedtime resistance and refusal to sleep alone, dreams and nightmares of separation, school refusal, physical or somatic complaints, and disobedience whenever separation is perceived as a possibility.

Specific Phobia

Phobias are fears of particular objects or situations that are either avoided or tolerated with great discomfort. Phobic children and adolescents often have more than one specific fear. Adolescents and adults typically recognize that their fears are unreasonable, but younger children most often do not. Children will commonly avoid situations wherein they feel phobic, which can be particularly disruptive and lead to a host of developmental difficulties.

Social Phobia

Some children are particularly scared in social or performance situations. They fear that they will embarrass themselves and have trouble speaking in class, reading aloud, conversing with people they do not know, and attending parties and social gatherings. Whereas children with phobias usually feel better when they are removed from the dreaded objects or situations, children suffering from other anxiety disorders tend to struggle most of the time.

Panic Attack

Panic attacks, as uncomfortable as they are, are a normative experience characterized by brief, intense fear in the absence of a genuine threat or danger along with a number of somatic and cognitive symptoms, such as shortness of breath, palpitations, sweating, dizziness, tremor, derealization, and a fear of going crazy, losing control, or dying. Attacks usually last 10 minutes or less, and individuals often report a desire to flee when they experience an episode. Most individuals will have at least one panic attack in their lifetime. Although uncommon in children, panic attacks are most often seen among those who suffer separation anxiety and social phobia.

Generalized Anxiety

Some children suffer from chronic, excessive, but nonspecific anxiety about many things. Unlike those with phobias, the anxiety these children experience is a moving target, shifting every so often from one thing to another. These children have trouble managing their anxiety and experience numerous manifestations and somatic symptoms.

Obsessions and Compulsions

Children who experience obsessive thoughts feel unable to control their worries and the compulsive behaviors they employ to neutralize their anxiety. These children and adolescents are universally very private about their thoughts and behaviors, which even they experience as strange and out of the ordinary. In fact, these children are so secretive and ashamed of their thoughts and behaviors that symptoms commonly exist for years before reaching clinical attention, if ever. Parents often unwittingly collude with their children in worsening the symptoms by providing constant reassurance, which only tends to invigorate and perpetuate the anxiety.

Trauma

Children and adolescents who have been traumatized may present clinically with any or all of the anxiety symptoms already mentioned. Their symptoms may wax and wane but typically worsen when confronted with any reminders or situations reminiscent of the trauma they experienced.

ETIOLOGY

The etiology or cause of anxiety is highly complex and has roots in our genes, neuroanatomy, endocrine function, neurotransmitters, and environment. One measureable temperamental construct, *behavioral inhibition*, has been helpful in understanding the development of child and adolescent anxiety. Behavioral inhibition is defined as the tendency to be unusually withdrawn or timid and to show fear, avoidance, and withdrawal in novel or unfamiliar social and nonsocial situations (Smoller et al., 2005). Those who are withdrawn only in social situations are simply considered shy. Both behavioral inhibition and shyness are associated with anxiety disorders in children and adults (Van Ameringen, Mancini, & Oakman, 1998), and the tendency to approach or withdraw from novel situations appears to be an enduring temperamental trait (Moehler et al., 2008).

Behaviorally inhibited children demonstrate a host of physiological signs often associated with anxiety, including enhanced sympathetic nervous system tone (e.g., elevated resting heart rate and salivary corti-sol), increased tension in the vocal cords and larynx, and elevations in urinary catecholamines (Kagan, Reznick, & Snidman, 1988). Children who demonstrate behavioral inhibition in laboratory settings are more likely to suffer multiple psychiatric disorders and two or more anxiety disorders, particularly social phobia, separation anxiety disorder (SAD), and agoraphobia (Biederman et al., 1993; Hirshfeld et al., 1992; Kagan & Snidman, 1999). These children have also been found to be at higher risk for panic disorder and phobias as they age (Smoller et al., 2005). Behavioral inhibition is also associated with a family history of anxiety, and children of parents with panic disorder with agoraphobia are at increased risk for behavioral inhibition (Rosenbaum et al., 1993). In summary, studies of behavioral inhibition demonstrate that these traits are heritable and predict the later onset of anxiety disorders. Whether behavioral inhibition is due to genes or the environment, however, remains unclear.

The neurobiology of anxiety is under active investigation, and numerous neural structures and networks appear to have important roles. In order to promote survival, the brain has many redundant mechanisms for sensing threat and responding rapidly. The reticular activating system, a group of neural systems involved in arousal, appears to be at the center of these networks. The locus coeruleus, the seat of noradrenergic neurons that project throughout the brain, is important in mobilizing the body in response to a perceived threat. The dorsal raphe nucleus, which houses the serotonin neuron cell bodies, can affect the sensitivity of the locus coeruleus. Cholinergic neuron projections, found within the lateral dorsal tegmentum, comprise yet another component of the reticular activating system, as do the dopamine neurons emanating from the substantia nigra, which project into mesolimbic and mesocortical areas, playing a vital role in the brain's sensation and interpretation of threat (Perry, 1998). Various drugs and medications that affect these brain structures, including the alpha-2 agonists, the SSRIs, tricyclic antidepressants, and stimulants, have major effects on anxiety by modulating these systems.

The limbic system, the brain's emotional processing hub, is a complicated network of subcortical structures, which include the amygdala, hippocampus, cingulate gyrus, hypothalamus, fornix, and thalamus. The amygdala receives neural projections from many areas (e.g., the sensory thalamus, the hippocampus, the entorhinal cortex) and plays a central role in orchestrating the brain's response to this sensory input by sending projections to motor, autonomic, and neuroendocrine systems. Although anxiety is believed to be recognized at the site of the amygdala, the hippocampus is likely to be the storage site of cognitive and emotional memories. The hippocampus itself is highly sensitive to stress, which impairs its ability to accurately store certain types of information and may promote some of the cognitive distortions associated with anxiety disorders (Perry, 1998). The human brain is designed to allow for pairing of cues, such as the honk of a car's horn and fear of harm. Once the horn is heard, the brain rapidly assesses for any real threat and responds. It is precisely this amazing ability of the brain to generalize from a common event, such as a horn honking, to a specific action, such as jumping out of the way, however, that makes us vulnerable to false associations and overgeneralizations. The brain is evolutionarily primed to make associations between threats and outcomes to promote survival; but once these cues (e.g., heights) become paired with emotions (e.g., anxiety), it is up to the individual's limbic sensitivity and cortex-mediated subjective appraisal to determine the appropriate response (Perry, 1998).

Family studies demonstrate that anxiety disorders tend to run in families. However, as yet, few twin studies have been completed (Kendler, 2001) and candidate genes for anxiety disorders are few (Donner et al., 2008). Heritability estimates exist for some illnesses, such as panic disorder at 48% and generalized anxiety disorder (GAD) at 32% (Hettema, Neale, & Kendler, 2001). Given these estimates, it is clear that genes account for only some portion of the increase in risk among family members of an affected individual. Environmental factors, then, such as perinatal exposures and developmental experience, must play a major role.

Some anxieties may be due to genetically fixed patterns developed over eons of evolution. For example, it is likely that many humans are afraid of snakes because fear of snakes or fear of slithering reptiles has been passed down and has become almost a part of our genetic code. Children mirror their parents' responses when interpreting internal states of pain, arousal, and anxiety. Consequently, children who grow up in a home with snakes or with parents who are comfortable handling snakes themselves will quite likely have no difficulties in this regard. Thus, it appears that while some anxiety is learned or easily built upon a genetically vulnerable substrate, anxiety can also be unlearned. Over time, children may come to pair a host of external cues, such as snakes, to anxiety following upon their parents' worries. When exposed to these cues, the child will perceive the situation as potentially threatening and will experience symptoms of anxiety. This *learned response* hypothesis is thought to be important in many cases of specific phobias, some types of posttraumatic stress disorder (PTSD), and GAD (Ronan & Kendall, 1990).

In an effort to put these various etiological perspectives together, let us consider obsessive-compulsive disorder (OCD) as a modal anxiety disorder. First, we recognize a genetic component, given the elevated concordance between monozygotes or identical twins (versus dizygotes or nonidentical twins) and the increased rates seen among first-degree relatives of affected individuals or probands (Towbin & Riddle, 1996). Physiologically, we know that individuals with OCD have increased brain metabolic activity in the orbitofrontal cortex and caudate nucleus when they actively obsess, as demonstrated by positron emission tomography (PET) scans (Baxter et al., 1992). We also know that the endocrine system is somehow involved in OCD, as affected individuals have been shown to have elevated levels of cerebrospinal oxytocin, a hormone that is typically released in large amounts when a woman is breast-feeding and that appears to increase bonding behavior between mother and child (Towbin & Riddle, 1996). Some of the behaviors associated with OCD are similar to the behavioral effects of oxytocin, such as repetitive grooming and obsessive worrying (Leckman et al., 1994). Finally, the neurotransmitter serotonin figures prominently in our understanding of OCD, as moderate to high dosages of medications that promote serotonin are highly effective in the treatment of this disorder.

EPIDEMIOLOGY

Anxiety disorders may be the most prevalent mental illness affecting children and teens. Various large epidemiological studies tell us that somewhere between 6% and 20% of children suffer at least one major anxiety disorder prior to age 18 (Costello, Egger, & Angold, 2004). We generally accept that about 13% of 9- to 17-year-olds meet diagnostic criteria (U.S. Department of Health and Human Services, 1999). While impressive, these numbers are themselves somewhat deceiving because we know that many additional children experience subclinical anxiety not meeting formal *DSM-IV* criteria but causing significant impairment and disability (Angold, Costello, Farmer, Burns, & Erkanli, 1999). In a study of nearly 800 11-year-olds, Anderson, Williams, McGee, and Silva (1987) reported that 3.5% suffered from separation anxiety disorder (SAD), 2.9% from overanxious disorder (a *DSM-III* diagnosis for what we now call GAD), 2.4% from specific phobia, and 1% from social phobia. Other studies have found similar rates (Bowen, Offord, & Boyle, 1990). In a study of over 5,000 14- to 17-year-olds, the lifetime prevalence of panic disorder was 0.6% (Whitaker et al., 1990).

Although anxiety disorders often lessen over time, one disorder may simply substitute or replace another (Last et al., 1996). Untreated anxiety leads to an increased risk of additional anxiety disorders, depression, educational underachievement, and substance abuse in childhood (Connolly & Bernstein, 2007) and an increased risk of anxiety and depression in adulthood (Pine, Cohen, Gurley, Brook, & Ma, 1998). Girls are more commonly affected by anxiety than boys (U.S. Department of Health and Human Services, 1999), and anxiety in the first grade has been shown to predict anxiety and low academic achievement in reading and math by fifth grade (Ialongo, Edelsohn, Werthamer-Larsson, Crockett, & Kellam, 1995).

Risk factors for the development of anxiety disorders include shyness and behavioral inhibition (Biederman et al., 1993; Van Ameringen et al., 1998) and parental anxiety disorder (Biederman et al., 2001). Anxious, critical, and overprotective parenting styles also increase a child's risk for anxiety, as does an insecure attachment to the primary caregivers (Connolly & Bernstein, 2007). Sophisticated coping skills, such as distraction and problem-solving strategies rather than avoidance, are considered protective for children (Ayers, Sandler, West, & Roosa, 1996).

CLINICAL COURSE

Generally speaking, childhood anxiety disorders do not readily remit, and the majority of affected adults report retrospectively that they suffered significant difficulties with anxiety as children (Angst & Vollrath, 1991). Given that adolescents often report a greater severity of anxiety than children with the same diagnosis, it is likely that without treatment symptoms persist and worsen over time (Kendall, Safford, Flannery-Schroeder, & Webb, 2004).

The usual course of most anxiety disorders is chronic, with waxing and waning. As the months and years go by, some individuals will improve, but many may simply "trade" one anxiety disorder for another. Children with a prior anxiety disorder appear to be not only more likely to suffer another anxiety disorder in the future, however, but also other nonanxiety psychiatric disorders (Last et al., 1996).

Depression, suicidal ideation and suicide attempts, and substance abuse have all been linked to a childhood history of anxiety disorders (Brent et al., 1986; Last et al., 1993). Studies suggest that anxiety commonly precedes the development of depression and substance abuse and that in at least some cases drugs and alcohol are used to self-medicate the anxiety (Kendall et al., 2004; Manassis & Monga, 2001). The lifetime comorbidity estimates of substance use and anxiety disorders are quite high, ranging from 33% to 45% (Kessler et al., 1996; Regier et al., 1990). In addition to these comorbidities, we must also consider the demoralization and damage to one's self-esteem that anxiety sufferers commonly endure. The frustration that these children feel often negatively impacts their peer and family relationships and academic functioning (Kendall et al., 2004).

DIAGNOSIS

The *DSM-III-R* (*Diagnostic and Statistical Manual of Mental Disorders,* 3rd edition, revised) included only three childhood anxiety disorders— SAD, overanxious disorder (now known as GAD), and avoidant disorder (now known as social phobia) (American Psychiatric Association, 1987). As our knowledge of childhood anxiety has increased in recent years, the *DSM* has allowed for an expansion of childhood diagnoses into areas previously reserved only for adults, including panic disorder, specific phobia, OCD, and acute stress and PTSD. In addition to these primary anxiety disorders, there are a number of other difficulties that children commonly face, which are not defined by the *DSM-IV* as anxiety disorders per se but are commonly characterized by extreme anxiety; these include selective mutism (which some researchers suggest should be a subtype of social phobia) and trichotillomania (categorized as an impulse-control disorder in the *DSM-IV*).

Separation Anxiety Disorder

Given that some degree of separation anxiety is normative for most children prior to 3 years of age, SAD is understandably the earliest anxiety disorder usually observed. The *DSM-IV* defines SAD as developmentally inappropriate and unwarranted anxiety regarding separation from home or major attachment figures. Three or more additional symptoms are required for the diagnosis, including excessive distress on separation; extreme worry about losing, or harm coming to, an attachment figure; fears of somehow being separated from an attachment figure, such as by kidnapping or getting lost; refusal to attend school; refusal to sleep alone at home or away from home; fear of being alone at home or in new situations without attachment figures present; continual nightmares of being separated from attachment figures; and frequent physical complaints upon separation or when planning such events. Finally, the *DSM-IV* requires at least 4 weeks of symptoms and an onset before age 18 (American Psychiatric Association, 2000).

Children with SAD often grow up within closely knit families. Upon separation, however, they become sad, withdrawn, and apathetic, and have difficulty concentrating. The specific fears that children with SAD report commonly mirror their developmental level, such that younger children may fear monsters and older children airplanes or natural disasters. Death or dying is a frequent concern among these children as well, who are often viewed as demanding because of their need for constant reassurance. Adults with SAD are generally fearful of changes, such as starting a new job or moving, and are overly worried about their children and spouses.

SAD may develop after a major life change or stress, such as the death of a family member or move to a new home. Approximately 4% of children and adolescents are believed to be affected, and it is more common among first-degree relatives and in children of mothers with panic disorder than in the general population. Adolescent onset is rare, and girls appear to be affected somewhat more frequently than boys. Typically, the anxiety waxes and wanes over time, with most children being free from anxiety by adulthood. However, some individuals appear to be at greater risk of depression and dysthymia, and SAD may precede the onset of panic disorder with agoraphobia among other anxiety disorders (American Psychiatric Association, 2000).

Panic Disorder

Panic attacks per se are not considered a psychiatric diagnosis, given the preponderance of individuals who experience at least one such episode in their lifetime. Furthermore, panic attacks are ubiquitous among a host of medical and psychiatric conditions, including mood, substance use, and anxiety disorders, as well as cardiac, respiratory, vestibular, and gastrointestinal disorders.

Two types of panic attacks are typically described, those that are unexpected or uncued and those that are situationally bound or cued. In the former the attacks are always unexpected and occur "out of the blue," as opposed to the latter, which generally occur during or in anticipation of a feared situation, such as a school examination or flying in an airplane. Unexpected panic attacks are required for a *DSM-IV* diagnosis of panic disorder. Cued or situationally bound panic attacks are also common in panic disorder but do occur in the context of other anxiety disorders, such as social phobia and PTSD. In addition to recurrent, unexpected panic attacks, the *DSM-IV* requires that at least one of the panic attacks was followed by 1 month or more of persistent fear of having additional attacks, fear of the implications of the attack (e.g., having a heart attack or going insane), or a major behavior change following the attack (American Psychiatric Association, 2000). Agoraphobia, literally a "fear of the open marketplace" but in actuality a fear of being in a place or situation from which one cannot easily exit or escape, may also accompany panic disorder.

The lifetime prevalence of panic disorder with or without agoraphobia is somewhere between 1% and 3.5%. Higher rates are generally found in clinical samples, with up to 10% of psychiatrically referred adults and up to 6% of psychiatrically referred children demonstrating diagnostic symptoms (Biederman et al., 1997). These numbers are considerably higher among adults in respiratory, vestibular, and gastrointestinal clinics, where up to 30% are affected, and cardiology clinics, where up to 60% are affected. Up to one half of community samples demonstrate comorbid agoraphobia, but the rate among clinical samples is higher (American Psychiatric Association, 2000).

Panic attacks are uncommon prior to puberty. Most cases set on between late adolescence and approximately 30 years of age. First-degree relatives are up to 8 times more likely to develop panic disorder; this number increases up to 20 times if the age of onset of the proband or index case is under 20 years. Panic disorder is often viewed as a chronic condition, although longitudinal studies have primarily been performed in psychiatric treatment centers where recidivism is generally elevated (American Psychiatric Association, 2000).

As previously noted, comorbidity with other anxiety disorders is high. Social phobia and GAD affect 15–30% of individuals with panic disorder, specific phobia affects 2–20%, and OCD as many as 10%. PTSD may occur in 10% or more of those affected, and SAD and hypochondriasis are common. Rates of coexisting major depressive disorder are also high, and studies vary with somewhere between 10% and 65% of panic sufferers being affected. In most individuals the depression co-occurs with or follows the panic. In a minority of cases the depression precedes the panic (American Psychiatric Association, 2000).

There are no diagnostic laboratory tests, although a number of abnormalities have been consistently found among groups of individuals with panic disorder. Most notably, some individuals demonstrate a compensated respiratory alkalosis (e.g., decreased carbon dioxide and bicarbonate levels in the presence of a nearly normal pH), and some are easily provoked into an attack with sodium lactate or carbon dioxide inhalation. Debate remains as to the role of mitral valve prolapse and thyroid disease in panic. Certainly, many individuals with panic disorder are hypersensitive to physical cues and medication side effects for fear of experiencing an attack (American Psychiatric Association, 2000).

Specific Phobia

A phobia is characterized by severe unreasonable and continual anxiety brought on by the presence or anticipation of a feared situation or object. In order for the *DSM-IV* definition to hold, the individual must always experience excessive anxiety, perhaps even a panic attack, after exposure to the feared object or situation or in anticipation of it. Children, however, may respond with a tantrum or by crying or clinging to an adult. Phobic adults recognize their fears as excessive, but this is often not the case for children. Affected individuals generally avoid those situations or objects that bother them but in some cases may suffer through exposure to the feared stimulus with great discomfort. The *DSM-IV* requires a symptom duration of at least 6 months prior to diagnosis (American Psychiatric Association, 2000).

The *DSM-IV* defines the four most common types of phobia as *animal type* (cued by animals or insects, with onset generally in childhood); *natural environmental type* (cued by naturally occurring objects in the environment, such as lightning or heights, with onset generally in childhood); *blood-injection-injury type* (cued by fear of injury, blood, injection, or venopuncture, often running in families and associated with a vasovagal response); and *situational type* (cued by feared situations, such as driving over a bridge or in a tunnel, flying, or being in an elevator). Other phobias are sometimes found in children, including fear of vomiting, choking, costumed characters, loud sounds, or getting sick (American Psychiatric Association, 2000).

Fears are common among children and adolescents but rarely cause enough difficulty to warrant a diagnosis of specific phobia. Community samples show point prevalence rates as high as 9% and lifetime prevalence rates as high as 11% with decline among the elderly. Females are affected about twice as often as males, and phobias tend to aggregate in families. The first symptoms usually occur in childhood or early adolescence but may not show up, particularly for situational phobias, until the mid-20s. Comorbidities are common, affecting as many as 80% of individuals. Typically the comorbid conditions cause more distress than the phobias themselves, which rarely bring individuals to treatment (American Psychiatric Association, 2000).

Social Phobia

Social phobia is characterized by consistent fear of social or performance situations in which the individual fears embarrassment or judgment by others. Affected individuals worry that they will be humiliated in performance situations or demonstrate symptoms of anxiety. The *DSM-IV* requires that children have an established capacity for age-appropriate social relationships and that the anxiety occur with peers as well as adults. As with specific phobia, the individual must always experience excessive anxiety, perhaps even a panic attack, after exposure to a feared social situation. Other common physical signs of anxiety include palpitations, sweating, tremors, and gastrointestinal symptoms such as diarrhea or vomiting. Children, however, may respond only with a tantrum or by crying or clinging to an adult. Socially phobic adults recognize their fears as excessive, but this is often not the case for children. Affected individuals generally avoid those situations that bother them but in some cases may suffer through exposure to the social situation with great discomfort. The *DSM-IV* requires a symptom duration of at least 6 months prior to diagnosis. Although not diagnostic, affected individuals are often passive, hypersensitive to criticism or rejection, and demonstrate low self-esteem and feelings of inferiority (American Psychiatric Association, 2000).

Although the ratio is not entirely clear, women appear to suffer more often than men. The lifetime prevalence ranges from 3% to 13%, and as with other anxiety disorders, social phobia typically occurs more frequently among first-degree relatives (American Psychiatric Association, 2000).

Obsessive-Compulsive Disorder

OCD is characterized by repeated obsessions and/or compulsions that require extensive time (more than 1 hour each day) or cause severe distress or impairment. Obsessions are defined as intrusive and inappropriate thoughts, impulses, or images that cause significant anguish. Affected individuals typically try to ignore or suppress the troubling obsessions and maintain good insight, realizing that these thoughts are due to anxiety. Unlike adults, children with OCD may not realize that the obsessions and compulsions are excessive or unreasonable. Compulsions, on the other hand, are the behavioral corollary of obsessions. They are defined as repeated behaviors, such as hand washing and checking, or mental acts, such as counting or praying, that an individual feels forced to do in response to an obsession or according to some rules that they feel must be followed. The compulsive behaviors or mental acts are consciously or unconsciously designed to prevent or reduce the stress that the individual feels but are not linked in any real way to the thoughts, images, or impulses they are trying to counteract or stop (American Psychiatric Association, 2000).

The most common obsessions are related to contamination (e.g., dirt, germs, or illness), aggression (e.g., fear of hurting oneself or others), hoarding, sexual content (e.g., having "forbidden" or perverse sexual thoughts), superstitions, and scrupulosity. As expected, the most common compulsions are behavioral manifestations of these same obsessions designed to neutralize these thoughts and include excessive cleaning and hand washing, checking to make sure that nothing is wrong, repeating, counting, ordering, arranging, hoarding, and engaging in superstitious acts. Unfortunately, these compulsive behaviors, the very acts designed to counteract the obsessions and relieve the anxiety (which they often very briefly do), rapidly become problems in their own right as the individual feels unable to stop them. In contrast to autism spectrum disorders, the obsessive thoughts and compulsive behaviors of OCD are *ego-dystonic* (see Chapter 7).

Epidemiological studies of children and adolescents worldwide estimate a lifetime prevalence of 1–2%. OCD typically begins in adolescence or early adulthood but may begin in childhood. Modal age at onset for males, 6–15 years of age, is typically earlier than for females, 20–29 years of age. In adults the disorder is equally common in males and females, but in childhood onset the disorder is more common in boys. OCD has a higher concordance among monozygotic (identical) as opposed to dizygotic (fraternal) twins. As with other anxiety disorders, there is a greater risk of OCD among first-degree relatives of affected individuals (American Psychiatric Association, 2000).

Onset is typically gradual, but acute onset can occur. Children often do not seek help, as the symptoms may not be as ego-dystonic or as uncomfortable as they are in adults. Some women experience new onset OCD after pregnancy and childbirth, which may have to do with elevated levels of oxytocin. PANDAS (pediatric autoimmune neuropsychiatric disorders associated with strep), as described in Chapter 8, may also be a cause of OCD.

Comorbidities are common among those with OCD. Coexisting conditions among adults may include depression, eating disorders, and other anxiety disorders; among children, OCD is more commonly associated with other anxiety disorders, learning disorders, and disruptive behavior disorders. As noted in Chapter 8, OCD is strongly linked with Tourette's disorder with up to 7% of referred children with OCD having comorbid Tourette's and 20% having comorbid tics. Comorbid obsessive-compulsive spectrum disorders such as trichotillomania, body dysmorphia, and habits, such as nail-biting, are not common but not rare among affected children (American Psychiatric Association, 2000).

Like other anxiety disorders, OCD generally has a waxing and waning course, with the vast majority of patients showing a continuous course of illness and about 15% of affected individuals showing progressive deterioration (Rasmussen & Tsuang, 1986). A review of long-term outcome studies comprising over 500 individuals with OCD first diagnosed in childhood found that 41% of individuals had full OCD and 60% had full or subthreshold OCD between 1 and 16 years postdiagnosis (Stewart et al., 2004).

Posttraumatic Stress Disorder

Physical, emotional, or sexual abuse, as well as witnessing such abuse, often results in significant trauma. When these events involve serious injury, death, or the threat of injury or death, the likelihood of a traumatic response increases. Symptoms of trauma can be particularly perplexing because they can present in virtually any form and look like almost any psychiatric disorder. In addition to experiencing or witnessing a traumatic event, individuals who suffer PTSD report feeling helpless and fearful during the event. A child may respond to a traumatic event, by contrast, with agitated and disorganized behavior (American Psychiatric Association, 2000).

Subsequent to the event, there are three requirements for a *DSM-IV* diagnosis of PTSD. First, the individual must regularly reexperience the event via, for example, flashbacks, nightmares, and recurrent thoughts, or have an overwhelming emotional or physiological response upon exposure to cues that symbolize or resemble the traumatic event. Children may demonstrate these symptoms by repetitive play with themes related to the trauma, frightening dreams unrelated to the content of the trauma, or trauma-specific reenactments. Second, the traumatized individual must avoid anything related to the trauma, including people, thoughts, and locations, that arouses memories of the traumatic event. Individuals may also have difficulty with memory recall related to the event, show less interest in routine activities, feel detached from others, appear emotionally blunted, and express a sense of doom for the future. Third, affected individuals must experience some symptoms of irritability, anger, attentional impairment, hypervigilance, exaggerated startle response, or trouble sleeping. Finally, the *DSM-IV* requires that the symptoms last for at least 1 month before a diagnosis is given (American Psychiatric Association, 2000).

The lifetime prevalence of PTSD in the United States is approximately 8%. Symptoms typically occur within about 3 months of the trauma, but a delay may occur in some cases. Partial symptoms are common, as are comorbid conditions. Girls generally tend to be more symptomatic than boys, and younger children demonstrate more avoidance while older children suffer more reexperiencing and accompanying increases in arousal (American Psychiatric Association, 2000).

The severity, extent, and proximity of an individual to the traumatic event are considered to be the most important features in determining the probability of developing PTSD. Social supports, preexisting psychiatric conditions, family history, childhood experiences, and personality traits may all affect the development of PTSD. Research suggests that heritability effects and having a first-degree relative with depression increase one's vulnerability to developing PTSD. The symptoms of PTSD often vary over time, with full recovery occurring within 3 months in about half of cases (American Psychiatric Association, 2000).

As expected, childhood trauma appears to cause more negative outcomes than adult trauma. Individuals who were sexually abused as children and again as adults, for example, have a greater risk of affect dysregulation, suicide attempts, and dissociative behavior than those individuals who were only sexually abused as adults. Individuals who were abused as children and again as adults also have more interpersonal problems as they age and more difficulties being assertive, sociable, responsible, and intimate. Finally, these individuals also have more difficulties with emotional control and are more likely to be submissive than those who were abused only as adults (Cloitre, Scarvalone, & Difede, 1997).

Acute Stress Disorder

As with PTSD, the diagnosis of acute stress disorder demands that individuals witness or experience a traumatic event and feel helpless and fearful during the event. Subsequently, affected individuals reexperience the event, avoid anything related to the trauma that might arouse memories of the event, and demonstrate notable symptoms of anxiety or increased arousal. Unlike PTSD, however, individuals suffering from acute stress disorder also tend to experience a number of dissociative symptoms during or after the event, such as derealization, depersonalization, amnesia for the event, a sense of being less aware of one's surroundings, or a sense of detachment. The keys to this diagnosis are exposure to a traumatic event, feeling unable to respond effectively to the event, and the dissociative symptoms that follow. Affected individuals are at increased risk of developing PTSD and may feel guilty or anhedonic. Up to 33% of individuals who are exposed to a severe trauma may develop an acute stress disorder, which by *DSM-IV* criteria must last for at least 2 days and resolve within a month. If symptoms persist beyond 4 weeks, a diagnosis of PTSD may be warranted (American Psychiatric Association, 2000).

Generalized Anxiety Disorder

GAD is characterized by extreme anxiety and apprehension about numerous events or activities, such as work or school, more days than not for at least 6 months. The *DSM-IV* diagnosis demands that the affected individual must find it difficult to manage the anxiety and have a number of symptoms (only one symptom is required in children), such as restlessness, fatigue, impairment in attention and concentration, irritability, muscle tension, or sleep disruption. Many affected individuals also suffer from other physical symptoms of anxiety, such as sweating, nausea, or diarrhea, in addition to being easily startled. Symptoms characteristic of panic, such as shortness of breath and palpitations, are not common in GAD (American Psychiatric Association, 2000).

The lifetime prevalence of GAD is about 5%. Epidemiological studies have found that roughly two-thirds of those affected are women. GAD is frequently comorbid with mood disorders, other anxiety disorders, and substance use disorders. Most affected individuals report having experienced symptoms of anxiety since childhood, but onset after 20 years of age is not uncommon (American Psychiatric Association, 2000).

Among children and adolescents, the worries they experience are usually developmentally age appropriate. Children commonly express concerns about school, athletics, peer relations, and catastrophic events such as plane crashes or hurricanes. Affected children may place a great deal of pressure on themselves, be perfectionistic, and seek reassurance from adults and teachers for whom they can be quite taxing (American Psychiatric Association, 2000).

Selective Mutism

Although not an anxiety disorder according to the *DSM-IV*, selective mutism is considered by many in the field to represent a subtype of social phobia (Black & Uhde, 1992; Yagenah, Beidel, Turner, Pina, & Silverman, 2003). More recent data, however, suggests that while social anxiety is a prominent feature of selective mutism, affected children are also likely to express communication delays and/or mild behavior problems (Cohan et al., 2008). Regardless of its categorization, the clinical presentation of selective mutism is reliable and characterized by repeated refusal to speak in social situations where speaking is expected, such as at school. Children with selective mutism do speak readily, however, with family members and familiar contacts. Affected children are generally shy, socially isolated, and withdrawn, sometimes teased by peers, fearful of embarrassment, and often oppositional at home. Selective mutism is usually evident by 5 years of age and affects fewer than 1% of children in mental health clinics (American Psychiatric Association, 2000).

Trichotillomania

Trichotillomania or chronic hair pulling is categorized as an impulse control disorder in the *DSM-IV*. Most cases begin in childhood or adolescence. As with motor and vocal tics, affected individuals commonly report a buildup of tension before hair pulling or when trying to resist hair pulling, along with a sense of satisfaction, release, and happiness while pulling or after pulling the hair. The eyebrows, eyelashes, and head are the most common sites of hair pulling, but all areas of the body can be affected. Hair pulling is typically scattered throughout the day. As with tics, it generally occurs more often when individuals are alone, relaxing, reading, or watching television, although stress can also exacerbate the behavior. Some affected individuals may eat their hair, known as *trichophagia*, which can result in hairballs or bezoars. Examination of the effected areas typically shows damage to the hair follicles and short, broken hairs (American Psychiatric Association, 2000).

Trichotillomania is equally common among boys and girls, but more common among women than men. The prevalence is unknown, but estimates vary greatly from a high of 4% to a low of 0.6%, with most researchers accepting a prevalence of about 1% (Diefenbach, Reitman, & Williamson, 2000).

There is typically a low concordance between child and parent reports of anxiety (Barbosa, Tannock, & Manassis, 2002; Choudhury, Pimentel, & Kendall, 2003). While parents tend to overreport symptoms of externalizing or disruptive behavior disorders, children tend to overreport symptoms of internalizing disorders, such as anxiety and depression (Kenny & Faust, 1997). Nonetheless, the best evidence comes from observation of the child and a series of collateral reports on his or her behavior. Older children can report more objectively on their own symptoms, but rating scales are often helpful as well. Two commonly used scales for general anxiety include the Screen for Child Anxiety Related Emotional Disorders (SCARED) and the Multidimensional Anxiety Scale for Children (MASC). For children with obsessive-compulsive symptoms, the most commonly employed scale is the Children's Yale-Brown Obsessive-Compulsive Scale (CYBOCS). The Leyton Obsessional Inventory is sometimes used as well for these children.

TREATMENT

Given the large variety of anxiety disorders, it is notable that the effective treatments are much the same regardless of diagnosis. Treatment should begin with psychoeducation. Parents and children often blame themselves for the anxiety they feel and are ashamed to discuss their symptoms for fears of ridicule, embarrassment, or sounding "crazy." The most important first step, then, is for the clinician to normalize the anxiety and remove the blame. Secondly, the clinician should inform the patient and family that anxiety disorders are extremely common, that the patient is not alone, and that these disorders are highly responsive to treatment.

Sometimes education and supportive counseling, oftentimes including a brief stint of family therapy, is all that is needed to improve the relationship between family members and relieve the anxiety. For infants and preschool children struggling with separation and other worries, an insecure bond between child and parent might lay behind the anxiety, and all efforts at strengthening this connection should be considered (Bernstein, Borchardt, & Perwien, 1996). Such interventions may be best achieved by working directly with the parents, who are likely to be anxious themselves, or with the parent and child together to strengthen their relationship. This method is generally more effective than working with the child alone (Bernstein et al., 1996). When a child or adolescent meets full diagnostic criteria for an anxiety disorder, however, or the child's function is significantly impaired, more intensive treatment is warranted.

The treatment of anxiety disorders in children and adolescents may incorporate psychotherapy, medication, or both. Psychodynamic psychotherapy, often termed *play therapy* with children, was previously utilized a great deal in the treatment of child anxiety disorders, but we have only a few small studies to support its use (Heinicke & Ramsey-Klee, 1986; Target & Fonagy, 1994). Although these studies have demonstrated improvements in adaptation and interpersonal relationships among the children receiving this treatment, the therapy is labor intensive, time consuming, and highly idiosyncratic. Furthermore, while these treatments often have great value, they are nonspecific and nearly impossible to replicate in a reliable fashion for a wide variety of patients because they are fraught with subjectivity by virtue of the unique nature of the therapist-child relationship, which will vary for each patient and practitioner.

Cognitive Behavior Therapy

In contrast to psychodynamic psychotherapy, cognitive behavior therapy (CBT) is an easily replicable form of psychotherapy that has been proven useful, expedient, and cost-effective in the treatment of a wide variety of child and adolescent anxiety disorders. In a large multistudy review, CBT was effective for 56% of children and adolescents suffering from an anxiety disorder versus 28% who improved in control groups (James, Soler, & Weatherall, 2005). Most studies report remission rates of anxiety disorders at 60–70% when using CBT (Hannesdottir & Ollendick, 2007), with rates as high as 85% for OCD (Barrett, Farrell, Pina, Peris, & Piacentini, 2008) and 84% for panic disorder (Landon & Barlow, 2004).

CBT rests upon the assertion that if one's thoughts and behaviors are changed, then one's feelings will follow suit. When treating anxiety disorders, the primary emphasis is on the behavioral component of CBT, and homework is always employed, in contrast to traditional psychotherapy. Behavioral therapy techniques for anxiety disorders can be likened to a vaccine or inoculation. Through a gradual process, the patient is exposed to toxic stimuli, precisely the things that cause distress. Over time, he becomes "immune" to the insult and is bothered to a much lesser extent, if at all. Essentially, this method relies upon the concept of *habituation.*

The theory of exposure and response prevention (ERP) emanates from the work of Victor Meyer (1966). He suggested that a prolonged confrontation with a feared "exposure," along with corresponding response prevention, would lead to a significant decrease in subjective distress. Meyer's initial conceptualization still forms the basis of ERP—the live or in vivo exposure to the feared object or situation must be extensive. The exposure must also be functional, in that the feared situation must be reenacted accurately in order to reflect what the patient really feels. For example, if an individual with OCD fears driving alone because he thinks that he may hit a pedestrian with the car, then driving with the therapist present is of little utility and does not truly simulate the real condition. Meyer's concept of response prevention incorporates stopping the individual from performing any act that would "undo" or lower his anxiety. For example, in an individual with a phobia of germs, one would therapeutically stop her from washing after a germ "exposure." Finally, since some fears simply cannot be acted out (e.g., an individual may fear leaving the stove on and burning down the house), *imaginal exposures* allow for certain scenarios to be only thought through.

ERP works because we can only stay intensely anxious for so long before our body tires and relaxes. With habituation, one's anxiety level comes down by itself. In the same way that only so much of a neurochemical (e.g., dopamine) can be released from a neuron before the neuron has to "recharge," our anxiety must reload before we can experience another intensive burst. A nice way of understanding this concept is to use a Subjective Units of Distress Scale, or SUDS, as in Figure 9.2.

In this example, an individual with OCD has a fear of germs. In the first curve (curve #1) the individual is exposed to a stressor at time zero (e.g., she touches a toilet seat in a public bathroom). She worries and

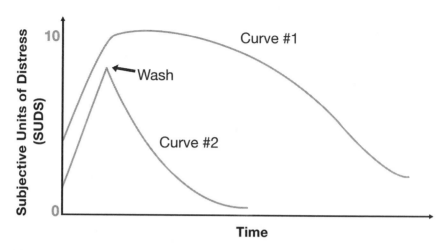

Figure 9.2.   Subjective Units of Distress (SUDS) Scale. As shown in Curve #1, exposure to a stressful situation (e.g., perceived contamination) at time zero results in a high level of distress that diminishes slowly over time. In Curve #2, the stress is relieved rapidly by compulsively washing.

worries, and her anxiety stays elevated for a considerable period of time, perhaps 30–90 minutes, before she calms down. In the second curve (curve #2) she washes her hands shortly after the exposure, allowing the anxiety to decrease relatively rapidly, perhaps in 10 minutes. Washing her hands has the immediate effect of calming her down, but it also provides a positive reinforcement, which inadvertently helps to perpetuate the germ phobia.

The CBT intervention is to stop the patient from washing her hands each time she experiences a given exposure. For example, ERP homework for this patient might be to touch a toilet seat in a public place three times each day and not wash her hands for 60 minutes after each exposure. What happens to the anxiety curve? As seen in Figure 9.3, the anxiety curve repeats itself but at a decreased level with each exposure because she becomes "habituated" to the exposure.

One of the first behavioral techniques employed in CBT is to develop a *fear hierarchy*. Without knowing one's fears, we cannot effectively design exposures. An added benefit of developing a hierarchy is that we learn more about the individual's anxiety and what causes him concern. This investigation is itself a therapeutic tool and often an opportunity for the therapist to challenge many of the cognitive distortions and assumptions of the patient (see Chapter 10). Various scales may be utilized for assessing what precisely increases an individual's anxiety, such as the Reiss-Epstein-Gursky Anxiety Sensitivity Index for Panic Disorder or the

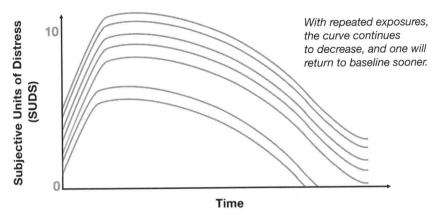

With repeated exposures, the curve continues to decrease, and one will return to baseline sooner.

Figure 9.3.   Exposure and Response Prevention (ERP).

CYBOCS for OCD. These tools can also be used to grade the intensity of the anxiety and how much it interferes with the patient's life. Furthermore, the instrument can be used to monitor treatment progress over time.

Once a list of fears has been compiled, they are placed in order of intensity. We often use numbers (e.g., on a scale of 1 to 10) to indicate the degree of distress that a certain exposure might cause for a given individual. A number value can be assessed by asking the individual questions, such as "How much distress would you feel if you did not wash after touching a toilet seat? Would you call that a 7? Would you call that an 8?" Alternatively, one could ask, "Which of these items we've discussed is the most difficult? We'll call that a 10." A child with a needle phobia may create the fear hierarchy seen in Table 9.1.

In an effort to work through to the upper levels of anxiety and not to rush the patient, one may need to add many steps in the hierarchy. This process is often creative and even enjoyable for both the patient and the

Table 9.1.   Example of a Needle Phobia Fear Hierarchy for a Child

Action	Level of distress
Driving past a hospital	0
Walking into a doctor's office	2
Holding an alcohol swab	4
Rubbing an alcohol swab on the arm	6
Holding a syringe with needle attached	8
Receiving an injection	10

Table 9.2.   Example of an HIV Fear Hierarchy for a Male Teen

Action	Level of distress
Being anywhere someone with HIV may have been	20
Touching shopping carts	25
Using public phones	30
Opening doors	45
Shaking hands	50
Leaving the house without bandages on cuts	55
Bumping into people	60
Eating at restaurants	65
Touching something in my house with dirty hands	65
Sitting down without checking what I sit on	70
Drinking from a public fountain	80
Wearing shorts or a bathing suit and touching someone	80
Kissing a girl	85
Taking food from anyone	90
Using a public toilet	95
Touching anything that appears to be blood	99

clinician. For the above individual, we may add "walking into a doctor's office and asking directions to a nearby store" (distress level = 1), "drawing a picture of a syringe" (distress level = 3), "watching a medical drama on television" (distress level = 5), and so forth. Many examples may be needed in order to keep the therapy moving along until the higher levels of intensity can be reached. A male teenager with a fear of AIDS may develop the fear hierarchy in Table 9.2.

Although some patients will move through their fear hierarchies quickly, it is important not to push the patient too hard in order to maintain adherence to the treatment plan. The lower the patient starts on the hierarchy, the greater the chances of initial success, and the more likely he will be to complete the therapy. Many therapists create their own scales or develop fear thermometers to help children rate the degree of discomfort they feel from a given exposure (see Figure 9.4).

For an individual with panic disorder, it should first be determined whether the panic attacks are cued or noncued. If they are cued, then an exposure hierarchy similar to those above can be produced. For example, if panic attacks are cued by being alone, a variety of scenarios can be created whereby the individual spends more and more time alone (e.g., alone in his room for 5 minutes, alone in a grocery store for 5 minutes, etc.). If the panic attacks are random, then the focus of treatment should be on the symptoms that the panic attacks produce (e.g., shortness of breath, elevated heart rate, sweating, dizziness), as these are often the most frightening for

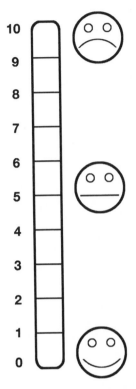

Feels the Worst/Very Scary

Feels the Best/Not Scary at All

Figure 9.4.   Fear thermometer. Fear thermometers and other similar tools are useful in helping children to describe their anxiety.

the patient. These symptoms can be reproduced on a fear hierarchy scale by engaging in activities, such as running in place, being spun in a chair, breathing through a straw, and so forth. Once the fear or anxiety hierarchy is complete, the in vivo therapy can commence.

Each CBT therapy session using ERP should start with a discussion of the past week. The clinician should ask if any new anxieties or problems arose; review the last week's homework; identify strengths and successes from the past week; provide positive reinforcement; and determine how to make the sessions and homework more functional and directly related to the fears the individual is having. The therapist and patient should then engage in some ERP together, selecting tasks from the fear hierarchy that may be perceived as too difficult for the patient to accomplish alone. The therapist should monitor closely for obstacles and provide adequate positive feedback. Finally, the session ends with the assigning of new homework for the coming week. Assigning homework is a collaborative effort between the therapist and patient and should constitute just enough of a challenge without overwhelming the patient.

Imaginal exposures are considerably more difficult to create but are often effective for those situations that are impossible to re-create. After it has been determined that certain fears are not amenable to in vivo exposure, a hierarchy of all anxieties requiring imaginal exposure should be created. Once the starting point on the hierarchy is determined, a scene for the imagined fear is developed, and the patient records the scene in his own voice on audiotape. The patient then listens to the scene repeatedly until he is able to tolerate the anxiety that the imagined exposure creates within him. As with in vivo exposures, the method is repeated until the most feared item on the hierarchy produces only minimal anxiety.

There are numerous potential pitfalls and problems with implementing ERP. Commonly, for example, patients report that they experienced too much anxiety to follow through on the homework. In this case, the therapist should make certain that the homework is adequately functional and addresses the correct exposure. Perhaps the assignment needs to be reworked, or perhaps this is an exposure that the therapist and patient should do together during a session. The therapist should make certain that the patient is not simply stalling or trying to use a subtle avoidance technique. Conversely, the therapist may need to consider decreasing the use of relaxation techniques or even anxiolytic medications so that the patient feels adequate distress during the exposures. Only by feeling a significant degree of anxiety during exposures will ERP ultimately work.

Another common problem with ERP is patient reports that the anxiety does not adequately decrease during the exposure, thereby not allowing habituation to the anxiety. In this case, the therapist should consider increasing the length of the exposure; or if the obsession is future oriented, using imaginal exposure. Perhaps better still is choosing an item lower on the fear hierarchy.

For patients who do not practice their exposures enough, consider additional sessions with the therapist or involving a significant other, such as a parent, older sibling, or babysitter in helping to make sure the exposures are practiced. The therapist should always exercise caution when incorporating family members, however, as this technique may lead to more conflict between the patient and parents. If the child still refuses to engage in treatment, a day or after-school treatment program may be necessary. Alternatively, for children who will engage in exposures only with the therapist, decreasing therapy sessions and further incorporating parents or other family members may be useful.

CBT should be employed for as long as necessary, but in the vast majority of cases, CBT is a time-limited therapeutic approach. For the treatment of anxiety, patients typically receive 12–16 weeks of treatment with periodic boosters thereafter if necessary. For particularly difficult cases, the therapy may be extended for many more weeks or months.

Psychopharmacological Treatment of Anxiety

Medications are commonly employed to treat anxiety in children and adolescents when therapy is unavailable or only partially effective. Some children and their families prefer medication to psychotherapy, which may be reasonable at times but should be carefully considered. While medication may address the symptoms of anxiety, without therapy the patient may never learn to manage the anxiety on his or her own, and medication may always be necessary. There are certainly many cases where medication is a key part of the treatment plan. However, we hope that by engaging in CBT, the patient will learn to recognize the signs of anxiety and to employ these skills when necessary.

There is little data to suggest that tricyclic antidepressants (TCAs), the "older" antidepressants, are effective for most child and adolescent anxiety disorders. While clomipramine (Anafranil) is one of the gold-standard treatments for OCD (DeVeaugh-Geiss et al., 1992; Flament et al., 1985; Leonard et al., 1989), studies of TCAs in other anxiety disorders have yielded mixed results. Randomized, double-blind, placebo-controlled studies of imipramine (Tofranil) combined with behavioral therapy for school refusal and SAD have been contradictory (Bernstein et al., 2000; Bernstein, Garfinkel, & Borchardt, 1990; Gittelman-Klein & Klein, 1973; Klein, Koplewicz, & Kanner, 1992). One study of clomipramine (Anafranil) found no benefit for the treatment of school phobia (Berney et al., 1981), and questions have been raised about the stability of treatment gains with TCAs for these children (Bernstein, Hektner, Borchardt, & McMillan, 2001). Furthermore, there are a variety of reasons that TCAs may not be as effective in children as they are in adults, and the safety concerns of these medications are significant and sufficiently concerning to limit their use (see Chapter 10). In general, TCAs should only be prescribed for children and adolescents by an experienced practitioner and, even then, under very limited circumstances.

More commonly utilized for anxiety disorders are the selective serotenin reuptake inhibitors (SSRIs). These medications have a preferable safety profile to the TCAs and are relatively easy for practitioners to prescribe and patients to tolerate. Three of these medications have been approved by the Food and Drug Administration (FDA) for the treatment of OCD in children and adolescents—sertraline (Zoloft) has been approved down to age 6; fluoxetine (Prozac) has been approved down to age 7; and fluvoxamine (Luvox) has been approved down to age 8. The FDA approval for these medications is based upon randomized, double-blind, placebo-controlled studies (Geller et al., 2001; Liebowitz et al., 2002; March et al., 1998; Pediatric OCD Treatment Study [POTS] Team, 2004; Riddle, Reeve, et al., 2001; Riddle, Scahill, et al., 1992). Paroxetine (Paxil) has also demonstrated efficacy in the treatment of pediatric OCD but generally causes more side effects and has not been FDA approved (Geller, Biederman, et al., 2003; Geller, Wagner, et al., 2004).

Though the data supporting SSRIs in the treatment of non-OCD anxiety disorders is not as robust, these medications have shown utility in treating a broad range of adult and child anxiety disorders and are frequently employed for this purpose. A handful of randomized, double-blind, placebo-controlled studies support the use of SSRIs for SAD, GAD, social phobia, and selective mutism. Fluvoxamine is supported by at least one study (Research Units for Pediatric Psychopharmacology [RUPP] Anxiety Study Group, 2001); fluoxetine is supported by at least two studies (Birmaher et al., 2003; Black & Uhde, 1994); paroxetine is supported by at least one study (Wagner et al., 2004); and sertraline (Zoloft) is supported by at least two studies (Rynn, Siqueland, & Rickels, 2001; Walkup et al., 2008).

The most recent and largest of these investigations, the Child and Adolescent Anxiety Multimodal Study (CAMS), published its first data in 2008 (Walkup et al., 2008). This study has sought to determine whether CBT, medications, or their combined action is the preferred treatment for pediatric anxiety disorders. The study randomly assigned 488 children and adolescents with SAD, social phobia, or GAD, aged 7 to 17 years, to one of four treatment groups for 12 weeks. The first group received CBT for 14 sessions; the second group received sertraline up to a dosage of 200 mg per day; the third group received both CBT and sertraline (Zoloft); and the fourth group received only placebo. Over 80% of children who received combined treatment, medication plus CBT, improved, as opposed to 60% receiving CBT only and 55% receiving medication only; although there was no statistical separation between the CBT and medication groups, and the 5% difference in efficacy between these two treatments could be due to chance. All treatments were statistically more effective than placebo, which led to improvement in only 24% of subjects. Consequently, the CAMS study demonstrates that medication and CBT both work well for pediatric anxiety disorders and that their combination is the best form of treatment.

SSRIs are generally viewed as safe for children, adolescents, and adults, though recent concerns about their ability to induce depression and suicidal thoughts have been raised (these issues are addressed fully in the Appendix). As yet, there are no direct head-to-head studies among different SSRIs for the treatment of anxiety. Consequently, the practitioner has few guideposts by which to choose the specific SSRI an anxious child should take. These decisions are commonly made by weighing the various side effect profiles of the medications. Many practitioners will select an SSRI based upon family members who may have taken and successfully tolerated one of these medications. However, we have no evidence to support this metric as a means of making this decision.

Another area for which we have little guidance is the dosage of SSRIs in children and adolescents with various anxiety disorders. In general, we titrate these medications to the highest and most beneficial dose that is well tolerated with minimal or no side effects. For panic disorder and particularly nervous children, we must often titrate the dosage upward very slowly and a low dose is frequently sufficient because some of the potential side effects of the medications themselves (e.g., sweating, tremor, and derealization, for example) can be misinterpreted as physical symptoms of anxiety. For those with OCD, by contrast, the best clinical response typically occurs at a high dosage.

As above, three SSRIs have an FDA indication for the treatment of OCD in children and adolescents, in addition to one TCA, clomipramine, which is approved by the FDA for OCD down to 11 years of age. Unfortunately, CBT along with an SSRI or clomipramine is still too often insufficient to adequately treat the OCD. Studies vary, but only about 50% of all individuals with OCD treated with an SSRI or clomipramine demonstrate an adequate response, and many of these individuals continue to suffer significant impairment. In addition to aggressive CBT and high-dose SSRI treatment, augmentation of the medication regimen with an antipsychotic results in significant symptom improvement in about one-third of individuals (Bloch et al., 2006). It is not entirely clear at this time which antipsychotic should be utilized, but the most impressive data is with haloperidol (Haldol) and risperidone (Risperdal). For a complete discussion of antipsychotic medication in children and adolescents, see Chapter 12.

In addition to the antipsychotic medications, clonazepam (Klonipin) and lithium may be effective for augmenting SSRIs and clomipramine (Anafranil) in the treatment of OCD (Leonard et al., 1994; Rasmussen, 1984). However, the supporting data for these interventions are based only upon case reports. The data at the present time favors antipsychotic medications for augmentation. Nonetheless, no augmentation should be attempted until after an adequate trial of an SSRI or clomipramine at a sufficient dose because a significant minority of patients will not respond until they have received 8–12 weeks of treatment with the initial agent.

For the treatment of GAD in children and adolescents, extended-release venlafaxine (Effexor XR) has demonstrated efficacy. Rynn, Riddle, Yeung, and Kunz (2007) reported on two separate multicenter randomized, double-blind, placebo-controlled trials involving more than 300 children, ages 6–17 years, with GAD who were treated with extended-release venlafaxine for 8 weeks. The first study showed improvement in specific GAD symptoms, but the second study only showed improvement on secondary measures. The combined response rates for the studies were 69% for active drug versus 48% for placebo. While positive overall, more data is needed before we can presume that extended-release venlafaxine is truly effective for GAD. The remarkably high placebo rate, relatively small difference between response rates among those taking active drug versus placebo, and the fact that only when combined did the two studies show statistical significance suggest that extended-release venlafaxine may not be a robust treatment for GAD.

Extended-release venlafaxine has also been found effective in the treatment of social phobia in a randomized, double-blind, placebo-controlled study of children and adolescents, ages 8–17 years (March, Entusah, Rynn, Albano, & Tourian, 2007). In this large sample of nearly 300 subjects who were treated for 16 weeks, 56% of children responded to active drug versus 37% who responded to placebo. While statistically significant, once again the split between active treatment and placebo is not particularly large.

Other medications utilized for children and adolescents with anxiety disorders have historically included barbiturates and benzodiazepines. Barbiturates, however, are concerning because of their safety profile and toxicity in overdose and are rarely used for treating childhood anxiety any longer. Benzodiazepines, which inhibit the nervous system by their action on gamma-aminobutyric acid (GABA) receptors, are much safer and highly effective for anxiety in adults, but in children and adolescents they not infrequently cause paradoxical dysinhibition and irritability. The agitation so commonly seen among children taking benzodiazepines is believed to be due to the fact that children do not have a full compliment of GABA receptors until the late teen years and therefore cannot properly utilize these treatments.

For the treatment of PTSD, we sometimes employ a type of CBT known as debriefing therapy. This popular approach helps the child transform his self-concept from victim to survivor. Interventions often involve helping the child to focus on recovery, leading to an eventual sense of mastery. The scientific literature suggests that desensitization, relaxation, and other behavioral techniques may be beneficial in the treatment of children with PTSD, but firm research is lacking. Revenge fantasies, in particular, commonly complicate the emotional resolution of symptoms and are discouraged. Propranolol (Inderal) and clonidine (Catapres), antihypertensives that work by different mechanisms, have been utilized for the treatment of adults with PTSD and the persistent arousal they often report. Sertraline and paroxetine have been approved for the treatment of PTSD in adults, but studies in children have not been performed. Gabapentin (Neurontin) and various antipsychotic medications are sometimes reportedly useful in adults, as is eye movement desensitization retraining (EMDR), but parallel studies in children have not been done.

Data supporting the use of medications for the treatment of panic disorder, selective mutism, and specific phobias is generally lacking for children and adolescents, but a sufficient number of studies has yet to be completed. Due to the paucity of empirical studies from which to draw upon, we have little to guide us. CBT remains the first treatment of choice for these disorders, but when medications are necessary, we must draw upon our experience with adults and extrapolate to children and adolescents.

Anxiety disorders are perhaps the most common psychiatric problems in children and adolescents. While we have some wonderful psychotherapeutic and medication treatments, nowhere is our lack of knowledge of child mental health as tragically evident as with anxiety disorders. OCD, one of the best recognized anxiety disorders, remains one of the top 10 causes of disability worldwide, and at present time we are only effective in treating about half of all cases when gold-standard treatment is even available (Murray & Lopez, 1996). The ubiquitous nature of these problems demands that we invest more resources into educating the public, researching etiology, and identifying effective treatments.

10

Depression

Case reports of childhood depression date to the early 17th century. Melancholia was first reported in children in the mid-19th century. Still, the existence of depression in children prior to 1960 was seriously doubted because it was felt that a child's immature *superego* would not permit the development of mood disorders. To Freud and other psychoanalysts of his day, the superego was understood to be the part of the psyche that, among other things, punished bad behavior with feelings of guilt (Reber, 1985). Thus, psychoanalytic theory suggested that children were unable to feel profound guilt, shame, and a sense of absolute right and wrong and were, therefore, unable to develop clinical depression. Research from Europe and the United States in the 1960s and '70s, however, led to an increasing awareness of precisely how children and adolescents experience depression and express its symptoms. We now clearly recognize that children and adolescents are vulnerable to depression, although the symptom expression often differs somewhat from adults.

CLINICAL PRESENTATION

According to the *DSM-IV*, the criteria for *major depressive disorder (MDD)* do not differ appreciably for children, adolescents, and adults. In place of depressed mood, the *DSM-IV* suggests that children and adolescents may experience an irritable mood, which may be expressed as temper tantrums and oppositional behavior; and in place of a significant decrease in weight, the *DSM-IV* suggests that children and adolescents may simply fail to make expected weight gains (American Psychiatric

Association, 2000). Though not described in the diagnostic criteria, depressed children and adolescents also tend to suffer fewer neurovegetative problems or impairments in sleep, appetite, energy, and concentration than do depressed adults. In addition, there are other differences in child and adolescent depression not fully appreciated by the *DSM-IV* criteria.

Young children tend to demonstrate more symptoms of anxiety when depressed, commonly expressed as phobias, separation anxiety, or somatic complaints, such as headache and stomachache. Though not common, these children may also experience auditory hallucinations, such as hearing their own named being called (Chambers, Puig-Antich, Tabrizi, & Davies, 1982). Describing their depression and labeling the symptoms is often difficult for prepubertal children, particularly given their relative inability to think in an abstract fashion and report upon their own mood state in an introspective and reflective manner. Rather, children may simply recognize the detachment, boredom, anger, and anxiety they feel. Unlike depressed adults, their negative mood may not entirely consume them, and they may still be able to enjoy numerous activities, engage with peers effectively, and complete their work relatively well at times, while demonstrating severe discomfort and behavior problems at other times. This inconsistency in mood is often confusing to parents, friends, and teachers, who may wonder about the validity of the diagnosis.

Mood lability, which is not uncommon among normally developing children and is particularly frequent among those with attention-deficit/hyperactivity disorder (ADHD), disruptive behavior disorders, anxiety disorders, bipolar disorder, and MDD, is not a good marker of depression in children. By mid-childhood, or ages 8 through 12 years, depressed children may begin to experience preoccupations with death, lowered self-esteem, social withdrawal, peer rejection, and poor school performance (Mitchell, McCauley, Burke, & Moss, 1988; Ryan et al., 1987), yet depressed children under the age of 15 years express few delusional beliefs and rarely attempt suicide (Centers for Disease Control and Prevention, 2003).

Depressed adolescents look considerably more like their adult counterparts. Adolescents typically demonstrate more cognitive components to their depression than do children. Guilt and hopelessness now become apparent. Major behavioral changes, such as a decrease in academic performance, loss of friends, and lack of interest in formerly pleasurable activities, may also be indicative of mood changes or speak to the severity of an adolescent's depression. Adolescents, like adults, demonstrate more sleep and appetite disturbances, are more likely than children to experience psychotic symptoms, and may express significant suicidal ideation and make bona fide suicide attempts. Despite our advances in recognition

and treatment, suicide remains the third leading cause of death in adolescents in the United States (Centers for Disease Control and Prevention,
2003). Compared to adults, however, adolescents still demonstrate more
behavior problems and fewer neurovegetative difficulties associated with
their depression.

ETIOLOGY

The cause of depression remains unclear, but numerous theories have
proven themselves useful to clinicians in considering their approach to
the patient. Psychodynamic theory, for example, suggests that those who
are depressed suffer from a severe and unrelenting superego and are extremely critical and prohibitive of their own fantasies, feelings, and actions. By contrast, attachment theory asserts that those with depression
had insecure early attachments, were never adequately bonded to their
primary caregivers, and as a result feel adrift and alone. Behavioral theorists
believe that depressed individuals never learned to obtain adequate reinforcement and, therefore, cannot gain pleasure from life. Cognitive theorists
argue that depressed individuals struggle with a negative or depressive
mind-set and see the world in a distorted fashion. Others view self-control
as the crux of depression, suggesting that deficits in self-monitoring and
self-evaluation cause depression. Most would agree that environmental
and social stressors, such as loss of a spouse, parent, or job, along with
other negative circumstances, can, at the very least, predispose one to depression. Finally, there are a host of biological theories, ranging from
neurochemical to endocrine, suggestive of an etiological explanation.

Regardless of which approach or theory one finds most attractive
and useful in treating patients, at this time we do not have a unifying explanation for why people get depressed. Still, these theoretical constructs
are often useful in helping the clinician to consider which aspects of an
individual and his life may be worth focusing on in psychotherapy and
amenable to change. Of note, these theories apply largely to adults, as
relatively little work has been done with children and adolescents.

A number of biological markers have been identified which, while
not explanatory, are suggestive of a biological effect in depression. Perhaps as many as 70% of adult patients suffering from severe depression
do not show normal suppression of cortisol secretion following the Dexamethasone Suppression Test (DST), suggesting an alteration in their
stress response. This test is not, however, a useful tool for diagnosing depression, as there are relatively high rates of DST nonsuppression in other
psychiatric conditions, such as anorexia nervosa, dementia, and substance

abuse (Díaz-Marsá et al., 2008; Murialdo et al., 2000; Sher, 2006). In addition, the data on children and the DST is not as impressive (Dahl et al., 1992). Both depressed children and adults, however, have a blunting of the normal growth hormone release in response to insulin challenge and a blunted production of thyroid-stimulating hormone in response to thyroid-releasing hormone (Dinan, 1998; Trimble, 1996). In addition, depressed girls secrete significantly more prolactin than girls who are not depressed (Hardan et al., 1999). The neuroendocrine abnormalities in depression are evident across various endocrine organs (e.g., adrenals, pancreas, and thyroid). Given this finding, the true neuroendocrine abnormality is likely at the level of the hypothalamus, a region largely regulated by monoamine neurotransmitters.

The biogenic amine or catecholamine hypothesis of mood disorders suggests that too much neurotransmitter causes mania and too little causes depression. While we realize that this explanation is an oversimplification, it is supported to some degree by the observation that medications that induce biogenic amine neurotransmitters, such as dopamine, norepinephrine, and serotonin, often improve depression and, likewise, worsen mania. There are, however, many limitations to this hypothesis, including the fact that direct precursors of amines, such as L-dopa and tryptophan, generally have no effect on mood and that compounds that block amine reuptake, such as cocaine and amphetamines, do not generally improve depression.

Studies have shown that typical changes found in the electroencephalogram (EEG) recordings of depressed adults, such as decreased slow-wave sleep, decreased REM latency, and longer periods of REM sleep, occur less often in depressed children and adolescents (Ivanenko, Crabtree, & Gozal, 2005). Studies of adolescents and adults do, however, share the finding that those with pervasive suicidal thoughts and intent have less of the major serotonin metabolite, 5-hydroxy-indoleacetic acid (5-HIAA), in their central nervous system, suggesting that the serotonin system may be impaired (Mann, Oquendo, Underwood, & Arango, 1999). Research also suggests that a significant portion of the vulnerability to depression may be based upon an inherited serotonin gene.

Adults with one or two copies of the short allele of the serotonin transporter gene exhibit more depressive symptoms, diagnosable depression, and suicidality in response to stressful life events than adults with two copies of the long allele (Caspi et al., 2003). Family studies suggest a moderate genetic influence on the heritability of depression based upon investigations of identical twins, 35–75% of whom will share the diagnosis (Eley & Stevenson, 1999; Glowinski, Madden, Bucholz, Lynskey, & Heath, 2003). In order to quantify the precise genetic influence, identical twin adoption studies would need to be completed, but even without these studies we have impressive data supporting the familial transmission of depression. In one study children whose parents suffered depression as children, for example, were up to 14 times more likely than controls to become depressed prior to age 13 (Weissman, Warner, Wickramaratne, & Prusoff, 1988). This relationship also moves in the opposite direction, as mothers of children with MDD are themselves about 50–75% likely to develop the disorder at some point in their lifetimes (Kovacs, Devlin, Pollock, Richards, & Mukerji, 1997).

A family history of depression is a major risk factor for the development of depression in other family members. First-degree relatives of a child with MDD, for example, are more likely to suffer depression, and prevalence rates vary between 30% and 50% (Harrington et al., 1997; Wickramaratne, Greenwald, & Weissman, 2000). In addition, children of parents with depression are two to three times more likely to suffer depression themselves, and these children have an earlier age of onset for their depression by approximately 3 years (Beardslee, Versage, & Gladstone, 1998; Weissman, Warner, Wickramaratne, Moreau, & Olfson, 1997). A recent 20-year follow-up of offspring of depressed and nondepressed parents found that the risks for anxiety disorder, major depression, and substance dependence were about three times higher in the offspring of depressed parents versus nondepressed parents. These children also suffered greater social impairments. All of these difficulties became much more evident when the children were about 15–20 years of age, particularly among females. The data also suggested higher rates of medical problems and mortality among the children of depressed parents as the children enter middle age (Weissman et al., 2006b).

EPIDEMIOLOGY

Varying prevalence rates of MDD in children and adolescents have been reported, and as yet there is no definitive study. We generally accept the prevalence to be about 1% for preschool children, 2% for school-age prepubertal children, and 4–8% for adolescents. The gender ratio is about 1:1, male to female, during childhood, reaching 1:2 by mid/late adolescence (Fleming & Offord, 1990; Kashani & Carlson, 1987; Kashani et al., 1987; Lewinsohn, Clarke, Seeley, & Rohde, 1994; Lewinsohn, Hops, Roberts, Seeley, & Andrews, 1993). The prevalence of MDD increases during adolescence such that by 18 years of age the lifetime prevalence (or the chance that a child will have experienced an episode of MDD by this point in his or her life) is approximately 15%, just two percentage points shy of the prevalence for adults over age 18 (Kessler & Walters, 1998; Kessler et al., 2005a).

Hospitalized children and adolescents and those with certain comorbidities demonstrate particularly high rates of MDD. As many as 40% of children on neurology wards with unexplained headaches have been diagnosed with depression (Ling, Oftedal, & Weinberg, 1970) as have 7% of general pediatric inpatients (Kashani, Barbero, & Bolander, 1981), 28% of child psychiatry outpatients (Carlson & Cantwell, 1980), 59% of child psychiatry inpatients (Petti, 1978), and 27% of adolescent inpatients (Robbins, Alessi, Cook, Poznanski, & Yanchyshyn, 1982).

Dysthymic disorder, a chronic, low-grade depression which can be just as severely disruptive for a child as MDD, has a wide range in prevalence depending upon the study. The frequency of occurrence in prepubertal children ranges from 0.6% to 1.7% and in adolescents from 1.6% to 8% (Garrison, Addy, Jackson, McKeown, & Waller, 1992; Kashani et al., 1987; Lewinsohn et al., 1993; Lewinsohn et al., 1994). Such variation in prevalence is not uncommonly seen in epidemiological studies, the discrepancy being largely due to study design and the patient population sampled.

The prevalence of depression increases during adolescence for reasons that are not entirely clear. We assume that hormonal and other maturational changes have something to do with the adolescent increase in depression, even though we do not fully understand the effect of puberty on the psyche of a developing child. Environmental factors, such as increased social and academic expectations, also presumably play a role as these youths are preparing for life in the adult world. It is also true that the longer one lives, the more likely he will encounter negative life events, such as friends and family getting sick, injured, or dying, witnessing the effects of poverty and injustice, and so forth. These experiences are sometimes too much for teens to process and understand with ease and can have an impact upon mood.

As teens age, they embrace increasing freedoms while struggling with establishing independence and a sense of who they are and wish to be. Erikson termed this stage of development *identity vs. role diffusion* and noted that as adolescents develop their unique identities, they are often preoccupied with appearance, hero worship, and ideology (Erikson & Erikson, 1997). Piaget viewed adolescence in terms of cognitive development and the ability to establish "formal operations" and abstract thought (Flavell, 1963). Once a child can think abstractly, in many ways the world becomes a much more frightening place. The adolescent now begins to see much of the inequity and brutality within society and realizes that she must advance further in her education, learn a skill, eventually earn a living, and possibly raise a family. Without proper adult guidance and support, this realization can be overly daunting and may contribute to the increase in depression.

CLINICAL COURSE

Among clinically referred children and adolescents, the median duration of depression is somewhere between 7 and 9 months. For samples drawn from the community, the median duration is about 1 to 2 months. These numbers suggest that the most severe and recalcitrant cases—those that last longer—find their way to specialty clinics and that those found within the community either get better on their own or receive treatment from a local therapist or physician. Approximately 90% of MDD episodes remit within 1 to 2 years of onset, where "remission" is defined as a 2-week-to-2-month period with only one or fewer clinically significant symptoms. Approximately 6–10% of MDD episodes become chronic. Predictors of a longer episode of MDD include increased severity of depression, comorbidities, negative life events (e.g., academic troubles, family conflict, abuse, or neglect), parental psychiatric illness, personality disorder, and poor psychosocial functioning (Birmaher & Brent, 1998).

About 50% of children and adolescents who suffer from MDD will experience a relapse or second episode after acute treatment during a period of remission, indicating the need for close observation and ongoing treatment after the initial episode has remitted. Given that up to 60% of children relapse in some studies, it may simply be the nature of depression to return, particularly with early childhood onset, which presumably indicates that the illness is more virulent in these cases. Factors likely to predict relapse include lack of treatment adherence and increased negative life events (Birmaher & Brent, 1998).

A patient is considered in "recovery" after an asymptomatic period of at least 2 months. "Recurrence" is defined as the reemergence of major depressive symptoms during a period of recovery; in other words, a recurrence is essentially a new episode of MDD. Both clinical and community samples have found the probability of recurrence to be somewhere between 20% and 60% within 1 to 2 years postremission and approximately 70% after 5 years. These numbers are higher than those found in adults and likely reflect the virulence of early-onset MDD. Recurrence is predicted by earlier age at onset, greater number of prior episodes, severity of the initial episode, presence of psychosis, psychosocial stressors, coexisting dysthymic disorder or other comorbidities, and treatment noncompliance (Birmaher & Brent, 1998).

The risk of ultimately developing bipolar disorder for children with a first episode of depression is extraordinarily high. Depending upon the study, somewhere between 20% and 40% of children and adolescents initially diagnosed with MDD will subsequently be diagnosed with bipolar disorder within 5 years. Risk factors among these children for developing bipolar disorder Type I include early-onset MDD, psychomotor retardation, psychosis, pharmacologically induced hypomania, a family history of bipolar disorder or psychotic depression, and a significant family history of mood disorders (Birmaher & Brent, 1998).

DIAGNOSIS

The *DSM-IV* requires five of nine symptoms present for 2 weeks to establish a diagnosis of MDD (American Psychiatric Association, 2000). The diagnosis for children and adolescents differs only slightly from adults; as previously noted, irritability can substitute for depressed mood, and failure to make expected weight gains can substitute for significant weight loss (see Table 10.1).

Dysthymic disorder, as previously described, is a chronic, low-grade form of depression that also takes a great toll on those affected. The word *dysthymia* comes from the Greek, meaning "bad state of mind" or "ill humor," and draws upon the antiquated idea that mood is controlled and balanced by the thymus gland. Though considerably milder than depression, symptoms of dysthymic disorder can be every bit as disruptive as MDD in the life of a child or adolescent and are often a precursor to MDD. The *DSM-IV* diagnosis of dysthymic disorder requires a depressed or irritable mood on most days for at least 1 year in children and adolescents or

Table 10.1. Diagnostic Symptoms of Major Depressive Disorder

1. Depressed or irritable mood most of the day, nearly every day.
2. Anhedonia or lack of interest in previously pleasurable activities.
3. Significant weight loss or failure to make expected weight gains.
4. Insomnia or hypersomnia.
5. Psychomotor agitation or retardation.
6. Fatigue or loss of energy.
7. Feelings of hopelessness, worthlessness, or guilt.
8. Difficulty with attention and concentration.
9. Recurrent thoughts of death or suicidal ideation.

Adapted from *DSM-IV* (American Psychiatric Association, 2000).

Table 10.2. Diagnostic Symptoms of Dysthymic Disorder

Depressed or irritable mood most days for at least 1 year, in addition to 2 or more of the following symptoms:

1. Lack of appetite or overeating.
2. Insomnia or hypersomnia.
3. Fatigue or loss of energy.
4. Poor self-esteem.
5. Inability to concentrate or make decisions.
6. Hopelessness.

Adapted from *DSM-IV* (American Psychiatric Association, 2000).

at least 2 years in adults, in addition to two or more of six symptoms (see Table 10.2).

Depression can present in many different guises, and the *DSM-IV* has defined a number of depressive variants. These include bipolar depression, psychotic depression, and atypical depression (characterized by mood reactivity, weight gain, hypersomnia, leaden paralysis, and rejection hypersensitivity). Most commonly, however, children and adolescents are diagnosed simply with MDD or dysthymic disorder.

Comorbidities are more often the rule than the exception in childhood onset depression. Although studies vary greatly, somewhere between 40% and 90% of children and adolescents with depression have a second psychiatric disorder, and 20–50% have two or more comorbid disorders (Birmaher, Ryan, Williamson, Brent, & Kaufman, 1996). Even though the ranges are great, predictably dysthymic disorder (30–80%), anxiety disorders (30–80%), disruptive behavior disorders (10–80%), and substance use disorders (20–30%) affect the largest numbers of youth (Birmaher & Brent, 1998). MDD usually sets on after the commencement of other psychiatric disorders with the exception of substance abuse and occasionally conduct disorder, where the latter disorders may follow the onset of MDD.

The differential diagnosis of depression in children and adolescents includes a number of mood disorders, such as *adjustment disorder with depressed mood, bipolar disorder, dysthymic disorder, seasonal affective disorder,* or *bereavement.* There are also, however, a number of nonmood psychiatric conditions that should be considered and ruled out when depressive symptoms are present, including ADHD, anxiety disorders, disruptive behavior disorders (e.g., oppositional defiant disorder and conduct disorder), learning disorders, substance use disorders, eating disorders, personality disorders, and premenstrual dysphoric disorder. One of the most common causes of depression in young children under 7 years of age is severe neglect and abuse, which should be screened for in every young child with depressive symptoms (Elliott & Smiga, 2003). General medical conditions, such as HIV infection, anemia, hypothyroidism, seizure disorders, cancer, lupus, chronic fatigue syndrome, and diabetes, are also associated with higher than expected rates of depression (Birmaher & Brent, 1998). Finally, stimulants, antipsychotics, corticosteroids, and contraceptives, among other medications, may induce or contribute to depression. Consequently, the clinician must consider other potential causes of depression in the evaluation of any child or adolescent and should consider ordering a complete blood count (to rule out anemia), a thyroid-stimulating hormone and free T4 (to rule out hypothyroidism), a urine drug toxicology screen of adolescents to rule out drug abuse, and any additional testing that is suggested by the history and clinical examination.

Rating scales can be employed to assist in the management of childhood depression. Although numerous scales are available, due to their low specificity, they are more useful for assessing symptoms and severity of depression, along with monitoring change in mood over time, than they are for diagnosing MDD. The Children's Depression Rating Scale–Revised (CDRS-R) is the most commonly utilized scale in studies of depression and is considered the gold standard. This scale must be administered by a trained examiner and does not have great relevance for the practicing clinician. The most commonly utilized scale by clinicians is the Children's Depression Inventory (CDI), a 27-question, self-administered scale that takes about 5 to 10 minutes to complete and score (Kovacs, 1985). Other scales designed for self-report in adults, such as the Beck Depression Inventory (BDI) and the Center for Epidemiologic Studies Depression Scale (CES-D), are sometimes used with adolescents and appear to be reasonably reliable (Sawyer Radloff, 1991; Teri, 1982). Additional scales sometimes employed in studies of childhood depression include the Global Assessment of Functioning (GAF), Children's Global Assessment Scale (C-GAS), or Clinical Global Impression (CGI) Scale, all of which are nonspecific to depression and limited in their utility by their highly subjective nature.

TREATMENT

At present we cannot define a single best approach to the treatment of depressed children and adolescents. Too few studies of both medication and psychotherapy have demonstrated adequate efficacy. Consequently, our treatment approach is founded upon the limited data we have from studies of children and adolescents, our clinical experience, and evidence inferred from studies of depressed adults. Treatment should always begin in the least restrictive setting and take into consideration the duration and intensity of the patient's symptoms. The more chronic and severely affected children should receive both psychotherapy and medication, while those mildly affected and not suicidal may warrant a trial of psychotherapy and close monitoring first before a medication is employed. Educating the patient, family, and other important figures in the child's life, such as teachers, friends, and coaches, is critical in helping to build adequate support for the ill child. As depression is known to cluster within families, the clinician should make all efforts to identify and treat, or refer for treatment, other family members, particularly parents and siblings, who may themselves be depressed or suffering from another psychiatric condition.

Mothers with MDD and their children have been studied extensively, and we now know that effective treatment of such mothers is associated with a reduction in anxiety, depression, and disruptive behavior in their children. In one study of 151 mother-child pairs, such diagnoses dropped by 11% in those children whose mothers were successfully treated for MDD, as opposed to an 8% increase in diagnoses among those children whose mothers did not respond to medication treatment. Of the children with MDD themselves at baseline, remission occurred in 33% of those whose mothers' MDD remitted versus 12% of those whose mothers' MDD did not remit. Finally, of the mothers who did not respond to treatment, 17% of their children without a diagnosis at baseline later developed a psychiatric condition within 3 months, as opposed to none of the children whose mothers responded to treatment (Weissman et al., 2006a). As these data demonstrate, it is absolutely necessary to address the entire family in the treatment of a child with MDD.

Treatment studies of both medications and psychotherapies for MDD typically begin with a rarified sample of children and adolescents. In other words, the youths studied are screened very carefully to make sure that they are relatively free from comorbidities that would hinder or obscure the effect of the treatment being studied. For example, when treating a child with MDD and comorbid posttraumatic stress disorder (PTSD), it may be difficult to discern how much symptom improvement is due to the effect of the treatment under study, either psychotherapeutic or pharmacologic, on the MDD or on the PTSD. Even though these are different disorders, there is considerable symptom overlap between them, and the same psychiatric treatments are often effective for different disorders. As seen in Table 10.3, the numerous typical exclusion criteria limit to some degree our ability to interpret and generalize the data from treatment studies of depression because it is more commonly the exception

Table 10.3. Typical Exclusion Criteria for Pediatric Depression Studies

- Attention-deficit/hyperactivity disorder
- Posttraumatic stress disorder
- Bipolar disorder
- Autism spectrum disorders
- Mental retardation
- Disruptive behavior disorders
- Psychosis
- Any recent medication treatment (within 2–4 weeks)
- Current alcohol or drug abuse
- Eating disorder
- Recent initiation of psychotherapy
- Recent suicide attempts (past year)

rather than the rule to find a child or adolescent with MDD who does not also have one of these comorbid conditions.

Placebo responses in MDD are quite high, particularly among children and adolescents where in randomized, double-blind, placebo-controlled studies of antidepressants they have ranged between 33% and 57% (Bridge, Birmaher, Iyengar, Barbe, & Brent, 2008). In adult studies, approximately 25–35% of depressed subjects will experience a response to placebo. Overall response rates to antidepressants in adult trials of MDD are usually about 65–70% and in trials of children and adolescents sometimes no more than 55%. Consequently, only about half of individuals responding to an antidepressant in most drug trials are responding because of the medication itself. In other words, the true antidepressant response rate is usually around 25–35%, and the placebo response rate is about 25–35%, so the total response rate is about 50–70%. In studies of children and adolescents who tend to have a very high placebo response rate, it is therefore extremely difficult to demonstrate drug efficacy because the separation between active drug and placebo is most often negligible.

Tricyclic Antidepressants

Tricyclic antidepressants (TCAs) are typically thought of as the "older" antidepressants, as they were the first established group of effective medications for MDD. The TCAs were found serendipitously, subsequent to the synthesis of chlorpromazine in 1950 from synthetic antihistamines, which themselves were first discovered in the 1940s. Initially designed to be an antihistamine, chlorpromazine was found in 1952 to have profound antipsychotic effects. By 1955, chlorpromazine, also known as Thorazine, was widely accepted, and its ubiquitous use in asylums and psychiatric hospitals helped to pave the way for the reintegration of many chronically ill schizophrenic and bipolar patients back into society. Imipramine, the first TCA, is an analog of chlorpromazine, not initially designed for the treatment of depression but rather for psychosis. The drug's tendency to induce manic effects and generally worsen psychosis in schizophrenia, however, led to its testing with depressed patients. The first trial of imipramine, also known as Tofranil, took place in 1955, and the first report of its antidepressant effects was published in 1957. The second member of the tricyclic family, amitriptyline (Elavil), was introduced in 1961. There are numerous other TCAs available today, and those best known include desipramine (Norpramin), clomipramine (Anafranil), nortriptyline (Aventyl, Pamelor), and doxepin (Sinequan).

TCAs are presumed to exert their positive effects by blocking the reuptake of norepinephrine, serotonin, and dopamine to varying degrees by neuronal presynaptic receptors (see Figure 10.1). This effect thereby causes these neurochemicals to remain within the synapse longer. By increasing the amount of time that serotonin and norepinephrine stay in the synapse, we increase the likelihood that these neurochemicals will stimulate a postsynaptic receptor. Although we understand this mechanism of action, it is still unclear why antidepressants take many weeks to demonstrate any clinical benefit. In all likelihood, the beneficial effects are due to alterations in neuron receptors and cell proteins, which typically take 4 to 6 weeks for the body's DNA and RNA to transcribe and synthesize. Thus, the true effect of an antidepressant is probably many steps downstream from the simple mechanism demonstrated in this figure.

While highly effective for adult depression, TCAs have unfortunately shown little utility in the treatment of pediatric MDD. Open-label trials of TCAs have reported that up to 80% of children and adolescents respond positively. However, among at least 11 published randomized, double-blind, placebo-controlled trials, 5 in adolescents and 6 in children, only 1 study of 30 depressed children ages 6 to 14 years treated with imipramine demonstrated a positive result (Birmaher et al., 1996; Preskorn, Weller, Hughes, Weller, & Bolte, 1987). In addition, a meta-analysis of numerous studies likewise found no beneficial effect for TCAs in the treatment of MDD in children and adolescents (Hazell, O'Connell, Heathcote, Robertson, & Henry, 1995).

Numerous factors may have negatively biased the TCA studies of pediatric depression that have been performed. Small sample sizes with a great deal of diagnostic heterogeneity and levels of symptom impairment, the incorporation of patients with depression secondary to other primary

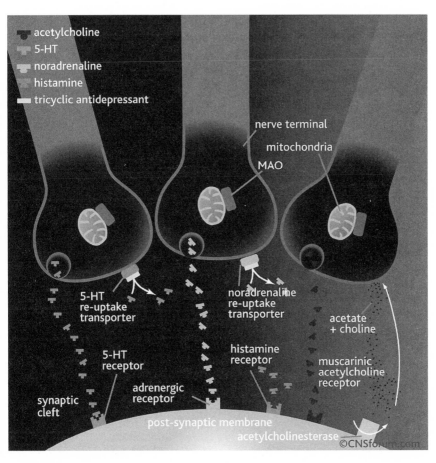

Figure 10.1. Tricyclic antidepressant mechanism of action. The tricyclic antidepressant blocks the 5-HT (serotonin) reuptake transporter and the noradrenaline reuptake transporter, thereby leaving more serotonin and noradrenaline within the synapse to stimulate the postsynaptic neuron.

psychiatric conditions (who may have had higher placebo response rates), and short trials of 6 to 8 weeks are but a few of the features that may have limited the data. Furthermore, lower doses of these medications were used because of understandable concerns about cardiac safety, yet children and adolescents may require higher dosages because of their more effective hepatic metabolism of drugs. Additionally, noradrenergic or secondary amine TCAs (see below) were most often employed, which are likely to be less favorable treatments for children. Since noradrenergic brain receptors may not be fully developed until early adulthood, children and adolescents may simply not be ready for noradrenergic (as opposed to serotonergic) antidepressants. Another potential factor is that more depressed children and adolescents than adults make the eventual transition into bipolar disorder, and TCAs are generally less effective for bipolar depression. Finally, the high prevalence of comorbid conditions in these studies may have interfered with ascertaining their true potential for the treatment of pediatric MDD (Birmaher et al., 1996).

Tricyclic antidepressants are classified as secondary or tertiary amines. Amines are organic compounds whose functional group contains a nitrogen atom with a loan pair of electrons. A primary amine has one of the three hydrogen atoms replaced by a carbon group, a secondary amine has two hydrogen atoms replaced by carbon groups, and a tertiary amine has three hydrogen atoms replaced by carbon groups. In general, the tertiary amines boost serotonin as well as norepinephrine and produce more sedation, anticholinergic effects (e.g., dry mouth and eyes, confusion, sedation), and orthostatic hypotension. The secondary amines act primarily on norepinephrine and tend to have a lower side-effect profile. The tertiary amines include amitriptyline (Elavil), imipramine (Tofranil), trimipramine (Surmontil), doxepin (Sinequan), clomipramine (Anafranil), and lofepramine (Gamanil); the secondary amines include nortriptyline (Pamelor), desipramine (Norpramin), protriptyline (Vivactil), and amoxapine (Asendin).

TCAs have demonstrated efficacy in the treatment of depression and anxiety in adults, obsessive-compulsive disorder (OCD) in children and adolescents, ADHD (particularly desipramine), analgesia for migraine headache prevention and neuropathic pain (particularly amitriptyline), and enuresis (particularly imipramine). For children and adolescents with these comorbidities, TCAs may be a reasonable treatment.

The most common side effects of TCAs are a result of their antimuscarinic and anticholinergic activity. Side effects include dry mouth, eyes, and nose, blurred vision, decreased gastrointestinal motility and constipation, urinary retention or hesitancy, sedation, and hyperthermia. Tolerance to these side effects often develops if treatment is continued. Side effects may also be less troublesome if the treatment is initiated at low dose and then gradually increased, although this approach will certainly delay the clinical effect. Other side effects of TCAs may include anxiety, restlessness, cognitive and memory difficulties, confusion, dizziness, akathisia (a sense of internal restlessness), increased appetite with weight gain, sweating, a decrease in sexual ability and desire, muscle twitches, weakness, nausea, vomiting, hypotension, tachycardia and, rarely, irregular heart rhythms.

There have been at least eight cases of sudden death reported in children and adolescents who have taken therapeutic doses of TCAs for the treatment of depression (Varley, 2001). More cases of sudden death have been reported among children and adolescents who took these medications in overdose (Amitai and Frischer, 2006). QT prolongation and subsequent *torsade de pointes* is the suggested cause of death in each case. The level of risk, however, remains unclear, as in many cases the children were taking other medications and their cardiac status had not been routinely monitored prior to treatment. Although infrequent, sudden death does occur in children regardless of medication treatment. Consequently, only experienced practitioners should prescribe TCAs, and even then only when all other reasonable alternatives have been exhausted. If a TCA is employed, the child and parents should be interviewed carefully. A history of sudden cardiac death in a first-degree relative and any symptoms of chest pain, exercise intolerance, syncope, shortness of breath, or dizziness in the child should be further explored and considered a possible contraindication to the initiation of treatment with a TCA. If a TCA is started, the child's cardiac status should be monitored before initiation of treatment, with each dosage adjustment, and regularly thereafter. (For a more extensive review of cardiac evaluation procedures prior to initiating potentially cardiotoxic medications, see Chapter 12.)

Monoamine Oxidase Inhibitors

Monoamine oxidase inhibitors (MAOIs) are a class of powerful antidepressants. The first MAOI, iproniazid, was designed to treat tuberculosis but was serendipitously found to improve patients' moods. Subsequent research led to its marketing in 1958 as an antidepressant, although it was later replaced by less hepatotoxic medications, including isocarboxazid (Marplan) in 1959. MAOIs are believed to work by decreasing the function of monoamine oxidase, an intracellular enzyme that metabolizes neurotransmitters. By decreasing the effect of this enzyme, the neurotransmitters, including norepinephrine, dopamine, and serotonin, are allowed to stay in the synapse longer and stimulate the postsynaptic neuron to a greater extent. Due to potentially lethal dietary and drug interactions, however, MAOIs have been reserved as a later line of defense to be used only when other classes of antidepressant drugs have been unsuccessful.

Recently, a patch form of the drug selegiline (Emsam) was developed. When applied transdermally in low dosages, the drug does not enter the gastrointestinal tract as it does when taken orally, thereby decreasing the dangers of dietary interactions associated with MAOIs taken orally. The four available MAIOs in the United States are isocarboxazid (Marplan), phenelzine (Nardil), tranylcypromine (Parnate), and selegiline (available as Eldepryl in tablet form and Emsam in patch form). In the past MAOIs were prescribed for those resistant to TCAs, but the newer MAOIs are now sometimes used as a first-line treatment by some practitioners for adult depression, social anxiety, smoking cessation, and atypical depression. Still, there remain no convincing studies of these medications in depressed children and adolescents.

The side effects of MAOIs can be significant and lethal. Of greatest concern is the hypertensive crisis that can occur when foods containing the amino acid tyramine are consumed. Monoamine oxidase typically degrades this protein, but if this enzyme system is inhibited by an MAOI, tyramine is free to enter the bloodstream where it is taken up by sympathetic nervous system terminals from where it can lead to release of endogenous catecholamines, such as norepinephrine and dopamine; these, in turn, can lead to hypertension, hyperpyrexia, tachycardia, diaphoresis, tremors, and cardiac arrhythmias. Similarly, when used in combination with selective serotonin reuptake inhibitors (SSRIs), clomipramine (Anafranil), or other serotonin-promoting drugs or foods high in tryptophan, the serotonin syndrome can result, characterized by tachycardia, hypertension, and fever. Both serotonin syndrome and tyramine ingestion can result, in the worst-case scenario, in coma, seizures, and death. For these reasons, MAOIs are infrequently used in children and adolescents, particularly given some data that suggest that 80% of adolescents do not follow the required diet (Ryan et al., 1988b). There is also great risk associated with MAOI use and over-the-counter medications, illicit drugs, and certain supplements, such as Saint-John's-wort.

Selective Serotonin Reuptake Inhibitors

SSRIs are much safer for use in children and adolescents, easier to prescribe, and generally better tolerated. The six available SSRIs include fluoxetine (Prozac), sertraline (Zoloft), paroxetine (Paxil), fluvoxamine (Luvox), citalopram (Celexa), and escitalopram (Lexapro). The presumed mechanism of action is similar to that with the TCAs, yet these medications exert their effects more specifically at the serotonin presynaptic receptors. By blocking the reuptake of serotonin by the presynaptic nerve, the SSRIs increase the amount of serotonin in the synapse to further stimulate the downstream neuron.

While generally useful for pediatric anxiety disorders, the SSRIs are perhaps less effective in treating pediatric depression. Although open-label studies have reported a 70–90% response rate in the treatment of adolescents with depression, more rigorous studies have not always been as impressive (Birmaher et al., 1996). Two large randomized, double-blind, placebo-controlled studies demonstrated the superiority of fluoxetine over placebo leading to Food and Drug Administration (FDA) approval of fluoxetine as the sole treatment for pediatric depression in children ages 7 to 17 years (Emslie, Heiligenstein, et al., 2002; Emslie, Rush, et al., 1997). Studies of the remaining SSRIs, however, have shown mixed results. Although most have demonstrated significant benefit in open-label studies, the randomized, double-blind, placebo-controlled studies that have been performed have not been robust (Keller et al., 2001; Berard, Fong, Carpenter, Thomason, & Wilkinson, 2006; Emslie et al., 2006; von Knorring, Olsson, Thomsen, Lemming, & Hultén, 2004; Wagner, Ambrosini, et al., 2003; Wagner, Berard, et al., 2004; Wagner, Jonas, Findling, Ventura, & Saikali, 2006a; Wagner, Robb, et al., 2004). Consequently, at this time fluoxetine is supported by the research for the treatment of pediatric depression, but other SSRIs have little evidence to suggest they are better than placebo.

Most common side effects of SSRIs tend to occur during the first few weeks of treatment, often becoming less apparent or bothersome thereafter. Sexual side effects, however, such as ejaculatory delay, anorgasmia, and decreased libido may set on after many weeks of treatment, although they generally improve over time. The transient side effects of SSRIs may include nausea, vomiting, diarrhea, drowsiness, headache, teeth clenching, vivid and strange dreams, dizziness, changes in appetite, weight loss or gain, increased feelings of depression and anxiety, tremors, autonomic dysfunction (including orthostatic hypotension or sweating), akathisia, hyponatremia, liver or renal impairment, and photosensitivity. Suicidal ideation has also been reported among children and adolescents taking SSRIs and is discussed at length in the Appendix.

The practitioner is always advised to proceed cautiously with dosing antidepressants in children and adolescents. When treating with fluoxetine, most youth can be started on a dose of 10 mg or even 5 mg, advancing to 10 mg within a few weeks. Practitioners should always follow up with their patients within 1 to 2 weeks of starting an antidepressant to encourage adherence to the treatment regimen, answer questions, provide further education, and address any side effects. Although advancing the dosage of antidepressants beyond an initial therapeutic target (20 mg for fluoxetine) has not generally been demonstrated to lead to improved efficacy, clinical experience dictates that if the treatment response is only partial, the dosage should be increased. Because it takes 2 weeks at a minimum and perhaps as many as 12 weeks at a maximum to see any benefit from the treatment, the prescribing physician is advised to be patient and advance the dosage cautiously.

Mixed Antidepressants

The serotonin-norepinephrine reuptake inhibitors (SNRIs) have yet to demonstrate efficacy for the treatment of pediatric depression. Open-label studies and case studies support the use of bupropion (Wellbutrin), nefazodone (Serzone), and mirtazapine (Remeron), but no randomized, double-blind, placebo-controlled studies have been completed (Daviss et al., 2001; Findling et al., 2000; Haapasalo-Pesu, Vuola, Lahelma, & Marttunen, 2004; Wilens, Spencer, Biederman, & Schleifer, 1997). Venlafaxine (Effexor) has been studied in two randomized, double-blind, placebo-controlled trials, but neither has demonstrated treatment efficacy (Emslie, Findling, Yeung, Kunz, & Li, 2007; Mandoki, Tapia, Tapia, Sumner, & Parker, 1997).

Antidepressant Augmentation

When a patient is partially but not fully responding to antidepressant treatment, augmenting medications are sometimes employed. A number of medications have proven themselves at least partially useful for this purpose in adults, including lithium, triiodothyronine (T3 thyroid hormone), stimulants, pindolol (Visken), and buspirone (Buspar) (Nelson, 2007). Recently, antipsychotic medications have been employed more frequently, and aripiprazole (Abilify) was recently approved by the FDA for the augmentation of treatment-resistant unipolar, nonpsychotic depression (Philip, Carpenter, Tyrka, & Price, 2008). One additional strategy sometimes employed for treatment-resistant depression, but without supportive data other than clinical experience, is combining antidepressants, particularly those that act within different neurochemical systems; a common example is buproprion (Wellbutrin), which acts primarily in the norepinephrine system, with an SSRI. In children and adolescents, however, other than lithium, which has only scant data, there is no evidence to support antidepressant augmentation, although in practice it happens frequently (Ryan, Meyer, Dachille, Mazzie, & Puig-Antich, 1988a; Strober, Freeman, Rigali, Schmidt, & Diamond, 1992; Walter, Lyndon, & Kubb, 1998).

Electroconvulsive Therapy

Case reports of children and adolescents receiving electroconvulsive therapy (ECT) for treatment-resistant depression date back to 1942. Most case reports, however, suffer from a lack of diagnostic clarity, small sample sizes, and heterogeneous diagnoses. More recent retrospective studies have reported the success of ECT in adolescents with a variety of psychiatric disorders, primarily MDD, some acute psychotic states, catatonia, and mania associated with bipolar disorder. ECT has not demonstrated efficacy for the treatment of anxiety, substance abuse, personality disorders, or dysthymia. Response rates vary from 51% to 100% in studies of adolescents with higher response rates noted among those with mood disorders (Ghaziuddin et al., 2004). Only one study has compared adolescents treated with ECT with those who refused ECT. Kutcher and Robertson (1995) found significant improvements noted among those who received ECT. Treated patients had shorter hospital stays, averaging 74 versus 176 days.

International estimates of ECT utilization are nearly impossible to assess, and even in the United States no mandatory reporting system exists. However, a study by the National Institutes of Mental Health revealed that about 1.5% of all ECT performed in 1980 in the United States, or about 500 cases, was for children and adolescents ages 11–20 years (Thompson & Blaine, 1987).

ECT is generally viewed as a remarkably safe and effective treatment for adults. Remission rates are usually greater than those reported for antidepressants, averaging at least 60–70% and in some studies quite a bit higher (U.S. Surgeon General, 1999). A single case series of four adolescents who received ECT found that only one teen responded favorably, and three had prolonged seizures of greater than 4 minutes each (Guttmacher & Cretella, 1988). This finding, however, has not been replicated, and all other studies suggest ECT to be effective in children and adolescents with no greater side effect profile than in adults (Rey & Walter, 1997).

Medication Treatment Algorithm

Upon establishing a proper diagnosis that warrants antidepressant treatment, the treating practitioner is advised to consider the use of fluoxetine as a first measure, given its FDA approval and demonstrated efficacy. Beyond this point in treatment, the practitioner is essentially left with only clinical experience to guide decision-making. Other SSRIs may be perfectly acceptable as a starting point as well, but the research data does not strongly support this approach at present time. If fluoxetine is ineffective, a second SSRI or an alternate antidepressant, such as an SNRI, may be considered. If fluoxetine is partially effective, the practitioner should consider a dosage increase. If the dosage increase is ineffective, the practitioner should consider an alternate antidepressant of a different mechanism,

Table 10.4.   Suggested Antidepressant Treatment Algorithm

*Step 1:	Fluoxetine (Prozac)
*Step 2:	SNRI or alternate SSRI
*Step 3:	TCA
Step 4:	MAOI
Step 5:	ECT

*Augmentation for partial responders can be considered at any of these three steps.

such as an SNRI. If either the first or the second antidepressant is partially effective, augmentation may be considered and may include lithium, an antipsychotic, or another antidepressant. T3 thyroid hormone, pindolol, a stimulant, or buspirone may also be considered at this time, even though we have no objective data to support this strategy in children and adolescents. Should augmentation fail, treatment with a TCA is advised, followed by augmentation of the TCA. If the TCA is ineffective, an MAOI without augmentation followed by ECT should be considered (see Table 10.4). Only experienced and skilled practitioners are advised to treat beyond the first two steps, particularly if augmentation is involved. If the practitioner has any questions, he or she should refer to an experienced specialist for consultation.

Psychodynamic Psychotherapy

Psychotherapy for the treatment of child and adolescent depression was historically psychodynamic or analytic in nature, often focusing on play as a means of getting to know the inner experience of the child. The practice of such therapies, while often useful, however, is highly idiosyncratic, and the utility of the treatment depends largely upon the therapist's skills and the fit between the therapist and patient. Although there are no absolute inclusion or exclusion criteria for patients entering psychodynamic psychotherapy, there are some generalizations that can be made. First, the ability to think abstractly helps considerably. For children in play therapy, abstract conceptualization is not a requirement, but in the absence of play as a primary technique, the ability to think outside of oneself is of great utility. Second, the patient should have reasonably good *ego strength* or an ability to withstand observations of his behavior and thoughts and to receive criticism from both himself and the therapist. Third, psychologically minded, introspective individuals tend to do better in psychodynamic psychotherapy. Finally, patients without an overwhelming *superego* tend to do better, as they do not feel excessively restricted by external values and morays to the point that they are incapable of questioning their natural inclinations, principles, and ideas. Cognitive behavior therapy (CBT), by contrast, does not make such demands on the patient. CBT only demands that the patient be willing to do homework and be in enough distress to be motivated to change his thinking.

Cognitive Behavior Therapy

In recent years CBT has moved to the forefront of depression treatment. Initially described by Aaron Beck for the treatment of adults with depression, CBT has since been successfully applied to depressed children and adolescents (Beck, Rush, Shaw, & Emery, 1979). Other therapies derived in part from CBT, including interpersonal therapy (IPT) and dialectical behavior therapy (DBT), have also demonstrated some degree of efficacy in treating both adults and youth with depression. These therapies have the distinct advantage of being "manualized" or designed for application in a straightforward, almost algorithmic fashion, which allows them to be rationally structured, reliably taught, and effectively replicated.

CBT has been found more effective than a wait-list condition or non-CBT psychotherapy for the treatment of depression in children and adolescents (Curry, 2001). Harrington, Whittaker, and Shoebridge's (1998) review of CBT in depressed children and adolescents reported benefit for 62% of treated patients versus 36% in placebo groups. Most studies have also found CBT better than other manualized treatments, such as relaxation training, family and supportive therapy, and CBT results in more rapid symptom remission than family or supportive therapy (Brent et al., 1997). Unfortunately, CBT follow-up studies have found high rates of relapse, which suggests the need for continued treatment (Birmaher and Brent, 1998). While clearly a more effective acute treatment, long-term follow-up studies of depressed adolescents have shown no superiority for CBT over other psychotherapies (Birmaher et al., 2000; Curry, 2001). In other words, while CBT generally results in a more rapid resolution of symptoms, years after the initial episode of depression, it is not clear that CBT is more effective than other types of psychotherapy. Finally, no form of CBT has as yet shown superiority over others.

Both cognitive and behavioral strategies are employed when treating depression with CBT. CBT is based on the idea that learned thoughts and behavioral patterns lead to feelings. The cognitive model presumes that the way in which one interprets and thinks about the things around him determines the way in which he feels and reacts. We know, for example, that different individuals often have different reactions to precisely the same event. Imagine a child waiting to be picked up from school by her parent. The child waits and waits; all of the other children have already been picked up by their parents, and now she stands alone. Our child may fear that her mother and father have died, thereby leading to feelings of sadness, abandonment, or panic. Conversely, our child may believe that her dad simply got caught at work, which may lead to feelings of neglect or anger. Or perhaps our child has not even been paying much attention to the fact that she is the last one waiting, and she's turned her attention to a book that she is excited about, leading to feelings of relief or happiness. The basic tenant of cognitive therapy is "the thoughts create the feeling."

CBT is generally brief and time-limited, generally no more than 12–16 weeks. Homework is stressed and viewed as a necessary component of the therapeutic work. The patient is encouraged to stay focused on the homework as part of the therapy, to employ time management, and to focus on solvable problems. Handouts, tapes, and other materials are often used. A good therapeutic relationship is important for CBT, but in contrast to traditional psychodynamic psychotherapy, the therapist may even use self-disclosure at times and share his own thoughts and behavioral responses with the patient. CBT is collaborative, and there is no hidden agenda. The patient may even be encouraged to read about CBT to help him understand the process. CBT often employs the Socratic method, using questions to examine patients' thoughts and suggesting that they substitute less troublesome thoughts for those they feel are bogging them down. CBT is therapist-directed and problem-focused. Finally, teaching is actively used by the therapist as indicated, as is an inductive model of experimenting and searching for facts (e.g., actively questioning the patient's theories about his behavior and thoughts).

In order to evaluate a patient's thoughts, CBT utilizes a number of methodologies. Using record keeping, a patient can keep tabs on his thoughts or "activating experiences" throughout the day. These thoughts, often distorted by depression, can be reviewed with the therapist during sessions. One can also have patients act out certain activities or problems that cause them stress and then evaluate how they think about them. Another therapeutic method is "thought listing," whereby patients describe what they were thinking prior to an activating experience in an attempt to recognize cues or precursors to the feelings that are experienced. Some therapists use audio- or videotapes to observe a patient during a particularly difficult activity or role play. The tapes can then be played back during therapy, where the therapist and patient can focus on the patient's thoughts at that time. Relaxation techniques are also used at times to help

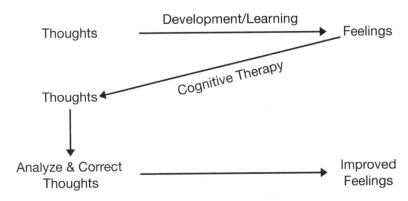

Figure 10.2.   Model of CBT for treatment of depression. Cognitive behavior theory hypothesizes that thoughts dictate feelings. Cognitive behavior therapy works by helping patients to analyze and correct their thoughts, which then leads to improved feelings.

patients who have difficulty expressing their thoughts. Using these and other methods, the therapist makes an effort to push "feelings" back into thoughts, which can then be analyzed and "corrected," resulting in improved feelings (see Figure 10.2).

For example, the adolescent may state, "I feel bad about myself in these situations." The proper therapist response using CBT techniques is not one of pure empathy (e.g., "You must have felt very sad."); further probing (e.g., "How did it feel to you to recognize that you cannot possibly do everything?"); or simple acknowledgment (e.g., "Tell me more."). Rather, the therapist's appropriate response using CBT is to focus on the evidence for the patient's feelings. A proper response might be, "Why do you *think* that you are bad?"

One of the key tenants of CBT for depression is to address patients' distorted thoughts. There are a number of so-called cognitive distortions to which depressed individuals commonly fall prey. These thought patterns are addressed directly in CBT. They include:

- *Filtering*—magnifying the negative details from a situation while filtering out all of the positive aspects.
- *Polarized thinking*—viewing everything as "good" or "bad" in an overly dogmatic fashion; believing that one must be perfect or a failure, allowing for no middle ground.
- *Overgeneralization*—coming to a conclusion about one's capabilities based upon a single incident or piece of evidence; when something bad happens once, the expectation is that it will happen over and over again.

- *Mind-reading*—presuming to understand how others feel and to know why they act as they do; particularly believing that one knows how others feel about him.
- *Catastrophizing*—expecting disaster from every interaction or situation.
- *Personalization*—thinking that everything people do or say is a reaction to oneself; constantly comparing oneself to others and trying to determine who is smarter, better-looking, and so forth.
- *Fallacy of control*—some individuals feel helpless and externally controlled by others, a victim of fate; alternatively, some individuals have a fallacy of internal control, which makes them feel as if they are responsible for the happiness and pain of everyone around them.
- *Fallacy of fairness*—feeling resentful because one thinks that he knows what is fair but others will not agree.
- *Fallacy of change*—expecting that others will change or respond if one only pressures or cajoles them adequately; one feels the need to change others because he feels that his happiness depends entirely upon them.
- *Heaven's reward fallacy*—expecting all of one's sacrifices and self-denial to pay off as if someone were keeping score; feeling bitter and angry when the reward does not come.
- *Blaming*—holding others responsible for the pain one feels, or blaming oneself for every problem in oneself and others.
- *Shoulds*—having a list of restrictive rules about how one and others should act; becoming angered when others break these rules or feeling guilty if one violates them.
- *Emotional reasoning*—believing that what one feels must be automatically true, such that if one feels bored or not intelligent in a given situation, then one must actually be "boring and stupid."
- *Global labeling*—generalizing one or two qualities into a negative global judgment.
- *Being right*—feeling continually on trial to prove that one's opinions and actions are correct; being wrong is impermissible and therefore going to great lengths to demonstrate one's correctness.

Interpersonal Therapy

Interpersonal therapy (IPT), another manualized therapy, has been shown to be more efficacious than a wait-list condition or minimal clinical management in a number of treatment studies of depressed adolescents (Miller, Gur, Shanok, & Weissman, 2008; Mufson, Weissman, Moreau, & Garfinkel,

1999; Rosselló & Bernal, 1999). Like CBT, IPT is a time-limited psychotherapy that uses a highly structured approach, along with homework assignments. IPT is based upon Harry Stack Sullivan's interpersonal theory, which suggests that individual relationships and interactions with others can provide the necessary insight into the causes and cures of mental dysfunction. IPT in its current form was developed by Gerald Klerman and Myrna Weissman in the 1980s for use in treatment studies of adult depression. IPT has since been modified for treatment of anorexia nervosa, bipolar disorder, PTSD, and anxiety disorders. The focus of IPT is generally on one or two personal issues or relationships most closely related to the depression. As with CBT, the therapist is the patient's advocate, not a neutral party.

IPT asserts that depression has three main features—symptom formation, social functioning, and personality contributions. IPT intervenes specifically in the realm of social functioning with the direct goal of alleviating symptoms. Problems in social functioning are hypothesized to occur in four ways—interpersonal disputes, role transitions, grief, and interpersonal deficits. IPT takes a very concrete approach by working with the patient to "solve" one specific problem with the belief that by so doing, the depression is likely to improve.

Both IPT and CBT have demonstrated efficacy in the treatment of adolescent depression when delivered either individually or in groups, making these treatments highly cost-effective and portable (David-Ferdon & Kaslow, 2008). Yet given the wealth of data supporting CBT for the treatment of adolescent depression, it remains the gold standard by which other psychotherapies should be judged (Rosselló, Bernal, & Rivera-Medina, 2008).

Dialectical Behavior Therapy

Dialectical behavior therapy (DBT), designed initially for the treatment of individuals with borderline personality disorder, has been effectively utilized for the treatment of suicidal and nonsuicidal self-injurious behavior in adults (Harley, Sprich, Safren, Jacobo, & Fava, 2008; Linehan, 1993; Stanley, Brodsky, Nelson, & Dulit, 2007). Although adequate scientific studies have not been performed in youth, DBT also appears to hold great promise for treating adolescents with MDD who are chronically suicidal or who self-injure (Fleischhaker, Munz, Böhme, Sixt, & Schulz, 2006; Miller, Rathus, & Linehan, 2006). At its core, DBT attempts to help individuals integrate opposing points of view or *dialectics* in an effort to become whole individuals. In addition to a reliance upon CBT strategies, DBT leans heavily upon Zen Buddhist philosophy, emphasizing the interrelatedness of opposing forces. From this perspective, typical borderline defenses, such as "splitting" and "projective identification," are viewed as a response to one's inability to allow contradictory feelings, such as love and anger. DBT aims to help affected individuals learn to regulate their emotions, tolerate distress without harming themselves, believe in their own interpersonal effectiveness, and engage in mindful ways of thinking. For those adolescents with MDD who self-injure or are chronically suicidal, referral for group or individual DBT is worth considering.

Combining Psychotherapy and Medication

Numerous recent studies have attempted to determine which treatment is "best" for child and adolescent depression—CBT, SSRIs, or a combination of the two. These large, federally funded multisite studies have compared CBT with various SSRIs and placebo for extended periods of time. The data from these studies is just now emerging.

The Treatment of Adolescents with Depression Study (TADS) is a multicenter, randomized clinical trial of 12–17-year-old adolescents with MDD, which enrolled over 430 youth. This ongoing study is comparing the efficacy of fluoxetine at dosages of 10–40 mg per day, CBT, their combination, and placebo for up to 1 year. Those receiving a medication were blinded, as were the treating physicians. Response rates at 12 weeks were 71% for combined treatment (fluoxetine plus CBT), 61% for fluoxetine alone, 43% for CBT alone, and 35% for placebo. Fluoxetine alone was superior to CBT alone, which did not itself separate from placebo. Remission rates totaled 23% for the study and included 37% of those receiving combined treatment, 23% of those receiving fluoxetine only, 17% of those receiving placebo, and 16% of those receiving CBT. Adolescents who were younger, were less chronically depressed, were higher functioning, were less hopeless with fewer indications of suicidal ideation, had fewer melancholic features and comorbid diagnoses, and those with greater expectations for improvement were more likely to benefit from treatment (March et al., 2004).

Data has now been published from the TADS study through 36 weeks of continued treatment (March, Silva, et al., 2007). This report indicates that 86% of those receiving combined treatment, 81% receiving fluoxetine, and 81% receiving CBT improved by week 36. Thus, most adolescents with depression who had not improved during acute treatment did so during the continuation and maintenance phases of the study. This continuation study also suggests that CBT is as effective as fluoxetine but takes somewhat longer to work.

Because only about 60% of adolescents demonstrate an adequate therapeutic response to SSRI treatment alone, the National Institutes of Mental Health sponsored the Treatment of Resistant Depression in Adolescents (TORDIA) study. This multisite clinical trial compared the efficacy of fluoxetine, paroxetine, citalopram, and venlafaxine, alone and in combination with CBT for 12–18-year-old adolescents with treatment-resistant depression. The study utilized a randomized, double-blind, placebo-controlled methodology by offering adolescents with MDD who did not respond to 2 months of initial treatment with an SSRI: (a) 12 additional weeks of a second, different SSRI (e.g., fluoxetine, paroxetine, or citalopram at 20–40 mg per day); (b) a switch to a second SSRI in addition to CBT; (c) a switch to venlafaxine alone at 150–225 mg per day; or (d) a switch to venlafaxine in addition to CBT. The study found that switching to an alternate medication plus CBT resulted in a higher response rate (55%) among these treatment-resistant adolescents than simply a medication switch alone (41%). While there were no differences in the response rates among those adolescents switching to a second SSRI versus venlafaxine, more side effects were noted among those taking venlafaxine, including slight blood pressure and heart rate increases, along with skin rashes (Brent et al., 2008).

When treating pediatric depression, the clinician is advised to evaluate all possible causes and comorbidities. If treatment for depression is indicated, CBT or IPT should be initiated for mild to moderate cases without suicidality. In the presence of chronic depression, suicidality, or moderate to severe symptoms, fluoxetine should be considered. Should this combination not result in significant symptom remission, an augmenting strategy and/or second medication (as above) should be considered, along with a referral to a child and adolescent psychiatrist for consultation.

11

Bipolar Disorder

Emil Kraepelin was among the first to comment on bipolar disorder in children and adolescents. In his observations of over 900 patients with manic depression (the prior term for bipolar disorder) in 1917, he reported that the illness most frequently set on between 15 and 20 years of age. Kraepelin also reported that onset prior to 10 years of age was rare and mild, if it occurred at all (Duffy, 2007). As happened with pediatric depression, psychoanalytic theory, which held great clout in American psychiatry through the 1970s, suggested that children lack the higher level cognitive structures required for a diagnosis of bipolar disorder. Thanks to research over the past three decades, however, we now once again recognize, as did Kraepelin, that bipolar disorder can affect children and adolescents. Nearly 60% of bipolar adults recall having symptoms prior to age 19 (Lish, Dime-Meenan, Whybrow, Price, & Hirschfeld, 1994), and up to 20% of adults recall having significant prodromal symptoms prior to age 10 years (Egeland, Hostetter, Pauls, & Sussex, 2000).

CLINICAL PRESENTATION

The classic adult presentation of bipolar disorder Type I (BP-I), with discrete episodes of mania and depression with clear onset and offset, is rare in children and younger adolescents (Goodwin & Jamison, 1990). In contrast, we more commonly see episodes of long duration characterized by rapid or continuous cycling and mixed mania among children. Among adolescents, BP-I more frequently resembles the adult presentation with euphoria, grandiosity, paranoid ideation, and flight of ideas, whereas younger children more frequently present with irritability, excitability, aggression, explosiveness, and significant mood lability. Those children with extensive mood disturbance who do not meet specific criteria for BP-I or bipolar disorder Type II (BP-II), characterized by episodes of hypomania alternating with depression, and whose symptoms are predominantly irritable and aggressive, are commonly diagnosed with bipolar disorder not otherwise specified (BP-NOS). The diagnosis of cyclothymia, which is rarely used for children and adolescents, describes a mood disorder with alternations between hypomania and low-grade depression.

The atypical presentation of bipolar disorder in prepubertal children has led many investigators and clinicians to doubt once again the existence of the illness in preadolescents. It has, after all, not yet been established that preteens currently diagnosed with bipolar disorder will develop the adult form (Chang, 2007), as characterized clearly in the *DSM-IV* (American Psychiatric Association, 2000). Perhaps the predominant irritability and aggression seen in these children is due to a different disorder or combination of disorders, such as attention-deficit/hyperactivity disorder (ADHD), learning disorders, and oppositional defiant disorder, along with poor parental monitoring. Because prepubertal children are simply not developmentally capable of expressing some of the classic *DSM-IV* symptoms of bipolar disorder (such as "engaging in unrestrained buying sprees, sexual indiscretions, or foolish business investments"), some parents, clinicians and researchers have been seen as zealots, embracing the disorder fervently to the exclusion of other reasonable explanations for a child's disruptive behavior. As is most often the case with such controversial issues, the truth probably lies somewhere in the middle. Certainly, irritability, aggression, and mood lability are frequent symptoms of many childhood psychiatric conditions and are most often not indicative of bipolar disorder (Stringaris & Goodman, 2008).

In order to properly diagnose the disorder as we currently understand it, clear symptoms of *DSM-IV* bipolar disorder must be present, but the symptoms in children will differ at least somewhat from those seen in adolescents and adults. Some investigators have argued that a bipolar elated mood may present in a child as repeated giggling in inappropriate places with an inability to stop; grandiosity may present as stealing and a child believing that rules do not apply to him or her; decreased need for sleep may present as staying awake late and keeping very busy, then needing only a few hours of sleep and awakening filled with energy for the day ahead; and risk-taking behavior may present as hypersexuality, including provocative speech, gestures, and inappropriate touching of oneself and others in public (Geller, Zimerman, Williams, DelBello,

Frazier, et al., 2002). Such symptom variants should be considered potentially diagnostic only if they are consistent with an overall clinical picture of bipolar disorder.

To further muddy the diagnostic water, rapid or complex cycling has been described in over 80% of children diagnosed with bipolar disorder in some studies (Geller et al., 2000). The *DSM-IV* defines "rapid cycling" bipolar disorder as four or more complete episodes of either (hypo)mania or depression per year with each episode meeting full diagnostic criteria for duration (e.g., 2 weeks for a major depressive episode, 1 week for a manic episode, and 4 days for a hypomanic episode). Although rapid cycling occurs in only about 10–20% of adults with bipolar disorder, it appears to be the rule in childhood manifestations of the disorder. In fact, investigators have termed the phrase "ultra rapid cycling" for those who have more than 4 but fewer than 365 cycles per year and "ultradian" for those who have numerous cycles every day or more than 365 per year (Geller, Tillman, Bolhofner, 2007). While these terms may not prove to be diagnostically valid in the years to come, researchers do agree that bipolar disorder in children is typically chronic with long, predominantly mixed symptoms of mania and depression and less clearly defined episodes than in adults.

ETIOLOGY

We currently envision the mood disorders as lying on a spectrum, with bipolar disorder being the most severe expression. Although not an etiological theory per se, the idea of *kindling*, generally applied to seizure disorders, has also been suggested as a way of understanding bipolar disorder (Mazza et al., 2007). Kindling theory suggests that repeated subthreshold stimulation of a nerve cell, or kindling a nerve cell, just as one would a campfire, eventually causes that nerve to activate or fire. Once this pattern of nerve activation is set in motion, repeated episodes of mood instability continue to stimulate those same tracts or pathways, resulting in a greater likelihood of repeated stimulation of these same nerve pathways over time, leading to repeated manic episodes (Post, 2007). Kindling is believed to be a function of the temporal lobes in bipolar disorder.

There are a number of interesting biological findings, which, taken as a whole, suggest a number of contributing etiological factors. Smaller hippocampal and total cerebral volumes have been found among children and adolescents with bipolar disorder (Frazier et al., 2005), although the meaning of these findings is unclear. Abnormalities have been found within the hypothalamic-pituitary-adrenal (HPA) axis among adults with bipolar disorder. Excess cortisol is suggested to contribute to depressive symptoms and neurotoxicity resulting in cognitive deficits, while mania has been proposed to be secondary to an increase in both ACTH and cortisol (Daban, Vieta, Mackin, & Young, 2005). Various gene mutations or associations have also been suggested as possible etiologies of bipolar disorder. A mutation in the G protein receptor kinase 3 (GRK3) gene may be responsible for up to 10% of cases. This GRK3 mutation is thought to lead to dopamine hypersensitivity, which in turn may cause mood swings (Barrett et al., 2003). Still, other research suggests that the portion of the genome that encodes diacylglycerol kinase eta (DGKH), an important protein in the lithium-sensitive phosphatidyl inositol pathway, may be involved in the genesis of bipolar disorder (Baum et al., 2008). Clearly, numerous biological factors are at play, and the genetic transmission of bipolar disorder is multifactorial.

Inheritance of bipolar disorder is most certain to be polygenic with no single responsible gene. Genetic transmission is probably greater for bipolar disorder than for major depressive disorder (MDD), with numerous studies suggesting an approximately 80% or greater concordance for monozygotic (identical) twins as opposed to about a 20% concordance for dizygotic (fraternal) twins (Cardno et al., 1999; Kieseppä, Partonen, Haukka, Kaprio, & Lönnqvist, 2004). In addition, the vast majority of children and adolescents with bipolar disorder have a relative with a major mood disorder, and a family history of bipolar disorder is a major risk factor for the same in children.

EPIDEMIOLOGY

BP-I has generally been thought to affect about 1% or slightly more of the adult population. When all forms of bipolar disorder are taken into account, that percentage may be as high as 3% (Angst, 1999). BP-I is diagnosed among adults considerably less than BP-II, BP-NOS, and cyclothymia. Among children and adolescents, this same pattern is followed, as establishing a clear diagnosis of BP-I in children is riddled with complications. In one large trial of older adolescents 14–18 years of age, the lifetime prevalence of bipolar disorder, primarily BP-II and cyclothymia, was 1%, but an additional 5.7% reported periods of abnormally and continually elevated, expansive, or irritable moods that never met criteria for BP-I or BP-II (Lewinsohn et al., 1995). In the present day, this group would undoubtedly be diagnosed by many with BP-NOS (National Institute of Mental Health Research Roundtable on Prepubertal Bipolar Disorder, 2001).

Family studies of parents with bipolar disorder have found that offspring have nearly a three times greater risk for developing any psychiatric condition and a four times greater risk for developing a mood disorder (Chang, Steiner, & Ketter, 2003). One study of children with at least one bipolar parent found a prevalence of 55% for any psychiatric disorder, 15% for depressive disorders, and 15% for bipolar disorder or cyclothymia among the offspring (Chang, Steiner, & Ketter, 2000). Gershon et al. (1982) found a 24% risk of developing a mood disorder for first-degree relatives of individuals with bipolar disorder, increasing to 27% if one parent and 74% if both parents have bipolar disorder. These studies suggest a high concordance among family members with bipolar disorder. By contrast, a Dutch study reported a prevalence of 44% for any psychiatric disorder, 23% for depressive disorders, but only 4% for bipolar spectrum disorders in offspring of adult bipolar patients (Wals et al., 2004). The reason for this discrepancy in bipolar disorder rates between these findings in the United States and Holland is not clear.

Finally, early age at onset of bipolar disorder appears to confer several risks. Children with earlier onset have more frequent suicidal ideation and attempts, substance use disorders, and rapid cycling (Carlson, Bromet, & Sievers, 2000; Carter, Mundo, Parikh, & Kennedy, 2003). In addition, younger age at onset confers a greater risk of bipolar disorder among first-degree relatives of an affected child (Geller et al., 2006).

CLINICAL COURSE

The onset of bipolar disorder generally occurs between 15 and 20 years of age. Males may present slightly earlier than females. In the largest study of children and adolescents with bipolar disorder to date (the Course and Outcome of Bipolar Illness in Youth, or COBY), approximately 25% of subjects converted to a more severe form of the disorder during the 2-year follow-up, such that children initially diagnosed with BP-II, for example, were later diagnosed with BP-I. Younger age at onset or longer duration of illness, BP-NOS, low socioeconomic status, and psychotic symptoms predicted a worse outcome among these youth (Birmaher et al., 2006).

Most children (70–100%) recover from their first or index episode, but recovery often takes many months or even years. Among those who do recover, 80% will experience one or more additional episodes within 5 years (Birmaher, 2007). A smaller naturalistic study of children and adolescents found that rate of recovery varied by polarity of the first episode, such that a more rapid recovery was observed in those with pure mania or mixed mania as opposed to those with pure depression at first presentation (Strober et al., 1995). Virtually all longitudinal studies in adults indicate that bipolar disorder is chronic, relapse is the rule, and fewer than

10% fully recover (American Psychiatric Association, 2000). Similar findings in children and adolescents are suggested but not yet substantiated.

Studies of bipolar adults suggest that over time episodes occur more frequently. Left untreated, the length of each cycle tends to decrease for each of the first four or five episodes until it stabilizes. As previously noted, cycling is a recognized characteristic of bipolar disorder and is a diagnostic specifier in the *DSM-IV*. Cycling may be transient or chronic. Risk factors for rapid cycling in adults include female gender, antidepressant use, thyroid disease, mental retardation, certain neurological conditions (e.g., multiple sclerosis), and head injury. The rapid cycling subtype in adults has a poorer prognosis (American Psychiatric Association, 2000). Risk factors for rapid cycling in children and adolescents are not known at this time, but, as previously noted, rapid cycling may affect 80% or more of youth with bipolar disorder (Geller et al., 2000).

"Mixed episode" is another specifier for bipolar disorder and can be understood as a combination of mania and depression present at the same time. Affected individuals may laugh and cry simultaneously, expressing both sadness and glee with equal intensity. Others may speak rapidly, be highly distractible, and make grandiose or euphoric statements, while reporting depression with suicidal ideation and paranoia. Mixed states appear to happen more commonly in children and adolescents with bipolar disorder than adults (Staton, Volness, & Beatty, 2008). However, we must remember that mixed emotional presentations are more common in children than adults even in the absence of psychopathology and that elevated and mixed emotions alone are not diagnostic.

The likelihood of "switching" diagnoses from MDD to bipolar disorder decreases with age. That is, the longer an individual has suffered from depression, the less likely he is to transition into bipolar disorder. The risk of conversion is greatest for children and adolescents (Othmer et al., 2007). Among adults, the risk of diagnostic conversion is greatest during the first 5 years after the onset of MDD, and about 10–15% of adults are affected. Risk factors for switching among adults include early onset, severity of MDD, family history of bipolar disorder, psychosis, and psychiatric comorbidity (Holma, Melartin, Holma, & Isometsä, 2008). The risk of converting to bipolar disorder from MDD probably increases with the number of these risk factors, such that those with two or more risk factors may be 50% or more likely to convert (Othmer et al., 2007).

As discussed in Chapter 10, a significant minority of children and adolescents, somewhere between 20% and 40%, who are initially diagnosed with MDD will later develop bipolar disorder within 5 years. Risk factors include early-onset MDD, psychomotor retardation, psychosis, pharmacologically induced hypomania, a family history of bipolar disorder or psychotic depression, and a significant family history of mood disorders (Birmaher & Brent, 1998).

Given the relatively small numbers of children and adolescents who are diagnosed with bipolar disorder and the controversies surrounding the diagnosis in this age group, predicting the course and prognosis of the illness is remarkably difficult (Strober et al., 2006). Based on the COBY and other studies, however, we do know that 20–30% of bipolar youths make at least one medically significant suicide attempt within 2 to 5 years of diagnosis (Goldstein et al., 2005; Strober et al., 1995), 20% suffer physical and/or sexual abuse (Romero et al., 2009), and 16% of adolescents suffer substance use disorders (Goldstein, Strober, et al., 2008). In addition, the COBY study found that 80% of subjects utilized mental health services in a 6-month period, illustrating only one of the many costs to our society of this illness (Rizzo et al., 2007).

Studies of both adults and children indicate severe psychosocial impairments among those with bipolar disorder. During episodes of mania and depression, all individuals suffer. However, between episodes, approximately one-third of adults with bipolar disorder continue to suffer major mood difficulties, and two-thirds struggle with chronic interpersonal and occupational troubles (American Psychiatric Association, 2000). The same appears true for children and adolescents, where even those in partial remission or full recovery continue to struggle interpersonally and with academic functioning. Predictors of impairment include adolescence (as opposed to childhood), symptom severity, psychosis, and comorbid conduct disorder (Goldstein, Birmaher, Axelson, Goldstein, Gill, Esposito Smythers, et al., 2008). Unquestionably, bipolar children and children of bipolar parents are more likely to be exposed to negative life events and psychosocial stressors because of their upbringing. Families with bipolar children, as well as families with bipolar parents, are characterized by poor cohesion and high conflict (Belardinelli et al., 2008; Chang, Blasey, Ketter, & Steiner, 2001).

DIAGNOSIS

The *DSM-IV* describes a number of bipolar variants, including BP-I, BP-II, BP-NOS, and cyclothymia. Both BP-I and BP-II have a characteristic manic phase alternating with periods of major depression. In addition, various specifiers, including "mixed episode" and "rapid cycling," are described. BP-I, the most virulent form of the illness, is characterized by at least 1 week (or less if hospitalization is required) of an abnormally elevated, expansive, or irritable mood. During this time, at least three of the following symptoms are present (four symptoms are required if the mood is only irritable): (a) decreased need for sleep; (b) grandiosity; (c) excessive talkativity or pressured speech; (d) excessive risk-taking behavior; (e) excessive goal-directed behavior; (f) excessive distractibility; or (g) racing thoughts. BP-II or hypomania is considered a more modest form of the disorder, where only 4 days of symptoms are required without hospitalization or psychosis. Cyclothymia, by contrast, demands at least 2 years (1 year in children and adolescents) of numerous hypomanic and depressive symptoms, never meeting criteria for MDD or bipolar disorder.

As previously noted, many of the hallmark symptoms of bipolar disorder are difficult to assess in children and adolescents. Grandiosity, for example, is developmentally normal in prepubertal children until about 8 years of age. Young children who report, and truly believe, that they can beat their father at chess or in a wrestling match are not grandiose in the psychotic sense. In fact, even as children age somewhat, grandiosity may still be viewed as more boastful or oppositional, rather than delusional, as is more common with adolescent-onset and adult-onset bipolar disorder. The examiner, then, must use many data points and be extremely cautious about the interpretation of symptoms. When adequately assessed, some investigators feel that grandiosity, hypersexuality, and an elated, euphoric mood are the most reliable indicators of true mania (Geller, Williams, et al., 1998).

We must understand that it is quite rare to see true *DSM-IV* bipolar disorder in children under 12 years of age. That is, we may witness true bipolar disorder, but its appearance is somewhat different than expected. Rapid mood fluctuations or lability, hyperactivity, disinhibition, and aggression are evident, but these are not the typical euphoria, grandiosity, or increase in goal-directed behavior seen in the adult presentation of bipolar disorder. Many of the symptoms reported by children and their families sound rather like ADHD than bipolar disorder, and this differential must be fully explored. Studies report that at least half and perhaps over 80% of bipolar children and adolescents suffer from comorbid ADHD symptoms and that over two-thirds have comorbid symptoms of conduct disorder (Borchardt & Bernstein, 1995; Faraone, Biederman, Jetton, & Tsuang, 1997a; Kovacs & Pollock, 1995; Milberger, Biederman, Faraone, Murphy, & Tsuang, 1995; West, McElroy, Strakowski, Keck, & McConville, 1995). Anxiety disorders are also highly comorbid with child and adolescent bipolar disorder, and studies typically show coexisting rates of 20–70% (Jolin, Weller, & Weller, 2008). Whether these symptoms truly represent comorbid conditions, however, or prodromal symptoms, current symptoms, or simply an overlap in *DSM-IV* diagnostic symptoms remains unclear. Certainly, this confusion appears to be a greater problem

Table 11.1. Symptom Crossover Between ADHD and Bipolar Disorder

DSM-IV symptoms of mania	Occurrence in ADHD
Elevated/expansive mood	No
Irritability	Common
Grandiosity	No
Decreased need for sleep	Common but relatively mild
Excessive talkativity	Criterion for diagnosis
Racing thoughts/flight-of-ideas	No
Excess goal-directed behavior	Hyperactivity criteria are similar
High-risk activities	Common
Distractibility	Criterion for diagnosis

with younger children, as adolescent-onset bipolar disorder has less reported comorbidity with ADHD and disruptive behavior disorders, appearing more like the adult form (Faraone et al., 1997b; Geller & Luby, 1997). As seen in Table 11.1, among the hallmark symptoms of bipolar disorder, only racing thoughts, grandiosity, and euphoria are not also symptoms of ADHD. However, irritability, another common feature of both disorders, further contributes to the confusion in making the diagnosis.

The centrality of irritability, or aggression and agitation, as a core symptom of bipolar disorder has taken main stage in the child bipolar controversy. Some clinicians support a diagnosis of bipolar disorder if a child meets DSM-IV criteria with irritability as a core symptom, even in the absence of elation, grandiosity, and cycling. Other clinicians believe that unmodified DSM-IV criteria should always be followed for a diagnosis of bipolar disorder in both children and adults. At this time it is likely that many prepubertal children, perhaps most, who have received the diagnosis of BP-NOS or cyclothymia will not go on to develop strictly defined DSM-IV bipolar disorder as adolescents or adults. Still, these children represent a greater conundrum to the clinician than simply a child with ADHD, disruptive behavior, poor social support, and learning disabilities. For while these features are extremely common among this cohort of children, regardless of how they are ultimately diagnosed, the fact remains that extensive treatments, including mood stabilizers and antipsychotics, along with intensive family, social, and individual psychosocial therapies, are often necessary to manage their symptoms (Meyer et al., 2009).

The differential diagnosis for bipolar disorder is extensive and includes psychotic, mood, anxiety, externalizing, and personality disorders. Schizophrenia and schizoaffective disorder, while equally difficult to diagnose in children as bipolar disorder, should be considered. Posttraumatic stress disorder, among other anxiety disorders such as obsessive-compulsive disorder, can also present with symptoms similar to bipolar disorder. ADHD, as already discussed, oppositional defiant disorder, and conduct disorder run so highly comorbid that these disorders are often difficult to distinguish from bipolar disorder. Finally, other mood and personality disorders should also be ruled out.

In addition to other psychiatric conditions, there are a number of general medical conditions that mimic mania. Although uncommon, neurologic conditions, including brain tumors, central nervous system infections, multiple sclerosis, temporal lobe epilepsy, and Kleine-Levin syndrome, can make children appear manic. Systemic conditions, including hyperthyroidism, uremia, Wilson's disease, and porphyria, while also infrequent occurrences, can present like bipolar disorder. Finally, numerous medications can induce a manic state, including antidepressants, stimulants, steroids, and various substances of abuse, such as amphetamines, cocaine, phencyclidine (PCP), inhalants, and ecstasy.

There are a number of rating scales that can be helpful in diagnosing child and adolescent bipolar disorder, but none should be relied upon as an absolute diagnostic tool. Perhaps the most useful method of determining if the presenting symptoms do, in fact, represent bipolar disorder is by maintaining a daily mood chart (see Table 11.2). Parents can be taught to log the fluctuations in their child's daily moods on a simple grid designed to follow extreme highs and lows. Parents should also be encouraged to enter how many hours of sleep the child received each day, any significantly stressful events that might explain mood changes, and any psychotic symptoms. Such mood charts allow a clinician to more accurately assess parent and child reports, determine the longitudinal course of the illness, clarify the diagnosis, and assist with tracking treatment response. Perhaps most important, a mood chart can help the clinician decide when to refer to a specialist. Mood charts are typically completed by parents, but collateral sources, such as teachers, and adolescents themselves can also maintain separate charts. Prior to employing a mood chart, the clinician must be certain to explain clearly what is meant by a "high" or manic and "low" or depressed mood to minimize inaccurate recordings.

The Parent Version of the Young Mania Rating Scale, an 11-question survey for parents about their child's mood, offers another method to help clinicians determine when to refer to specialist care. The scale, which is readily available on numerous Internet sites for free, is not intended to diagnose bipolar disorder and does not follow strict *DSM-IV* criteria for bipolar disorder. Average scores among manic children are

Table 11.2. Mood Chart

Day #	1	2	3	4	5	6	7	8	9	10	11	12	13	14	15	16	17	18	19	20	21	22	23	24	25	26	27	28	29	30	31
Agitated/manic																															
Hypomanic																															
Euthymic																															
Dysthymic																															
Depressed																															
Sleep (hours)																															
Psychosis																															
Stressful events																															

approximately 25 and among hypomanic children approximately 20. Scores above 13 are considered suggestive of bipolar disorder, and scores over 21 are considered probable (Gracious, Youngstrom, Findling, & Calabrese, 2002).

Finally, the Children's Mania Rating Scale (see Figure 11.1) can also aid in diagnosis and be particularly helpful in distinguishing bipolar disorder from ADHD. In research trials, scores over 21 were considered suggestive of a bipolar diagnosis as opposed to ADHD (Pavuluri, Henry, Devineni, Carbray, & Birmaher, 2006).

TREATMENT

The first step in treatment is education about the disorder for the affected individual, family, and important collaterals, such as teachers, friends, and coaches. An enormous amount can be gained by teaching youth with bipolar disorder and their families about associated risks and the need for adherence to the treatment regimen. Much of this instruction can be accomplished by individual supportive psychotherapy and family therapy. Helping a child or adolescent to reckon with the diagnosis is, perhaps, the most difficult part of treatment and can take months or even years. Once achieved, however, acceptance of the diagnosis is immensely useful because it allows the individual to identify the warning signs of an impending mood episode and to address the problems immediately.

Mood hygiene is also an extremely important component of treatment, and those with bipolar disorder must learn how fragile their moods can be. Even small changes in their sleep cycle, nutrition, and stress can cause imbalance and agitation, and can predispose them to a major mood episode. To this end, children, adolescents, and their parents should keep mood charts, as described above, particularly when establishing the diagnosis and making major changes in treatment. The data gathered will aid in maintaining mood hygiene and further educating the child and family about the disorder.

In establishing a treatment plan, it is vital to understand the factors that interfere with symptom resolution. While we have little data to guide us in this regard at present time, we do recognize that effective treatment should address all comorbidities. ADHD, conduct disorder, anxiety, and aggression have clearly been shown to interfere with treatment efficacy and must be addressed within a comprehensive treatment plan (Jolin et al., 2008; Masi et al., 2004; Papolos, Hennen, & Cockerham, 2005). In addition, low socioeconomic status, ADHD, anxiety, and poor adherence to

INSTRUCTIONS

The following questions concern your child's mood and behavior in the **past month**. Please place a checkmark or an "x" in a box for each item. Please consider it a problem if it is **causing trouble** and is beyond what is normal for your child's age. Otherwise, check "rare or never" if the behavior is not causing trouble.

Does your child . . .

	NEVER/ RARELY	SOMETIMES	OFTEN	VERY OFTEN
1. Have periods of feeling super happy for hours or days at a time, extremely wound up and excited, such as feeling "on top of the world"	0	1	2	3
2. Feel irritable, cranky, or mad for hours or days at a time	0	1	2	3
3. Think that he or she can be anything or do anything (e.g., leader, best basket ball player, rap singer, millionaire, princess) beyond what is usual for that age	0	1	2	3
4. Believe that he or she has unrealistic abilities or powers that are unusual, and may try to act upon them, which causes trouble	0	1	2	3
5. Need less sleep than usual; yet does not feel tired the next day	0	1	2	3
6. Have periods of too much energy	0	1	2	3
7. Have periods when she or he talks too much or too loud or talks a mile-a-minute	0	1	2	3
8. Have periods of racing thoughts that his or her mind cannot slow down , and it seems that your child's mouth cannot keep up with his or her mind	0	1	2	3
9. Talk so fast that he or she jumps from topic to topic	0	1	2	3
10. Rush around doing things nonstop	0	1	2	3
11. Have trouble staying on track and is easily drawn to what is happening around him or her	0	1	2	3
12. Do many more things than usual, or is unusually productive or highly creative	0	1	2	3
13. Behave in a sexually inappropriate way (e.g., talks dirty, exposing, playing with private parts, masturbating, making sex phone calls, humping on dogs, playing sex games, touches others sexually)	0	1	2	3
14. Go and talk to strangers inappropriately, is more socially outgoing than usual	0	1	2	3

Does your child . . .

	NEVER/ RARELY	SOMETIMES	OFTEN	VERY OFTEN
15. Do things that are unusual for him or her that are foolish or risky (e.g., jumping off heights, ordering CDs with your credit cards, giving things away)	0	1	2	3
16. Have rage attacks, intense and prolonged temper tantrums	0	1	2	3
17. Crack jokes or pun more than usual, laugh loud, or act silly in a way that is out of the ordinary	0	1	2	3
18. Experience rapid mood swings	0	1	2	3
19. Have any suspicious or strange thoughts	0	1	2	3
20. Hear voices that nobody else can hear	0	1	2	3
21. See things that nobody else can see	0	1	2	3

TOTAL SCORE _____

*Used with permission of
Manu Pavuluri, MD*

Figure 11.1. Children's mania rating scale, parent version.

medication treatment are associated with delayed recovery. More rapid symptom recurrence is observed among those who abuse alcohol and do not receive psychotherapy (DelBello, Hanseman, Adler, Fleck, & Strakowski, 2007). Finally, we recognize that early onset, long illness duration, mixed episodes, rapid cycling, psychosis, negative life events, subsyndromal symptoms, and family psychopathology are associated with worse long-term outcomes (Birmaher, 2007). Given these factors, treatment should address each of these areas and commence immediately upon suspected diagnosis.

Among bipolar adults with even mild symptom impairment, delays in necessary medication treatment are correlated with worse psychosocial functioning, more hospitalizations, and a greater likelihood of making a suicide attempt (Goldberg & Ernst, 2002). Though parallel data in children and adolescents is not yet available, we suspect the same to be true. Furthermore, children diagnosed with ADHD and/or MDD who have a significant family history of bipolar disorder may be experiencing a prodromal bipolar state. For such children, we anticipate that early psychotherapeutic and medication interventions may even help prevent the more severe manifestations of the illness (Chang, Howe, Gallelli, & Miklowitz, 2006).

If the disease course can be altered by recurrence (e.g., kindling), then repeated episodes of the illness are likely to affect gene expression. If we presume that the kindling theory is valid, then it follows that illness progression can also be altered by rapidly halting a manic episode, and, in fact, this pattern is precisely what we see in clinical practice. The more rapid and aggressive our treatment, the longer the individual is likely to stay well. Lack of treatment or rapid discontinuation of treatment may then, alternatively, promote advancement of the illness, leading to longer episodes with greater frequency. It is quite clear that one's risk of recurrence is increased with inadequate treatment and decreased with proper treatment.

Psychotherapeutic Treatment of Bipolar Disorder

As noted above, psychotherapy may be useful early in the course of illness to provide patient education and support acceptance of the diagnosis. Therapy can also help the affected individual to recognize episode triggers, identify symptoms early before a full-blown mood episode ensues, and help family members to reduce "expressed emotion," or excessive criticism expressed toward the affected individual. As yet, no single type of psychotherapy or other psychosocial treatment has emerged as superior to others. Some methods have, however, shown early promise.

Family-focused therapy (FFT), which emphasizes psychoeducation, communication enhancement, and problem-solving skills, has been shown to prolong time to relapse in randomized clinical trials of adults. One small open trial of FFT in bipolar adolescents, who were also receiving mood-stabilizing medications, demonstrated improvements in subjects' symptoms of depression, mania, and general behavior problems over 1 year (Miklowitz et al., 2004). In a follow-up to this study, the only randomized controlled psychotherapeutic trial in youths with bipolar disorder, teens treated with mood stabilizers were randomly assigned to 21 sessions of FFT or 3 sessions of "enhanced care," a relapse prevention, treatment adherence, and psychoeducation program. Here again, those in FFT had more rapid recovery from depression, shorter episodes of depression, and lower scores on depression ratings for 2 years (Miklowitz et al., 2008).

Feeny, Danielson, Schwartz, Youngstrom, and Findling (2006) have reported the successful development of a manualized cognitive behavior therapy (CBT) for adolescents with bipolar disorder receiving adjunctive psychopharmacological treatment. In their small preliminary study, those receiving CBT demonstrated more symptom improvement than those teens in the matched group who did not receive any psychosocial treatment. (For a complete review of CBT, see Chapters 9 and 10.)

Multifamily psychoeducation groups have been explored for children ages 8 to 11 as an adjunctive therapy (Fristad, Goldberg-Arnold, & Gavazzi, 2003). Compared to those with treatment as usual, families in the psychoeducation groups reported greater knowledge about their child's mood symptoms, more positive family interactions, greater parental support as perceived by children, and increased utilization of appropriate services by the families. In contrast to expectations, no impact was found on decreasing negative family interactions. Nonetheless, this study does point to the vital need for psychoeducation for all family members.

Pavuluri, Graczyk, et al. (2004) designed a child- and family-focused CBT intended to be used along with adjunctive medication treatment. This treatment incorporates both CBT and family-focused therapy. After 12 sessions, participants engaged in the therapy, which focuses on the specific problems that bipolar children face and the role of environmental stressors, demonstrated improvements in mood symptoms, psychosocial functioning, and medication adherence.

Finally, Goldstein, Axelson, Birmaher, and Brent (2007) developed a modified dialectical behavior therapy (DBT) for adolescents with bipolar disorder. This small, open trial consisted of a 1-year intervention focused on family skills training and individual therapy as an adjunct to medication treatment. The treatment was well accepted by participants who demonstrated decreases in suicidal ideation, nonsuicidal self-injurious behavior, depressive symptoms, and emotional dysregulation. Particularly given the high comorbidity of bipolar disorder with conduct disorder among teens and personality disorders among adults (Fan & Hassell, 2008), this study should pave the way for further investigations of DBT. (For a review of DBT, see Chapter 10.)

Psychopharmacological Treatment of Bipolar Disorder

Medications have proven themselves remarkably helpful in the treatment of bipolar disorder. Though we have much more data on effective treatments for adults, emerging data suggests parallel findings for the same medications among children and adolescents. The sine qua non of bipolar treatment is the mood stabilizer, which is often augmented with an antipsychotic and/or antidepressant. Lithium and divalproex sodium (Depakote) are the two mood stabilizers approved by the Food and Drug Administration (FDA) for the treatment of acute mania in adults, and aripiprazole (Abilify), olanzapine (Zyprexa), risperidone (Risperdal), quetiapine (Seroquel), ziprasidone (Geodon), and chlorpromazine (Thorazine) are all FDA-approved antipsychotics for the same indication. Both lamotrigine (Lamictal) and olanzapine are approved for maintenance therapy of adult bipolar disorder, and the combination of olanzapine and fluoxetine (Symbyax) and quetiapine extended release (Seroquel XR) are approved for the treatment of adult bipolar depression.

A mood stabilizer is essentially any psychiatric medication that is used to treat bipolar disorder. We think of mood stabilizers as something akin to Dolby Sound—these medications take out some of the extreme highs and extreme lows in one's mood. The mood stabilizers consist of lithium carbonate, various anticonvulsants, and a number of antipsychotics. Most mood stabilizers are pure antimanic agents, but both lithium and lamotrigine (Lamictal) have notable antidepressant effects often employed in the treatment of bipolar depression (Patel et al., 2006). Beyond bipolar disorder, mood stabilizers are sometimes used as augmenting medications for aggression, irritability, anxiety, borderline personality, depression, conduct disorder, and ADHD.

Lithium Carbonate

Lithium carbonate, available under many trade names, is the "classic" and first mood stabilizer described. Lithium is highly effective for the treatment of mania associated with bipolar disorder, for bipolar depression, and as an augmenting medication for treatment-resistant MDD. Lithium has a narrow therapeutic index, meaning that its therapeutic dose is not far afield from its toxic dose. Consequently, lithium should only be prescribed by an experienced practitioner, who follows blood levels and other lab values regularly.

Prescreening for lithium treatment includes an electrocardiogram to rule out sick sinus syndrome, along with a complete blood count, thyroid panel, kidney panel, and electrolytes. Lab values should be followed every 3 to 6 months and after every dosage adjustment. Therapeutic blood levels of lithium in children and adolescents are generally the same as those for adults. Excessive fluid loss, as by strenuous exercise, diarrhea, or vomiting, can result in a rapid increase in blood lithium to potentially toxic levels. Thus, the medication must be carefully monitored over time. Side effects can include tremor, sedation, weight gain, various gastrointestinal effects, acne, white blood cell count elevation, and thyroid and kidney damage.

Lithium is presumed to work by blocking the synthesis of inositol from glucose and the recycling of inositol phosphates, thereby inhibiting the neurons from creating the second messengers, diacylglycerol and inositol triphosphate. This mechanism dampens the ability of a rapidly firing neuron (e.g., an overactive or "manic" neuron) to respond to further stimulation.

Dozens of studies have established the efficacy of lithium for the treatment of adult bipolar disorder (Fountoulakis & Vieta, 2008). Far fewer studies have been completed in bipolar youth, and most of these have been case series and open-label studies (Delong & Nieman, 1983; Strober, Morrell, Lampert, & Burroughs, 1990; Varanka, Weller, Weller, & Fristad, 1988) along with a few small and short-term double-blind efforts (Geller, Cooper, et al., 1998; Kafantaris et al., 2004). Given the benefits of lithium in randomized, double-blind, placebo-controlled studies of adults with bipolar disorder and the benefits suggested for youth in the aforementioned trials, lithium has been approved by the FDA for the treatment of adolescent bipolar disorder down to age 13. In addition, guidelines published by the American Academy of Child and Adolescent Psychiatry recommend lithium for the treatment of manic or mixed-episode pediatric bipolar disorder (Kowatch et al., 2005). Given the promise of lithium for bipolar youth but the many uncertainties regarding it use, including dosage, monitoring, short- and long-term efficacy, safety, and pharmacokinetics, large multisite studies are currently ongoing (Findling et al., 2008).

Antipsychotics

In addition to lithium, the FDA has approved two antipsychotics, aripiprazole (Abilify) and risperidone (Risperdal), for the treatment of pediatric bipolar disorder down to age 10. Both medications have demonstrated efficacy in treating manic and mixed-episode symptoms in children and adolescents suffering from bipolar disorder in multisite, randomized controlled trials. Risperidone (Risperdal) separated from placebo by week one in a 3-week study of over 150 children within two dosage ranges, 0.5–2.5 mg and 3–6 mg per day (Pandina et al., 2007). Of note, those taking the higher dose did no better than those within the lower dosage range, although they did experience more side effects. Aripiprazole separated from placebo by the end point in a 4-week study of nearly 300 children also at two different dosages, 10 and 30 mg per day (Chang et al., 2007). A 30-week extension of this study found continued efficacy (Wagner et al., 2007). Though not FDA approved, quetiapine (Seroquel) has also recently been studied in acute mania versus placebo at dosages of 400 and 600 mg per day in a study of nearly 300 subjects. Results show separation of drug from placebo by day four for the higher dose with maintained efficacy throughout the length of the 3-week study (DelBello, Findling, Earley, Stankowski, & Acevedo, 2007). Olanzapine has also been found efficacious, at dosages of 2.5–20 mg per day, in a 3-week blinded, placebo-controlled study of just over 100 bipolar teens for the treatment of acute mania and mixed episodes (Tohen et al., 2007). Finally, 150 children with bipolar disorder were treated with ziprasidone, which also showed significant improvement over placebo (DelBello, Findling, Wang, Gundapaneni, & Versael, 2008).

Other antipsychotic medications are frequently employed for mood stabilization as well and may also be efficacious. Consequently, there is now considerable evidence that numerous atypical antipsychotic medications are effective at suppressing acute manic and mixed episodes of pediatric bipolar disorder. With the exception of the aripiprazole extension study, however, these medications have not been studied in long-term trials for both efficacy and safety. Practitioners prescribing antipsychotic medications to children and adolescents should always start with modest doses and proceed cautiously because of the potential for significant side effects (see Chapter 12 for a complete discussion of antipsychotic medications).

Anticonvulsants

Anticonvulsants have also proven useful for the treatment of bipolar disorder in adults, where they are presumed to function via cellular membrane stabilization. Most frequently used for rapid-cycling bipolar disorder, divalproex sodium (Depakote) and to a lesser extent carbamazepine (Tegretol) have strong supporting data in adults and are used routinely, but as expected, studies in children and adolescents are few in number. Open-label trials, case reports, and retrospective chart reviews have found divalproex sodium and carbemazepine to be effective for acute manic and mixed episodes in children and adolescents (Davanzo et al., 2003; McClellan, Kowatch, & Findling, 2007; Papatheodorou, Kutcher, Katic, & Szalai, 1995; Wagner et al., 2002). There is also some support for lamotrigine in the treatment of adolescent bipolar depression (Carandang, Robbins, Mullany, Yazbek, & Minot, 2007; Chang, Saxena, & Howe, 2006).

Few comparison studies between medications have been completed. One open-label comparison among lithium, divalproex sodium, and carbamazepine found no statistically significant difference between the three after 8 weeks in 42 youth with BP-I or BP-II in a manic or mixed episode. The effect sizes were more robust than the response rates—for divalproex sodium, the response rate was 53% (effect size of 1.63); the response rate to lithium was 38% (effect size of 1.06); and the response rate to carbamazepine was 38% (effect size 1.00) (Kowatch et al., 2000). Another study comparing lithium and divalproex sodium for maintenance treatment in a double-blind fashion for up to 18 months found no differences in survival time until relapse or until patients discontinued their medications for any reason (Findling et al., 2005). A recent, as yet unpublished, double-blind study compared lithium, divalproex sodium, and placebo in over 150 subjects for 8 weeks and found that only divalproex sodium separated from placebo (Kowatch, Findling, Scheffer, & Stanford, 2007). Finally, one randomized, double-blind, placebo-controlled trial of oxcarbazepine (Trileptal) for manic or mixed episodes of over 100 children and adolescents found no benefit for active medication at an average dose of 1,500 mg per day for 7 weeks (Wagner et al., 2006).

Combined treatment with both an antipsychotic and a mood stabilizer is a common strategy for both adults and youth with bipolar disorder who are in a manic or mixed episode, but scant data is available to guide this practice in youth. One 12-month open-label trial of risperidone augmentation in lithium nonresponders with preschool onset bipolar disorder found that 86% of the 21 subjects demonstrated a greater than 50% improvement from baseline. Predictors of inadequate response to lithium monotherapy included ADHD, severity at baseline, history of sexual or physical abuse, and young or preschool age (Pavuluri, Henry, Carbray, et al., 2006). Another study looked at augmenting both divalproex sodium and lithium with risperidone (Risperdal). Both augmented treatments were highly effective with very large effect sizes and response rates in excess of 80% (Pavuluri, Henry, et al., 2004).

Selecting between an antipsychotic or alternate mood stabilizer for the acute treatment of a manic or mixed episode is not always an easy task. One randomized, double-blind study of 50 hospitalized adolescents with BP-I in a manic or mixed episode compared quetiapine at dosages of 400–600 mg per day with divalproex sodium at therapeutic serum levels of 80–120 mcg per milliliter for 28 days. Both groups showed statistically significant improvements in functioning, although quetiapine may have acted more rapidly (DelBello et al., 2006). This study notwithstanding, it is reasonable to begin treatment of a manic or mixed episode of BP-I or BP-II with an antipsychotic, particularly if psychosis is present. Although some data support lithium and anticonvulsants for this practice, the preponderance of current studies supporting the use of antipsychotics strongly suggests that treatment should start here. Augmentation with a second mood stabilizer is also entirely reasonable, especially for a severe episode. Once the manic episode is stabilized, the patient may be transitioned over to lithium or an anticonvulsant, either alone or in combination with an antipsychotic. An antidepressant may be added later if the mood subsequently becomes depressed.

Medication Monitoring

The use of mood stabilizers requires significant safety precautions and monitoring. Prior to treatment with lithium, thyroid function, kidney function, electrolytes including calcium, and a complete blood count including white cells should be ordered. In addition, the patient should undergo a 12-lead electrocardiogram (ECG) to rule out sick sinus syndrome or any sinus node abnormalities that would contradict treatment with lithium. The practitioner should also be aware that lithium can induce benign T-wave flattening in the ECG over time. As lithium can impact both the thyroid and parathyroid glands, it may alter the set point at which the gland responds to the presence of calcium by an internal feedback mechanism. Thus, treatment with lithium raises the risk of increasing calcium beyond safe levels and must be monitored. During treatment with lithium, the use of nonsteroidal anti-inflammatory medications, such as aspirin and ibuprofen, should be discontinued or severely limited, given the propensity for these medications to elevate the blood level of lithium. There are numerous other medications that are contraindicated with lithium treatment, and these must be reviewed carefully with the patient. Thyroid function and calcium should be rechecked at 2 and 6 months after initiating treatment and annually thereafter. Lithium should be discontinued if calcium levels surpass 11.5 mg per deciliter. Renal function should be monitored every 6 months, and the complete blood count should be checked annually. Lithium levels should be followed at 6-month intervals and before and after any dosage adjustments. ECGs should be followed annually.

Prior to treatment with an anticonvulsant, a complete blood count, including platelets and white cells, electrolytes and a chemistry panel including fasting glucose and lipids, liver function, amylase, lipase, and thyroid tests should be performed. For divalproex sodium, a menstrual history is necessary, along with a pregnancy test in any female of reproductive age, given the risk of birth defects to a developing fetus. Sexually active females taking anticonvulsants should be advised to use two forms of contraception, such as condoms along with oral contraception, an intrauterine device, or a diaphragm. During treatment, divalproex sodium and carbamazepine levels should be checked every 6 to 12 months and before and after any dosage adjustments. Other laboratory values as noted above should be followed annually. Given concerns about the possibility of a relationship between divalproex sodium and the development of polycystic ovary syndrome (PCOS), practitioners should regularly monitor for irregular menses, hirsutism, and acne and refer to an endocrinologist should any concern arise. Lamotrigine is generally well tolerated, but a small number of individuals will suffer dermatitis and in rare cases Stevens-Johnson syndrome, which can be fatal. The practitioner should review carefully all additional medications the patient is taking and pay particular attention to potential drug-drug interactions. For safety precautions and monitoring of atypical antipsychotics, see Chapter 12.

Given the frequent comorbidity of ADHD with bipolar disorder among children and adolescents, it is reasonable to wonder about the possibility of inducing mania or mood instability by giving stimulant treatment to a bipolar child. However, as numerous studies have shown, bipolar children and adolescents with ADHD generally respond favorably to stimulants and are not likely to be pushed into a manic episode (Carlson, Loney, Salisbury, Kramer, & Arthur, 2000; Craney & Geller, 2003; Galanter et al., 2003; Geller, Zimmerman, Williams, DelBello, Bolhofner, et al., 2002). The clinician is advised, however, to treat comorbid ADHD only in children and adolescents who are already receiving adequate mood-stabilizing treatment.

In conclusion, when evaluating children and adolescents for bipolar disorder, we must remember to apply *DSM-IV* criteria in a developmentally sensitive manner. Irritability is a core feature of the illness, but in and of itself is not sufficient to warrant a diagnosis. The high comorbidity with ADHD, anxiety, oppositional defiant disorder, and conduct disorder must be appreciated and treated as necessary. A number of psychotherapies show promising data, and at least lithium, aripiprazole, and risperidone have adequate evidence to support their use. Most important, the child and family must be educated about the mood disorder, and a close working relationship must be established between the clinician and family.

12

Schizophrenia and Psychosis

Psychosis is not a distinct disorder, but rather a symptom found among many disorders, both psychiatric and medical. The core symptoms of *schizophrenia* and *schizoaffective disorder* are psychotic in nature, in contrast to bipolar disorder, major depressive disorder, posttraumatic stress, and other anxiety disorders, where psychotic symptoms sometimes occur. Even though schizophrenia and schizoaffective disorder are the primary psychotic illnesses, mood and anxiety disorders are, in fact, the most common causes of psychotic symptoms in children and adolescents. Psychosis can also occur in the context of drug and alcohol abuse, seizure disorders, metabolic illnesses, central nervous system tumors and infections, and delirium.

The second edition of the *Diagnostic and Statistical Manual of Mental Disorders* of the American Psychiatric Association (*DSM-II*) grouped all psychoses in childhood under the rubric of childhood schizophrenia, thus obscuring both our understanding of schizophrenia and psychosis itself. At that time psychosis was a highly inclusive term that included any mental disorder that grossly interfered with one's ability to meet life's typical demands; psychosis was also meant to indicate a loss of ego boundaries or profound difficulties with reality testing (American Psychiatric Association, 1968). As a result, much of the early work on childhood schizophrenia was muddied by overlap with autism and other disorders that are sometimes characterized by these broadly defined psychotic symptoms. It was not until publication of the *DSM-III* in 1980 that the criteria used to diagnose adult schizophrenia were applied to child and adolescent schizophrenia. Psychosis is now viewed as a constellation of symptoms that include both the so-called positive symptoms (e.g., hallucinations, delusions, disorganized speech, and grossly disorganized or catatonic be-havior) and the negative symptoms (e.g., affective blunting, poverty of thought and speech or alogia, and difficulty initiating goal-directed be-havior or avolition).

The impact of psychosis on children and adolescents is profound, but thankfully such symptoms are relatively rare. In order to help those affected children, the clinician must be able to distinguish developmen-tally normal from psychotic behavior and cognition. At the same time, one must be sensitive to the frequently subtle nuances in mood, cogni-tion, and behavior that indicate psychosis. Furthermore, the practitioner must be knowledgeable about antipsychotic medications as they are now commonly used for a variety of child and adolescent mental disorders, psychotic and nonpsychotic alike.

CLINICAL PRESENTATION

In order to understand psychosis in a child or adolescent, it is first neces-sary to understand what is developmentally "normal." As already stated, most children and adolescents who experience psychotic symptoms are not schizophrenic. Transient hallucinations are sometimes seen in pre-school children, visual and tactile being the most common, and are prog-nostically benign. These symptoms are generally exacerbated by stress or anxiety. Hypnogogic hallucinations (e.g., false perceptions experienced while falling off to sleep) or hypnopomic hallucinations (e.g., false per-ceptions upon awakening) are normal and occur in both children and adults. Loosening of associations and illogical thinking decrease consider-ably after about age 6 or 7 years in children but are common and expected before that time (Volkmar, 1996a).

Psychotic thought content among children tends to reflect their de-velopmental stage and concerns. For example, a grade-school child may experience hallucinations relating to monsters or toys, while an adoles-cent may experience command auditory hallucinations that tell him to harm himself, reflecting the increased cognitive capacity of his age. The onset of schizophrenia is usually insidious, and in addition to hallucina-tions and delusions, the attendant signs of psychosis may include bizarre or unusual thinking and behavior, moodiness, paranoia, poor peer rela-tions and social withdrawal, and decline in personal hygiene. Auditory hallucinations are common in childhood schizophrenia, but delusions are less frequent, affecting only about half of diagnosed children. Other psy-chotic symptoms may be congruent with the cause of the primary illness. For example, a child suffering from bipolar disorder is more likely to experience psychosis in the context of his mood, such that during a manic episode he may exhibit extreme grandiosity and during a depressive episode, suicidal ideation and paranoia.

During the premorbid phase of schizophrenia, there may be nonspecific concerns until school age. By this time, impairments in attention and behavior, along with behavioral problems and developmental delays in language and motor skills, may be noted. Interpersonal relations and problem-solving skills may begin to suffer, and lower IQ, solitary play, and excessive anxiety may be observed. During the prodromal phase, just prior to the onset of illness, psychosis will gradually develop. The best predictor of outcome in childhood-onset schizophrenia is premorbid functioning (Schaeffer & Ross, 2002).

Schizophrenia and schizoaffective disorder are extremely rare in preteens. There may be at least two clinical phenotypes or presentations of schizophrenia, one characterized by long-standing neurobehavioral difficulties of early onset and the other that occurs in a previously "normal" person. Age at diagnosis distinguishes very early onset schizophrenia (VEOS), prior to age 13, from early-onset schizophrenia (EOS), between 13 and 18 years. Those children at increased risk of VEOS may show abnormalities of gait, posture, and muscle tone, the so-called neurological soft signs. Hallucinations, disordered thinking, and a flattened or blunted affect are other common features and are generally more easily detected. Children with VEOS tend to show characteristic communication deficits, including loose associations, illogical thinking, and impaired discourse skills. They may also be unaware that they are experiencing psychotic phenomena and soon disengage socially or are ostracized by peers, particularly if they share their thoughts with others. Among children with VEOS, it is commonly the behavior of the child that is more telling of the psychotic disorder than any overtly delusional thinking. For example, these children may regularly start fights with much larger kids, or consistently confuse television and dreams with reality. Such repeated displays of reckless judgment and bizarre behavior may be more indicative of a psychotic thought disorder than anything a young child actually reports. EOS, by contrast, tends to mirror much more closely the late teen and adult presentations of schizophrenia with which most clinicians are much more familiar.

ETIOLOGY

Numerous theories and associations have been suggested as possible etiological factors in the development of schizophrenia. A history of obstetrical complications at birth, for example, appears to be more common among schizophrenics (Preti et al., 2000). It remains unclear, however, which birth events and which factors, genetic or otherwise, account for these findings. There are mixed reports of increased frequency of schizophrenia among offspring of mothers who were pregnant during influenza epidemics, received poor nutrition, experienced high prenatal stress, or suffered intrapartum maternal infections (Brown et al., 2004; Clarke, Harley, & Cannon, 2006; Susser & Lin, 1992). Other associated risk factors include advanced paternal age (Brown et al., 2002) and birth in late winter (Messias & Kirkpatrick, 2001). While each is compelling in its own way, none of these findings has adequately clarified the etiology of schizophrenia.

A number of neurobiological findings in the brains of schizophrenics further clarify some aspects of the illness. The best recognized and replicated neurological finding is increased size of the cerebral ventricles and overall decreased brain volume, which were first observed in the 1800s (Brown et al., 1986; Hecker, 1871). One review found that lateral ventricular enlargement, third ventricular enlargement, and cortical changes occur in 67–83% of subjects across numerous studies (Shelton & Weinberger, 1986). Studies of first-break schizophrenia among twins suggest that these findings are not due to medication treatment or hospitalization (Cardno et al., 1999; Nybäck, Wiesel, Berggren, & Hindmarsh, 1982; Reveley, Reveley, Clifford, & Murray, 1982). Magnetic resonance imaging (MRI) studies have also now validated these findings (McDonald et al., 2006). Some investigators have reported clinical correlations between larger ventricles among schizophrenics and poor premorbid adjustment, cognitive impairment, increased severity of negative symptoms, poor response to antipsychotics, and more frequent movement disorders, although these reports are disputed by others (Cleghorn, Zipursky, & List, 1991).

MRI brain scans of adolescent schizophrenics reveal the same neurological changes observed in adults. Abnormally enlarged ventricles are seen as early as 9 years of age (Sowell et al., 2000). As the ventricles increase in size, these children lose about four to five times as much cortical gray matter as do normal teens. The gray matter loss progressively engulfs the brain from back to front, beginning in parietal structures involved in visuospatial and associative thinking and eventually moving forward to the temporal and dorsolateral prefrontal cortices involved in sensorimotor and visual function. The loss of tissue in these areas corresponds directly to clinical impairments, mirroring the neuromotor, auditory, visual search, and executive functioning (e.g., organization, planning, and attention) deficits found in schizophrenics. This research has controlled for the effects of antipsychotic medication, IQ, and gender, and the findings hold. While healthy teens lose an average of 1% of cortical gray matter per year, these schizophrenic teens lost 5% per year, with the greatest loss occurring among individuals with the most severe symptoms. By age 18, these teens had lost up to 25% of their gray matter in certain brain regions (Thompson et al., 2001).

A number of additional, sometimes contradictory, neuroanatomical findings have been made by studying brains of schizophrenics. Reduced cell size and total neurons, along with altered volume, have been reported in the basal ganglia. Abnormalities of the medial temporal lobe have also been reported and are not surprising, given the deficits in memory on neuropsychological testing commonly evidenced among schizophrenics. In addition, reduced amygdala, hippocampal, and parahippocampal volume has been widely noted. Finally, reduced prefrontal activity, thalamic abnormalities, and a reduction in the size of the cerebellar vermis have also been reported (Knable, Kleinman, & Weinberger, 1998).

The structural abnormalities in the brains of schizophrenics are suspected to have their foundation in fetal development, because of the noted lack of gliosis. Gliosis is a normal inflammatory response to cell damage that begins to take place by the third trimester of pregnancy. Neuronal damage after this time results in a classic pattern of observable inflammation. The fact that gliosis is not found in postmortem studies of schizophrenic brains suggests that any neuroanatomical damage occurs during the first and second trimesters (Fruntes & Limosin, 2008).

In addition to neuroanatomical data, there are a number of neurochemical findings in schizophrenia suggestive of etiology. Decreased metabolism in the prefrontal cortex, particularly during cognitive tasks, has been noted by many researchers, suggesting a "hypofrontality" in schizophrenia (Ben-Shachar et al., 2007). Additionally, the neurotransmitters dopamine, glutamate, serotonin, norepinephrine, and gamma-aminobutyric acid (GABA) have all been implicated for different reasons. Dopamine and norepinephrine agonists, such as cocaine and amphetamine, can potentiate or even induce psychosis. The same is true for the glutamate receptor, N-methyl D-aspartate (NMDA), antagonists, phencyclidine (PCP), and ketamine. The so-called dopamine hypothesis of schizophrenia has been particularly attractive for the past 40 years, given the fact that dozens of studies have identified elevated levels of dopamine D2 receptors in the caudate nucleus, putamen, and nucleus accumbens of schizophrenic brains and the fact that virtually all effective antipsychotic medications antagonize dopamine in some fashion (Knable et al., 1998). However, we now realize that while dopamine is a key player in schizophrenia, the dopamine hypothesis is an oversimplification.

Decreased prefrontal brain activity has been consistently found in schizophrenic patients as compared to normal controls, in addition to associated deficits in cognitive performance (Andreason et al., 1992). Auditory and visual working memory, attention, and eye-tracking are the most typical impairments seen among schizophrenics, but emotional perception, verbal abilities, perceptual-motor speed, and visuospatial skills have also been found to be impaired in schizophrenic children and their otherwise well siblings (Davalos et al., 2003; Niendam, 2003). Related alterations in glucose metabolism and irregular autonomic nervous system arousal, as noted in adult schizophrenics, have also been found in children with schizophrenia (Jacobsen et al., 1997; Zahn et al., 1997).

The baseline population rate of schizophrenia is about 1% in adulthood. Family studies of schizophrenia, however, have generally reported about a 50% concordance rate for monozygotic (identical) twins and a 15% concordance for dizygotic (nonidentical) twins (Cardno et al., 1999). Additionally, the risk for a first-degree relative of an affected individual is about 10 times that of the general population (American Psychiatric Association, 2000). The rate of schizophrenia among parents of an affected child is about 10%, also considerably greater than the population base rate (Volkmar, 1996b). These findings indicate that schizophrenia is highly genetically bound but also highly susceptible to environmental influences, such as drug abuse, head injury, birth complications, paternal age at conception, and stressful life events (Sagud et al., 2008). Heritability estimates vary greatly but suggest that over 80% of the risk of becoming schizophrenic may be due to genetics (Cardno & Gottesman, 2000). Regardless of risk, we now recognize that schizophrenia is a polygenetic disorder and is not inherited in simple Mendelian fashion.

EPIDEMIOLOGY

Fewer than 1 in 10,000 children will develop schizophrenia. The rate then steadily increases during adolescence until hitting a peak incidence of 1% among adults. About 4% of all cases present prior to age 15. The average age of onset is 18–25 years for men and 23–35 years for women (Gorwood, Leboyer, Jay, Payan, & Feingold, 1995). A second but much smaller peak in incidence after 40 years of age, considered late-onset schizophrenia, occurs among females, accounting for as many as 10% of all female cases. Affected females tend to experience more affective symptoms, paranoid delusions, and hallucinations, in contrast to men who experience more negative symptoms. Women generally have a better prognosis than men, based upon length of hospital stay and rehospitalizations (American

Psychiatric Association, 2000). Males are more commonly diagnosed in childhood and throughout the teen years, but by mid-adulthood the gender ratio equalizes. Although men and women are believed to be equally affected by schizophrenia, a diagnostic bias may result in more psychotic females being diagnosed with a mood disorder and more psychotic males with schizophrenia (Beauchamp & Gagnon, 2004).

Risk factors for the later development of psychosis have been suggested. Cannon et al. (2008) followed nearly 300 teens deemed to be at high risk of psychosis based on experiencing prodromal symptoms in one or more of the following five categories in the 12 months prior to study entry: (a) unusual thought content, (b) suspicion/paranoia, (c) perceptual anomalies, (d) grandiosity, and (e) disorganized communication. At the end of 30 months of observation, the team identified five factors assessed at baseline that contributed to the prediction of psychosis: (a) a genetic risk for schizophrenia with recent deterioration in functioning; (b) higher levels of unusual thought content; (c) higher levels of suspicion/paranoia; (d) greater social impairment; and (e) a history of substance abuse. Algorithms combining two or three of these factors were 68–80% predictive of psychosis as compared to the prodromal risk criteria alone. This multisite North American study represents the largest prodromal population followed to date worldwide and suggests strongly that clinicians should be assessing these predictive risk factors.

CLINICAL COURSE

Early-onset schizophrenia more commonly occurs among males with poor premorbid adjustment, lower academic achievement, and significant negative psychotic symptoms. These individuals also display more signs of neuroanatomical abnormalities and cognitive impairment and suffer a worse outcome. By contrast, those with later-onset illness are more commonly female, have fewer signs of neuroanatomical abnormalities and cognitive impairment, and have a better outcome (American Psychiatric Association, 2000). A number of additional prognostic indicators for schizophrenia have been identified, as seen in Table 12.1.

Schizophrenia is virtually always a chronic illness with variable periods of exacerbation and remission. Over time the illness may stabilize but is unlikely to ever fully remit. Most clinicians concur that EOS, particularly VEOS, has a poor prognosis. The longitudinal course of the illness, as classically described by Bleuler, is believed to follow a cyclic pattern of acute psychosis, followed by longer periods of recuperation, and then remission. Bleuler described increasing deterioration with each cycle,

Table 12.1. Prognostic Indicators for Schizophrenia

Good	Bad
Acute onset	Insidious onset
Short duration of illness	Long duration of illness
Lack of prior psychiatric history	Psychiatric history
Presence of affective symptoms, confusion,	Poor insight
or mood symptoms	Obsessive-compulsive symptoms
Good premorbid adjustment	History of violence
Steady work history	Poor insight
Marriage	Premorbid personality disorder
Older age at onset	Poor work history
Female	Celibacy
	Young age at onset
	Family history of schizophrenia

leading to an eventual burnout around 10 years into the active phase of the illness, leaving individuals with various degrees of disability and pre-dominately negative residual symptoms (Bleuler, 1978). Affected individuals may occasionally find satisfying work and relationships but virtually always require extensive assistance. Most schizophrenics live with their families of origin as long as possible or in assisted group homes. Perhaps a smaller number will progressively deteriorate, becoming increasingly disabled and necessitating long-term inpatient treatment and institutional support. A high level of "expressed emotion" within the family of origin, a measure of hostility, emotional overinvolvement, and criticism, is known to be damaging for affected individuals (Goldstein, 1989).

Up to 75% of schizophrenics may develop the neurological soft signs previously mentioned either early in the course of the illness or over time. These include abnormalities in stereognosis, the ability to perceive the form of an object with only the sense of touch; graphesthesia, the ability to recognize writing on the skin purely by the sense of touch; balance; ocular abilities, such as eye-tracking; and proprioception, a sense of the relative positioning of various parts of the body, most commonly measured by closing one's eyes and bringing the index finger to the nose or following and tapping another's finger in the visual plane. Some studies also report a reduction in Stage 4 sleep in schizophrenics, and a lack of interest in sex is common.

DIAGNOSIS

Emile Kraepelin, a German psychiatrist, first named *dementia praecox* (early dementia) in 1887, distinguishing it from manic depression (now bipolar disorder). Paul Eugen Bleuler, a Swiss psychiatrist, renamed dementia praecox, given his observation that it was not a dementia and did not exclusively affect the young. He coined the term *schizophrenia* (from the Greek, meaning literally "to split the mind") in 1912 to emphasize the cognitive impairments, which he conceptualized as a "splitting" of the psychic processes. Bleuler believed that the characteristic symptoms could be described by what he labeled as the 4 As of schizophrenia: (a) affective blunting; (b) loosening of associations (speech characterized by shifting between topics that are only minimally related to one another, a feature indicative of cognitive disorganization); (c) autism, another term he invented to describe the self-centered nature of these individuals (see Chapter 7); and (d) ambivalence or indecisiveness. Bleuler clearly believed that the negative symptoms of schizophrenia, the 4 As, were the true defining features of the illness and regarded positive symptoms of schizophrenia, such as delusions and hallucinations, as accessory because they occurred in other disorders, such as bipolar disorder and psychotic depression (Bleuler, 1978).

Kurt Schneider, another German psychiatrist, followed upon the heels of Kraepelin and Bleuler and was also interested in differentiating schizophrenia from other psychotic illnesses. Unlike Bleuler, however, he felt that it was the unique positive symptoms of psychosis—or first-rank symptoms, as they came to be known—that were the true hallmark of schizophrenia. Schneider felt that all first-rank symptoms involved ego boundaries and did not regularly occur in patients with mood disorders. The symptoms he described included hearing one's own thoughts, hearing voices arguing in one's head, hearing voices commenting on one's behavior, and believing that an external force is acting upon one's body. Other first-rank symptoms include "thought withdrawal," or the idea that thoughts can be taken out of one's head; "thought insertion," or the idea that others' thoughts can be placed inside of one's head; "thought broadcasting," or the idea that one's thoughts can be broadcast out loud for others to hear; and ideas of reference, the idea that unrelated phenomena refer directly to the affected individual (e.g., believing that radio broadcasts, media articles, and television programs are produced especially for or about them) (Schneider, 1959). Although Schneider's work was influential in its time and had the effect of placing the diagnostic focus of schizophrenia on the positive symptoms, mental health practitioners today incorporate both positive and negative symptoms into the diagnostic understanding of schizophrenia.

The *DSM-IV* requires at least two of the following symptoms in order to meet criteria for a diagnosis of schizophrenia: (a) delusions (false beliefs); (b) hallucinations (false sensations); (c) disorganized speech, sounding confused and disjointed; (d) grossly disorganized or catatonic behavior; and (e) negative symptoms, such as affective blunting, poverty of thought and speech (alogia), or difficulty initiating goal-directed behavior (avolition). The *DSM-IV* also requires that the illness be functionally impairing and extend for at least 6 months before a diagnosis is given (American Psychiatric Association, 2000).

Five subtypes of schizophrenia are described. The most common is the *chronic paranoid type*, affecting about 85% of those with schizophrenia. Chronic paranoid schizophrenics suffer troublesome paranoid delusions and auditory hallucinations, while maintaining relatively intact cognitive function and affect. *Disorganized type schizophrenia* is characterized by disorganized speech, behavior, and an affect that is flat or inappropriate to the situation. *Catatonic type schizophrenia* is characterized by psychological and motor impairments affecting movement and speech. Affected individuals may be immobile or cataplectic and may exhibit odd movements and posturing, excessive and purposeless motor activity, extreme negativism or mutism, and echolalia and echopraxia. Those individuals who suffer at least one episode of schizophrenia but who subsequently only suffer negative symptoms or negative symptoms with only mild and minimally impairing positive symptoms are described as having *residual type schizophrenia*. Finally, those affected individuals whose schizophrenia is not better characterized by paranoid, disorganized, or catatonic types are considered to be of the *undifferentiated type* (American Psychiatric Association, 2000).

Upon presentation, children with psychotic symptoms should receive a full medical and neurological evaluation. Any evidence of neurological impairment should be followed with specific testing, including an electroencephalogram and neuroimaging studies. Delirium, seizure disorders, central nervous system lesions (e.g., tumors, malformations, and head trauma), neurodegenerative disorders (e.g., Huntington's chorea), metabolic disorders (e.g., Wilson's disease), infectious diseases (e.g., encephalitis, HIV, meningitis), and toxic encephalopathies (e.g., substances of abuse, industrial chemicals, toxins) should be ruled out as potential causes. Rates of comorbid substance abuse among adolescents presenting with psychotic symptoms are as high as 50% in some studies. In fact, first-break psychotic episodes commonly occur in the context of substance abuse, which may exacerbate or trigger the psychosis, even if it is not the primary etiological factor (McClellan & Werry, 1997).

The differential diagnosis of schizophrenia includes a broad range of disorders. Schizoaffective disorder, bipolar disorder, and major depressive disorder can all present with psychosis and must be considered. Following the patient longitudinally and obtaining collateral information is absolutely vital in establishing this differential, along with establishing a complete family history. Conduct and other disruptive behavior disorders can also present with psychotic-like symptoms, although these youths tend to have lower rates of delusions and thought disorder. Autism spectrum disorders are best differentiated by their early age at onset and transient psychotic symptoms, if present at all. Anxiety disorders, particularly obsessive-compulsive disorder (OCD), can be difficult to differentiate because schizophrenics themselves can also display significant obsessive-compulsive symptoms; however, most often those affected by OCD recognize their anxieties as unreasonable and excessive. Other anxiety disorders, such as posttraumatic stress disorder, can present with psychotic features, particularly among those children who have been physically and sexually abused. Here again, it is the history and longitudinal course that provides the greatest help in differentiating this disorder from a primary psychotic process. Various speech and language disorders, which can present with disordered speech, and personality disorders, which can present with paranoia and mildly psychotic behavior, must also be ruled out (McClellan & Werry, 1997).

Because young children are concrete in their cognition and cannot easily abstract, they may misunderstand direct questions about psychotic phenomena during an interview. As expected, questions regarding rare occurrences, such as psychosis, typically have the highest rates of false-positive responses in structured interviews. From a child's perspective, normal thought and memory processes may include hearing internal voices and experiencing odd or false beliefs. Consequently, assessing and understanding a child's symptoms are particularly difficult, and in many cases it is virtually impossible to obtain a reliable answer to a direct question about hallucinations or delusions. Obtaining collateral information about the child's behavior at home, at school, and with friends from parents, teachers, and other individuals in the child's life, therefore, is absolutely necessary. As previously noted, behavioral observations are often more useful than direct interview questions when assessing childhood psychosis. In addition, the clinician should interact more loosely with the child, playing if indicated, or discussing popular culture, friendships, hobbies, and interests. Such interactions can provide great insight into a child's psyche.

When asking children directly about psychotic phenomena, the questions should be couched in developmentally appropriate language. Asking questions about hallucinations and delusions successfully is tricky for even the most seasoned examiner. Some good examples of specific questions that clinicians might employ follow:

- *"Sometimes when it's quiet or when people are alone, they see or hear things that other people cannot see or hear. Has that ever happened to you? Will you tell me about it?"*

- *"Do you sometimes hear your own thoughts or hear yourself thinking? Lots of people say they do. But have you ever actually heard, like with your own ears, voices that other people could not hear? What did they say?"*
- *"Have you ever heard your name being called when no one else was around?"*
- *"Have you ever seen things that other people cannot see? What did you see?"*
- *"Do you know what imagination is? Can you tell me? Has your imagination ever played tricks on you? What was that like?"*
- *"Have you ever felt like anybody else knew just what you were thinking? Did it ever feel like they could take thoughts out of your head or put thoughts into your head?"*
- *"Does it ever feel like songs on the radio or shows on the TV are being put there just for you?"*
- *"Have you ever had thoughts that you were afraid to tell other people about, even your parents? Can you tell me about that?"*
- *"Do you sometimes believe things that nobody else seems to believe?"*
- *"Do you ever worry that someone is trying to hurt you? Do you ever feel like someone is following you around?"*
- *"Do you ever worry that people might be talking about you or saying bad things about you?"*
- *"What do you want to be when you're a grown-up? Do you ever think that you're destined to be a great or really special person?"*

Affirmative responses to these questions do not provide absolute confirmation of psychosis, but with some practice the clinician will get a sense of which responses are typical or "normal" and which are aberrant. Depending upon the child's age, self-report of psychotic symptoms can be fraught with confusion. The validity of self-report should be questioned when the details are inconsistent and when there is no documented evidence to support the assertion (e.g., no observed odd behavior) other than the child's statement. Self-report should also be questioned when the nature of the report is not typical of psychosis, such as highly detailed descriptions of delusions and hallucinations that are more suggestive of fantasy, imagination, or attention-seeking. Finally, self-report should be questioned when the symptoms only occur at specific times or are reinforced by current circumstances, such that, for example, one hears voices only when angry or after an argument or fight.

Neuropsychological testing can also sometimes be useful in evaluating psychosis. Schizophrenics tend to do poorly on most psychological tests but have particular difficulty with tests of frontal lobe function that assess problem solving, judgment, working memory, attention, concentration, and eye-tracking. Temporal lobe function is also typically impaired, as evidenced by the language and thought disorders identified by testing, and deficient long-term memory functioning, which is thought to be both medial temporal lobe and hippocampal in nature (Knable et al., 1998). Finally, as described in Chapter 4, projective tests are often useful for assessing hidden and unconscious thoughts and emotions.

TREATMENT

The interval between onset of psychosis and initiation of treatment varies greatly but generally averages 1 to 2 years. The duration of untreated psychosis depends upon a variety of factors. Those who are more severely affected and those with more social support tend to receive services sooner, but other factors influencing when people begin to receive treatment remain unknown (Ho & Andreason, 2001). Increasing evidence indicates that a delay in treatment exerts at least a modest negative influence upon clinical outcome and that earlier treatment leads to a better prognosis and treatment response (Addington, Van Mastrigt, & Addington, 2004; Marshall et al., 2005; Novak Sarotar, Pesek, Agius, & Kocmur, 2008). Among schizophrenics in one study, delays in treatment resulted in greater negative, positive, and general psychopathological symptoms, along with global functioning deficits, 15 years after the first psychiatric admission, even after other factors possibly related to long-term outcome were controlled for (Bottlender et al., 2003). Additionally, prolonged untreated psychosis commonly creates problems that go well beyond the psychosis itself, including both psychosocial and neurological difficulties.

Historically, the neurological deficits associated with psychosis were thought to be due to toxicity associated with the psychosis itself; however, more recently it has been suggested that those parts of the brain involved in the production of psychotic symptoms may become somewhat hypertrophic whereas other areas that are not utilized during these times of intense symptomatology become somewhat atrophic. The result of this combined overuse hypertrophy and disuse atrophy might be a net loss in brain interconnectivity, synaptic plasticity, and cognitive capacity (McGlashan, 2006). It is becoming increasingly clear, therefore, that clinicians should take great pains to identify and aggressively treat psychotic symptoms from the moment they are evident.

The Food and Drug Administration (FDA) has approved various antipsychotic medications for the treatment of schizophrenia, acute mania associated with bipolar disorder, irritability associated with autistic disorder, and Tourette's disorder in children and adolescents. The FDA has not validated the efficacy of these medications for the treatment of aggression, anxiety, attention-deficit/hyperactivity disorder (ADHD), personality disorders, oppositional defiant and conduct disorder, and major depressive disorder in children and adolescents, yet we often use them for these indications as well. Practitioners vary in their degree of comfort in prescribing antipsychotics for off-label purposes, either as primary or adjunctive medications, but many practitioners agree that the antipsychotics do have a place in the treatment of many conditions for which they do not have an FDA indication, as is shown by prescribing practices.

Antipsychotics have been increasingly prescribed for the treatment of a wide variety of conditions in children and adolescents over the past decade. The number of children prescribed antipsychotics increased five times between 1995 and 2002, to an estimated 2.5 million children per year by 2002; or from 8.6 per 1,000 children in 1995 to 39.4 per 1,000 in 2002. The rate of increase in the use of antipsychotics has also been greater among children in recent years than among adults. Antipsychotic use saw a 73% increase between 2001 and 2005 in those under 18 years of age, as opposed to a 13% increase among adults during this same time. Fifteen percent of all antipsychotics are now prescribed to those 18 years and younger, most often for disorders of mood and behavior (Cooper et al., 2006).

Risperidone (Risperdal) has been approved by the FDA for the treatment of irritability associated with autistic disorder in children, ages 5 to 16 years (McCracken et al., 2002; Shea et al., 2004). Risperidone has also been approved for the acute treatment of schizophrenia in adolescents, ages 13–17, and bipolar mania, ages 10–17 (Pandina et al., 2007). The two studies of risperidone in schizophrenia lasted 6 and 8 weeks, respectively, and included over 400 subjects. Dosages ranged from 0.25 mg per day to 6 mg per day. Dosages higher than 3 mg per day did not increase efficacy but did increase the number of side effects. Aripiprazole (Abilify) has also been FDA approved for the acute treatment of schizophrenia in adolescents, ages 13–17, and bipolar mania, ages 10–17 (Chang et al., 2007). The aripiprazole study of schizophrenia lasted 6 weeks and included over 300 subjects, and both dosages utilized, 10 mg and 30 mg, were efficacious. With the exception of these well-designed studies, however, most research reports of child and adolescent psychosis have been open-label and case studies, including only a small number of subjects.

Previously described as neuroleptics, which quite literally means to "seize the neuron," antipsychotics work by antagonizing dopamine-mediated synaptic transmission by blocking postsynaptic dopamine receptors. The primary effect of most antipsychotics is to block the dopamine D2 receptor, although other dopamine receptors, such as D3, and a host of serotonin, histamine, muscarine, and other receptors are often purposefully and inadvertently blocked by these medications. The medications are hypothesized to exert their effects via *depolarization inactivation*; that is, chronic treatment is believed to push the dopamine neurons in the substantia nigra and ventral tegmental area beyond their physiological limits and drive them into quiescence secondary to excessive membrane depolarization (Mereu et al., 1995). The clinical potency of most, but not all, antipsychotics correlates well with their relative blocking of the D2 receptor. The first generation or typical antipsychotics exert their beneficial effects by acting exclusively on dopamine. The second generation or atypical antipsychotics are unique in that they act on both dopamine and serotonin.

First-Generation Antipsychotics

The first typical antipsychotic invented was chlorpromazine (Thorazine) in 1950, released for general distribution in 1955. Medications in this class are highly lipophilic, membrane- or protein-bound, and accumulate in the brain, lung, and other highly vascularized tissues. The usual half-life of the typical antipsychotics is about 20–40 hours, depending on the medication. Consequently, the biological effects of a single dose can last 24 hours or more.

Dopamine neurons project throughout the brain from the substantia nigra and ventral tegmentum, the primary dopamine hubs. Dopamine neurons follow four main pathways, each of which is blocked to some degree by antipsychotic medications. The typical antipsychotics exert their beneficial clinical impact by blocking dopamine D2 receptors in the mesolimbic pathway, which is highly involved in emotion. Because these medications are not particularly selective, however, they also block dopamine receptors in other areas of the brain, such as the mesocortical area, where they can interfere with memory, cognition, and motivation; the tuberoinfundibular pathway, where they can interfere with hormonal regulation and lead to increases in prolactin; and the nigrostriatal pathway, where they can interfere with physical movement and motor control, resulting in tremors, stiffness, dyskinesias, and dystonias.

The first-generation antipsychotics are described as either low or high potency, depending on the strength of their dopamine D2 binding. The best-known high-potency medications are haloperidol (Haldol) and fluphenazine (Prolixin). Higher-potency antipsychotics are given in dosages of a few milligrams, induce less sedation than low-potency anti-psychotics, but lead to more extrapyramidal side effects or difficulties with movement because they block dopamine more severely. Lower-potency antipsychotics, such as thioridazine (Mellaril) and chlorpromaz-ine, are given in dosages of several hundred milligrams and induce greater sedation and calming because of their increased anticholinergic and anti-histaminergic activity, which can counteract some of their dopamine blockade–related side effects.

Second-Generation Antipsychotics

The second-generation antipsychotics, or "atypicals," arrived in 1993 with the release of risperidone. These drugs are unique in that they not only block dopamine D2 receptors, but they also block or partially block sero-tonin receptors, particularly 5HT2A, 5HT2C, and 5HT1A. One of these medications, aripiprazole, also stimulates or agonizes dopamine recep-tors, in addition to blocking them. Still other atypicals, such as olanzapine (Zyprexa), also block dopamine D1, D3, and D4 receptors, in addition to D2. When initially released, these medications were believed to be at least equally effective to the first-generation antipsychotics for the treatment of positive symptoms but of greater utility for negative symptoms, in large part, it was thought, because of their effects on serotonin (Stahl, 2002). Recent trials among both psychotic adults and children and adolescents, however, have demonstrated no significant difference in efficacy between the first- and second-generation antipsychotics in at least the acute treat-ment of psychosis (Lieberman et al., 2005; Sikich et al., 2008). Because the atypical antipsychotics cause fewer extrapyramidal side effects, they are sometimes initially easier for patients to tolerate. However, no medication is free from side effects, and what the atypicals lack in the extrapyramidal domain, they often make up for in metabolic complications, including weight gain and insulin resistance.

Antipsychotic Side Effects

Antipsychotics can cause numerous adverse effects, many of which are a nuisance but not always a cause for discontinuation. Sedation, dry mouth, tremor, dizziness, and nausea, for example, are relatively common, albeit troubling, side effects; yet many, perhaps most, children and adolescents quickly become accustomed to these disturbances, particularly if mild or time-limited, and may continue on the medication without complaints.

Other side effects, however, are more significant and may necessitate medication adjustments or discontinuation.

The most common difficulties with the first-generation antipsychotics are the extrapyramidal side effects, so named because the "extrapyramidal" motor neuron network lies outside of the motor tracts that travel through the "pyramids" of the medulla. The extrapyramidal system modulates motor activity in areas of the brain highly vulnerable to antipsychotic medications but does not directly innervate motor neurons. There are four primary extrapyramidal problems that can arise secondary to the use of antipsychotics—dystonias, akathisia, Parkinsonism, and dyskinesias. Dystonias are movements in which sustained muscle contractions cause bending or twisting, recurring movements, or abnormal postures. Some of the more common dystonias include torticollis (a rotation of the neck), blepharospasm (rapid eye-blinking), and oculogyric crisis (an upward deviation of the eyes). Dystonias are extremely uncomfortable at the least but can be painful and incapacitating. Akathisia is characterized by a sense of internal restlessness and an inability to sit still and is often confused with anxiety. Parkinsonism represents a series of side effects that mirror the effects of Parkinson's syndrome, including stiffness, rigidity, tremor, and an unsteady posture. Parkinsonism is so called because the hypodopaminergic state induced by some antipsychotics mirrors that found in Parkinson's syndrome. Finally, dyskinesias are repetitive, involuntary, and purposeless movements of the lips, face, legs, or torso.

Dyskinesias are similar to tics and are more likely to happen with repeated exposure to antipsychotics over time. When they set on after chronic exposure to an antipsychotic, they are termed tardive dyskinesia (TD), tardive being derived from the French word for late. The risk of developing TD is not clearly established but is estimated to be about 3–5% per year, at least for the first 5 years of treatment. Untreated schizophrenics have a significant risk of developing TD as well, although antipsychotic treatment clearly increases that risk. The atypical antipsychotics were initially thought to result in less TD, although some recent studies dispute this assumption (Kane, 2006). The most common expression of TD among antipsychotic users is movements of the mouth and tongue.

Children are generally more vulnerable than adults to extrapyramidal side effects, particularly with the first-generation antipsychotics (Correll & Kane, 2007; Nasrallah, 2006). Both the first-generation and atypical antipsychotics can also cause cardiac toxicity, prolactin elevation, and weight gain. The atypicals, however, are particularly troublesome in this regard.

Finally, antipsychotic medications can also rarely induce fatal side effects, including seizures and neuroleptic malignant syndrome (NMS).

NMS is the most severe of the antipsychotic side effects with a mortality rate approaching 30%. The presentation of NMS is characterized by muscular rigidity, elevated body temperature, unstable vital signs, elevations in creatine phosphokinase, and eventually altered consciousness (Marder, 1998). When caught early, NMS is highly treatable.

Medication Monitoring

Any child or adolescent taking an antipsychotic medication requires extensive and continued monitoring. Baseline blood work should include a fasting glucose and lipid profile, complete blood count, electrolytes (including calcium and magnesium), BUN (blood urea nitrogen), creatinine, liver function tests, thyroid function tests, and prolactin, in addition to height, weight, and a urine drug screen if there is even a remote possibility of substance abuse. The body mass index (BMI) should be calculated from the height and weight, as it represents a highly reliable measure of body fat. A physical examination should have been performed in the past 12 months, and an electrocardiogram (EKG) is also advised.

There are a number of features of the heart rhythm that antipsychotics can alter. In most cases, these alterations, when they occur, are mild and cause no notable concerns. However, in rare cases they can result in arrhythmias and death. Virtually all of the antipsychotics can extend the time it takes for the ventricles of the heart to both depolarize and repolarize, a gap known as the QT interval or the QTc when corrected for heart rate. The QT duration is the single best parameter for assessing unstable ventricular depolarization. A QTc of less than 450 milliseconds is considered normal (Zareba & Lin, 2003). EKGs should be assessed both before and during treatment with an antipsychotic, and any increases beyond 450 milliseconds or greater than 10% over baseline suggests the need for further investigation. In addition, hypokalemia, hypermagnesemia, or hypercalcemia should be treated prior to starting a child or adolescent on an antipsychotic, as these abnormalities can cause prolongation of the QT interval. Finally, delayed cardiac conduction, as observed by a PR interval of greater than 200 milliseconds or a QRS interval of greater than 120 milliseconds, may necessitate a dosage or medication change (Kaplan & Sadock, 2007).

Given that excessive weight gain and Type II diabetes can result from antipsychotic use, practitioners sometimes struggle with how to monitor their patients. The American Diabetes Association, along with a number of other professional groups including the American Psychiatric Association, has endorsed recommendations for monitoring individuals taking

Table 12.2. Monitoring Protocol for Patients on Second-Generation Antipsychotics

Lab Value	Baseline	4 weeks	8 weeks	12 weeks	Quarterly	Annually	Every 5 years
Personal/ family history	X					X	
Weight (BMI)	X	X	X	X	X		
Waist circumference	X					X	
Blood pressure	X			X		X	
Fasting plasma glucose	X			X		X	
Fasting lipid profile	X			X			X

American Diabetes Association (2004).

second-generation antipsychotics (American Diabetes Association, 2004). Although these guidelines were designed for adults taking antipsychotics over extended periods of time, they are also reasonable for children and adolescents, as the antipsychotics have a similar and often immediate metabolic impact on youth (see Table 12.2). In addition, the practitioner should regularly inquire about clinical signs of diabetes, such as unintended weight loss, polydipsia, and polyuria.

Prior to treating a female, a menstrual history should be ascertained. During treatment, it is also important to inquire regularly about menstruation and amenorrhea among females, as antipsychotic-induced prolactin elevation can have severe long-term consequences. Among both males and females, nipple discharge, sexual dysfunction, and pubertal development should be regularly assessed as well. If serum prolactin is elevated in a female, pregnancy or oral contraceptives could be the culprit, in addition to the antipsychotic, and all possibilities should be evaluated. Additionally, thyroid-stimulating hormone (TSH) and serum creatinine should be rechecked because both hypothyroidism and renal failure can result in an increase in prolactin. Sexually active females taking antipsychotics should be advised to use two forms of contraception, such as condoms along with oral contraception, an intrauterine device, or a diaphragm, given the risk of possible birth defects to a developing fetus. If the prolactin is repeatedly over 200 nanograms per milliliter or does not decrease even after changing to a prolactin-sparing antipsychotic such as quetiapine (Seroquel), aripiprazole, or clozapine (Clozaril), then a brain MRI of the sella turcica should be performed to rule out a pituitary adenoma or a parasellar tumor. Because prolactin levels may rise early in response to antipsychotic treatment and then taper off to normal levels over 12 months, it may be prudent to follow levels for 6 to 12 months before making major changes in regimen unless side effects are troubling (Pandina et al., 2006).

Psychosocial Treatments for Psychotic Disorders

Multimodal psychosocial treatment approaches that incorporate medication management, family and collateral psychoeducation, vocational rehabilitation, and supportive psychotherapy are effective in reducing relapse rates and morbidity due to psychosis among adults (McClellan & Werry, 1997). In contrast, insight-oriented psychotherapy by itself has not proven useful for psychotic individuals, and it would be rare indeed to find a psychiatrist or therapist these days providing such treatment as the sole intervention (Goldstein, 1989).

Most psychotherapeutic approaches to the treatment of psychosis have been studied in adults and will generalize reasonably well to older adolescents but perhaps not as well to children. High-functioning rehabilitation programs that support social and vocational skills training have proven useful. These programs are particularly necessary for those diagnosed with EOS and VEOS because the earlier one is affected by a chronic psychotic illness, the greater not only the morbidity from the psychosis itself, but also from the resulting deviations in normal development (McClellan & Werry, 1997).

Most psychotic children and adolescents will not do well in a regular academic setting and will require specialized supports. For those who are unable to continue academically beyond a certain point for whatever reason, training in problem solving, life skills, and independent living has proven remarkably helpful. Other program components, such as vocational counseling, job training, educational support, money management skills, use of public transportation, and social skills training are all key components that have been shown to be effective for those with schizophrenia (Kopelowicz, Liberman, & Wallace, 2003). These approaches are typically community centered and attempt to provide patients with the skills necessary to lead productive lives outside of hospitals and chronic care facilities.

Cognitive behavior therapy (CBT) has proven useful with schizophrenic adults (Lecomte et al., 2008). In addition, family therapy focused on improving family interactions and reducing "expressed emotion," or excessive criticism expressed toward the affected individual, has been shown to decrease relapse rates among schizophrenic adults (Goldstein, 1989; McClellan & Werry, 1997). Neither CBT nor family therapy, however, has been adequately tested in children and adolescents (Muñoz-Solomando, Kendall, & Whittington, 2008).

Family education is vital and must begin the moment the diagnosis is established. The family should be taught about the illness itself and how to support the affected member. Most important, all efforts to support the family in maintaining relapse prevention must be employed. Teaching coping strategies and problem-solving skills to both the patient and the family is also a major tenant of family education. Families can also help the affected individual by supporting adherence to the medication regimen and regular visits with the treating physician.

Self-help groups have sometimes been used effectively for those with schizophrenia and are becoming more common. These groups can provide support and comfort for patients and may serve other important functions by acting, for example, as a surrogate family and source of friendships. Community-based clubhouse programs for those with chronic mental illness provide a gathering place and a setting in which to teach social and life skills. Finally, intensive case management and assertive community treatment (ACT) programs, which provide community-based mobile mental health treatment, have been shown to decrease recidivism among adults with severe and persistent psychotic illness (Weisbrod, 1983). The ACT service delivery model uses a team of clinical professionals from various disciplines, including psychiatry, nursing, addiction counseling, and vocational rehabilitation, to provide treatment, rehabilitation, and support services on a 24-hour, 7-day-a-week basis. Regardless of the therapeutic approach selected, it is important to remember that psychosocial treatment approaches are not a substitute for medication, which is clearly the first-line treatment for those with psychosis.

13

Substance Use Disorders

Gambling, eating, sex, and drug and alcohol use are all normal behaviors. When done in excess, however, each can cause major impairments. Though rarely a problem in children, drug and alcohol use among adolescents and adults takes a tremendous toll on the affected individuals, their families, and society. We might rather think of these behaviors as lying on a spectrum, where engaging in some drug and alcohol use is typical but engaging in excessive use is impairing. Clinicians and physicians must ask themselves the difficult question of what constitutes normative substance use in adolescents before they can effectively diagnose and treat these disorders.

As humans we have a universal desire to alter our consciousness, which is evident from childhood. Some children hold their breath or spin in circles to make themselves feel dizzy. Recall the merry-go-rounds in parks and playgrounds and the thrill of swinging. Consider how much children enjoy amusement parks and fast rides. Adults also enjoy mind-altering experiences, as clearly seen by their extensive use of alcohol and drugs. Far from benign, coffee is an $80 billion industry and the second most frequently traded commodity in the world (Avery, 2009).

CLINICAL PRESENTATION

In order to help children or adolescents who are struggling with *substance use disorders (SUDS)*, we must first identify the problem. Given that some level of use is normative, particularly during adolescence when many teens experiment, it can be particularly difficult to determine when use becomes abuse. Furthermore, most adolescents who abuse drugs and alcohol with any regularity tend to deny it and will not seek help unless forced to do so (Indig, Copeland, & Conigrave, 2008).

The clinical presentation of SUDS may take many forms and will vary to some degree, depending upon which substance the adolescent is abusing. The most apparent feature is a child or adolescent's failure to meet academic, occupational, and social expectations and mandates. These persistent and recurrent social and interpersonal problems that occur as a result of alcohol and substance abuse, or are exacerbated by the effects of the substance, are commonly the first features noted. Still, parents and other family members, peers, teachers, and clinicians must maintain some degree of vigilance and suspicion in order to detect substance abuse early.

ETIOLOGY

Before we can effectively diagnose and treat SUDS, it helps to understand why individuals abuse alcohol and substances. There are numerous theories, none of which fully explains the issue in its entirety, but each of which contributes something to our understanding and perspective. Many individuals use drugs and alcohol in order to fit in with their peers (Pilkington, 2007). Some children and adolescents try drugs and alcohol to relieve boredom, feel good, challenge parental authority, escape parental pressure, forget their troubles, relax, satisfy their curiosity, have fun, ease physical or emotional pain, or take a risk. Others insist that the media is at least partially responsible.

Numerous well-known celebrities and popular music stars, whom many adolescents view as role models, are known to have used drugs and alcohol. In addition, many popular films portray images of alcohol, drugs, and tobacco. Sixteen of the most popular R-rated films in the mid-1980s, for example, contained alcohol use and averaged 16 episodes of use per film (Greenberg et al., 1993). Ninety-three percent of the 200 most popular video rentals from 1996–97 depicted alcohol use, and 22% depicted illicit drugs (Roberts, Henriksen, & Christenson, 1999). Over one-quarter of these films depicted graphic portrayals of drug preparation and/or ingestion. Few of these movies gave any indication as to the reason for drug use among the characters. Fewer than 50% of the films portrayed short-term consequences of substance abuse, and only 12% depicted long-term consequences. Films between 1960 and 1990 showed characters smoking at a rate of three times the national average for American adults (Hazan, Lipton, & Glantz, 1994). Among the 25 top-grossing films each year between

1988 and 1997, over 75% of them contained tobacco use. Likewise, nearly 90% of the 200 most popular movie rentals from 1996–97 depicted tobacco use (Roberts et al., 1999). These films tend to portray smoking in a positive fashion, and the characters who smoke are sexier and more romantic than other characters in the films (McIntosh, Bazzini, Smith, & Wayne, 1998). Another study reviewed all G-rated animated feature films released between 1937 and 2000 and found that 47% portrayed alcohol use and 43% portrayed tobacco use, but the movies are not alone (Thompson & Yokota, 2001).

Primack, Dalton, Carroll, Agarwal, and Fine (2008) analyzed 279 of the most popular songs of 2005, according to *Billboard* magazine, and found that 33% contained explicit references to drug or alcohol use. This percentage translates into 35.2 substance references per hour of listening to music. Given that adolescents listen to an average of nearly 2.5 hours of music per day, the typical teen is exposed to approximately 84 references to explicit substance use daily in songs. The number of references varied by genre—about 9% of pop songs had lyrics relating to drugs or alcohol, 14% of rock songs, 20% of rhythm and blues and hip-hop songs, 36% of country songs, and 77% of rap songs. Only 4% of songs contained explicit antidrug-use messages, and none portrayed refusal of substance use. The authors also found that the substance use depicted in popular music was generally motivated by a desire for peer acceptance and sex and usually had positive associations and consequences. While there is no doubt that the media's influence is important in the equation of why adolescents abuse substances, these data are correlative only and not convincing as a causal factor (Petraitis, Flay, Miller, Torpy, & Greiner, 1998).

Since virtually all children and adolescents struggle with peer acceptance, periodic boredom, and parental pressure, and are exposed to the media, yet only a minority become dependent upon drugs and alcohol, additional factors must be at play. Research supports the assertion that emotional vulnerability makes some children and adolescents more susceptible to the influence of peers and may help to explain why at least some portion of adolescents become drug dependent (Nuño-Gutiérrez, Rodriguez-Cerda, & Alvarez-Nemegyei, 2006). We must ask ourselves, however, why some children and adolescents are more emotionally vulnerable than others. Various risk factors, including family strife, psychopathology, academic troubles, and even neurobiology, may hold the answer (Rumpold et al., 2006).

From a neurobiological perspective it appears that the use of drugs and alcohol increases dopamine in the limbic system, the emotional center of the brain. As a neurotransmitter, dopamine helps to regulate the motivation of behaviors necessary for survival. Food intake increases dopamine, which gives us a good feeling and leads us to seek it out; sexual behavior increases dopamine, which gives us a good feeling and leads us to seek it out; and social interaction also increases dopamine, leading us to seek that out as well. Drugs of abuse, by nature of their dopamine effects, also make us feel good, which is crucial to their reinforcing and addictive effects (Volkow, 2004).

We now understand that individuals who use drugs, such as cocaine, amphetamines, heroine, and alcohol, generally have a lower number of dopamine receptors, particularly D2 dopamine receptors, in their brains in key limbic areas that appear to be involved in addiction. We can even watch as individuals continue to abuse drugs and alcohol over time, observing their dopamine D2 receptors decrease with increased abuse.

Dopamine D2 receptor density appears to matter because, as already noted, dopamine neurons turn our attention to what is salient, fun, sad, aversive, and important for survival. If the dopamine D2 density is naturally lower among those who abuse drugs and alcohol, they may experience less of a signal from the firing of dopamine neurons in a given situation. For example, natural reinforcers, such as food, sex, and getting an "A" on an exam, may be less rewarding for some than for others because the increase in dopamine is simply not enough to signal them as salient stimuli. Drugs of abuse, however, provide a much more powerful dopamine signal that triggers the D2 receptors, making drugs and alcohol highly reinforcing.

It is difficult to know which came first among those who abuse drugs and alcohol—the low D2 dopamine receptor density or the addiction. In studies of randomly selected individuals who do not abuse drugs, those with a low compliment of dopamine D2 receptors at baseline typically experience drugs, such as intravenous stimulants, as pleasurable, whereas those with high levels of dopamine D2 receptors experience drugs as unpleasant. One possible conclusion, then, is that low levels of dopamine D2 receptors may make individuals more vulnerable to taking drugs because the experience is pleasant, which increases the probability of trying it again. Conversely, high levels of receptors may protect against drug abuse because the reaction to the drugs tends to be aversive, which decreases the probability of trying it again.

Increases in dopamine within the dopamine neuron synapses are 5 to 10 times greater with drugs of abuse than with natural reinforcers, such as food and sex. Moreover, drugs like cocaine, amphetamines, and methamphetamine block the reuptake transporter so that dopamine stays in the synapse longer than with natural reinforcers. Thus, despite the fact that the number of dopamine D2 receptors may be decreased among drug abusers, the probability of interaction between dopamine and the receptors is increased by the drugs themselves and because the drugs force dopamine to stay in the synapse longer. For the drug abuser, natural rein-forcers no longer generate a salient "feel good" signal; but abusing drugs does. This fact perpetuates addictive behavior (Volkow, 2004).

Still, dopamine is not enough to explain addiction. If you were to give drugs to an individual who is not addicted, you would see an increase in dopamine in the brain that would be equal to or even larger than that seen in the brain of an addicted individual; yet most individuals who ex-periment with drugs do not become addicted. Thus, dopamine in and of itself is not a sufficient explanation (Volkow, 2004).

Most would agree that the environment in which children are raised has a major impact upon their personality development and behavior. Studies of macaque monkeys have found that dominant monkeys have higher levels of dopamine D2 receptors than subordinate monkeys, yet these dopamine levels are not predetermined. That is, the D2 levels ap-pear to rise among the dominant monkeys only once they enter a social group and establish their hierarchy. Consequently, it appears that the en-vironment somehow triggered higher dopamine D2 receptor levels in the dominant monkeys. It is also notable that the subordinate animals not only had lower D2 receptor density, but also readily self-administered high doses of cocaine, whereas the dominant monkeys had relatively no interest in the drug (Morgan et al., 2005).

EPIDEMIOLOGY

Approximately 8% of adolescents ages 12–17 are considered in need of treatment for alcohol and substance abuse. About 10–20% of individuals will at some point be addicted to a drug or alcohol in their lifetime. Over 22 million Americans—nearly 10% of the total population age 12 and older—meet criteria for substance dependence or abuse; 3.2 million are dependent on or abuse both alcohol and illicit drugs; 3.7 million are de-pendent on or abuse illicit drugs but not alcohol; and 15.5 million are dependent on or abuse alcohol but not illicit drugs (Substance Abuse and Mental Health Services Administration [SAMHSA], 2008b).

Illicit drug use peaks in late adolescence and early adulthood with nearly 22% of 18–20-year-olds reporting use in the past month and simi-larly high percentages of 16–17-year-olds (16%) and 21–25-year-olds (nearly 19%) reporting the same. Nearly 12% of 12–17-year-olds used an illicit drug in the past month, with marijuana being the most common (over 6%). Abuse of prescription medications (3.3%), inhalants (1.2%), and hallucinogens (0.7%) follow behind (Substance Abuse and Mental Health Services Administration [SAMHSA], 2008b). The majority of teens who abuse prescription drugs get them easily and for free, primarily from friends and relatives (University of Michigan, 2008). The prescription drugs most commonly abused by teens are stimulants, painkillers, sedatives, and tranquilizers.

The Monitoring the Future Study surveys approximately 50,000 8th, 10th, and 12th graders annually to determine their drug and alcohol use patterns. In 2008, 47% of 12th graders, 34% of 10th graders, and 20% of 8th graders reported having used an illicit substance on at least one occasion in their lifetime; 22% of 12th graders, 16% of 10th graders, and 8% of 8th graders reported using an illicit substance within the past month; and 5% of 12th graders, 3% of 10th graders, and 1% of 8th graders reported using an illicit substance daily. Daily cigarette use was reported by nearly 11% of 12th graders, 6% of 10th graders, and 3% of 8th graders. Alcohol was used by 43% of 12th graders, 29% of 10th graders, and 16% of 8th graders in the past month, and 3% of 12th graders, 1% of 10th graders, and just under 1% of 8th graders reported daily use; while 55% of 12th graders, 37% of 10th graders, and 18% of 8th graders reported having been drunk at least once in their lifetime (University of Michigan, 2008). In 2006, more than 13% of high school seniors acknowledged driving under the influence of marijuana in the 2 weeks prior to the survey, and 30% reported driving drugged or drunk or with a drugged or drunk driver. Only 20% of those students with an A or A- grade point average exposed themselves to these situations, as opposed to almost 39% with a grade point average of B- or below (O'Malley & Johnston, 2007).

Nearly 10 million people reported driving under the influence of an illicit drug in 2007 or 4% of the population 12 years and older. The rate was highest (13%) among young adults, ages 18–25. In 2005, over 13% of individuals 12 years of age and older drove under the influence of an illicit drug or alcohol at least once. Driving under the influence is associated with age—over 7% of 16-year-olds drove under the influence, but nearly 32% of 22-year-olds did. Rates decline beyond this age. Males are nearly twice as likely as females (17.6% versus 9.3%) to drive under the influence of an illicit drug or alcohol (Substance Abuse and Mental Health Services Administration [SAMHSA], 2007).

Marijuana is the most widely used illicit drug but rarely the first substance used (Gfroerer, Wu, & Penne, 2002). Over 90% of new marijuana initiates have first used cigarettes and/or alcohol before trying marijuana, making cigarettes and alcohol true gateway drugs (Substance Abuse and Mental Health Services Administration [SAMHSA], 2003).

Teens are also using over-the-counter drugs with increasing frequency, mostly cough and cold remedies containing dextromethorphan (DXM), a cough suppressant. In 2006, approximately 3.1 million people, or 5.3% of the population, ages 12–25 years reported a lifetime history of using an over-the-counter cough or cold medicine to get high, and nearly 1 million had done so in the past year (Substance Abuse and Mental Health Services Administration [SAMHSA], 2008a). Six percent of 12th graders, 5% of 10th graders, and 4% of 8th graders abused a cough or cold medicine within the past year (University of Michigan, 2008). Products with DXM are found in more than 140 over-the-counter cough and cold preparations, including Nyquil, Coricidin, and Robitussin.

The younger one is at initiation of drug and alcohol use or experimentation, the greater the risk for adult abuse and dependence (Chen, Storr, & Anthony, 2009). Other risk factors include early aggressive behavior, lack of parental supervision, drug availability, and poverty. Association with peers who abuse drugs is perhaps the most robust predictor of adolescent substance abuse (National Institute on Drug Abuse [NIDA], 2008; Rowe, Liddle, Caruso, & Dakof, 2004). Difficult temperament, lack of self-control, and aggressive behavior are risk factors that can be noted as early as infancy. Family conflict, lack of nurturing and attachment, and caregiver drug abuse are also frequently cited as risks for later substance abuse. In addition, individuals who abuse alcohol and drugs have high rates of physical, sexual, and emotional abuse, often live in disorganized and violent neighborhoods, have frequent psychiatric diagnoses, and experience high rates of chronic pain and disability. Education level is also associated with drug abuse. Regular illicit drug use is lower for college graduates (5.1%) than for those who do not graduate from high school (9.3%), high school graduates (8.6%), and those with some college (8.9%). By contrast, college graduates are more likely to try illicit drugs in their lifetime than adults who have not completed high school (52% vs. 36%) (Substance Abuse and Mental Health Services Administration [SAMHSA], 2008b).

CLINICAL COURSE

As noted above, most individuals experiment with drugs and alcohol to some degree, but most do not become addicted. For those who do become addicted, they often struggle for many years, and effective treatment programs typically describe these individuals as perpetually "in recovery." Among the greatest risk factors for chronicity are early onset and childhood vulnerabilities, as has been found in studies of adult alcoholics.

Two stereotyped groups of chronic alcoholics, Type A and Type B, have been described (Babor et al., 1992). Type A alcoholics have a later onset, fewer childhood risk factors, less severe dependence, less psychopathological dysfunction, and better treatment outcomes than Type B.

By contrast, Type B alcoholics have more childhood risk factors, a family history of alcoholism, early onset of alcohol-related problems, more severe dependence, polydrug use, a more chronic treatment history, greater psychopathological dysfunction, and more stress. This typology has been replicated with adult drug abusers, suggesting the same impact with early-onset drug abuse. Similarly, the earlier an adolescent begins abusing substances, the greater the likelihood of conduct problems and family dysfunction and the more likely one is to experience chronic problems into adulthood (Zucker et al., 1996).

Long-term follow-up studies of alcoholics have found that 20% or more eventually become permanently abstinent, generally after a major life stressor, such as incarceration or life-threatening complications related to alcohol abuse. Relapse rates are particularly high during the first 12 months of abstinence (American Psychiatric Association, 2000). Recovery among adolescent drug and alcohol abusers varies greatly and is impacted by many factors, including motivation to change, access to resources, and severity of abuse and dependence. A recent 25-year longitudinal study of adolescents who began using marijuana prior to 21 years of age found that high levels of cannabis use in adolescence were related to worse educational outcomes, lower income, greater welfare dependence and unemployment, and less relationship and general life satisfaction (Fergusson & Boden, 2008). All manner of risky behavior, including early sexual activity, accidents and motor vehicle accidents, violence, and school dropout, are more common among teens who abuse drugs and alcohol (Weinberg, Rahdert, Colliver, & Glantz, 1998).

We are increasingly aware of the health consequences of drug and alcohol abuse as well. Methamphetamine, for example, is known to cause cell damage and even dopamine neuron cell death in animals. Methamphetamine addicts are known to have significant reductions in dopamine transporters, and the lower the number of dopamine transporters, the worse addicts tend to perform on neuropsychological tests of gross memory speed and fine motor and memory function. After detoxification and sustained abstinence, many addicts appear to recover roughly their full complement of dopamine transporters. There may be a less marked trend, however, toward recovery of motor and memory function, and in some cases there appears to be permanent damage (Volkow, 2004).

DIAGNOSIS

According to the *DSM-IV*, the diagnosis of alcohol and substance abuse and dependence incorporates six primary categories: *substance dependence, substance abuse, substance intoxication, substance withdrawal, polysubstance dependence,* and *substance-induced psychiatric disorders,* causing mood, anxiety, or psychotic symptoms (American Psychiatric Association, 2000). These categories can be applied to virtually any drug.

In order to diagnose, we must first define the terms. Addiction is generally viewed as a cluster of cognitive, affective, behavioral, and physiologic signs that indicate compulsive use of a substance and inability to control intake, despite negative consequences, such as medical illness, failure in life roles, and interpersonal difficulties. Similarly, dependence is defined by the *DSM-IV* as a maladaptive pattern of substance use, which leads to clinically significant impairment or distress, as manifested by three or more of the following: tolerance; withdrawal symptoms; using more of the substance or for a longer period of time than intended; persistent and unsuccessful efforts to control use; spending extensive time trying to procure the substance, using it, or recovering from its effects; impairment in social, occupational, or recreational activities; or continued use despite knowledge of its negative impact (American Psychiatric Association, 2000). Tolerance is defined as a need for increased amounts of the substance to achieve the desired effect or diminished effect with use of the same amount; and withdrawal is defined by a characteristic drug discontinuation syndrome or taking more of the substance or a similar substance to avoid the discontinuation symptoms.

Polysubstance dependence is defined by *DSM-IV* as a disorder in which one is dependent upon at least three substances but no single substance predominates. The *DSM-IV* does not list polysubstance abuse as a diagnosis, yet we commonly see it described clinically. Substance abuse, according to the *DSM-IV,* is a pattern of use leading to impairment in fulfilling major role obligations; use in physically hazardous situations; recurrent legal problems; or continued use despite persistent social and interpersonal problems. Finally, substance intoxication is defined as a reversible substance-specific syndrome due to drug use (American Psychiatric Association, 2000).

Psychiatric comorbidities abound among adolescents with SUDS. In one study of over 200 adolescents at an inpatient drug treatment program, over 80% had an additional Axis I disorder, and 75% had more than one additional disorder. Among the disorders identified, 61% had a mood disorder, 54% had conduct disorder, and 43% had an anxiety disorder (Stowell & Estroff, 1992). Another study found that among over 150 adolescents on an inpatient dual-diagnosis unit, 71% had conduct disorder and 31% had a major depressive disorder (Bukstein, Glancy, & Kaminer, 1992). Attention-deficit/hyperactivity disorder (ADHD) has been frequently

Table 13.1. CRAFFT Screening Protocol

C   Have you ever gotten into a *car* driven by someone including yourself who was high
    or using alcohol or drugs?

R   Do you ever use alcohol or drugs to *relax*?

A   Do you ever use alcohol or drugs while you are by yourself or *alone*?

F   Has a *friend, family member*, or other person every thought you had a problem with
    alcohol or drugs?

F   Do you ever *forget* (or regret) things you did while using?

T   Have you ever gotten into *trouble* while using alcohol or drugs, or done something
    you would not normally do—for example, break the laws, rules, or curfew, or engage
    in risky behavior?

noted to be comorbid with SUDS as well, although its association may have more to do with its mutual association with conduct disorder than a true relation to SUDS (Weinberg et al., 1998).

Assessing substance use is difficult. For those individuals who abuse drugs and are engaged in inpatient or outpatient treatment programs or individual treatment, urine drug toxicology screens are commonly employed to monitor progress. However, most drugs dissipate within about 1 to 3 days, after which time finding traces of their presence is very difficult, with the exception of marijuana, which can be accurately measured for up to 7 weeks after the last use.

Fewer than half of pediatricians screen adolescents for tobacco, alcohol, and drug use, and fewer than one-quarter report that they are comfortable asking about these issues (Kulig, 2005). Yet simply asking about the frequency and quantity of alcohol and drug use has not shown great validity as a screening tool. Yes/no questions about substance use can be useful, but these questions do not address the quantity of use. Although there are a number of well-designed and validated self-report measures available for purchase, one of the most clinically relevant tools is the CRAFFT (Griswold, Aronoff, Kernan, & Kahn, 2008). This six-item verbally administered screening tool is quick, easy to employ, and effective in identifying children and adolescents at risk (see Table 13.1).

TREATMENT

Numerous medications exist for helping adults with addiction. None of these has been approved by the Food and Drug Administration for use in children or adolescents, although they are sometimes employed. These medications include acamprosate (Campral) for alcohol abstinence, which decreases cravings; buprenorphine (Subutex) for opioid dependence; disulfiram (Antabuse) for the maintenance of sobriety; methadone (Dolophine or Methadose) for opioid dependence; naltrexone (Revia, Depade, Vivitrol) for alcohol and opioid dependence; bupropion (Zyban or Buproban) and varenicline (Chantix) for smoking cessation; and buprenorphine plus naloxone (Suboxone) for opioid dependence. There are numerous nicotine replacements available, including nicotine gum (Nicorette), a nicotine inhalation system (Nicotrol inhaler), a nicotine lozenge (Commit), a nicotine nasal spray (Nicotrol-NS), and a nicotine patch (Habitrol, Nicoderm, and Nicotrol). All of these products are designed to replace nicotine and thereby decrease cravings.

Although adolescents experiment a great deal with drugs and alcohol, we are fortunate that most do not require intensive medication treatment for the addiction itself. More commonly, children and adolescents will require treatment for comorbid Axis I conditions, such as conduct disorder, anxiety, depression, and ADHD. These treatments often include medications and therapeutic interventions aimed at the individual, family, peer, and social network.

The five key steps in the treatment of addiction include: (a) detoxification; (b) inpatient hospitalization; (c) therapeutic community; (d) outpatient treatment; and (e) self-help programs. If detoxification is necessary, it is best performed during an inpatient hospital stay. Depending upon the drug, the level of addiction, and the patient's social support, however, outpatient detoxification is sometimes possible. Thankfully, for most adolescents who abuse drugs and alcohol, detoxification is not generally required.

Inpatient hospitalization is commonly employed for those who have severe drug or alcohol dependence. Hospitalization typically begins with a thorough assessment of all presenting problems and may include neuropsychological testing to identify cognitive impairments that preceded or were caused by the substance abuse. Inpatient programs are generally administered by physicians, drug counselors, therapists, and psychologists, who can provide multimodal care to the drug-dependent individual. Along with general medical care, Axis I comorbidities are a key focus of treatment during an inpatient hospitalization, as are individual drug counseling and peer group and family education. There are no standard inpatient admission criteria for adolescent drug addiction. Admission is generally based upon the severity of comorbid psychiatric conditions, a clear determination that the individual will continue to use unabated without hospitalization, or the belief that the individual is at great risk to himself or others.

Therapeutic communities are designed to isolate an addicted individual from the influence of his peer group and place him in a drug-free, supportive environment. The goal of a therapeutic community is to teach individuals how to cope, function, and socialize without drugs. These programs are commonly based upon mutual help or self-help philosophies and are often staffed by prior addicts. Treatment may take months or even more than a year, although the dropout rate is often quite high, as individuals frequently relapse. Therapeutic communities are supportive and emphasize intensive therapy, counseling to build self-esteem, the establishment of social skills, education, and job training. As these programs are not standardized in their treatment approach, it is difficult to accurately assess outcomes, although some adolescent programs have shown remarkable success in decreasing substance abuse, improving psychological functioning, and reducing crime (Morral, McCaffrey, & Ridgeway, 2004). Families also anecdotally often report that these programs are effective.

A more modern form of the therapeutic community, and one often employed with adolescents, is a wilderness camp or retreat in which a child is separated from his family and peer group to live in relative isolation. Length of stay for these programs is generally about 30 days but may extend to 3 or 4 months or even longer in some cases. Wilderness programs lack the intensive group process that takes place in treatment programs with a longer length of stay; additionally, the family is largely unable to be involved in these programs. Consequently, a child may go off to a wilderness program, have a good experience, but then come home to an unchanged family, home life, and peer group. Regardless of their efficacy, adolescent admissions to substance-abuse treatment programs have increased greatly in recent years. Between 1995 and 1998, for example, admissions increased by 46%, almost entirely due to referrals from the criminal justice system (Substance Abuse and Mental Health Services Administration [SAMHSA], 2001).

Whereas therapeutic communities emphasize mutual self-help, behavioral consequences, and shared values regarding "right living," another community-based adolescent treatment approach, the Minnesota Model, takes a slightly different theoretical perspective. The Minnesota Model derives its approach from Alcoholics Anonymous and incorporates techniques of both individual and group psychotherapy (Morral et al., 2004). The Minnesota Model has also proven useful among adolescents and leads to higher rates of abstinence among those who complete the program as opposed to those who drop out or are placed on a wait list (Winters, Stinchfield, Opland, Weller, & Latimer, 2000). While the therapeutic community views substance dependence as a behavioral and personality problem and the community as the effective change agent, the Minnesota Model views substance dependence as a disease and the counselor as the treatment director. As yet, no head-to-head studies comparing these treatment programs exist.

The vast majority of adolescent substance-abuse treatment programs are outpatient. These programs generally incorporate individual and group counseling, aftercare services for those who have already been to a residential treatment program or therapeutic community, structured day treatment as an alternative to inpatient care, and family therapy. Adolescents without major medical or psychiatric comorbidities and who are motivated and cooperative are good candidates for outpatient treatment programs. In addition, willingness to submit to random urine drug testing and a family commitment to engage in treatment and therapy are vitally important. Outpatient programs often employ a variety of therapeutic interventions, including individual and group, family, and behavioral therapy, crisis and emergency services, and sometimes even hypnosis and biofeedback.

A number of specific therapies are currently utilized for the treatment of adolescent substance abuse. Numerous family therapies, including multidimensional family therapy, brief strategic family therapy, multisystemic therapy, Purdue brief family therapy, and various forms of family therapy integrated with cognitive behavior therapy (CBT) have proven efficacious (Deas, 2008; Liddle, Rowe, Dakof, Henderson, & Greenbaum, 2009; Santisteban, Suarez-Morales, Robbins, & Szapocznik, 2006). Perhaps more than the specific details of the therapies themselves, these findings point to the importance of the family in understanding and treating adolescent substance abuse.

Much recent attention has been paid to motivational enhancement therapy, also known as motivational interviewing (MI). MI is a brief treatment designed to increase an individual's motivation to make changes about substance abuse and aspects of his or her life that trigger or perpetuate substance abuse. This treatment has been successful with teens and adults, in part because substance abusers benefit from efforts to motivate their engagement in treatment as they have difficulties motivating themselves. There are four major therapeutic principles that encompass the fundamental tenants of MI: (a) employ empathy to listen and accept the individual; (b) develop discrepancy between the patient's behavior and their greater values and goals as a way to motivate change; (c) roll with resistance and do not argue with the patient or directly oppose the resistance; rather reframe the resistance to create a new perspective; and (d) support self-efficacy by encouraging the patient's belief in himself or herself.

The final strategy in the treatment of substance abuse and dependence, self-help, may be employed as a stand-alone treatment but is also commonly integrated into the aforementioned venues, including inpatient and outpatient care and therapeutic communities. The prototypical self-help program is Alcoholics Anonymous, but many 12-step and similar programs exist today. Self-help programs rely in large part on the idea that one's participation is willing and voluntary. However, this core tenant lies in opposition to the reality of many adolescents, whose participation is often mandatory and at the discretion of their parents or the criminal justice system. Another roadblock to the success of self-help programs is the fact that the first and fundamental step of a 12-step program is to acknowledge that one is helpless or powerless in the face of substance abuse. This principle lies in contrast to the natural striving for independence that is developmentally normative at this age. The 12-step idea, that of hitting "rock bottom" before one can recover, also may not be easily accepted by an adolescent who feels he has his whole life ahead of him. Consequently, although 12-step programs can be used successfully with adolescents, expectations and structure must often be redesigned or developmentally adapted (Dusenbury, Khuri, & Millman, 1992).

While many of the aforementioned treatment interventions are helpful, we do not yet know when it is absolutely best to employ each modality. We also do not know which types of addictions and which types of teens and families benefit most from each type of treatment. We do know, however, that particular therapeutic skills are helpful and that treatment must address not only the child, but also the family, peer group, and community. Regardless of the ultimate treatment plan, we also know that across all types of treatment programs, both inpatient and outpatient, slightly more than one-third of adolescents maintain abstinence at 6 months and slightly less than one-third after 12 months. The factors most closely related to good outcome include completing the treatment program, low pretreatment substance use, and peer, parent, and social support of nonuse (Williams & Chang, 2000).

In working with adolescents, it is vital to remember that the majority will use alcohol and drugs at some time but that most will not develop SUDS. Perhaps more important than abstinence, then, is close parental and societal monitoring while helping adolescents to establish guidelines for reasonable choices. Paracelsus (1493–1541) stated, "All substances are poisons; there is none which is not a poison. The right dose differentiates a poison and a remedy." Paracelsus's words ring as true today as they did 500 years ago. The issue for most children and adolescents is not abstinence but rather the establishment of good judgment and learning moderation.

Eating Disorders

The modern obsession with body weight and dieting is stunning: 40–60% of normal-weight adolescents see themselves as overweight; up to 60% of teens regularly diet to lose weight; over 50% of teens report that they exercise in order to improve their shape or lose weight; nearly 50% of teens periodically smoke cigarettes to lose weight; the majority of teens acknowledge being preoccupied with how much they eat; and roughly 70% of girls report that their body shape is important to their self-esteem (Strober & Schneider, 2005). Although often thought to be a product of modern society, eating disorders have a long history.

In Western Europe in the 12th and 13th centuries, "miracle maidens," or women who starved themselves, were highly regarded, and their behavior was imbued with religious interpretations. Catherine of Siena (1347–1380), whose complete control over her food intake was seen as a sign of religious devotion, was regarded as a saint (Heywood, 1996). This period of "holy anorexia" was, however, short-lived, and in the 16th century the Catholic Church began to disapprove of asceticism. Some anorexics were subsequently viewed as witches and burned at the stake (Brumberg, 2000).

The English physician Richard Morton described two cases, one male and one female, of a "wasting" disease of nervous etiology in 1689 that may mark the first clinical portrayal of anorexia nervosa (AN) in a medical text (Gordon, 2000). The first formal description of AN, however, is credited to Sir William Gull, physician to Queen Victoria, who in 1868 named the disorder anorexia hysterica, emphasizing what he believed to be its psychogenic origins. He later changed the name to anorexia nervosa to avoid confusion with the psychological umbrella term *hysteria* (Hepworth,

ruite descriptive, the word *anorexia* is a misnomer, as
eans "lack of appetite," which is, in fact, rare.
a (BN), by contrast, was first clinically described in
torical accounts it, too, does not appear to be a new
'9). The word *bulimia* is derived from Greek and
unger," quite the opposite of anorexia. Bulimic behav-
a in case reports as far back as 1398 when "true boulimus" was
scribed in an individual having an intense preoccupation with food and
overeating at very short intervals, terminated by vomiting (Stein & Laakso,
1988). Regardless, much less has been historically made of bulimic behavior,
and consequently, we have significantly less knowledge of this disorder.

CLINICAL PRESENTATION

One of the most notable features of individuals affected by AN is the
number and variety of odd and self-destructive behaviors in which they
willingly engage in order to lose weight. Extreme diets, refusing to eat
with others or in public places, radically changing their eating patterns,
and adopting unusual food choices are but a few examples. Perhaps paradoxically, affected individuals show an extraordinary interest in food that
belies their fear of gaining weight. They may, for example, prepare elabo-
rate meals for others, hoard food, develop an interest in nutrition, and
collect recipes. Many patients ultimately abuse laxatives, diuretics, and
stimulants in an effort to lose weight. Others develop an intense interest
in exercise and maintain strict workout regimens. All eating-disordered
patients tend to carry on these behaviors in secrecy or privacy if at all
possible.

Both AN and BN tend to have a stereotypic clinical presentation, age
at onset, and gender distribution (Kaye, Klump, Frank, & Strober, 2000).
Anorexic children tend to come from families that are characterized as
nonconflictive and intrusive. By example, the parents may tend to be
overprotective and answer for the children, maintaining rigid and inflexible rules at home. The anorexic temperament is classically risk averse,
emotionally restrained, socially constricted, obsessional, compliant, con-
ventional, and perfectionistic. Affected children are not typically resilient
and prefer order and routine in an effort to maintain control of their environment and emotions. These children are often academically successful but have poor social and sexual adjustment.

While anorexics restrict their food intake, bulimics typically overeat
foods high in carbohydrates. The binge may bring with it feelings of relief, but it is almost always followed by feelings of self-disgust and guilt,

Table 14.1.   Anorexia vs. Bulimia

Anorexia	Bulimia
Denies abnormal eating behavior	Recognizes abnormal eating behavior
Introverted	Extroverted
Turns away from food in order to cope	Turns to food in order to cope
Preoccupation with losing more weight	Preoccupation with attaining an ideal but often unrealistic weight

which lead to the compensatory purging. In addition to laxatives, diuretics, and stimulants, some patients abuse Ipecac or other emetics in order to promote vomiting.

The bulimic temperament is classically impulsive and affectively unstable. Substance abuse, nonsuicidal self-injurious behavior, and shoplifting are not uncommon, as are personality disorders. Whereas the families of children with AN tend to be highly rigid and inflexible, the families of children with BN are characterized by a notable lack of control, low levels of parental affection, negative, hostile, and disengaged interactions between members, and parental impulsivity, alcoholism, obesity, and even chaos (see Table 14.1).

ETIOLOGY

Early psychological theories proposed that AN represented a phobic avoidance of food (Crisp & Bhat, 1982). Psychoanalytic formulations suggested that anorexic patients avoid food because they have fantasies of oral impregnation (Masserman, 1941). Self-psychology suggested that the disorder arose when a child subordinated her needs to those of her mother (Geist, 1985), and still others have argued that AN is the result of an undue emphasis upon female independence and autonomy (Steiner-Adair, 1986).

More modern psychological theory on the etiology of AN began with the work of Hilda Bruch (1962), who viewed self-starvation as a representation of an effort to gain control. She posited that the mother's failure to recognize and confirm a child's independence produced difficulties in three areas: (a) a propensity to overestimate body size; (b) an inability to correctly identify internal sensations, such as hunger, satiety, mood, and sexual feelings; and (c) a general sense of feeling ineffective in one's life and a loss of control. Bruch's observations and writings were timely and coincided with greater societal recognition of eating disorders.

Current psychological theories stress that anorexics are avoidant of normal maturational challenges, which are perceived as insurmountable. Concretization and avoidance of psychological discord follow thereafter. These children aim for the antithesis of puberty. They feel unprepared for adolescence and adulthood and exert control by not eating, thereby staying young, immature, and prepubescent. They experience profound self-loathing along with the illusion of competence because of their ability to follow rules, dietary and otherwise (Crisp, 1980).

Other points of influence are also worthy of exploration and include the role of the family, cognition, and social influences. Minuchin, Rosman, and Baker (1978) have suggested that anorexia amounts to a cry for help from a child who is enmeshed within a conflicted and dysfunctional family. Furthermore, they suggest that family members unconsciously collude to perpetuate the child's symptoms because focus on the child defuses the parental conflicts. Cognitive-behavior theory, meanwhile, proposes that individuals are rewarded by peers and society for being slender, which for some can be sufficiently powerful to maintain the illness despite the health risks. Finally, the social and cultural emphasis upon being thin and the associated pressures that are overtly and covertly placed upon children by the fashion industry and reflected in every aspect of media are believed to contribute in some way to the genesis of eating disorders (Brumberg, 1988). The stress to conform to the American ideal of youth, beauty, and slimness is an enduring characteristic of our society.

It is no wonder that the media has been targeted in the war on eating disorders. Ninety percent of all girls ages 3–11 in the United States own a Barbie doll. If Barbie were a real woman, her measurements would be 38″-18″-34″ (Brownell & Napolitano, 1995). This body shape portrayed in toys and advertising as the ideal for women is possessed naturally by only about 1 in 100,000 women (Norton, 1996). Consequently, most women in our society maintain a body shape that is very different from that which is idealized, and through media images they are constantly reminded of this fact. There is no doubt that these images have an effect on girls and boys. The degree of impact, however, remains unknown.

Over 60 years ago it was proposed that AN had a biological basis and might be the result of a pituitary or hypothalamic disturbance. More recently, the role of neurotransmitters in both AN and BN has been studied with some interesting results. A number of neuroendocrine abnormalities have been observed in both disorders, including alteration in the hypothalamic-pituitary-gonadal axis, hypothalamic-pituitary-adrenal axis, thyroid system, growth hormone, fluid conservation, metabolism, and autonomic nervous system (Kaye et al., 2000). Most of these observed changes, however, appear to occur as a result of the malnutrition of the eating disorder itself and normalize readily once nutrition is restored. The occurrence of amenorrhea, or loss of the menstrual period, also suggests a hypothalamic disturbance. Most commonly, amenorrhea appears to occur as a consequence of weight loss. However, in about 20% of patients the amenorrhea occurs before the onset of dietary restriction (Kaplan, Sadock, & Greb, 1994a).

Studies of the cerebrospinal fluid of anorexic patients have found an increase in corticotrophin releasing factor (CRF). When administered to rats, CRF leads to a reduction in food intake, feeding time, and feeding episodes. CRF also leads to an increase in grooming time, decreased sexual activity, and hyperactivity, all of which are also noted among anorexics (Kaye et al., 2000). Another hormone, leptin, appears to play a key role in anorexia as well, as several symptoms of anorexia, including amenorrhea and semistarvation-induced hyperactivity, are related to low levels of circulating leptin. Leptin is secreted by adipose tissue, and once the body fat drops precipitously low, no more leptin is released; this, in turn, leads to down regulation of the hypothalamic-pituitary-gonadal and thyroid axes and an up regulation of the hypothalamic-pituitary-adrenal axis (Müller, Föcker, Holtkamp, Herpertz-Dahlmann, & Hebebrand, 2009). Other peptides, including adiponectin, resistin, ghrelin, peptide YY (PYY), neurotrophin brain-derived neurotrophic factor (BDNF), and endocannabinoid substances may also play some as yet unidentified role in the etiology of both AN and BN (Monteleone, Castaldo, & Maj, 2008).

Other evidence supports neurotransmitter system dysregulation in eating disorders, which affects serotonin, norepinephrine, and dopamine. Serotonin pathways are important in the pathological behaviors generally observed in people with eating disorders, such as obsessionality and disturbance in mood, eating, and impulse control. Numerous studies have shown altered levels of serotonin among those with eating disorders, and it appears that these disturbances persist even after recovery (Kaye et al., 2000). While theories of serotonergic hyperfunctioning in AN and serotonergic hypofunctioning in BN are attractive, they do not explain why selective serotonin reuptake inhibitors (SSRIs) can be helpful for both disorders. Additional evidence suggests that reduced norepinephrine activity and turnover play a role in eating disorders, resulting in hypotension, bradycardia, hypothermia, and depression (Pirke, 1996). Finally, vomiting leads to an increase in dopamine levels in the area postrema, which ironically rewards and reinforces vomiting behavior.

Eating disorders are familial. The risk of AN among mothers and sisters of probands is estimated at 4% or about eight times the rate among the general population (Strober, Freeman, Lampert, Diamond, & Kaye, 2000). A large twin registry study appears to confirm that BN and AN are related. This study found that the co-twin of a child with AN was 2.6 times more likely to have a diagnosis of BN than were co-twins of children without an eating disorder (Walters & Kendler, 1995). Twin studies confirm a genetic link. Studies of identical or monozygotic twins show concordance of up to 90% for AN and 83% for BN (Kaye et al., 2000). Nearly all women in Western society diet at some point in adolescence or young adulthood, yet fewer than 1% develop AN. While not entirely causal, a genetic predisposition must play a significant role.

EPIDEMIOLOGY

While the prevalence of AN lies somewhere between 0.3% and 0.8%, the annual incidence or number of new cases per year is less than 0.1%. The prevalence of BN is considerably higher, affecting somewhere between 1.7% and 2.5% of the population, but with an annual incidence of also less than 0.1% (American Psychiatric Association, 2000; Kaye et al., 2000). These figures demonstrate that eating disorders are highly chronic because even though only small numbers of new cases occur each year, much higher percentages of affected individuals maintain their disorders. The prevalence of both disorders among men is about one-tenth that of women.

The symptoms of eating disorders, such as binge eating, purging, fasting, use of laxatives, and excessive exercise, are much more common than the disorders themselves. Most individuals, in fact, who employ these behaviors at one time or another do not go on to develop a full-blown eating disorder. The typical age of onset for AN is 14–18 years and for BN, late adolescence and early adulthood. AN is more prevalent in industrialized societies where food is abundant and the cultural norm links beauty to thinness. Immigrants who move from countries with low rates of AN to Western cultures increase their vulnerability to the disorder as they assimilate to the new culture (American Psychiatric Association, 2000).

The onset of puberty is a major risk factor for AN. Other risks include a perfectionistic personality; a history of mood disorder; obsessive-compulsive or other anxiety disorder; impaired family interactions; and stressful life events, such as a history of sexual abuse or moving away from home for the first time. Risk factors for BN include dieting, puberty, and transitions, such as starting college, a new job, or the breakup of a relationship. Certain jobs and activities carry a particularly high risk of bulimia. Athletes who must maintain their weight class, such as wrestlers and ballerinas, and actors and models are prime examples. A history of AN, impulsivity, and anxiety are also risk factors for the development of BN.

CLINICAL COURSE

Long-term follow-up studies show varying rates of recovery for both AN and BN, much of which has to do with the design of each study and the length of follow-up. Studies referenced here ranged from 2 months to 20 years. Approximately 50% of anorexics achieve a normal weight, and fewer than 10% are overweight at follow-up. Consequently, only about half of anorexics eventually achieve a normal weight, defined as within 10–15% of ideal body weight. Also unfortunate is the fact that only about one-third of anorexics maintain a normal diet upon follow-up, whereas one-half avoid high-calorie foods and up to one-half display evidence of bulimic behaviors, including binge eating, vomiting, and laxative abuse. Menstrual functioning returns in about 40–90% of affected women but typically only after 90% of ideal body weight is attained. Psychosocial impairments are common at follow-up, including difficulties with educational, vocational, psychological, social, and sexual functioning. Even among those who improve, many continue to display characteristic symptoms of the illness, such as a distorted body image. Within the first 5 years of the illness, as many as 30% of anorexics begin to engage in bulimic behavior. Finally, mortality has generally been accepted to be 10% after 10 years, but longer-term studies now suggest higher rates of up to 15% after 20 years. AN, therefore, has the highest mortality rate in psychiatry. About 50% of deaths are due to complications from the illness, 25% die by suicide, and 25% die of unrelated causes (American Psychiatric Association, 2000; Fisher, 2003). In general terms, those who are doing poorly at 5-to-10-year follow-up most often continue to do poorly or die within the following years.

BN typically begins in the context of a diet. In most cases the illness continues for years after onset and may take a waxing and waning course. We have considerably less long-term follow-up data available on BN, but behaviors often persist, such as vomiting (28–77%), binge eating (29–67%), and laxative abuse (3–13%). Furthermore, depression commonly affects somewhere between 15% and 36% at follow-up (Fisher, 2003).

Poor outcome in AN is generally associated with a longer duration and greater severity of illness, lowest weight achieved, duration of inpatient admissions, number of readmissions, and comorbid bulimic behaviors. In addition, psychiatric comorbidity, particularly borderline personality disorder, and, to a lesser extent, depression and anxiety, predict a worse outcome. Very early onset AN, under 12 years of age, predicts a bad outcome, as is expected for a highly virulent disorder that would set on so early. Paradoxically, however, onset between 12 and 18 years of age is better than adult onset, as measured by long-term outcome, normalization of body weight, menstruation, eating behaviors, and psychiatric comorbidity. Outcome is better for adolescents because they are still minors, and families can mandate treatment for them (Fisher, 2003).

Though we know considerably less about the prognosis of BN, certainly the long-term outcome is better than with AN. Approximately one-half of affected individuals recover, one-quarter improve but still suffer bulimic symptoms, and one-quarter remain chronically ill. After 10 years, about two-thirds to three-quarters of bulimics are in at least partial recovery. Relatively few bulimics cross over into AN, with rates no higher than 15% at long-term follow-up. Comorbid psychiatric conditions, particularly borderline personality disorder, but also depression, anxiety, and alcohol abuse, have a negative impact on outcome. Social adjustment and personal relationships tend to normalize over time for bulimics, but many women continue to suffer from social and sexual impairments. Finally, the mortality of BN ranges from 1% to 6% after many years of follow-up (Steinhausen, 2009).

AN wreaks havoc on the entire body. Weight loss is not the only outcome, although most secondary effects are due to the malnourished state. Hypothermia, dependent edema, anemia, impaired renal function, bradycardia, hypotension, cardiac arrhythmias, lanugo (soft downy hair on the skin), osteoporosis, and even brain atrophy are common for those who are chronically ill. Hormonal abnormalities may include elevated growth hormone and plasma cortisol levels, along with reduced gonadotropin, follicle-stimulating hormone, luteinizing hormone, and estrogen levels (testosterone in males). Triiodothyronine (T3 thyroid hormone) is often decreased, although T4 and TSH (thyroid-stimulating hormone) levels are often normal. In addition to amenorrhea, physical symptoms commonly include constipation, abdominal pain, cold intolerance, lethargy, and excessive energy (see Figure 14.1).

Bulimics, by contrast, frequently develop many symptoms secondary to the purging behaviors, such as calluses on the dorsal surface of their hands from self-induced vomiting and the biting or clamping down of their jaw that follows a gag reflex. Additionally, dental caries due to corrosion of the enamel from stomach acid are often observed, along with esophageal erosion and a risk of rupture, which, while rare, can be fatal. Enlarged parotid glands and a resultant "chipmunk" face are due to the increased amylase released from the parotid glands, which accompanies vomiting. Bradycardia, hypotension, and cardiac arrhythmias secondary to hypokalemia (low potassium) may follow. Bulimic patients may also develop lanugo hair, as in AN. Medical complications include hypocalcemia (low calcium), hypochloridemia (low chloride), hypokalemia, metabolic alkalosis, electrolyte disturbances, serum transaminase

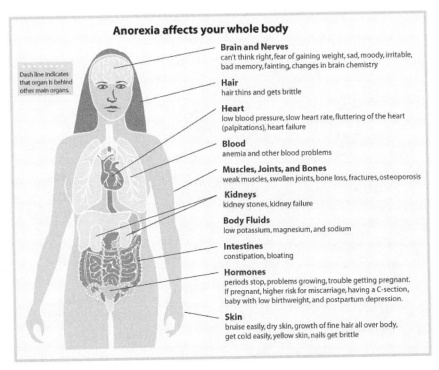

Figure 14.1.   Impact of anorexia nervosa on the body. Anorexia nervosa literally starves the body of needed protein and calories, resulting in a plethora of impairments to virtually all major body systems.
U.S. Department of Health and Human Services.

increases reflecting fatty degeneration of the liver, lethargy, and seizures (see Figure 14.2).

DIAGNOSIS

The *DSM-IV* defines three eating disorders: AN, BN, and *eating disorder NOS* (not otherwise specified). AN is further subcategorized into *restricting type* (e.g., those who only restrict their food intake) and *binge-eating/ purging type* (e.g., those who restrict food intake but also engage in binge-eating and/or purging behaviors, such as self-induced vomiting or the misuse of laxatives, diuretics, or enemas). Binge-eating/purging type anorexics often demonstrate many of the typical eating behaviors, personality characteristics, and family troubles of "classic" bulimics. Likewise, BN is also subcategorized into *purging type* (e.g., those who self-induce vomiting and/or misuse laxatives, diuretics, or enemas to purge) and *nonpurging type*

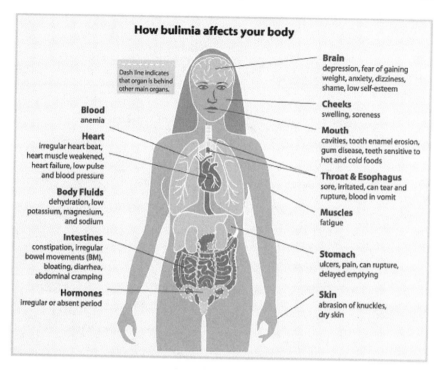

Figure 14.2. Impact of bulimia nervosa on the body. The binging and purging of bulimia nervosa commonly result in damage to many major body systems. U.S. Department of Health and Human Services.

(e.g., those who use other compensatory behaviors after binge eating, such as excessive exercise or fasting). Eating disorder NOS captures all other variants of abnormal eating behavior, including binge-eating disorder (American Psychiatric Association, 2000).

The *DSM-IV* diagnosis of AN requires four features: (a) a marked self-induced weight loss or failure to make expected weight gain during growth, resulting in a body weight of less than 85% of that expected; (b) an intense fear of weight gain or becoming fat, despite being underweight; (c) a fundamental disturbance in the way in which one perceives his or her body weight or shape, such that one feels overweight despite evidence to the contrary, and harshly evaluates oneself based on body weight or shape; and (d) endocrine changes resulting in amenorrhea in females for at least three consecutive months and a lack of sexual interest, virulence, and potency in males (American Psychiatric Association, 2000).

The discrepancy between body weight and perceived body image is key to the diagnosis of AN. Anorexics take great joy in their weight loss and feel highly competent as dieters. Even at subnormal weights, anorexics perceive themselves as fat and are driven to lose more weight. They are intensely fearful of gaining weight and becoming fat and are extraordinarily preoccupied with body shape and size. All of their efforts are aimed at lowering their body weight still further, and the illness entirely distorts their self-perception and takes all of their time. Sexual development is also commonly delayed, and physical growth slows or ceases entirely due to lack of nutrition and altered hormone levels.

The *DSM-IV* diagnosis of BN requires recurrent episodes of binge eating, which is defined as eating more than one would normally within a discrete period of time and feeling a lack of control during eating. The diagnosis also requires repeated compensatory behaviors in an effort to counteract the weight gain, such as vomiting, misusing laxatives, diuretics, enemas, or other medications, fasting, or exercising excessively. The binge eating and compensatory behaviors must occur on average at least twice a week for at least 3 months. Finally, the *DSM-IV* also requires that, as with AN, one's self-evaluation is overly influenced by body weight and shape (American Psychiatric Association, 2000).

Bulimics feel overwhelmed by the urge to binge and often only stop eating when they become too physically uncomfortable to continue. Although binge eating may briefly elevate one's mood, the episodes are generally triggered by stress and dysphoria, and after the binge these feelings immediately return. Subsequent feelings of guilt, anxiety, and depression follow because of their perceived inability to control intake and appetite. In an effort to regain control over their prior eating episode, the compensatory behaviors take hold. The most common method is vomiting, but as previously noted, laxatives, diuretics, appetite suppressants, enemas, fasting, stimulants, and excessive exercise are not uncommon.

Individuals with a diagnosis of eating disorder NOS generally represent those who have either been effectively treated for their eating disorder but maintain some residual symptoms, or those who are on the way toward the development of a full-blown eating disorder. Additionally, this category may represent those who vomit after eating small amounts of "guilty" foods (e.g., a cupcake), chew their food and then spit it out before swallowing, or binge eat without then using compensatory behaviors to purge the food (American Psychiatric Association, 2000).

According to the *DSM-IV*, obesity is not an eating disorder. The National Institutes of Health (2000) defines obesity in adults as a body mass index (BMI) of greater than or equal to 30 kg/meter^2 and in youth as a BMI of greater than the 95th percentile. By this definition, one in three adults in America is obese, a doubling in prevalence since 1980 (Hedley et al., 2004). Approximately 17% of American youth are obese and another 17%

are at risk of being overweight, as defined by a BMI greater than the 85th percentile, representing a tripling in prevalence over the past 30 years (Hedley et al., 2004; Ogden et al., 2006). Although not an eating disorder per se, obesity is associated with a greatly increased rate of not only many medical and physical complications (e.g., diabetes, cardiovascular disease, sleep apnea, hypertension, stroke, and even some cancers), but also depression and lowered self-esteem (Bean, Stewart, & Olbrisch, 2008).

The differential diagnosis of AN includes a number of psychiatric and medical illnesses. Obsessive-compulsive disorder (OCD) is not only a potential alternate diagnosis, but also a common comorbidity, particularly given the ritualistic eating behaviors so often in evidence. Some have even argued that AN may be a variant of OCD, as obsessive-compulsive symptoms are so common among anorexics and ritualistic eating behaviors seen among anorexics can be experimentally induced in lab animals by starvation (Herpertz-Dahlmann, 2009). Major depressive disorder (MDD) is also characterized by weight loss, and given the seemingly delusional aspects of AN, schizophrenia is sometimes considered in the differential as well. However, in both mood and psychotic disorders the weight loss is not desired, nor is there a fear of gaining weight. Aspects of both social phobia and body dysmorphic disorder (BDD) are frequently present in AN. BDD can be distinguished from AN by the presence of distortions unrelated to body weight and shape. Anorexics may be socially phobic, but this diagnosis is only valid if the individual is phobic about a variety of social behaviors and situations and not just eating in public. Numerous medical disorders can also cause excessive weight loss, including HIV, cancer, and gastrointestinal disease. In each case, however, the weight loss is not desired, and the affected individuals do not typically have a distorted body image.

The differential diagnosis for BN includes anxiety and mood disorders, particularly MDD with atypical features, along with borderline personality disorder. Important general medical conditions to rule out include Kleine-Levin syndrome, which is characterized by periodic hyperphagia, hypersomnia, and irritability in male adolescents and typically has a self-limiting course; and Klüver-Bucy syndrome, a limbic system dysfunction with resulting visual and auditory agnosia, placidity, hyperorality, hypersexuality, and hyperphagia. Klüver-Bucy is sometimes seen in Pick's disease, HIV encephalopathy, herpes encephalitis, and brain tumors.

Psychiatric comorbidities are extremely common among eating disorders, and the majority of affected individuals will meet criteria for another disorder during either the acute stage of the illness and/or over the long-term course. Up to 80% of adolescents with AN suffer MDD, and similar rates have been found among bulimics. Up to 20% of anorexics and 35% of bulimics acknowledge having attempted suicide with a greater likelihood among those who engage in binge/purge behavior. Suicidal behavior is associated with the severity of the eating disorder and the presence of cluster B personality disorders. Up to 60% of anorexics and 75% of bulimics have a comorbid anxiety disorder, among which social phobia, panic disorder, agoraphobia, generalized anxiety disorder, and posttraumatic stress disorder are particularly common. Studies of adults with both AN and BN indicate a 40% lifetime comorbidity of OCD, while studies of adolescents reveal rates of about 20%. Alcohol and substance abuse affect upward of 25% of all individuals with eating disorders and 30% among binge/purge anorexics and bulimics. Personality disorders, particularly cluster C among restricting anorexics and cluster B among binge/purge anorexics and bulimics, are also elevated among individuals with eating disorders (Herpertz-Dahlmann, 2009).

Both AN and BN commonly lead to a variety of endocrine changes, which are generally a result of starvation or abnormal eating behavior. By definition, amenorrhea is a core symptom of anorexia, but other endocrine changes affecting the adrenal and thyroid glands, as well as neuropeptides such as leptin and ghrelin, are well established. Adolescents with eating disorders are at increased risk of osteopenia and osteoporosis, as most bone mass is built up during adolescence, and this process cannot be adequately achieved in the presence of starvation (Herpertz-Dahlmann, 2009).

Warning Signs of an Eating Disorder

There are numerous warning signs that indicate a child may be at risk of developing an eating disorder. These include dissatisfaction with body shape, weight, or size; skipping meals; fasting for 24 hours; losing weight to the bottom of the healthy range for age and size; exercising excessively; preferring to eat in private and not in public; demonstrating a tendency toward perfectionism; developing odd eating habits, such as chewing each bite for extensive periods of time or cutting food into very small pieces; vomiting after an occasional large meal; most often choosing low-fat or low-carbohydrate foods or becoming a vegetarian; demonstrating sudden episodes of binging; overeating and then starving in regular cycles; studying food labels for nutritional content; rigidly applying diet plans such as Weight Watcher's, Jenny Craig, South Beach, or Atkins; and being physically and emotionally uncomfortable after eating because of anxiety about the calories ingested. For AN specifically, additional signs include excessive weight loss, odd food rituals, lack of menstrual cycles, lanugo hair on the face, arms, and torso, wearing baggy clothing, exercising vigorously at odd hours, appearing pale or dizzy, and fainting. Additional signs of BN include fluctuating weight, missing food around the house, secret eating, cuts or scrapes on the back of the hand from purging, tooth decay from vomiting, using the bathroom after meals, taking diet pills or abusing laxatives, emetics, or enemas, demonstrating self-disparaging talk related to food intake, and having swollen glands, puffy cheeks, or broken blood vessels under the eyes (Strober & Schneider, 2005).

During a clinical evaluation, questions may include:

- *Do you constantly think about food?*
- *Do you find it hard to concentrate because you are thinking about food and your weight?*
- *Do you worry about how the food you eat is affecting your body?*
- *Do you feel guilt and shame after you eat?*
- *Do you find it hard to eat in public? Do you prefer eating alone?*
- *Are you constantly counting calories?*
- *Do you feel fat regardless of what others say about your body?*
- *Even if you're thin, do you find that you still obsess about parts of your body and how they look (e.g., stomach, hips, thighs, etc.)?*
- *Do you feel like you're constantly weighing yourself?*
- *Does your mood change with the number on the scale?*
- *Do you punish yourself with more exercise and food restriction if you don't like the number on the scale?*
- *Do you exercise more than 1 hour five times each week with the goal of burning calories?*
- *Do you exercise even if you are ill or injured?*
- *Do you think of foods as "good" and "bad?"*
- *Do you vomit after eating or use laxatives or diuretics?*

TREATMENT

Anorexia Nervosa

The treatment of AN must focus on three primary issues: (a) restoring weight; (b) modifying distorted eating behavior; and (c) addressing the psychological and family issues. Treatment methods typically include nutritional rehabilitation, psychotherapy, and medication. Many individuals with an eating disorder can be treated on an outpatient basis, which sometimes includes periods of intensive day treatment, but in the United States about half of all patients with AN who seek treatment are hospitalized

(Herpertz-Dahlmann & Salback-Andrae, 2009). Hospitalization is typically encouraged when the patient is severely malnourished, dehydrated, suffering from an electrolyte imbalance, or facing other physically threatening complications. Hospitalization is also indicated when outpatient treatment has not been effective, there is a risk of suicide, psychosis is present, or there is a major lack of motivation toward resolving the eating disorder. The benefits of inpatient versus outpatient treatment remain unclear, however, and as yet we have no evidence-based criteria for inpatient admission. Additionally, adequate controlled studies comparing day treatment to inpatient programs have not been performed (Herpertz-Dahlmann & Salback-Andrae, 2009).

Although systematic studies are lacking, there is general support for a multimodal treatment approach that incorporates nutritional rehabilitation, nutritional counseling, individual psychotherapy to help correct cognitive distortions and improve self-esteem, group therapy, and family or parent therapy. Comorbid medical and psychiatric conditions should also be addressed concurrently.

The goals of nutritional rehabilitation are to restore weight, normalize eating patterns, reestablish normal perceptions of hunger and satiety, and correct the biological and psychological sequelae of malnutrition. The treatment plan should establish clear goals for target weight gain, which are generally accepted to be 1–2 pounds per week for inpatients and 0.5–1 pound per week for outpatients. Nutritionists and pediatricians are often involved in this phase of treatment, and routine lab parameters must be followed. Physical activity must be monitored as well and restricted if it interferes with weight gain. All reasonable steps should be taken to avoid forced feeding, but severely malnourished patients who refuse to eat must be aggressively managed (American Psychiatric Association, 2006).

Nutritional counseling involves the establishment of meal plans, proper food choices, and balanced nutrition. Both individual and group psychoeducation is often employed, as are group cooking sessions and meals in order to combat the shame that many anorexics feel when eating with others. Involving the family in this process is also important, as is supporting parents in their efforts to speak with their children about food.

Many different types of individual psychotherapy have been evaluated among adults with AN, but no controlled studies have been performed in children and adolescents. Cognitive behavior therapy (CBT), interpersonal therapy (IPT), cognitive analytic therapy, focal psychoanalytic therapy, and specialist supportive clinical management have all shown utility in adults, and it is not clear that any one method is superior to others. Regardless of the technique, the establishment of a trusting and accepting relationship with the therapist is vital. Additionally, therapists are generally more effective with anorexics when they actively engage the patient and directly address body image and concept, growth and development, and family and peer interactions. Typical cognitive distortions affecting those with anorexia should also be addressed in therapy and include personalization, polarized thinking, mind reading, catastrophizing, shoulds, overgeneralizing, and global labeling (see Chapter 10).

Group psychotherapy is also a mainstay of treatment for AN in both inpatient and outpatient settings. Still, only one randomized controlled trial has examined the efficacy of group therapy for anorexia, and no studies have compared individual versus group psychotherapy. Pilot studies of dialectical behavior therapy (DBT) in adolescents suggest utility in the treatment of both AN and BN, but further study is required (Herpertz-Dahlmann & Salback-Andrae, 2009).

Finally, family-based therapy (FBT), which grew out of the work of Minuchin and has been developed at the Maudsley Institute in London, is a problem-focused therapy that aims to change behavior through unified parental action. The family in FBT is not viewed as the cause of the disorder, but rather as a positive resource in the adolescent's weight restoration and return to normal eating and health. In fact, FBT takes no stance on disease etiology and tries instead to separate the pathology of AN from the adolescent herself. FBT posits that figuring out the strengths of the family and finding new solutions are much more helpful than pursuing the search for an etiology of the illness within the family. The first phase of treatment supports the parents in their efforts to restore their child's weight. The second phase begins when the child has reached 90% of ideal body weight and is eating without much resistance; at this point the parents are supported in returning the responsibility for their child's eating back to the child. The final phase generally begins when the adolescent has achieved a healthy weight for age and height and focuses on the general issues of adolescent development and how the eating disorder affected this process. There are few contraindications to FBT, but in families where there is significant parental psychopathology or a very critical environment, family therapy has been found less useful (le Grange & Eisler, 2009). FBT, or the so-called Maudsley Method, has been shown effective in 50–75% of adolescents, who in randomized trials achieved weight restoration by the end of treatment and maintained it for up to 5 years. In one trial of adolescents with a short history of illness, the response rate reached 90% (Eisler et al., 1997).

Medication Treatment

Medications have not generally proven themselves to be remarkably effective for the treatment of AN. However, tricyclic antidepressants (TCAs), monoamine oxidase inhibitors (MAOIs), trazodone (Desyrel), and the selective serotonin reuptake inhibitors (SSRIs) have demonstrated benefit in the treatment of binge/purge behavior in BN. The greatest evidence of benefit lies with fluoxetine (Prozac), which has been approved by the FDA for the treatment of adults with BN in both acute and maintenance treatment at a dosage of 60 mg per day (Fichter et al., 1991; Fluoxetine Bulimia Nervosa Collaborative Study Group, 1992). Follow-up studies suggest that fluoxetine should be continued for at least 1 year among those who respond positively to the medication within the first 8 weeks, as it extends the time to relapse. Much less data supports the use of fluoxetine and other antidepressants for children and adolescents with BN. The most impressive study is an open-label investigation, which treated adolescents for 8 weeks with 60 mg of fluoxetine per day, along with supportive psychotherapy. The study found decreases in binge and purge episodes, and 70% of subjects were rated as improved or much improved by study's end (Kotler, Devlin, Davies, & Walsh, 2003). While fluoxetine can also be used to treat comorbidities, such as depression and OCD among patients with eating disorders, the medication appears to treat binge-and-purge behavior regardless of the presence of comorbid depression (Goldstein, Wilson, Ascroft, & al-Banna, 1999). Although other medications may be employed to treat the comorbidities of BN, no other medications are indicated in the treatment of BN itself. Certainly, bupropion (Wellbutrin) is contraindicated given the elevated risk of seizures in patients with BN.

Medications considered for the treatment of AN have generally included antidepressants and antipsychotics. Scant data, however, supports their use in adults, and virtually nothing other than a few case reports suggests their utility in children and adolescents (Couturier & Lock, 2007). Both TCAs and SSRIs have shown little promise in the treatment of adult AN. Kaye et al. (2001) did find an increased time to relapse with fluoxetine compared to placebo in 35 patients, but a larger randomized controlled trial of 93 adults found the opposite (Walsh et al., 2006).

As with antidepressants, there is little data to support the use of antipsychotics among patients with AN. Case reports of olanzapine (Zyprexa) among children and adolescents and risperidone (Risperdal) have reported greater treatment compliance and weight gain, along with decreased anxiety and agitation (Boachie, Goldfield, & Spettigue, 2003; Newman-Toker, 2000).

Among adults, one small randomized trial compared 10 mg of olanzapine with 50 mg of chlorpromazine (Thorazine) and found decreases in rumination with olanzapine but no differences in weight gain (Mondraty et al., 2005). Consequently, limited data suggest that olanzapine and perhaps other atypical antipsychotics may be helpful with reducing eating-related anxiety and perhaps supporting weight gain. There is a small amount of evidence supporting the use of SSRIs for relapse prevention, but in general medications for AN should be addressed at treatment co-morbidities. The practitioner must be cautious, however, as symptoms of depression and OCD often resolve independently once the AN is treated and weight is restored.

Bulimia Nervosa

Although medications can have a significant role in the treatment of BN, as with AN, effective treatment is largely psychotherapeutic. The main issues of concern in the treatment of BN are: (a) reducing or eliminating binge eating and purging; (b) modifying distorted eating behavior; and (c) addressing the psychological and family issues. Hospitalization is less commonly necessary than with AN but is sometimes employed, particularly for those affected individuals who have comorbid conditions that are interfering with recovery from the BN.

Nutritional rehabilitation in the case of BN generally involves the design of structured meal planning to reduce episodes of dietary restriction and the urge to binge, along with adequate nutrition to promote satiety and reduce craving. Simply being of normal or expected BMI or weight for age and size does not equate to adequate nutrition or normal body composition. Finally, nutritional counseling is helpful for all affected individuals to assist with food restriction, expand the variety of foods eaten, and encourage healthy exercise habits (American Psychiatric Association, 2006).

CBT has demonstrated efficacy for the treatment of adults with BN in both individual and group settings with little difference between the two approaches. Preliminary evidence suggests that DBT, too, may be effective for BN in adults (Herpertz-Dahlmann & Salbach-Andrae, 2009). CBT has been modified specifically for the treatment of BN (CBT-BN) by placing emphasis upon bulimic behaviors and cognitions, such as distortions about weight, shape, and appearance (Fairburn, Marcus, & Wilson, 1993). Among adults with BN, CBT-BN is at least as effective as other psychotherapies if not superior in producing recovery. The National Institute for Health and Clinical Excellence of the United Kingdom now recommends CBT-BN as the treatment of choice for BN and binge eating disorder. After a course of treatment, 30–40% of patients are free of symptoms and maintain these gains at long-term follow-up. Studies of CBT-BN in adolescents, however, are few in number and supported only by anecdotal report and case studies (Schmidt, 2009).

Other psychotherapy studies of adolescents have reported mixed results. One randomized controlled study compared family therapy with a manualized form of CBT. Results indicate that CBT leads to earlier improvements in bingeing but few other differences in clinical outcomes compared to family therapy. Another group adapted CBT for individual Internet access by adolescents and found after eight interactive online sessions that the treatment was acceptable and effective in reducing bingeing, vomiting, global eating disorder problems, and service contacts at 3 and 6 months posttreatment (Schmidt, 2009). For patients who do not respond to CBT, both IPT and family therapy have shown some, although generally less, utility (American Psychiatric Association, 2006).

Eating Disorder Not Otherwise Specified

Given the variety of symptoms and presentations that can accompany a diagnosis of eating disorder NOS, the most sensible approach is to treat the patient for the disorder that most closely approximates her symptoms (National Institute for Clinical Excellence, 2004). Consequently, if the patient is binge eating or purging, then a treatment protocol for BN may be most appropriate. Alternatively, if food restriction is the greatest problem, then treating for AN is suggested.

15

Sleep Disorders

Although we have some general understanding of the biochemical, neurophysiological, and neuroendocrine activities during sleep, we still do not entirely understand the function of sleep. Certainly, sleep appears to be both restorative and homeostatic, helping us to conserve energy and maintain our body temperature. Sleep is also important in the consolidation of learning and memory and for healthy neurocognitive functioning (Brawn, Fenn, Nusbaum, & Margoliash, 2008). It has been suggested that the programming of species-specific behaviors occurs during sleep, such that animals and humans rehearse instinctual behaviors during sleep (Tauber & Glovinsky, 1987). Regardless of its function, problems with sleep are ubiquitous but rarely a cause for great concern. Although individuals with diagnosable sleep problems generally have higher rates of mood and anxiety disorders than the general population, the vast majority do not suffer major psychiatric impairments.

CLINICAL PRESENTATION

Most parents struggle to help their infants, children, and adolescents establish habits of good sleep hygiene. Parents must teach infants to self-soothe and put themselves back to sleep in the middle of the night, for no child truly sleeps through the night. Infants awaken every few hours, as do children and adults, simply to roll over and fall back to sleep. If we do not teach our infants to fall asleep on their own, however, they will never be able to soothe themselves back to sleep during these normal nighttime awakenings.

Some parents prefer a family bed, where all members co-sleep in the same bed or sleep separately but share the same room. Unlike our psychoanalytic forefathers, psychiatrists today have no reason to suspect that sleeping in the same bed or room is damaging in any way to our children's psyche. Yet children must still learn the skill of falling asleep on their own even in a family bed. Without this training, our children's sleep will be disrupted by their awakenings, during which time they will search out a parent to soothe them back down, which leads to even more awakenings and fracturing of a normal night's sleep. The only situation in which sleeping with an infant or child is potentially dangerous is when the parent has been drinking alcohol or taking medications or drugs that can impair their ability to awaken easily. In these situations, the risk of sudden infant death syndrome (SIDS) is increased, as the parent may roll over on top of the infant and suffocate the child without awakening.

Children and adolescents have additional issues with sleep. Children may bed wet, or experience nightmares, narcolepsy, night terrors, or insomnia; others may sleepwalk, talk in their sleep, grind their teeth, or suffer breathing difficulties during sleep; still others may simply refuse to go to bed. Adolescents may experience these difficulties as well, in addition to a delayed sleep phase, such that their sleep cycle becomes shifted to later in the evening. Sleep-phase disorders can lead to severe difficulties with awakening on time for school or other activities.

Infants, children, and adolescents traverse most sleep problems without seeking professional consultation. Still, most parents will benefit from learning about sleep and proper sleep hygiene, which will allow them to teach their children good sleep habits, which, in turn, will promote a more refreshing night's sleep and better daytime energy and concentration (Weiss, Wasdell, Bomben, Rea, & Freeman, 2006).

Sleep Problems Associated with Psychiatric Conditions

Sleep difficulties are common in a number of psychiatric disorders and a core *DSM-IV* symptom among other psychiatric conditions. Disrupted sleep has long been recognized as a feature of children diagnosed with attention-deficit/hyperactivity disorder (ADHD), for example. The *Diagnostic and Statistical Manual of Mental Disorders*, third edition (*DSM-III*), in fact, considered excessive movements during sleep to be a criterion for hyperactivity in children (American Psychiatric Association, 1980). Children with ADHD usually show greater variation in sleep onset time, wake time, and sleep duration; significantly more bedtime struggles with parents than other children; an increase in the frequency of habitual snoring to 3 times that among the general population; and a greater frequency of periodic leg movement disorder (PLMD) and sleep-disordered breathing (SDB) (Sung, Hiscock, Sciberras, & Efron, 2008).

Children, adolescents, and adults diagnosed with autism spectrum disorders also commonly experience sleep difficulties. The clinical presentation of these children may include difficulties falling asleep, frequent awakenings with difficulty returning to sleep, early-morning awakening, irregular sleep-wake patterns, a shortened duration of sleep, and dyssomnias and parasomnias (Johnson & Malow, 2008).

The clinical presentation of children with mood disorders may include bedtime resistance or anxiety, early and middle insomnia, a desire to co-sleep with parents because of fears or bad moods, enuresis, nightmares, sleepwalking, early-morning awakening, and excessive daytime sleepiness. Over 50% of depressed adolescents report difficulties falling and staying asleep with extended evening awakenings, excessive daytime sleepiness, and unrefreshing sleep, while a much smaller percentage report hypersomnia (Liu et al., 2007). Adolescents who report sleep problems are also much more likely to report symptoms of depression, anxiety, poor self-esteem, lethargy, irritability, and emotional lability even in the absence of a proper mood disorder (Ivanenko, Crabtree, & Gozal, 2005). Adolescents who report sleep problems are also much more likely to consume caffeine, nicotine, alcohol, and drugs, which themselves cause difficulties with sleep (Roane & Taylor, 2008). Consequently, sleep problems should be viewed as a potential early marker for adolescents at risk of developing some sort of psychopathology.

The clinical presentation of anxiety in children includes nighttime fears that commonly take the form of animals and age appropriate fictitious characters, such as witches and monsters. Children may also fear being kidnapped or being teased by peers. Anxiety also appears to predispose children to parasomnias and nightmares (Muris, Merckelbach, Gadet, & Moulaert, 2000).

ETIOLOGY

The electroencephalogram (EEG) provides a reliable and reproducible measure of brain waves during sleep and allows us to define various sleep stages. While awake and alert, the brain is predominantly generating beta waves. As seen in Figure 15.1, beta waves are of low amplitude and are the fastest of the four types of brain waves, running at a frequency of 15–40 cycles per second (or Hz). The presence of beta waves indicates an active and engaged mind. Someone in conversation would be producing lots of

Figure 15.1. EEG sleep patterns. Figure 15.1 illustrates the characteristic brain waves of each sleep stage. Adapted from Kaplan and Sadock (1994b).

beta waves; during an argument, an individual would be in high beta. When not aroused or when drowsy, the EEG shows a slightly higher voltage and slower (8–12 Hz) brain wave pattern, characterized by the presence of alpha waves. Someone resting or relaxed is often in alpha; during a work break or while taking a walk along the beach, one is likely to be in alpha.

Stage 1 sleep is characterized by brain waves of still greater amplitude and lower frequency, around 3–7 Hz. Theta waves are the predominant EEG brain wave pattern evident during this stage of sleep. Theta waves appear during daydreaming, while drowsy, or even when we are engaged in a repetitive task, such as freeway driving. As opposed to city driving where one is always concentrating on the traffic and beta waves are largely in evidence, theta waves appear during freeway driving because the task requires a lower level of concentration and is sometimes performed while in a trancelike state. At anytime when one is involved in an automatic task from which one can mentally disengage while still performing the task (e.g., brushing teeth, taking a shower, jogging, swimming laps, meditation, or yoga), the predominant theta waves are hypothesized to place one in a state of "flow," in which many individuals report the generation of good ideas and mental well-being (Csikszentmihalyi, 1991; Wachsmuth & Dolce, 1980). Jerking movements or sudden twitches, known as positive myoclonus, along with hallucinations upon drifting off to sleep, known as hypnagogic hallucinations, are common during Stage 1, as is some degree of muscle tone loss and decreased conscious awareness of the external environment. Stage 1 sleep occupies about 2–5% of total sleep time in children.

Stage 2 sleep is notable for high-amplitude waves at 12–16 Hz, along with sleep spindles, which are characteristic jagged runs on the EEG. In addition, larger spikes, known as K-complexes, are present. Sleep spindles may represent efforts by the brain to inhibit processing in order to maintain the individual in a tranquil state. They appear to result from interactions between cells of the thalamus and the cortex. K-complexes are brief, high-voltage peaks, usually followed by bursts of sleep spindles, which may occur in response to auditory stimuli during sleep. Stage 2 sleep is notable for reduced muscle tone and decelerations in respiration and heart rate. Children can move about freely and reposition themselves during Stage 2, which occupies about 50% of total sleep time.

Stages 3 and 4 are characterized by high-amplitude slow delta waves occurring at 0.5–2 Hz. Previously distinguished by the predominance of delta waves (e.g., in Stage 3 delta waves accounted for less than 50% of the total wave patterns and in Stage 4 more than 50%), the American

Academy of Sleep Medicine has now eliminated this distinction from their staging system. Currently, all delta wave, slow wave, or deep sleep is categorized as Stage 3, and Stage 4 no longer exists (Schulz, 2008). Parasomnias, such as night terrors, sleepwalking, sleep talking, and bruxism, commonly occur during deep sleep, which accounts for about 20% of total sleep time.

Finally, REM sleep, commonly thought of as dream sleep, is the final sleep stage. So named because of the frequent flickering of the eyelids observed as the eyes move underneath, REM sleep is characterized by low-voltage random waves with a periodic sawtooth pattern. More than any other sleep stage, the brain waves during REM sleep look a great deal like those during the awake state. REM comprises the greatest proportion of sleep in infants (approximately 55%), declining to about 25% by 5 years of age. Both REM and Stage 3 are homeostatic, meaning that when deprived of sleep, the body will preferentially "rebound" into these stages once sleep is allowed. This observation suggests that both deep sleep and REM are essential. Although certain brain waves predominate at different stages of sleep, alpha, beta, theta, and delta are all present, if only in trace amounts, throughout the day and in each sleep stage.

In order to understand sleep pathology, one must first understand some basic terms utilized in the study of sleep:

- *Sleep latency* is the period of time required to fall asleep, typically taken as the amount of time it takes to enter Stage 1.
- *REM latency* is defined as the amount of time between the onset of sleep and the first REM period.
- *REM density* is defined as the number of eye movement bursts or frequency of eye movements per minute of REM sleep.
- *REM rebound* describes the body's preference for REM when in a sleep-deprived state and the fact that the body will more rapidly "rebound" into REM when under slept.
- *Sleep onset REM* occurs when one lapses immediately into REM upon falling asleep, bypassing Stages 1, 2, and 3, as occurs with narcolepsy.

For purposes of understanding sleep physiology and pathology, it is useful to think of sleep as being subdivided into REM and non-REM (Stages 1–3). During non-REM, there is generally reduced physiological activity, as evidenced by slowing of the heart rate and respiration, decreased metabolic function, and a decrease in the activation of the autonomic nervous system, yet the body maintains a steady internal temperature. During non-REM sleep, one can move about freely and may pull up the blankets if too cold or kick off the sheets if too warm. Non-REM is also notable for episodic involuntary and sometimes jerky movements. Finally, during non-REM there is a slowing of blood flow, few penile erections, and little vaginal lubrication. REM sleep physiological changes, by contrast, are the opposite of those in non-REM sleep.

REM sleep is notable for increased physiological activity and autonomic nervous system activation. Altered thermoregulation, such that the body does not maintain a steady internal body temperature, and partial or full penile erections and significant vaginal lubrication are also characteristic. Skeletal muscle paralysis and numerous REMs are also evident. It is theorized that skeletal muscle paralysis is necessary during REM sleep because we would otherwise stand up and act out our dreams, which tend to occur in greatest density during REM.

During REM sleep, cells in the preoptic/anterior hypothalamus, which are responsible for maintaining a steady body temperature, cease firing, causing us to experience poikilothermia or to respond like cold-blooded animals. Since our thermoregulatory cells stop functioning during REM, our body temperatures tend to approach the temperature of the ambient environment. Interestingly, when the ambient temperature is at an extreme of hot or cold, REM sleep is lost, as if the body is refusing to let such an uncomfortable temperature be imposed upon itself. Likewise, animals kept in thermoneutral zones during sleep, or temperature ranges of greatest comfort for their species, show a maximal amount of REM (Alam, McGinty, & Szymusiak, 1995; Buguet, 2007).

The cyclical nature of sleep is reliable. REM periods occur about every 90–120 minutes. The first REM period is the shortest. Most deep sleep, Stage 3, occurs early in the evening while most REM sleep occurs later. The normal sleep cycle for children is portrayed in Figure 15.2. In contrast to adult sleep, the density of deep sleep early in the evening is somewhat greater during childhood. In the elderly population there is little Stage 3 sleep, particularly after age 70. Sleep becomes more fragmented by this age, and there are numerous awakenings throughout the evening, particularly toward the morning. It is this relative lack of deep sleep that causes the elderly to feel sleepy throughout the day and accounts for their frequent naps.

There is no clear single center that regulates sleep, but we do recognize numerous brain structures, neurochemicals, and hormones that are involved. The neurochemicals serotonin, norepinephrine, dopamine, histamine, glutamate, aspartate, acetylcholine, and gamma aminobutyric acid (GABA) all play a role. The suprachiasmatic nucleus, located within the hypothalamus, is responsible for controlling endogenous circadian rhythms. The suprachiasmatic nucleus contains several cell types and releases several different peptide hormones, including vasopressin

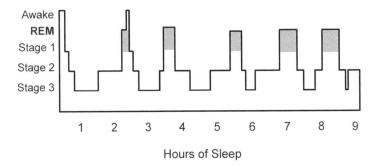

Figure 15.2. Normal sleep cycle in children. Figure 15.2 illustrates the relative time spent in each sleep stage throughout a typical evening.

(antidiuretic hormone) and vasoactive intestinal peptide. Numerous other hormones are also involved in sleep.

Orexin, a pair of excitatory neuropeptide hormones, so named because of their orexigenic (appetite-stimulating) activity, are synthesized in the hypothalamus and involved in narcolepsy. Dogs lacking an orexin receptor have narcolepsy while people and other animals lacking the orexin neuropeptide itself also have narcolepsy. Another hormone, melatonin, is synthesized by the pineal gland and is released at night and inhibited by ambient light. While exogenous administration increases total sleep time and decreases sleep latency, the exact role of melatonin in sleep has yet to be elucidated. Growth hormone is released during Stage 3 sleep in children. Consequently, those children who do not obtain adequate deep sleep are at risk of growth retardation.

Perhaps the purpose of sleep is to dream. Until just recently, we believed that dreams only occurred during REM sleep. This observation was founded upon the fact that when individuals were awoken during REM they could rapidly and easily recount their dreams, whereas when awoken in other stages of sleep, dreams were not easily recalled. In recent years we have come to understand that individuals do, in fact, dream during non-REM sleep, but these dreams are often brief, fragmented, and not as vivid and well remembered.

Neurocognitive Effects of Sleep Disruption

We have limited data on the neurocognitive effects of sleep disruption on children's attention and memory. Most of our information is based upon studies of the daytime performance of children with sleep-disordered breathing (SDB). The most common cause of SDB is sleep apnea, which can affect both children and adults. When an individual is apneic, the brain does not receive sufficient oxygen, and sleep is interrupted. These individuals generally do not reach deep sleep or REM and are constantly awoken throughout the night as they gasp for air (Gozal, O'Brien, & Row, 2004). Sleep restriction in experimental settings causes daytime inattention and changes in cortical EEG responses even after only 1 hour of restriction the night before (Randazzo, Muehlbach, Schweitzer, & Walsh, 1998). Data are inconsistent regarding the effects of sleep disruption on memory performance, yet children suffering from obstructive sleep apnea (OSA), periodic limb movement disorder (PLMD), and restless legs syndrome (RLS) with resulting sleep fragmentation have been shown to suffer academic deficits, learning problems, and symptoms that mirror attention-deficit/hyperactivity disorder (ADHD). In the case of OSA at least, symptoms are generally reversible after treatment (Chervin & Archbold, 2001; Chervin et al., 2002).

Neuropsychological testing has been useful in demonstrating the acute effects of sleep restriction on children and adolescents. Sleep restriction and total sleep deprivation reduce computational speed, impair verbal fluency, and decrease creativity and abstract problem-solving ability (Engleman & Joffe, 1999; Fallone, Acebo, Arnedt, Seifer, & Carskadon, 2001). Severe sleep fragmentation, as seen in OSA, may even result in reduced IQ scores. Sleep disruption can also have clear effects on academic achievement (Gozal, 1998). In fact, children with OSA suffer lower academic achievement even when age, race, gender, socioeconomic status, and school attended are controlled for. The treatment of OSA results in significant improvement in school performance. Even children who snore loudly and consistently in their early years are at a greater risk for academic delays in later years, suggesting some residual effects on learning that continue even after resolution of symptoms (Blunden et al., 2000). Animal models show increased locomotor activity and neuron cell loss in the hippocampus and prefrontal cortex in rats exposed to intermittent hypoxia, along with decreases in special task acquisition and retention compared to controls (O'Brien & Gozal, 2004).

EPIDEMIOLOGY

Approximately 25% of youth will suffer a sleep problem at some point during childhood (Owens & Witmans, 2004). Complaints range from bedtime resistance and anxiety to primary sleep disorders, such as OSA and narcolepsy. Research is remarkably consistent with parents reporting about 50% of preschool children (Kerr & Jowett, 1994), 30% of school-age children (Stein, Mendelson, Obermeyer, Amronin, & Benca, 2001), and 40% of adolescents as having sleep difficulties (Smedje, Broman, & Hetta, 2001). Self report among adolescents reveals that up to one-third complain of frequent or extended nighttime awakenings, excessive day-time sleepiness, unrefreshing sleep, trouble falling asleep, and a subjective need for more sleep (Patten, Choi, Gillin, & Pierce, 2000; Saarenpää-Heikkilä, Laippala, & Koivikko, 2001).

Perhaps the most frightening sleep disorder, SIDS has seen a world-wide decline in the past decade. The incidence is estimated at about 0.77 per 1,000 live births in Great Britain. The incidence in the United States has dropped more than 50%, from 1.53 per 1,000 live births in 1980 to 0.56 per 1,000 live births in 2001 (Arias, MacDorman, Strobino, & Guyer, 2002; Leach et al., 1999). Still, SIDS accounted for 8% of all infant deaths in the United States in 2002 and ranks as the third leading cause of infant death in the United States (Hoyert et al., 2006). In the United States the SIDS rate for African and Native American infants remains at more than twice that of Caucasian infants, reflecting a long-standing racial disparity.

Narcolepsy occurs at a rate of about 1.37 per 100,000 and has a prevalence of 56 per 100,000 in the United States (Kotagal, 2008). Narcolepsy most commonly sets on during the second decade of life but is not un-commonly diagnosed in the third and fourth decades. Cataplexy, or the sudden loss of muscle tone, which commonly occurs secondary to an emotional trigger such as anger or laughter, affects 50–70% of those with narcolepsy.

The prevalence of pediatric insomnia is estimated at between 1% and 6% in the general pediatric population but considerably higher among those children with neurodevelopmental delays and chronic medi-cal and psychiatric conditions (Ivanenko, Crabtree, & Gozal, 2004; Manni et al., 1997; Stein et al., 2001). A recent study of children ages 5–16 found that 50% of those presenting to a pediatric sleep center for insomnia had a preexisting psychiatric diagnosis, while the remaining 50% had elevated psychiatric impairment scores on psychometric measures and diagnostic interview. Perhaps the majority of children with pediatric insomnia, then, may have at least psychiatric symptoms, if not an actual disorder (Ivanenko, Barnes, Crabtree, & Gozal, 2005).

The prevalence of snoring among children is somewhere between 7% and 12%, while OSA is much less frequent with a prevalence of 1–2% (Ersu et al., 2004; Gozal, 1998). The frequency of upper airway resistance syndrome, a relatively newer category of SDB, has been as yet difficult to ascertain.

Enuresis occurs in approximately 30% of 4-year-olds, 10% of 6-year-olds, 5% of 10-year-olds, 3% of 12-year-olds, and about 1% of those 15 years of age and over (Byrd, Weitzman, Lanphear, & Auinger, 1996; Essen & Peckham, 1976; Feehan, Mcgee, Stanton, & Silva, 1990; Fergusson & Horwood, 1994; Hellström, Hanson, Hansson, Hjalmas, & Jodal, 1990; Kalo & Bella, 1986; Klackenberg, 1981; Rahim & Cederblad, 1986). Although not satisfying *DSM-IV* criteria for a diagnosis, between 10% and 20% of 5-year-olds continue to have at least one episode of nocturnal enuresis per month (Klein, 2001).

Non-REM parasomnias are common among children and adolescents. As an example, *night terrors* affect somewhere between 3% and 7% of children and 1–3% of adults (American Psychiatric Association, 2000). Sleepwalking is a much more common occurrence with a prevalence of somewhere between 6% and 17% in children and a lifetime incidence of as high as 40% in the general population. The prevalence in adults is about 1–2% (Mahowald & Rosen, 1990). Although not a formal *DSM-IV* diagnosis, *confusional arousals* are described in the International Classification of Sleep Disorders (American Sleep Disorders Association, 2007). Confusional arousals are essentially sleepwalking episodes during which an individual becomes confused and disruptive. The epidemiology of such events is unclear. In one Stockholm study a 4% incidence was noted (Klackenberg, 1981).

Sleep Problems Associated with Psychiatric Conditions

All variety of sleep disorders are more common among children with ADHD than healthy controls, controls with other psychiatric disorders, and healthy siblings by about five times (Corkum, Tannock, & Brewer, 1998). It is estimated that up to 25% of children with severe sleep problems in infancy will later meet criteria for a diagnosis of ADHD (Thunström, 2002). Up to 83% of children with a diagnosis of frank autistic disorder are reported to suffer sleep difficulties, as are up to 86% of children with autism spectrum disorders (Patzold, Richdale, & Tonge, 1998; Richdale & Prior, 1995; Wiggs & Stores, 1996). Younger children and those with more significant cognitive delay or disability tend to demonstrate increased problems. Sleep problems are often long-standing. A recent study of adults with Asperger's syndrome, for example, demonstrated that 90% continue to complain of frequent insomnia (Tani et al., 2003).

Mood disorders too are commonly comorbid with sleep problems. Up to two-thirds of children with a diagnosis of major depressive disorder have early and middle insomnia, and half of these children also report late insomnia or early-morning awakening (Puig-Antich et al., 1982).

Nearly 90% of depressed adolescents report sleep disturbances, usually insomnia, with up to 25% of these teens reporting hypersomnia (Goetz et al., 1987). About 10% experience continued insomnia even after the depression is lifted (Goetz et al., 1983). One study of bipolar children found that 40% had a dramatically reduced need for sleep versus controls and those with ADHD (Geller et al., 2002b).

Anxiety and sleep are intimately tied in childhood. Sleep problems by age 4 are correlated with later-onset depression and anxiety by age 15 (Ivanenko et al., 2004). Nighttime fears are common and are reported by up to 75% of typical children (Muris et al., 2000). Sleep problems generally follow for those children with *DSM-IV*-diagnosed anxiety disorders. Occasional nightmares occur in 80% of children; 15% report frequent nightmares (e.g., more than one a month); and up to 70% of children report that the content of their nightmares is influenced by frightening material viewed on television or at the movies (Hawkins & Williams, 1992; Muris et al., 2000). This statistic should not go unheeded by clinicians and parents. It is vital to acknowledge that the media has a major impact on children's thoughts and subsequent behavior and that parents must carefully monitor their children's media exposure, limiting that which frightens them or is not age-appropriate.

CLINICAL COURSE

Most sleep disorders in children and adolescents are developmental and dissipate with time as the children outgrow them. Only a fraction of affected children, as already noted, continue to sleepwalk, bed wet, or experience night terrors as adults, and the same is true with nightmares. SDB in children is most often due to enlarged tonsils and will generally be less troublesome as children age and their tonsils naturally shrink. Alternatively, tonsillectomy and adenoidectomy are almost always effective in treating the problem immediately. By contrast, narcolepsy is generally a lifelong condition with a stable course over time.

Primary insomnia is typically of sudden onset with continuation due to negative conditioning and the development of maladaptive sleep patterns. Individuals who have a series of nights or weeks with difficulty falling or staying asleep become rapidly conditioned into fearing that they will have difficulty falling or staying asleep; they then often develop a series of maladaptive behaviors, such as watching television in bed, sleeping on the couch, reading in bed, or drinking alcohol before sleep, all of which ultimately interfere further with their ability to maintain a good night's sleep.

DIAGNOSIS

Sleep is most often studied by observation in a sleep lab, where the patient stays overnight. The gold standard of sleep studies is the polysomnogram (PSG). PSG is simply a term for describing the conglomeration of tests employed to study an individual during sleep. These measures usually include videotaped observation, EEG, electromyogram (monitors muscle movements), electro-oculogram (monitors eye movements), vital signs, and any other physiological parameters that may be relevant, such as an electrocardiogram to follow heart rate and rhythm.

Newer methods to study sleep allow an investigator to observe a patient not simply in a sleep lab, but also in their home. The most common ambulatory technique involves actigraphy. This method was developed in the early 1970s and has come into increasing use in both research and clinical practice. Actigraphy allows for the study of sleep-wake patterns and circadian rhythms via the assessment of body movements. The device is worn on the wrist like a watch and can easily be adapted for home use. It is reliable and valid for the study of sleep in normal healthy populations but less reliable for detecting disturbed sleep.

A number of survey instruments, such as sleep diaries and questionnaires, also exist for detecting problematic sleep in children and adolescents. Self-report measures, such as the Sleep Disturbance Scale for Children, the Child Sleep Questionnaire, and the Child and Family Sleep History Questionnaire, along with parent report forms, are frequently helpful (Blader, Koplewicz, Abikoff, & Foley, 1997; Corkum, Moldofsky, Hogg-Johnson, Humphries, & Tannock, 1999).

Sudden Infant Death Syndrome

The most widely accepted definitions of SIDS require that all other possible causes of death be ruled out by death scene investigation, review of the clinical history, and autopsy prior to accepting SIDS as the diagnosis (Krous et al., 2004). Intentional or nonintentional injury and suffocation must also be considered.

DSM-IV Sleep Disorders

The *DSM-IV* defines six sleep disorders under the category of dyssomnias. These include *primary insomnia, primary hyperinsomnia, narcolepsy, breathing-related sleep disorder, circadian rhythm sleep disorder,* and *dyssomnia not otherwise specified (NOS)*. The *DSM-IV* also defines a series of parasomnias or disorders characterized by abnormal behavioral or physiological events that occur during sleep. These disorders include *nightmare disorder, sleep (night) terror disorder, sleepwalking disorder,* and *parasomnia not otherwise specified (NOS)*. As with all *DSM-IV* diagnoses, in order to be considered a "disorder," significant functional impairment must be present.

Narcolepsy

Narcolepsy is diagnosed by nocturnal polysomnogram, sleep history, and the multiple sleep latency test, which measures how long it takes the patient to fall asleep in a sleep lab during repeated nap opportunities. Symptoms of narcolepsy may set on all at once or gradually over a series of years.

Insomnia

Insomnia among adults most commonly occurs in the early and mid-evening hours. Affected individuals have difficulties falling and staying asleep. In the vast majority of individuals with a diagnosis of primary insomnia, PSG studies are negative. Although many of these individuals display subclinical symptoms of psychiatric illness, most do not have another primary psychiatric diagnosis but are at greater risk than the general population (American Psychiatric Association, 2000).

Although long recognized among adults, until 2005 no clear definition existed for pediatric insomnia. According to the International Classification of Sleep Disorders, pediatric insomnia is now defined as "frequent problems with sleep initiation, duration, consolidation, and/or quality that occurs despite adequate opportunity for sleep, resulting in daytime functional impairment for the child and/or family" (American Sleep Disorders Association, 2005, p. 26).

Behavioral insomnia is another recently introduced diagnostic category to describe the sleep difficulties resulting from inadequate parental limit-setting or sleep associations, such as rocking a child to bed at night, allowing a child to fall asleep in the parent's bed, or allowing children to watch television to fall asleep. Behavioral insomnia is characterized by the inability of the child to fall asleep in the absence of these conditions at both bedtime and following nocturnal awakenings.

Sleep Disordered Breathing

Many children and adolescents snore. As long as there are no changes in sleep architecture, alveolar ventilation, blood oxygenation, and the child is not awakening frequently and experiencing difficulties throughout the day, there is no concern. OSA is the most impairing of the sleep breathing difficulties faced by children and is characterized by frequent awakenings, blood oxygen desaturations, and poor sleep quality, resulting in excessive daytime sleepiness and many of the neurocognitive impairments previously noted. Upper airway resistance syndrome, which causes frequent awakenings, does not result in blood oxygen desaturations and is therefore less impairing.

Parents whose child suffers from SDB will commonly complain of hearing their child snore, frequent awakenings, excessive daytime sleepiness, poor academic performance, irritability, poor executive functioning, and general inattention or cognitive impairment. Lab results for children who are severely affected by SDB will demonstrate a reduction in air flow and lowered hemoglobin oxygen saturation, along with an increase in total hemoglobin. Sinus arrhythmias, premature ventricular contractions (PVCs), atrioventricular (AV) block, sinus arrest, and a preponderance of Stage 1 sleep signify severe impairment. Physical examination may show adenotonsillar enlargement, pectus excavatum, obesity, hypertension, and cor pulmonale or right heart enlargement.

Parasomnias

Parasomnias can occur during REM and non-REM sleep. Non-REM parasomnias include somnambulism (sleepwalking), night terrors, somniloquy (sleep talking), and sleep-related involuntary movement disorders such as PLMD, body rocking, and bruxism (jaw clenching or tooth grinding throughout the night). The non-REM sleep disorders have many features in common. They are of short duration, lasting somewhere between 1 and 30 minutes; affected individuals do not recall the events subsequently upon awakening due to retrograde amnesia; there is a high potential for injury to oneself or others; and there is often a personal or family history of such events. Non-REM parasomnias occur during slow-wave deep sleep (e.g., Stage 3). As already discussed, they are more common in childhood than adulthood. Psychopathology among affected children is rare. Precipitating factors include a preexisting dyssomnia, sleep deprivation, medications that interrupt or alter sleep architecture, magnesium deficiency, and hormonal factors. There is, in fact, a slight increase in occurrence around puberty.

Somnambulists are typically docile. Some affected individuals begin sleepwalking after an episode of enuresis. Somnambulists may engage in simple behaviors, such as walking into another room and falling back to sleep on the couch, or more complex behaviors, such as getting dressed, taking a walk outside, or preparing and eating food. Sleepwalking episodes that include irrational acts, incoherence, and significant disorientation are called confusional arousals and are considered a variant of sleepwalking. As with all non-REM parasomnias, autonomic arousal is characteristic, as is complete amnesia for the event. Premeditated acts are believed to be impossible, although there have been episodes of life-threatening behavior, murder, and even attempted suicide during these events (Broughton et al., 1994; Guilleminault, Moscovitch, & Leger, 1995; Shatkin, Feinfeld, & Strober, 2002).

The hallmark of a night terror is extreme autonomic nervous system activation. A rapid increase in pulse, blood pressure, heart rate, and respiratory rate, along with profuse sweating, is always observed. Affected children sit bolt upright in bed, scream loudly for a few seconds or minutes, and then promptly fall right back to sleep. They experience complete amnesia for the event and are not harmed in any way.

Though thankfully less frequent, there are a number of REM parasomnias to which children are sometimes vulnerable as well. The most severe of these, REM sleep behavior disorder, occurs when the body is not adequately paralyzed during REM sleep. Affected individuals commonly act out their dreams, which can result in threatening behavior to themselves and others. Another REM parasomnia, sleep paralysis, occurs when an individual awakens during a REM period while the body is paralyzed. These episodes are highly frightening, as individuals often feel that they are unable to move, breathe, or even open their eyes, yet their brain is actively awake.

Enuresis

Bed-wetting or enuresis can occur during both REM and non-REM sleep. Most children are dry during the evening by about 4 or 5 years of age, yet some children take longer to train. For a *DSM-IV* diagnosis of enuresis, bed-wetting must occur at least twice a week for at least 3 months, and the child must be at least 5 years of age (American Psychiatric Association, 2000). Enuresis is described as either "primary," indicating that the child has never been regularly dry, or "secondary," when enuresis occurs in a child who was previously dry for at least 6 months.

TREATMENT

Before engaging in treatment, it is important to obtain a complete sleep history. Key components include how many hours the child sleeps each day (including both naps and evening sleep), when he goes to sleep, how long it takes him to fall asleep, notable awakenings, and any rituals or practices necessary to put him to sleep. Special attention should be paid to difficulties falling asleep (early insomnia), staying asleep (middle insomnia), and awakening too early (late insomnia). Parents and children should also be asked directly about sleep pathologies, including enuresis, parasomnias, SDB, family history of sleep problems, and any medications or other methods utilized to promote sleep. A sleep diary is often useful for tracking sleep and helping parents to determine their child's precise vulnerabilities. Sleep diaries generally assess sleep patterns and disruptions, exercise, caffeine use, drugs and alcohol, and stressors that can interfere with sleep. Sample sleep diaries are readily available on the Internet.

Sudden Infant Death Syndrome

Reducing modifiable risk factors for infants, such as sleeping in a prone position, overbundling, and secondary smoke exposure, has decreased the incidence of SIDS by more than 60% in most parts of the world (Halbower & Marcus, 2003). Other strategies, such as sleeping solitary in a supine position, not allowing infants to sleep on their sides, and using a pacifier, may ultimately reduce the incidence still further (Alm, Lagercrantz, & Wennergren, 2006).

Narcolepsy

As narcolepsy is a lifelong disorder, extensive education of the affected child and his family is of great importance. Methods to increase daytime alertness and enhance psychomotor functioning are of great importance. Maintaining a regular sleep-wake schedule, avoiding alcohol and drugs, taking one or two brief, planned naps each day, and engaging in regular exercise are helpful strategies. Avoiding driving and other high-risk activities is also advised. Stimulants, such as modafinil (Provigil) and methylphenidate (Ritalin), are often employed to help with wakefulness, and anticholinergic drugs, such as protriptyline (Vivactil) and clomipramine (Anafranil) are often effective for cataplexy (Kotagal, 2008).

Insomnia

The treatment of insomnia, adult or pediatric, should begin with an adequate history and understanding of the environment within which the child sleeps and lives. Certainly, all other potential Axis I disorders and psychosocial disturbances should be considered in the history, along with any medical illnesses and medications that can interfere with sleep. Proper sleep hygiene, which is often curative for insomnia, should be reviewed with the family and emphasized as a first intervention (see Table 15.1).

The techniques of sleep hygiene, when employed appropriately, are commonly helpful in settling children and adults back to sleep without further need for treatment. The importance of a sleep-wake schedule, particularly for children, cannot be overemphasized. The folk saying, "sleep begets sleep," appears to be the experience of most parents. Consequently, if we wish for our children to sleep well, we should be making sure that they receive plenty of opportunity. Establishing a standard bedtime and routine, which for a child may include bathing, reading a book, or engaging in a quiet and comforting family ritual, is often helpful. Allowing the child to fall asleep in the parents' bed or, conversely, parents falling asleep with their children in the child's bed, while commonly enjoyable and comforting for both parents and children, often leaves the child without the confidence necessary to put himself back to sleep when he awakens naturally throughout the night. Consequently, when overused, these methods of putting children to sleep almost invariably result in the child calling for the parent each time he awakens throughout the night, resulting in unsatisfactory sleep for both.

For those parents who have fallen asleep with their children every night and now find themselves in a maladaptive pattern with which they are frustrated, behavioral methods are very helpful and typically resolve the problem rapidly. One useful methodology involves leaving the child alone in his room for one additional minute each night until the child is able to fall asleep on his own. For example, on night #1, the parent explains

Table 15.1. Sleep Hygiene

- Set a routine sleep-wake schedule.
- Encourage regular exercise and physical activity, but not at night.
- Avoid caffeine within six hours of bedtime.
- Invent a relaxing bedtime ritual, such as bathing and reading together.
- Avoid large meals and large amounts of fluid prior to bedtime.
- Adjust the room temperature as desired.
- Keep noise levels low and the bedroom dark. Use a nightlight if necessary.

the plan, noting that he or she is going to help the child to learn to fall asleep on his own. The parent then kisses the child good night and leaves the room for 1 minute. The parent then comes back to the room, rejoins the child, and lies with him until he falls asleep, as any other night. On night #2 the parent steps out for 2 minutes before lying with the child, and on night #3, the parent steps out for 3 minutes, and so forth. This method is often effective within a matter of days, as long as the parent is consistent. Because young children are not generally oriented to time, by the fourth or fifth evening, many parents can stay out of the room for 10 minutes or more, and the child by this time will have fallen asleep on his own.

In the event that a child experiences a new onset of insomnia, the parent may find it helpful to soothe the child by sitting with him for a brief period of time, perhaps reading for a few moments or telling a story, before leaving the room once again so that the child can fall asleep. Adults with insomnia are advised not to read in bed but rather to get up and read on the couch or in another room under dim light for 10–15 minutes before once again going back to the bed to try and fall asleep. This method is not necessary for children who can be read to in their beds.

Medications are rarely used for pediatric insomnia, and the Food and Drug Administration (FDA) has not approved any such treatments for children suffering from insomnia. Sedatives are rarely necessary, as behavioral methods most always work well. For those children with psychiatric or medical comorbidities that are causing the insomnia, short half-life medications (e.g., those rapidly metabolized by the body) are sometimes utilized. The medications typically useful in adults with insomnia are rarely employed with children and younger adolescents. Benzodiazepines, such as lorazepam (Ativan), diazepam (Valium), clonazepam (Klonopin), flurazepam (Dalmane), and temazepam (Restoril), are commonly effective for adults with insomnia, as are related agents, such as zaleplon (Sonata), zolpidem (Ambien), and eszopiclone (Lunesta). Barbiturates are almost never given any longer because of their narrow therapeutic index, abuse and addictive potential, and significant side effects. While tolerance to the somnolent effects of benzodiazepines develops in about 4 weeks, the anxiolytic effects persist. In the long run, then, these medications are often more useful for anxiety than they are for sleep. In children the GABA receptors, the primary site of action for these medications, are not fully mature until somewhere between the ages of 15 and 18 years, depending upon the child. As a result, a significant minority of children who are given benzodiazepines and similar medications respond paradoxically in a belligerent, agitated, and almost "drunken" manner.

When medications are necessary for the treatment of pediatric insomnia, antihistamines, alpha-2 agonists, and sedating antidepressants are sometimes employed. The antihistamines diphenhydramine (Benadryl), hydroxyzine (Vistaril), and cyproheptadine (Periactin) are all sedating but not without side effects, which can include dry mouth and eyes, tachycardia, urinary retention, paradoxical agitation, confusion, and residual sedation upon awakening, to name just a few. In spite of these side effects, antihistamines are generally well tolerated by children and adolescents. Dosages of both diphenhydramine and hydroxyzine would usually start somewhere between 6.25 and 25 mg, depending upon the child, and between 1 and 2 mg for cyproheptadine. Perhaps more commonly used, at least among children with ADHD, is the alpha-2 agonist antihypertensive, clonidine (Catapres). Clonidine is generally initiated at 0.05 mg at bedtime and can be titrated up to 0.2 mg as needed (see Chapter 2). Sedating antidepressants, such as trazodone (Desyrel) at dosages of 12.5–100 mg and mirtazapine (Remeron) at dosages of 7.5–15 mg, are also sometimes employed for pediatric insomnia. Increasingly, and perhaps unfortunately, antipsychotics, such as quetiapine (Serzone) and risperidone (Risperdal), are also being used to treat pediatric insomnia, although in the absence of a major psychiatric comorbidity, such as bipolar disorder, this type of aggressive treatment is rarely indicated.

Finally, we are beginning to see an influx in the use of herbal medications and dietary supplements, such as melatonin, which has been found effective for treating insomnia in certain groups of children at dosages between 300 mcg and 10 mg. Kava kava, valerian, L-tryptophan, chamomile, passion flower, and lavender are also sometimes marketed and used for pediatric insomnia. With the exception of melatonin, however, which is a reasonable treatment without frequent side effects for most children and adolescents, these medications have not been studied and should be avoided.

Sleep-Disordered Breathing

The treatment of OSA and other forms of severe SDB among children typically involves tonsillectomy and adenoidectomy, which almost always resolves the problem. Among adults with OSA, weight loss, sleeping on one's side and stomach (as opposed to the back), and using an air mask that provides continuous positive airway pressure (C-PAP) and keeps the airway patent and free of obstruction by the uvula, soft palate, and tongue are often helpful. In more severe cases, septoplasty, to repair a deviated nasal septum, or tonsillectomy and adenoidectomy, for those with residually enlarged tonsils, may be necessary.

Parasomnias

The treatment of non-REM parasomnias involves first a series of psychosocial interventions. Educating the family and patient about the pathology itself is of the utmost importance so that they can make any necessary changes to avoid possible recurrences. Violent episodes, as can occur during a confusional arousal, are rarely repeated. However, somnambulism and night terrors do commonly recur. Once educated, the family and patient should identify and then avoid possible precipitants, such as sleep disruption and intermittent sleep deprivation. Disruptions will include loud noises while the child is asleep. Limiting evening fluid intake in an effort to decrease the likelihood of awakening to the cues of bladder fullness is also a commonly employed strategy. Locking windows and doors, removing lethal objects (such as knives) from the child's reach, and even placing a movement sensor on the doorpost of a child's room will help to safeguard the house for an active sleepwalker. For those younger children who sleepwalk or experience frequent night terrors, enforcing an afternoon nap may be protective, as naps typically decrease the density of Stage 3 sleep in the evening, during which time these parasomnias occur.

Medications may also be employed in the treatment of non-REM parasomnias but are rarely necessary. Although antidepressants tend to decrease REM density, they have been shown to be helpful in non-REM sleep disorders (Mahowald & Schenck, 1996). Their utility may simply rest upon the fact that they disrupt the normal sleep architecture. Benzodiazepines with long half-lives, such as clonazepam and diazepam, are also sometimes helpful. Benzodiazepines tend to decrease non-REM sleep, in contrast to barbiturates, which tend to decrease REM. As above, some children and adolescents will have a paradoxical reaction to benzodiazepines, however, and cannot tolerate their effects. For these children, antidepressants, such as the SSRIs and trazodone, may be useful.

The REM parasomnias, such as sleep paralysis and nightmare disorder, are generally treated simply with psychoeducation. Neither is life-threatening, and rarely do they result in significant functional impairment. For those rare cases of REM sleep behavior disorder, a board-certified sleep specialist should be consulted immediately.

Enuresis

The etiology of enuresis is likely to be multifactorial and includes difficulties with bladder muscular stability, central nervous system arousability, pontine reflex function, internal sphincter tone, functional bladder capacity, nocturnal urine production, and a maturational delay in anti-diuretic hormone (ADH) secretion, which inhibits urination. The final factor is perhaps the most important as numerous medications seem to work at this level. Affected individuals probably either do not produce sufficient ADH or do not respond adequately to the ADH that they do produce, resulting in enuresis. Secondary enuresis is commonly caused by urinary tract infections, diabetes mellitus, and in some cases psychological factors.

The treatment of enuresis, as with all sleep disorders, begins with a full and complete history. Any prior treatment efforts, behavioral or otherwise, should be ascertained. Education is then provided for the family and patient. Enuresis commonly occurs within families and is more often seen in males than females. Most children will outgrow enuresis by 10–12 years of age, and about 12–16% of children become asymptomatic each year, even without treatment. Consequently, education rests upon supporting the family, helping them to consider behavioral strategies that may be useful, and emphasizing that the family should not blame, embarrass, or shame the child.

Behavioral treatment efforts begin by discontinuing all caffeine and alcohol use within 6 hours of bedtime, as both will inhibit ADH production. Restricting late-night fluid intake to less than 4 ounces of liquid after dinner is also commonly employed, although we have no data to support this practice. Some families find it useful to briefly awaken the child just before the parents go to bed, place him on the toilet, and run the tap water in order to stimulate the flow of urine. Allowing the child to void in this manner before placing him back to bed is often helpful in decreasing early-morning enuresis.

The "bell and pad" or bed-wetting alarm has the highest effective treatment rate and the lowest relapse rate of the behavioral methods (Thiedke, 2003). This practice employs a moisture-sensitive monitor, often a pad placed atop the mattress or smaller monitors placed on the child's underwear, which sounds a loud alarm if the child wets. Once the alarm is triggered, the parents can help the child get to the bathroom to urinate. This method typically takes about 3–4 weeks to work. Some children will naturally relapse after achieving nighttime bladder control, but if the bell and pad method is used subsequently, they can generally be easily retrained. Other behavioral treatments have not been as consistent in their utility; these include training to increase the functional capacity of the bladder to hold urine; reward systems for children who successfully sleep through the night without urinating in the bed; cognitive and motivational therapies; pelvic floor muscle training; and biofeedback (Abdelghany et al., 2001; Glazener & Evans, 2002; Robson & Leung, 2002; Van Kampen et al., 2002; Yeung, 2003).

The most commonly utilized medication for the treatment of enuresis is desmopressin acetate (DDAVP), a synthetic ADH analog. Desmopressin acetate (DDAVP) can be given either by oral tablet or intranasal spray. Doses typically range between 0.1 and 0.6 mg per evening for the oral tablet and 10–60 mcg for the intranasal preparation. Concerns about hyponatremia (low blood sodium) that have rarely resulted in seizures among a small number of children who have received the intranasal form only have recently prompted the FDA to issue a warning advising children receiving intranasal DDAVP to have their blood sodium levels followed both before and during treatment.

Other common medications for the treatment of enuresis include the tricyclic antidepressants (TCAs), in particular imipramine (Tofranil). Although most commonly used to treat adult depression, at dosages of 25–50 mg, imipramine is often effective for the treatment of enuresis in children and adults. The anticholinergic effects are clearly not the reason for the antienuretic effects, given the fact that other anticholinergic medications are not generally helpful for enuresis. Some suggest that children with enuresis excrete a smaller amount of ADH during sleep and that imipramine restores normal levels of nocturnal ADH secretion (Tomasi, Siracusano, Monni, Mela, & Delitala, 2001). Whenever treating children with TCAs, however, as discussed in Chapter 10, routine electrocardiograms must be performed before and during treatment. Although the dosage of imipramine employed in treating enuresis is much lower than that used to treat depression, and is therefore likely to be considerably safer, cardiac parameters must still be followed.

Various antispasmodics are useful for adults who suffer enuresis. These medications include oxybutynin (Ditropan) at a dosage of 2.5–5 mg per evening or tolterodine (Detrol) at a dosage of 0.5–1 mg per evening. We generally try not to use these medications in children, however, as they can cause excessive sedation and even confusion. In children with particularly difficult-to-treat enuresis, we may sometimes combine treatments, such as desmopressin acetate plus imipramine or oxybutynin. More recently studies have found that atomoxetine (Strattera), an ADHD treatment, is also effective for enuresis. This serendipitous finding was first reported in a case series (Shatkin, 2004) and has now been replicated in a randomized, double-blind, placebo-controlled trial (Sumner, Schuh, Sutton, Lipetz, & Kelsey, 2006).

Treating Sleep Problems Associated with Psychiatric Conditions

As previously noted, many children with ADHD have difficulties with falling asleep or staying asleep. Treatment for these children should begin by reviewing proper sleep hygiene with the parents. Stimulant medications used to treat ADHD also commonly cause sleep impairments. If a stimulant is the cause of the insomnia, the practitioner should consider lowering the dosage of the stimulant or changing to another preparation, perhaps a shorter-acting medication. Paradoxically, for some children with ADHD, adding a low dose of stimulant in the evening may help them to settle to sleep by decreasing their hyperactivity. Changing to a nonstimulant, such as atomoxetine, or using adjunctive agents, particularly clonidine but sometimes sedating antihistamines, antidepressants, or melatonin, is also often useful.

Children with autism spectrum disorders (ASD) often fail to recognize environmental and social cues indicating bedtime. These children may also suffer from poorly developed circadian rhythms because of their social deficits, altered melatonin production, and abnormalities in the hypothalamic-pituitary-adrenal axis (Kulman et al., 2000; Nir et al., 1995; Wiggs & Stores, 1998). Regardless, many of these children require help getting to sleep. As with children diagnosed with ADHD, proper sleep hygiene should be the first intervention. Chronotherapy, or systematically delaying bedtime each night until an age-appropriate bedtime is reached, is sometimes helpful (Piazza, Hagopian, Hughes, & Fisher, 1998). Unstudied medications, but those often utilized for sleep in these children, may include antihistamines, sedating antidepressants, clonidine, benzodiazepines, and antipsychotics. As above, melatonin has been studied in small numbers of children affected with developmental disabilities and ASD and has been found effective (Garstang & Wallis, 2006).

Children with depression often exhibit a decreased REM latency, increased total REM, and increased sleep-onset time, all of which tend to dissipate for most children once the depression is treated (Emslie, Rush, Weinberg, Rintelmann, & Roffwarg, 1990). Beyond sleep hygiene and treating all comorbid conditions, no clear data exist on whether or not to treat the symptom of insomnia independent from the mood disorder. For milder cases, a combination of improved sleep hygiene and CBT has been proven effective in managing the insomnia and awakenings associated with depression (Ivanenko et al., 2004). In more severe cases, effective drug therapy may require a combination of an antidepressant with the short-term use of a sedative or hypnotic. Borrowing from adult studies, at the very least practitioners should aggressively treat insomnia associated with bipolar disorder, as a decreased need for sleep is one of the earliest and cardinal symptoms of mania.

The treatment of sleep difficulties in children and adolescents with anxiety disorders involves identifying and treating the primary Axis I disorder, utilizing sleep hygiene, and then medications as indicated. As with depression, it is not clear how much benefit is gained from treating the symptom of insomnia as a separate entity.

Appendix

Child and Adolescent Psychopharmacology

HISTORY

In 1937, Charles Bradley published "The Behavior of Children Receiving Benzedrine" in the *American Journal of Psychiatry* (Bradley, 1937). Bradley stumbled upon stimulants as a treatment for hyperactive behavior. Amphetamine sulfate (Benzedrine) was marketed in 1928 as an inhaled bronchodilator for children with asthma. Bradley thought that Benzedrine could be useful for the headaches that commonly accompany lumbar punctures. Teachers, however, gave him the feedback that the children who had received Benzedrine were calmer at school and had less disruptive behavior. Bradley observed 30 children ages 5–14 years medicated with Benzedrine for 1 week. He found that the medication calmed and settled hyperactive and impulsive behavior, noting a "spectacular change in behavior ... remarkably improved school performance" (Bradley, 1937). Bradley's observation marks the beginning of child psychopharmacology. The Emma Pendleton Bradley Hospital in Providence, Rhode Island, is named for his uncle's daughter, Emma Pendleton Bradley, who was stricken with encephalitis at age 7 and became permanently disabled. The Bradley Hospital is the first neuropsychiatric hospital for children in the United States and opened in 1931.

Later that same year, Matthew Molitch published three papers on the use of amphetamine sulfate in children, including two placebo controlled studies (Molitch & Eccles, 1937; Molitch & Poliakoff, 1937; Molitch & Sullivan, 1937). Two of the studies noted improvements in intelligence testing among those children who had taken medication, and the third report found that 86% of the enuretic boys who were taking the medication stopped bed-wetting but reverted when the medication was discontinued. In 1958 the Conference on Child Research in Psychopharmacology was sponsored by the National Institute of Mental Health. The following year, *Child Research in Psychopharmacology*, the first book devoted to psychopharmacological research in child mental health and based upon the proceedings of the 1958 conference, was edited by Seymour Fisher (Fisher, 1959). The 1958 conference on child research was important because it was the first time that national scientific attention was focused specifically on the issue of child and adolescent mental health.

Methylphenidate was patented in 1954 but first used to treat "minimal brain dysfunction," or what we now call attention-deficit/hyperactivity disorder (ADHD), in the early 1960s. In 1997 the federal government passed the Food and Drug Administration (FDA) Modernization Act (FDAMA), which encouraged the pharmaceutical industry to voluntarily conduct pediatric drug testing by providing manufacturers with the possibility of an additional 6 months of patent or marketing exclusivity on their drugs. FDAMA was important because it provided federal support and encouragement for research into the pediatric applications of prescription medications, both psychiatric and general medical.

Only about 20% of the medications available to prescribers in the United States, both psychiatric and general medical, have been FDA approved for use in children and adolescents. Pharmaceutical manufacturers realize that physicians will prescribe medications for children and adolescents regardless of FDA approval because of their need for effective treatments. Once a medication is approved by the FDA for any purpose, a physician may legally prescribe that drug for any indication that he sees fit. Consequently, physicians often rely solely on clinical and anecdotal experience and without the benefits of research data when prescribing medications to children and adolescents.

PHARMACOLOGY

There are numerous pharmacological principles that must be understood in order to properly prescribe psychotropic medications. The two most important principles are pharmacokinetics and pharmacodynamics. In simple terms, pharmacokinetics describes how the body processes a medication. The four primary steps include: (a) absorption of the drug; (b) distribution of the drug throughout the body; (c) metabolism of the drug; and (d) excretion or elimination of the drug. Pharmacodynamics describes what the medication does to the body, which results in the therapeutic and unintended side effects of the drug. Stated another way, pharmacokinetics describes the entry of the drug into the body and its elimination from the body, and pharmacodynamics explains the drug's effects on the body.

Absorption and distribution help to determine a drug's speed of onset, whereas metabolism and elimination determine how long a drug will last. Considerable pharmacokinetic variation exists between individuals, and there is a stronger relationship between the concentration of the drug in the plasma and drug effects than the drug dose and drug effects. That is, drug distribution in the body fluids is more important than the dosage taken. There are a number of characteristics that favor absorption of a drug by the body, and generally the opposing characteristics favor excretion. Well-absorbed drugs are usually lipid soluble, nonpolar, and of small molecular size; in contrast to drugs that are not well absorbed and are generally nonlipid soluble, highly polar, and of large molecular size. The body favors nonpolar substances for absorption but typically polarizes them for excretion.

Metabolism is the key to changing drugs into a form that allows their excretion. Covalent bonds occur when atoms share electrons. A polar bond occurs when the electrons are unequally shared. Polar bonds occur when two or more different atoms come together to form a molecule, such as a carbon and an oxygen forming carbon monoxide. Each atom has a different strength of attraction for the electrons circulating around them. The strength of their pull on the electrons is their electronegativity. A greater variation in electronegativity between atoms makes a molecule more polar and favors excretion.

Most cells within the body have a lipid bilayer or a two-layered cell wall that is polar on the outside and nonpolar on the inside. For all practical purposes, the bilayer is impermeable to most water-soluble and polar molecules and ions. Complex proteins and ion channels within the bilayer allow selected molecules and ions to float in and out of the cell. All medications must be able to pass through the lipid bilayer and into the cell if they are to be effective.

Most psychotropic medications are orally administered and absorbed into the circulation through the gastrointestinal tract. Oral administration of drugs, however, is the least reliable and predictable due to the "first-pass effect." Once ingested, contents from the stomach and small intestine are gathered up in the portal venous circulation and passed directly to the liver, the body's detoxification station. After being absorbed by the intestine, most food, drugs, and other gut contents will be metabolized by the liver before entering the body's systemic circulation. The amount of drug making it through the liver on the "first pass" and entering the circulatory system is thereby reduced and accompanied by metabolites of varying pharmacological activity.

The fraction of a drug that reaches the systemic circulation, or that which survives beyond the first-pass effect and is available to exert a biological effect on target tissues, is known as the *bioavailable fraction*. It is only this portion of the drug that actually has a chance of asserting an impact on the body. For many drugs, 80–90% is destroyed by the liver during the first pass. The amount of drug that binds to the receptor at the site of action determines the magnitude of the drug effect. Because children have highly metabolically active hepatic enzymes and an increased renal glomerular filtration rate, they metabolize drugs more rapidly than do adults per unit body weight.

Once a drug or its active metabolite arrives at its target, it must bind to its intended receptor. A receptor is a protein on the cell membrane or within the cell cytoplasm or nucleus that binds to a specific molecule known as a *ligand*, such as a neurotransmitter, hormone, or drug, and initiates a cellular response. The ligand, then, induces a change in the behavior of receptor proteins, resulting in physiological changes within the body. Virtually all biological ligand/receptor bonds are reversible.

The distribution of a drug within the body is determined by a number of factors, including the drug's lipid solubility, the rate of drug absorption from the gastrointestinal tract, the pH of the body fluids, differences in regional blood flow, and the *blood-brain barrier*. The blood-brain barrier is a membrane structure that acts to protect the brain from chemicals in the blood while still allowing essential metabolic functions. It is composed of endothelial cells that are packed very tightly in brain capillaries. This high density of endothelial cells restricts passage of substances from the bloodstream. Finally, the amount of albumin or blood protein can also affect drug distribution, particularly for strongly protein bound drugs, such as divalproex sodium (Depakote). Protein binding leaves only the free and unbound portion to act on the body. A significant decrease in albumin, for example, leads to an increase in free drug within the plasma, greater receptor binding, and a risk of drug toxicity. Conversely, a significant increase in albumin can lead to more protein binding and less drug activity.

Most psychotropic drugs are lipid soluble and must undergo extensive metabolism to make them more polar and water-soluble for excretion. Metabolism involves both Phase I and Phase II reactions. During Phase I reactions, oxidation, reduction, or hydrolysis of the parent drug occurs via various enzymes at different tissue sites. Examples include the cytochrome P450 enzymes, which metabolize many drugs; plasma esterases, which metabolize stimulants; microsomal epoxide hydrolases, which metabolize carbamazepine (Tegretol); and flavin-containing monooxygenases, which degrade clozapine (Clozaril) and olanzapine (Zyprexa). Polar metabolites sometimes have pharmacological activity as well, which can be of greater, lesser, or equal potency to that of the parent drug. Norfluoxetine, for example, a metabolite of fluoxetine (Prozac), has a longer half-life and may be up to five times more potent than the parent drug (Pinna, Costa, & Guidotti, 2006).

The cytochrome P450 (CYP) proteins are a large family of iron- or heme-containing enzymes. The CYP 3A family is the most significant CYP 450 enzyme group, found primarily in the liver and small intestine. The CYP 3A family alone metabolizes approximately 30–40% of drugs known to be metabolized by human CYP enzymes. Some drugs are not only *substrates* for a CYP enzyme (e.g., metabolized by the enzyme), but also *inducers* or *inhibitors*, which increase or decrease, respectively, the activity of the enzyme or a related enzyme. Carbamazepine is a well-known inducer of CYP 3A4, for example, which when given with oral contraceptives and other drugs metabolized by this enzyme, increases their metabolism and renders them less effective. Conversely, fluoxetine is a well-known inhibitor of CYP 2D6, which when given with other antidepressants and atomoxetine (Strattera), for example, decreases their metabolism and increases their plasma levels.

Phase II pharmacokinetic reactions involve conjugation of Phase I metabolites or certain parent drugs with endogenous substrates, such as sulfate, acetate, or glucuronic acid, to produce more water-soluble metabolites for excretion. The products of Phase II reactions rarely exhibit pharmacological activity.

Most psychotropic drugs follow *first-order elimination kinetics*. In other words, a constant fraction or percentage of the drug is eliminated per unit time. The rate of drug elimination is proportional to the amount of drug in the body, and the rate will increase or decrease with greater or lesser concentrations, respectively, of the drug. First-order elimination kinetics allow for predictions of the impact of dose changes on plasma drug concentrations. The majority of drugs are eliminated in this way. A first-order reaction depends upon the concentration of only one reactant, the drug itself. Whereas a constant fraction of a drug is eliminated per unit time when following first-order kinetics, a constant amount of a drug is eliminated per unit time when following zero-order kinetics.

Zero-order elimination kinetics occur for drugs for which there are a very limited number of metabolizing enzymes, leading to quick saturation of enzyme sites even at normal therapeutic drug concentrations. In other words, zero-order elimination kinetics occur when there is a drug without a lot of enzymes to break it down or when the enzymes present have been overwhelmed or supersaturated. Elimination here is constant over time. There is nothing one can do to change the elimination rate. Zero-order elimination kinetics are followed with alcohol, for example, which is why we can metabolize only approximately 8–10 grams per hour or one standard drink (e.g., 1 ounce of hard liquor, 4 ounces of wine, or 12 ounces of beer). A zero-order reaction has a rate that is independent of the concentration of the reactants or amount of the drug. Increasing the concentration of the reacting species or the amount of drug will not speed up the rate of the reaction. Though uncommon, the body will resort to zero-order elimination kinetics even for drugs that typically follow first-order elimination kinetics when enzyme saturation occurs at very high concentrations of any drug.

The *steady state* is the point at which an equilibrium is reached between the amount of drug ingested and the amount of drug eliminated, resulting in no net change in plasma concentration over time. Steady state typically occurs after about 4½ half-lives. Likewise, a drug is essentially entirely eliminated from the body, if no more drug is given, after about 4½ half-lives. The *half-life* $(T_{1/2})$ is the time it takes for the plasma concentration to fall by 50% from the initial plasma concentration of the drug. Half-lives are very helpful in determining dosage intervals, and medications are commonly dosed on a schedule equivalent to the half-life of the drug (see Table A.1). Once the drug reaches steady state, it is not generally necessary to keep to a strict schedule of dosing on the half-life, but it is the surest way of maintaining a steady state with minimal fluctuation.

Most clinicians have observed that children and young adolescents often require larger, weight-adjusted dosages and more frequent dosing than adults in order to achieve comparable blood levels and therapeutic effects with most medications. This variation appears to be due to increased rates of metabolism and elimination in children. There are other differences as well in pediatric pharmacokinetics, including children's metabolic capacity, renal elimination, tissue differences, and whole-body water. Children and adolescents have greater metabolic capacity than adults and more rapidly eliminate drugs that utilize hepatic pathways, such as tricyclic antidepressants, antipsychotics, and methylphenidate. After the first year of life, the younger the child, the more rapidly the drug will be metabolized

Table A.1   Drug Half-Life

Fraction of drug eliminated and fraction remaining in the body as a function of half-life

Half-lives (n)	Fraction eliminated (%)	Fraction remaining (%)
1	50.0	50.0
2	75.0	25.0
3	87.5	12.5
4	93.8	6.2
5	96.9	3.1

in the liver. Children and adolescents are also more efficient in their renal elimination and excrete drugs that rely solely upon renal clearance and are not metabolized by the liver, such as lithium, more rapidly than adults. In addition, younger children have a greater glomerular filtration rate and, therefore, more rapidly move plasma through the kidneys.

Children also differ from adults in terms of body tissue. The proportion of body fat is highest in the first year of life, followed by a steady decrease until another increase at puberty. Compared to adults, most children and adolescents have relatively less fatty tissue, which can lead to differences in drug distribution and increased accumulation of lipophilic or fatty agents and their metabolites in their plasma. Although we might predict higher plasma drug levels in children and adolescents because they have fewer fat stores, their increased metabolic rate often more than compensates for the lower fat stores and leads to a lower plasma drug level than in adults.

Finally, as compared to adults, children have a greater volume of extracellular water. For drugs like lithium that are distributed largely throughout the body water, children will generally have a lower plasma concentration than adults because the volume of water distribution is higher in children. Total body water gradually decreases during childhood to adult values of approximately 55% of body weight by 12 years of age. By approximately 15 years of age, adolescent pharmacokinetic parameters resemble those of adults more so than those of children.

Target receptors on the neural substrates that bind drugs may also be different in children. Children are neurobiologically immature when compared to adults. As discussed in Chapter 9, for example, gamma aminobutyric acid (GABA) receptors are not fully mature until later adolescence. Consequently, children who receive benzodiazepine drugs may have a paradoxical reaction to them. Instead of being calmed or relaxed by these medications, children may become agitated, irritable, or belligerent. Additionally, as discussed in Chapter 10, catecholamine receptors in the central nervous system may not be fully developed until adulthood. The fact that children's immature noradrenergic receptors cannot adequately utilize the tricyclic antidepressants may explain the failure of these medications to treat depression in most studies of youth. Likewise, serotonin neural networks continue to develop throughout the third decade of life, which may explain why serotonergic antidepressants appear to be more effective in adults than in children.

EVALUATION AND TREATMENT

Children and adolescents should have a complete psychiatric and medical evaluation prior to starting psychotropic medications in order to determine the potential risks and benefits of treatment. The standard of care for psychiatric disorders requires a careful diagnostic assessment before the introduction of therapy. Because we lack sufficient data in many areas of child psychiatry, we cannot always rely on research to determine the most efficacious treatments and must borrow heavily from our clinical experience. If a practitioner does not have adequate clinical experience and is not confident in his abilities to diagnose and treat child and adolescent mental illness, consultation with or referral to a specialist is advised. Although our diagnostic nosology and evaluation methods remain imperfect, without an adequate diagnosis an accurate treatment plan cannot be formulated. Appropriate laboratory examinations should also be completed as indicated before the initiation of pharmacotherapy.

Typically, we demand that a child has received a full physical and neurological exam within the past 12 months prior to initiating treatment. The practitioner, if not completing a physical examination himself, should contact the individual who did the last physical examination prior to prescribing medication. In addition to any indicated blood and urine laboratory examinations, routine vital signs, including blood pressure, pulse, height, and weight, should be ascertained in order to follow growth and cardiac parameters. For children and adolescents taking antipsychotics, routine lab work as described in Chapter 12 should be obtained.

Once psychotropic treatment has been agreed upon, the practitioner should provide extensive psychoeducation to the child or adolescent and the family. Successful treatment may also require educating the teacher, coach, and other important collaterals in the child's life. If the grandmother, for example, spends a great deal of time with the child or has particular influence within the family, she should be educated about the need for treatment as well because without her support the treatment plan is likely to fail.

Parents must be told about all medication options to treat the target symptoms, in addition to the possible benefits and risks of each treatment being considered. Parents should also be educated about the therapeutic dosage range of medication; the medication schedule and dosage titration; the duration of treatment to achieve the desired effect; plans for managing adverse drug reactions or any emergencies that may arise; and the anticipated length of treatment.

Once medication treatment is initiated, a full trial is advised unless the side effects make continued treatment untenable. Practitioners are encouraged to generally start with a low dosage and titrate upward slowly until the desired treatment effect or dosage is achieved. With the exception of stimulants, psychiatric medications commonly take weeks to exert their intended effects. Even with stimulants, it may take weeks or months to achieve the optimal dose and treatment schedule. Consequently, an adequate trial at a therapeutic dosage is required before an individual is considered a nonresponder.

Some parents will prefer that the practitioner not advise their child about medication side effects prior to initiating treatment. As the parent is the legal guardian, their wishes should be respected, but at the same time the prescriber must inform the child in some way that he will be taking a new medication that is designed to treat specific symptoms. Providing too much information on side effects to some children and adolescents, particularly those with high anxiety, is sometimes an error, as they will be so fearful of the potential side effects that they will not try the medication or maintain adherence with the treatment plan.

Finally, clinical management of patients being treated with psychotropic medications should include the following: monitoring the target symptoms; evaluating medication efficacy and the need for additional interventions, such as individual or family psychotherapy; providing ongoing support and education to the family and patient about not only the diagnosis, but also the medication and its use; evaluating the need for educational interventions and supports; and evaluating the need for additional case management services.

BLACK BOX WARNINGS

Subsequent to the passing of the FDAMA of 1997, a number of pharmaceutical companies began studies of their antidepressants in children and adolescents. In the midst of these studies, it was observed that some youth were reporting thoughts of suicide or self-harm after being treated with an antidepressant. Upon recognition that there appeared to be a pattern, the FDA engaged in a review of all studies of antidepressants in children. Nine medications were included in the FDA's review, including fluoxetine (Prozac), sertraline (Zoloft), paroxetine (Paxil), fluvoxamine (Luvox), citalopram (Celexa), bupropion (Wellbutrin), venlafaxine (Effexor), nefazodone (Serzone), and mirtazapine (Remeron). The FDA analysis comprised approximately 4,400 patients in 25 placebo-controlled trials, which ranged from 4 to 16 weeks in duration. Sixteen of these studies were for the treatment of major depressive disorder, four were for obsessive-compulsive disorder, two were for generalized anxiety disorder, two were for ADHD, and one was for social anxiety disorder.

Pooled analyses of these studies found an excess of suicidal ideation noted in children and adolescents taking antidepressants. Roughly 4% of those children and adolescents taking medication versus about 2% of those taking placebo reported thoughts of suicide (Hammad, Laughren, & Racoosin, 2006; U.S. Food and Drug Administration, 2004). A subsequent review incorporated additional studies of antidepressants into this analysis and found lower rates of associated suicidality (Bridge et al., 2007). Regardless, no suicides occurred in these trials, but the FDA could not rule out an increased risk of suicide when using these medications. Given these concerns, Black Box Warnings suggesting that children and adolescents treated with antidepressants "should be observed closely for clinical worsening, suicidality, or unusual changes in behavior" were added to the packaging of all antidepressants. The release of this data and the subsequent FDA response has had both practitioners and parents concerned.

Although we should be cautious when treating with any medication, additional analyses suggest that antidepressants do considerably more good than harm when treating child and adolescent depression. In a 12–16 week study of psychotherapy for the treatment of adolescent depression, for example, 12.5% of teens (11 of 88) reported suicidality at some point during treatment, even though no medications were used and they denied suicidality on initial intake interview (Bridge, Barbe, Birmaher, Kolko, & Brent, 2005). The detection of suicidality was improved by specific and systematic assessment, and self-reported suicidality in the week prior to intake predicted the onset of emergent suicidality more accurately than did interviewer-rated concern, treatment assignment, cognitive distortions, and severity of depression. By contrast, among the 25 studies that the FDA analyzed, the assessment instruments varied, as did the methods of assessing for suicidal ideation. Consequently, it is possible that among these 25 studies some of these youth would have acknowledged suicidal ideation prior to entry into the study were they systematically assessed.

Following the warnings about a possible association between antidepressants and suicidal ideation and behavior in 2003 and 2004, prescriptions for selective serotonin reuptake inhibitors (SSRIs) for the treatment of child and adolescent depression fell by 22% in both the United States and the Netherlands. Between 2003 and 2005, the youth suicide rate increased by 49% in the Netherlands; similarly, the rate increased by 14% in the United States between 2003 and 2004 (Gibbons et al., 2007). These data suggest that for every 20% decline in antidepressant use among patients of all ages in the United States, an additional 3,040 suicides per year would occur. Although not proof of causation, certainly the timing between the antidepressant warnings and subsequent decrease in prescriptions correlates well with the increases in suicide rates. Elevated rates of suicide among youth in the United States persisted between 2004 and

2005, suggesting that the increase seen in the United States between 2003 and 2004 was not an isolated event (Bridge, Greenhouse, Weldon, Campo, & Kelleher, 2008).

Additional data suggest that antidepressant sales of fluoxetine and other SSRIs may be tied to a decrease in overall suicide rate. The U.S. suicide rate held fairly steady for 15 years from 1973 to 1988 at between 12.2 and 13.7 per 100,000. After the introduction of fluoxetine in 1988, the suicide rate gradually declined to 10.4 per 100,000 by the year 2000. This drop was associated with an increase in fluoxetine prescriptions from 2.47 million in 1988 to 33.32 million in 2002. The estimated decrease in suicides during this period totals 33,600. This data suggests that it may have been the increased availability of antidepressants that led to the decrease in suicides (Licinio & Wong, 2005).

Regardless of these studies, we do know that the risk of suicide increases for those with chronic as opposed to acute depression and that the vast majority of teen suicide completers are not taking an antidepressant at the time of the event. About 32,000 Americans commit suicide each year. If antidepressants were responsible for large numbers of suicides, then the reduction in prescriptions should have caused a decrease in the suicide rate. Instead, we saw the opposite. It would appear, then, that the slight increased risk of suicidal thinking as reported by the FDA among children and adolescents is more than balanced out by the protective effect of these medications for the majority of those who take them.

References

AACAP Work Group on Stimulant Medications. (2002). Practice parameter for the use of stimulant medications in the treatment of children, adolescents, and adults. *Journal of the American Academy of Child and Adolescent Psychiatry, 41*(2), 26S–49S.

Abdelghany, S., Hughes, J., Lammers, J., Wellbrock, B., Buffington, P. J., & Shank, R. A. (2001). Biofeedback and electrical stimulation therapy for treating urinary incontinence and voiding dysfunction: One center's experience. *Urologic Nursing, 21*(6), 401–405, 410.

Abelson, J. F., Kwan, K. Y., O'Roak, B. J., Baek, D. Y., Stillman, A. A., Morgan, T. M., et al. (2005). Sequence variants in SLITRK1 are associated with Tourette's syndrome. *Science, 310,* 317–320.

Accreditation Council for Graduate Medical Education. (2007). *Child and adolescent psychiatry program requirements.* Retrieved April 5, 2009 from http://www.acgme.org/acWebsite/downloads/RRC_progReq/320pr0101 2006.pdf

Addington, J., Van Mastrigt, S., & Addington, D. (2004). Duration of untreated psychosis: Impact on 2-year outcome. *Psychological Medicine, 34*(2), 277–284.

Alam, M. N., McGinty, D., & Szymusiak, R. (1995). Neuronal discharge of preoptic/anterior hypothalamic thermosensitive neurons: Relation to NREM sleep. *American Journal of Physiology, 269*(5), R1240–R1249.

Alm, B., Lagercrantz, H., & Wennergren, G. (2006). Stop SIDS—sleeping solitary supine, sucking soother, stopping smoking substitutes. *Acta Paediatrica, 95*(3), 260–262.

Aman, M. G., Arnold, L. E., & Armstrong, S. C. (1999). Review of serotonergic agents and perseverative behavior in patients with developmental disabilities. *Mental Retardation and Developmental Disabilities, 5,* 279–289.

Aman, M. G., Collier-Crespin, A., & Lindsay, R. L. (2000). Pharmacotherapy of disorders in mental retardation. *European Child and Adolescent Psychiatry, 1,* 198–207.

Aman, M. G., De Smedt, G., Derivan, A., Lyons, B., & Findling, R. L. (2002). Double-blind, placebo-controlled study of risperidone for the treatment of disruptive behaviors in children with subaverage intelligence. *American Journal of Psychiatry, 159,* 1337–1346.

American Diabetes Association. (2004). Consensus development conference on antipsychotic drugs and obesity (consensus statement). *Diabetes Care, 27,* 596–601.

American Psychiatric Association. (1952). *Diagnostic and statistical manual of mental disorders.* Washington, DC: Author.

American Psychiatric Association. (1968). *Diagnostic and statistical manual of mental disorders* (2nd ed.). Washington, DC: Author.

American Psychiatric Association. (1980). *Diagnostic and statistical manual of mental disorders* (3rd ed.). Washington, DC: Author.

American Psychiatric Association. (1987). *Diagnostic and statistical manual of mental disorders* (3rd ed., revision). Washington, DC: Author.

American Psychiatric Association. (1994). *Diagnostic and statistical manual of mental disorders* (4th ed.). Washington, DC: Author.

American Psychiatric Association. (2000). *Diagnostic and statistical manual of mental disorders* (4th ed., text revision). Washington, DC: Author.

American Psychiatric Association. (2006). Treatment of patients with eating disorders. *American Journal of Psychiatry, 163*(7), 4–54.

American Sleep Disorders Association. (2007). *International classification of sleep disorders: Diagnostic and coding manual, ICSD-R.* Westchester, IL: American Academy of Sleep Medicine.

Amitai, Y., & Frischer, H. (2006). Excess fatality from desipramine in children and adolescents. *Journal of the American Academy of Child and Adolescent Psychiatry, 45*(1), 54–60.

Anderson, J. C., Williams, S., McGee, R., & Silva, P. A. (1987). DSM-III disorders in preadolescent children. Prevalence in a large sample from the general population. *Archives of General Psychiatry, 44*(1), 69–76.

Anderson, J. R. (2000). *Cognitive psychology and its implications* (5th ed.). New York: Worth.

Anderson, K. J., Revelle, W., & Lynch, M. J. (1989). Caffeine, impulsivity, and memory scanning: A comparison of two explanations for the Yerkes-Dodson Effect. *Motivation and Emotion, 13,* 1–20.

Anderson, R. N., & Smith, B. L. (2003). Deaths: Leading causes for 2001. *National Vital Statistics Report, 52*(9), 1–85.

Anderson, R. N., & Smith, B. L. (2005). Deaths: Leading causes for 2002. *National Vital Statistics Reports, 53*(17), 1–89.

Andreasen, N. C., Rezai, K., Alliger, R., Swayze, V. W., Flaum, M., Kirchner, P., et al. (1992). Hypofrontality in neuroleptic-naive patients and in patients with chronic schizophrenia. Assessment with xenon 133 single-photon emission computed tomography and the Tower of London. *Archives of General Psychiatry, 49*(12), 943–958.

Angold A., & Costello E. J. (1993). Depressive comorbidity in children and adolescents: Empirical, theoretical, and methodological issues. *American Journal of Psychiatry, 150,* 1779–1791.

Angold, A., Costello, E. J., Farmer, E. M., Burns, B. J., & Erkanli, A. (1999). Impaired but undiagnosed. *Journal of the American Academy of Child and Adolescent Psychiatry, 38*(2), 129–137.

Angst, J. (1999). Major depression in 1998: Are we providing optimal therapy? *Journal of Clinical Psychiatry, 60*(6), 5–9.

Angst, J., & Vollrath, M. (1991). The natural history of anxiety disorders. *Acta Psychiatrica Scandinavica, 84*(5), 446–452.

Antochi, R., Stavrakaki, C., & Emery, P. C. (2003). Psychopharmacological treatments in persons with dual diagnosis of psychiatric disorders and developmental disabilities. *Postgraduate Medicine Journal, 9,* 139–146.

Apter, A., Pauls, D. L., Bleich, A., Zohar, A. H., Kron, S., Ratzoni, G., et al. (1993). An epidemiologic study of Gilles de la Tourette's syndrome in Israel. *Archives of General Psychiatry, 50*(9), 734–738.

Arias, E., MacDorman, M. F., Strobino, D. M., & Guyer, B. (2003). Annual summary of vital statistics—2002. *Pediatrics, 112*(6), 1215–1230.

Aristotle. Bekker, A. I. Number II. 1109a27, *Nicomachean Ethics.*

Arnold, L. E. (2000). Methylphenidate vs. amphetamine: Comparative review. *Journal of Attention Disorders, 3*(4), 200–211.

Avery, K. (2009). The coffee trade and its MDG ramifications. *UN Chronicle Online Edition.* Retrieved January 28, 2009, from http://www.un.org/Pubs/chronicle/2007/webArticles/111407_coffee_trade.html

Ayers, T. S., Sandler, I. N., West, S. G., & Roosa, M. W. (1996). A dispositional and situational assessment of children's coping: Testing alternative models of coping. *Journal of Personality, 64*(4), 923–958.

Babor, T. F., Hofmann, M., DelBoca, F. K., Hesselbrock, V., Meyer, R. E., Dolinsky, Z. S., et al. (1992). Types of alcoholics, I. Evidence for an empirically derived typology based on indicators of vulnerability and severity. *Archives of General Psychiatry, 49*(8), 599–608.

Bailey, A., Le Couteur, A., Gottesman, I., Bolton, P., Simonoff, E., Yuzda, E., et al. (1995). Autism as a strongly genetic disorder: Evidence from a British twin study. *Psychological Medicine, 25*(1), 63–78.

Baird, G., Pickles, A., Simonoff, E., Charman, T., Sullivan, P., Chandler, S., et al. (2008). Measles vaccination and antibody response in autism spectrum disorders. *Archives of Disease in Childhood, 93,* 832–837.

Bangs, M. E., Jin, L., Zhang, S., Desaiah, D., Allen, A. J., Read, H. A., et al. (2008). Hepatic events associated with atomoxetine treatment for attention-deficit hyperactivity disorder. *Drug Safety, 31*(4), 345–354.

Barbosa, J., Tannock, R., & Manassis, K. (2002). Measuring anxiety: Parent-child reporting differences in clinical samples. *Depression and Anxiety, 15*(2), 61–65.

Barkley, R. A. (1998). *Attention-deficit hyperactivity disorder, a handbook for diagnosis and treatment* (2nd ed.). New York: Guilford Press.

Barkley, R. A., Murphy, K. R., & Kwasnik, D. (1996). Motor vehicle driving competencies and risks in teens and young adults with attention deficit hyperactivity disorder. *Pediatrics, 98*(6), 1089–1095.

Baron-Cohen, S., Allen, J., & Gillberg, C. (1992). Can autism be detected at 18 months? The needle, the haystack, and the CHAT. *British Journal of Psychiatry, 161*, 839–843.

Baron-Cohen, S., Cox, A., Baird, G., Swettenham, J., Nightingale, N., Morgan, K., et al. (1996). Psychological markers in the detection of autism in infancy in a large population. *British Journal of Psychiatry, 168*, 158–163.

Barrett, P. M., Farrell, L., Pina, A. A., Peris, T. S., & Piacentini, J. (2008). Evidence-based psychosocial treatments for child and adolescent obsessive-compulsive disorder. *Journal of Clinical Child and Adolescent Psychology, 37*(1), 131–155.

Barrett, T. B., Hauger, R. L., Kennedy, J. L., Sadovnick, A. D., Remick, R. A., Keck, P. E., et al. (2003). Evidence that a single nucleotide polymorphism in the promoter of the G protein receptor kinase 3 gene is associated with bipolar disorder. *Molecular Psychiatry, 8*(5), 546–557.

Batshaw, M. L. (1993). Mental retardation. *Pediatric Clinics of North America, 40*, 507–521.

Baum, A. E., Akula, N., Cabanero, M., Cardona, I., Corona, W., Klemens, B., et al. (2008). A genome-wide association study implicates diacylglycerol kinase eta (DGKH) and several other genes in the etiology of bipolar disorder. *Molecular Psychiatry, 13*(2), 197–207.

Bawden, H. N., Stokes, A., Camfield, C. S., Camfield, P. R., & Salisbury, S. (1998). Peer relationship problems in children with Tourette's disorder or diabetes mellitus. *Journal of Child Psychology and Psychiatry, 39*(5), 663–668.

Baxter, A. J., & Krenzelok, E. P. (2008). Pediatric fatality secondary to EDTA chelation. *Clinical Toxicology, 23*, 1–2.

Baxter, L. R., Schwartz, J. M., Bergman, K. S., Szuba, M. P., Guze, B. H., Mazziotta, J. C., et al. (1992). Caudate glucose metabolic rate changes with both drug and behavior therapy for obsessive-compulsive disorder. *Archives of General Psychiatry, 49*, 681–689.

Baxter, L. R., Schwartz, J. M., Mazziotta, J. C., Phelps, M. E., Pahl, J. J., Guze, B. H., et al. (1988). Cerebral glucose metabolic rates in nondepressed patients with obsessive-compulsive disorder. *American Journal of Psychiatry, 145*, 1560–1563.

Bean, M. K., Stewart, K., & Olbrisch, M. E. (2008). Obesity in America: Implications for clinical and health psychologists. *Journal of Clinical Psychology in Medical Settings, 15*(3), 214–224.

Beardslee, W. R., Versage, E. M., & Gladstone, T. R. (1998). Children of affectively ill parents: A review of the past 10 years. *Journal of the American Academy of Child and Adolescent Psychiatry, 37*(11), 1134–1141.

Beauchamp, G., & Gagnon, A. (2004). Influence of diagnostic classification on gender ratio in schizophrenia: A meta-analysis of youths hospitalized for psychosis. *Social Psychiatry and Psychiatric Epidemiology, 39*(12), 1017–1022.

Beck, A. T., Rush, J. A., Shaw, B. F., & Emery, G. (1979). *Cognitive therapy of depression*. New York: Guilford Press.

Beitchman, J. H., Cantwell, D. P., Forness, S. R., Kavale, K. A., & Kauffman, J. M. (1998). Practice parameters for the assessment and treatment of children and adolescents with language and learning disorders. *Journal of the American Academy of Child and Adolescent Psychiatry, 37*(10), 46S–62S.

Beitchman, J. H., & Youn, A. R. (1997). Learning disorders with a special emphasis on reading disorders: A review of the past 10 years. *Journal of the American Academy of Child and Adolescent Psychiatry, 36*(8), 1020–1032.

Belardinelli, C., Hatch, J. P., Olvera, R. L., Fonseca, M., Caetano, S. C., Nicoletti, M., et al. (2008). Family environment patterns in families with bipolar children. *Journal of Affective Disorders, 107*(1–3), 299–305.

Bell-Dolan, D. J., Last, C. G., & Strauss, C. C. (1990). Symptoms of anxiety disorders in normal children. *Journal of the American Academy of Child and Adolescent Psychiatry, 29*(5), 759–765.

Bellini, S., & Peters, J. K. (2008). Social skills training for youth with autism spectrum disorders. *Child and Adolescent Psychiatric Clinics of North America, 17*(4), 857–873.

Ben-Shachar, D., Bonne, O., Chisin, R., Klein, E., Lester, H., Aharon-Peretz, J., et al. (2007). Cerebral glucose utilization and platelet mitochondrial complex I activity in schizophrenia: A FDG-PET study. *Progress in Neuropsychopharmacology and Biological Psychiatry, 31*(4), 807–813.

Berard, R., Fong, R., Carpenter, D. J., Thomason, C., & Wilkinson, C. (2006). An international, multicenter, placebo-controlled trial of paroxetine in adolescents with major depressive disorder. *Journal of Child and Adolescent Psychopharmacology, 16*(1–2), 59–75.

Berney, T., Kolvin, I., Bhate, S. R., Garside, R. F., Jeans, J., Kay, B., et al. (1981). School phobia: A therapeutic trial with clomipramine and short-term outcome. *British Journal of Psychiatry, 138*, 110–118.

Bernstein, G. A., Borchardt, C. M., & Perwien, A. R. (1996). Anxiety disorders in children and adolescents: A review of the past 10 years. *Journal of the American Academy of Child and Adolescent Psychiatry, 35*(9), 1110–1119.

Bernstein, G. A., Borchardt, C. M., Perwien, A. R., Crosby, R. D., Kushner, M. G., Thuras, P. D., et al. (2000). Imipramine plus cognitive-behavioral therapy in the treatment of school refusal. *Journal of the American Academy of Child and Adolescent Psychiatry, 39*, 276–283.

Bernstein, G. A., Garfinkel, B. D., & Borchardt, C. M. (1990). Comparative studies of pharmacotherapy for school refusal. *Journal of the American Academy of Child and Adolescent Psychiatry, 29*(5), 773–781.

Bernstein, G. A., Hektner, J. M., Borchardt, C. M., & McMillan, M. H. (2001). Treatment of school refusal: One-year follow-up. *Journal of the American Academy of Child and Adolescent Psychiatry, 40*(2), 206–213.

Biederman, J., Faraone, S. V., Hirshfeld-Becker, D. R., Friedman, D., Robin, J. A., & Rosenbaum, J. F. (2001). Patterns of psychopathology and dysfunction in high-risk children of parents with panic disorder and major depression. *American Journal of Psychiatry, 158*, 49–57.

Biederman, J., Faraone, S. V., Marrs, A., Moore, P., Garcia, J., Ablon, S., et al. (1997). Panic disorder and agoraphobia in consecutively referred children and adolescents. *Journal of the American Academy of Child and Adolescent Psychiatry, 36*(2), 214–223.

Biederman, J., Faraone, S., Milberger, S., Guite, J., Mick, E., Chen, L., et al. (1996). A prospective 4-year follow-up study of attention-deficit hyperactivity and related disorders. *Archives of General Psychiatry, 53*(5), 437–446.

Biederman, J., Melmed, R. D., Patel, A., McBurnett, K., Konow, J., Lyne, A., et al. (2008a). A randomized, double-blind, placebo-controlled study of guanfacine extended release in children and adolescents with attention-deficit/hyperactivity disorder. *Pediatrics, 121*(1), e73–e84.

Biederman, J., Petty, C. R., Fried, R., Kaiser, R., Dolan, C. R., Schoenfeld, S., et al. (2008b). Educational and occupational underattainment in adults with attention-deficit/hyperactivity disorder: A controlled study. *Journal of Clinical Psychiatry, 69*(8), 1217–1222.

Biederman, J., & Pliszka, S. R. (2008). Modafinil improves symptoms of attention deficit/hyperactivity disorder across subtypes in children and adolescents. *Journal of Pediatrics, 152*(3), 394–399.

Biederman, J., Rosenbaum, J. F., Bolduc-Murphy, E. A., Faraone, S. V., Chaloff, J., Hirshfeld, D. R., et al. (1993). A 3-year follow-up of children with and without behavioral inhibition. *Journal of the American Academy of Child and Adolescent Psychiatry, 32*(4), 814–821.

Biederman, J., Spencer, T. J., Wilens, T. E., Prince, J. B., & Faraone, S. V. (2006). Treatment of ADHD with stimulant medications: Response to Nissen perspective in the *New England Journal of Medicine. Journal of the American Academy of Child and Adolescent Psychiatry, 45*(10), 1147–1150.

Biederman, J., Wilens, T. E., Mick, E., Faraone, S. V., & Spencer, T. (1998). Does attention-deficit hyperactivity disorder impact the developmental course of drug and alcohol abuse and dependence? *Biological Psychiatry, 44*(4), 269–273.

Birmaher, B. (2007). Longitudinal course of pediatric bipolar disorder. *American Journal of Psychiatry, 164*(4), 537–539.

Birmaher, B., Axelson, D. A., Monk, K., Kalas, C., Clark, D. B., Ehmann, M., et al. (2003). Fluoxetine for the treatment of childhood anxiety disorders. *Journal of the American Academy of Child and Adolescent Psychiatry, 42*, 415–423.

Birmaher, B., Axelson, D., Strober, M., Gill, M. K., Valeri, S., Chiappetta, L., et al. (2006). Clinical course of children and adolescents with bipolar spectrum disorders. *Archives of General Psychiatry, 63*(2), 175–183.

Birmaher, B., & Brent, D. (1998). Practice parameters for the assessment and treatment of children and adolescents with depressive disorders. *Journal of the American Academy of Child and Adolescent Psychiatry, 37*(10), 635–835.

Birmaher, B., Brent, D. A., Kolko, D., Baugher, M., Bridge, J., Holder, D. (2000). Clinical outcome after short-term psychotherapy for adolescents with major depressive disorder. *Archives of General Psychiatry, 57*(1), 29–36.

Birmaher, B., Ryan, N. D., Williamson, D. E., Brent, D. A., & Kaufman, J. (1996). Childhood and adolescent depression: A review of the past 10 years. Part II.

Journal of the American Academy of Child and Adolescent Psychiatry, 35(12), 1575–1583.

Black, B., & Uhde, T. W. (1992). Case study: Elective mutism as a variant of social phobia. *Journal of the American Academy of Child and Adolescent Psychiatry, 31*(6), 1090–1094.

Black, B., & Uhde, T. W. (1994). Treatment of elective mutism with fluoxetine: A double-blind, placebo-controlled study. *Journal of the American Academy of Child and Adolescent Psychiatry, 33*, 1000–1006.

Blackorby, J., & Wagner, M. (1996). Longitudinal post school outcomes of youth with disabilities: Findings from the National Longitudinal Transition Study. *Exceptional Children, 62*(5), 399–413.

Blader, J. C., Koplewicz, H. S., Abikoff, H., & Foley, C. (1997). Sleep problems of elementary school children. A community survey. *Archives of Pediatrics and Adolescent Medicine, 151*(5), 473–480.

Bleuler, M. (1978). *The schizophrenic disorders: Long-term patient and family studies.* London: Yale University Press.

Bloch, M. H., Landeros-Weisenberger, A., Kelmendi, B., Coric, V., Bracken, M. B., & Leckman, J. F. (2006). A systematic review: Antipsychotic augmentation with treatment refractory obsessive-compulsive disorder. *Molecular Psychiatry, 11*(7), 622–632.

Bloch, M. H., Leckman, J. F., Zhu, H., & Peterson, B. S. (2005). Caudate volumes in childhood predict symptom severity in adults with Tourette syndrome. *Neurology, 65*(8), 1253–1258.

Blunden, S., Lushington, K., Kennedy, D., Martin, J., & Dawson, D. (2000). Behavior and neurocognitive performance in children aged 5–10 years who snore compared to controls. *Journal of Clinical and Experimental Neuropsychology, 5*, 554.

Boachie, A., Goldfield, G. S., & Spettigue, W. (2003). Olanzapine use as an adjunctive treatment for hospitalized children with anorexia nervosa: Case reports. *International Journal of Eating Disorders, 33*(1), 98–103.

Boney-McCoy, S., & Finkelhor, D. (1995). Psychosocial sequelae of violent victimization in a national youth sample. *Journal of Consulting and Clinical Psychology, 63*, 726–736.

Bongers, I. L., Koot, H. M., van der Ende, J., & Verhulst, F. C. (2003). The normative development of child and adolescent problem behaviour. *Journal of Abnormal Psychology, 112*, 179–192.

Bookheimer, S. Y., Ting Wang, A., Scott, A., Sigman, M., & Dapretto, M. (2008). Frontal contributions to face processing differences in autism: Evidence from fMRI of inverted face processing. *Journal of the International Neuropsychological Society, 14*, 922–932.

Borchardt, C. M., & Bernstein, G. A. (1995). Comorbid disorders in hospitalized bipolar adolescents compared with unipolar depressed adolescents. *Child Psychiatry and Human Development, 26*(1), 11–18.

Borcherding, B. G., Keysor, C. S., Rapoport, J. L., Elia, J., & Amass, J. (1990). Motor/vocal tics and compulsive behaviors on stimulant drugs: Is there a common vulnerability? *Psychiatry Research, 33*, 83–94.

Bottlender, R., Sato, T., Jäger, M., Wegener, U., Wittmann, J., Strauss, A., et al. (2003). The impact of the duration of untreated psychosis prior to first psychiatric admission on the 15-year outcome in schizophrenia. *Schizophrenia Research, 62*(1–2), 37–44.

Bowen, R. C., Offord, D. R., & Boyle, M. H. (1990). The prevalence of overanxious disorder and separation anxiety disorder: Results from the Ontario Child Health Study. *Journal of the American Academy of Child and Adolescent Psychiatry, 29*(5), 753–758.

Bradley, C. (1937). The behavior of children receiving benzedrine. *American Journal of Psychiatry, 94*, 577–585.

Bradley, S. J., Jadaa, D. A., Brody, J., Landy, S., Tallett, S. E., Watson, W., et al. (2003). Brief psychoeducational parenting program: An evaluation and 1-year follow-up. *Journal of the American Academy of Child and Adolescent Psychiatry, 42*(10), 1171–1178.

Brady, J. P. (1991). The pharmacology of stuttering: A critical review. *American Journal of Psychiatry, 148*, 1309–1316.

Brawn, T. P., Fenn, K. M., Nusbaum, H. C., & Margoliash, D. (2008). Consolidation of sensorimotor learning during sleep. *Learning & Memory, 15*(11), 815–819.

Bregman, J. D. (1991). Current developments in the understanding of mental retardation. Part II: Psychopathology. *Journal of the American Academy of Child and Adolescent Psychiatry, 30*(6), 861–872.

Brent, D., Emslie, G., Clarke, G., Wagner, K. D., Asarnow, J. R., Keller, M., et al. (2008). Switching to another SSRI or to venlafaxine with or without cognitive behavioral therapy for adolescents with SSRI-resistant depression: The TORDIA randomized controlled trial. *Journal of the American Medical Association, 299*(8), 901–913.

Brent, D. A., Holder, D., Kolko, D., Birmaher, B., Baugher, M., Roth, C., et al. (1997). A clinical psychotherapy trial for adolescent depression comparing cognitive, family, and supportive therapy. *Archives of General Psychiatry, 54*(9), 877–885.

Brent, D. A., Kalas, R., Edelbrock, C., Costello, A. J., Dulcan, M. K., & Conover, N. (1986). Psychopathology and its relationship to suicidal ideation in childhood and adolescence. *Journal of the American Academy of Child and Adolescent Psychiatry, 25*, 666–673.

Bridge, J. A., Barbe, R. P., Birmaher, B., Kolko, D. J., & Brent D. A. (2005). Emergent suicidality in a clinical psychotherapy trial for adolescent depression. *American Journal of Psychiatry, 162*(11), 2173–2175.

Bridge, J. A., Birmaher, B., Iyengar, S., Barbe, R. P., & Brent, D. A. (2008a). Placebo response in randomized controlled trials of antidepressants for pediatric major depressive disorder. *American Journal of Psychiatry, 166*, 42–49.

Bridge, J. A., Greenhouse, J. B., Weldon, A. H., Campo, J. V., & Kelleher, K. J. (2008b). Suicide trends among youths aged 10 to 19 years in the United States, 1996–2005. *Journal of the American Medical Association, 300*(9), 1025–1026.

Bridge, J. A., Iyengar, S., Salary, C. B., Barbe, R. P., Birmaher, B., Pincus, H. A., et al. (2007). Clinical response and risk for reported suicidal ideation and suicide attempts in pediatric antidepressant treatment: A meta-analysis of randomized controlled trials. *Journal of the American Medical Association, 297*(15), 1683–1696.

Brizendine, L. (2006). *The Female Brain.* New York: Morgan Road Books.

Broadhurst, P. L. (1957). *Emotional Psychology, 54,* 345–352.

Brooks-Gunn, J., & Duncan, C. J. (1997). The effects of poverty on children. *The Future of Children, 7*(2), 55–71.

Broughton, R., Billings, R., Cartwright, R., Doucette, D., Edmeads, J., Edwardh, M., et al. (1994). Homicidal somnambulism: A case report. *Sleep, 17*(3), 253–264.

Brown, A. S., Begg, M. D., Gravenstein, S., Schaefer, C. A., Wyatt, R. J., Bresnahan, M., et al. (2004). Serologic evidence of prenatal influenza in the etiology of schizophrenia. *Archives of General Psychiatry, 61,* 774–780.

Brown, A. S., Schaefer, C. A., Wyatt, R. J., Begg, M. D., Goetz, R., Bresnahan, M. A., et al. (2002). Paternal age and risk of schizophrenia in adult offspring. *American Journal of Psychiatry, 159*(9), 1528–1533.

Brown, R., Colter, N., Corsellis, J. A., Crow, T. J., Frith, C. D., Jagoe, R., et al. (1986). Postmortem evidence of structural brain changes in schizophrenia. Differences in brain weight, temporal horn area, and parahippocampal gyrus compared with affective disorder. *Archives of General Psychiatry, 43*(1), 36–42.

Brownell, K. D., & Napolitano, M. A. (1995). Distorting reality for children: Body size proportions of Barbie and Ken dolls. *International Journal of Eating Disorders, 18*(3), 295–298.

Bruch, H. (1962). Perceptual and conceptual disturbances in anorexia nervosa. *Psychosomatic Medicine, 24,* 187–194.

Brumberg, J. J. (1988). *Fasting girls: The emergence of anorexia nervosa as a modern disease.* Cambridge, MA: Harvard University Press.

Brumberg, J. J. (2000). *Fasting girls: The history of anorexia nervosa.* New York: Vintage Books.

Bryan, T. (1991). Assessment of social cognition: Review of research in learning disabilities. In L. H. Swanson (Ed.), *Handbook on the assessment of learning disabilities: Theory, research and practice* (pp. 285–311). Austin, TX: Pro-Ed.

Buguet, A. (2007). Sleep under extreme environments: Effects of heat and cold exposure, altitude, hyperbaric pressure and microgravity in space. *Journal of the Neurological Sciences, 262*(1–2), 145–152.

Bukstein, O. G., Glancy, L. J., & Kaminer, Y. (1992). Patterns of affective comorbidity in a clinical population of dually diagnosed adolescent substance users. *Journal of the American Academy of Child and Adolescent Psychiatry, 31,* 1041–1045.

Burke, J. D., Loeber, R., & Birmaher, B. (2002). Oppositional defiant and conduct disorder: A review of the past 10 years, part II. *Journal of the American Academy of Child and Adolescent Psychiatry, 41*(11), 1275–1293.

Byrd, R. S., Weitzman, M., Lanphear, N. E., & Auinger, P. (1996). Bed-wetting in US children: Epidemiology and related behavior problems. *Pediatrics, 98,* 414–419.

Campbell, M., Cohen, I. L., & Small, A. M. (1982). Drugs in aggressive behavior. *Journal of the American Academy of Child and Adolescent Psychiatry, 21*, 107–117.

Campbell, M., Small, A. M., Green, W. H., Jennings, S. H., Perry, R., Bennett, W. G, et al. (1985). Behavioral efficacy of haloperidol and lithium carbonate: A comparison in hospitalized aggressive children with conduct disorder. *Archives of General Psychiatry, 41*, 650–656.

Cannon, T. D., Cadenhead, K., Cornblatt, B., Woods, S. W., Addington, J., Walker, E., et al. (2008). Prediction of psychosis in youth at high clinical risk: A multi-site longitudinal study in North America. *Archives of General Psychiatry, 65*(1), 28–37.

Cantwell, D. (1996). Attention deficit disorder: A review of the past 10 years. *Journal of the American Academy of Child and Adolescent Psychiatry, 35*(8), 978–987.

Carandang, C., Robbins, D., Mullany, E., Yazbek, M., & Minot, S. (2007). Lamotrigine in adolescent mood disorders: A retrospective chart review. *Journal of the Canadian Academy of Child and Adolescent Psychiatry, 16*(1), 1–8.

Cardno, A. G., & Gottesman, I. I. (2000). Twin studies of schizophrenia: From bow-and arrow concordances to star wars Mx and functional genomics. *American Journal of Medical Genetics, 97*(1), 12–17.

Cardno, A. G., Marshall, E. J., Coid, B., Macdonald, A. M., Ribchester, T. R., Davies, N. J., et al. (1999). Heritability estimates for psychotic disorders: The Maudsley twin psychosis series. *Archives of General Psychiatry, 56*(2), 162–168.

Carlson, G. A., Bromet, E. J., & Sievers, S. (2000a). Phenomenology and outcome of subjects with early- and adult-onset psychotic mania. *American Journal of Psychiatry, 157*(2), 213–219.

Carlson, G. A., & Cantwell, D. P. (1980). A survey of depressive symptoms, syndrome and disorder in a child psychiatric population. *Journal of Child Psychology and Psychiatry, 21*(1), 19–25.

Carlson, G. A., Loney, J., Salisbury, H., Kramer, J. R., & Arthur, C. (2000b). Stimulant treatment in young boys with symptoms suggesting childhood mania: A report from a longitudinal study. *Journal of Child and Adolescent Psychopharmacology, 10*(3), 175–184.

Carter, A. S., O'Donnell, D. A., Schultz, R. T., Scahill, L., Leckman, J. F., & Pauls, D. L. (2000). Social and emotional adjustment in children affected with Gilles de la Tourette's syndrome: Associations with ADHD and family functioning. *Journal of Child Psychology and Psychiatry, 41*(2), 215–223.

Carter, T. D., Mundo, E., Parikh, S. V., & Kennedy, J. L. (2003). Early age at onset as a risk factor for poor outcome of bipolar disorder. *Journal of Psychiatric Research, 37*(4), 297–303.

Caspi, A., Henry, B., McGee, R. O., Moffitt, T. E., & Silva, P. A. (1995). Temperamental origins of child and adolescent behavior problems: From age three to age fifteen. *Child Development, 66*, 55–68.

Caspi, A., Sugden, K., Moffitt, T. E., Taylor, A., Craig, I. W., Harrington, H., et al. (2003). Influence of life stress on depression: Moderation by a polymorphism in the 5-HTT gene. *Science, 301*(5631), 386–389.

Cass, H., Gringras, P., March, J., McKendrick, I., O'Hare, A. E., Owen, L., et al. (2008). Absence of urinary pioid peptides in children with autism. *Archives of Disease in Children, 93*(9), 745–750.

Castellanos, F. X., Lee, P. P., Sharp, W., Jeffries, N. O., Greenstein, D. K., Clasen, L. S., et al. (2002). Developmental trajectories of brain volume abnormalities in children and adolescents with attention deficit/hyperactivity disorder. *Journal of the American Medical Association, 288*(14), 1740–1748.

Centers for Disease Control. (2007). Prevalence of autism spectrum disorders: Autism and developmental disabilities onitoring network, 14 sites, United States. *Morbidity and Mortality Weekly Report, 56*(SS01), 12–28.

Centers for Disease Control. (2001). *National health interview surveys 1997–2001.* Retrieved from http://www.cdc.gov/nchs/nhis.htm

Centers for Disease Control and Prevention, Department of Health and Human Services, & WISQARSTM (Web-based Injury Statistics Query and Reporting System). (2003). Retrieved ftp://ftp.cdc.gov/pub/ncipc/10LC-2003/PDF/10lc-2003.pdf

Chambers, W. J., Puig-Antich, J., Tabrizi, M. A., & Davies, M. (1982). Psychotic symptoms in prepubertal major depressive disorder. *Archives of General Psychiatry, 39*(8), 921–927.

Chang, K. (2007). Adult bipolar disorder is continuous with pediatric bipolar disorder. *Canadian Journal of Psychiatry, 52*(7), 418–425.

Chang, K. D., Blasey, C., Ketter, T. A., & Steiner, H. (2001). Family environment of children and adolescents with bipolar parents. *Bipolar Disorder, 3*(2), 73–78.

Chang, K., Howe, M., Gallelli, K., & Miklowitz, D. (2006a). Prevention of pediatric bipolar disorder: Integration of neurobiological and psychosocial processes. *Annals of the New York Academy of Sciences, 1094,* 235–247.

Chang, K. D., Nyilas, M., Aurang, C., et al. (2007, October). *Efficacy of aripiprazole in children (10–17 years old) with mania.* Poster presented at the annual meeting of the American Academy of Child and Adolescent Psychiatry, Boston, Massachusetts.

Chang, K., Saxena, K., & Howe, M. (2006b). An open-label study of lamotrigine adjunct or monotherapy for the treatment of adolescents with bipolardepression. *Journal of the American Academy of Child and Adolescent Psychiatry, 4,* 298–304.

Chang, K. D., Steiner, H., & Ketter, T. A. (2000). Psychiatric phenomenology of child and adolescent bipolar offspring. *Journal of the American Academy of Child and Adolescent Psychiatry, 39*(4), 453–460.

Chang, K., Steiner, H., & Ketter, T. (2003). Studies of offspring of parents with bipolar disorder. *American Journal of Medical Genetics Part C: Seminars of Medical Genetics, 123C*(1), 26–35.

Chen, C. Y., Storr, C. L., & Anthony, J. C. (2009). Early-onset drug use and risk for drug dependence problems. *Addictive Behaviors, 34*(3), 319–322.

Chervin, R. D., & Archbold, K. H. (2001). Hyperactivity and polysomnographic findings in children evaluated for sleep-disordered breathing. *Sleep, 24*(3), 313.

Chervin, R. D., Archbold, K. H., Dillon, J. E., Panahi, P., Pituch, K. J., Dahl, R. E., et al. (2002). Inattention, hyperactivity, and symptoms of sleep-disordered breathing. *Pediatrics, 109*(3), 449.

Children's Defense Fund. (2002). *The state of children in America's union: A 2002 action guide to leave no child behind.* Retrieved from www.childrensdefense .org/pdf/minigreenbook.pdf

Choudhury, M. S., Pimentel, S. S., & Kendall, P. C. (2003). Childhood anxiety disorders: Parent-child (dis)agreement using a structured interview for the DSM-IV. *Journal of the American Academy of Child and Adolescent Psychiatry, 42*(8), 957–964.

Christison, G. W., & Ivany, K. (2006). Elimination diets in autism spectrum disorders: Any wheat amidst the chaff? *Journal of Developmental and Behavioral Pediatrics, 27*(2), 5162–5171.

Clarke, M. C., Harley, M., & Cannon, M. (2006). The role of obstetric events in schizophrenia. *Schizophrenia Bulletin, 32,* 3.

Cleghorn, J. M., Zipursky, R. B., & List, S. J. (1991). Structural and functional brain imaging in schizophrenia. *Journal of Psychiatry and Neuroscience, 16*(2), 53–74.

Cloitre, M., Scarvalone, P., & Difede, J. A. (1997). Posttraumatic stress disorder, self- and interpersonal dysfunction among sexually retraumatized women. *Journal of Traumatic Stress, 10*(3), 437–452.

Coffey, B. J., Biederman, J., Smoller, J. W., Geller, D. A., Sarin, P., Schwartz, S., & Kim, G. S. (2000). Anxiety disorders and tic severity in juveniles with Tourette's disorder. *Journal of the American Academy of Child and Adolescent Psychiatry, 39*(5), 562–568.

Coffey, B. J., & Park, K. S. (1997). Behavioral and emotional aspects of Tourette syndrome. *Neurologic Clinics, 15*(2), 277–289.

Cohan, S. L., Chavira, D. A., Shipon-Blum, E., Hitchcock, C., Roesch, S. C., & Stein, M. B. (2008). Refining the classification of children with selective mutism: A latent profile analysis. *Journal of Clinical Child and Adolescent Psychology, 37*(4), 770–784.

Cohen, N. J., Davine, M., Horodesky, N., Lipsett, L., & Isaacson, L. (1993). Unsuspected language impairment in psychiatrically disturbed children: Prevalence and language and behavioral characteristics. *Journal of the American Academy of Child and Adolescent Psychiatry, 32,* 595–603.

Conduct Problems Prevention Research Group. (1992). A developmental and clinical model for the prevention of conduct disorder: The FAST track program. *Development and Psychopathology, 4,* 509–527.

Conners, C. K., Casat, C. D., Gualtieri, C. T., Weller, E., Reader, M., Reiss, A., et al. (1996). Bupropion hydrochloride in attention deficit disorder with hyperactivity. *Journal of the American Academy of Child and Adolescent Psychiatry, 35*(10), 1314–1321.

Connolly, S. D., & Bernstein, G. A. (2007). Practice parameter for the assessment and treatment of children and adolescents with anxiety disorders. *Journal of the American Academy of Child and Adolescent Psychiatry, 46*(2), 267–283.

Connor, D. F. (2002). *Aggression and antisocial behavior in children and adolescents: Research and treatment.* New York: The Guilford Press.

Connor, D. F., Barkley, R. A., & Davis, H. T. (2000). A pilot study of methylphenidate, clonidine, or the combination in ADHD comorbid with aggressive oppositional defiant or conduct disorder. *Clinical Pediatrics, 39,* 15–25.

Connor, D. F., Fletcher, K. E., & Swanson, J. M. (1999). A meta-analysis of clonidine for symptoms of attention-deficit hyperactivity disorder. *Journal of the American Academy of Child and Adolescent Psychiatry, 38,* 12.

Conture, E. G., Schwartz, H. D., & Brewer, D. W. (1984). Laryngeal behavior during stuttering. *Journal of Speech and Hearing Research, 28,* 233–240.

Cooper, W. O., Arbogast, P. G., Ding, H., Hickson, G. B., Fuchs, D. C., & Ray, W. A. (2006). Trends in prescribing of antipsychotic medications for US children. *Ambulatory Pediatrics, 6*(2), 79–83.

Copur, M., Arpaci, B., Demir, T., & Narin, H. (2007). Clinical effectiveness of quetiapine in children and adolescents with Tourette's syndrome: A retrospective case-note survey. *Clinical Drug Investigation, 27*(2), 123–130.

Corkum, P., Moldofsky, H., Hogg-Johnson, S., Humphries, T., & Tannock, R. (1999). Sleep problems in children with attention-deficit/hyperactivity disorder: Impact of subtype, comorbidity, and stimulant medication. *Journal of the American Academy of Child and Adolescent Psychiatry, 38*(10), 1285–1293.

Corkum, P., Tannock, R., & Moldofsky, H. (1998). Sleep disturbances in children with attention-deficit/hyperactivity disorder. *Journal of the American Academy of Child and Adolescent Psychiatry, 37*(6), 637–646.

Correll, C. U., & Kane, J. M. (2007). One-year incidence rates of tardive dyskinesia in children and adolescents treated with second-generation antipsychotics: A systematic review. *Journal of Child and Adolescent Psychopharmacology, 17*(5), 647–656.

Costello, E. J., Egger, H. L., & Angold, A. (2004). Developmental epidemiology of anxiety disorders. In T. H. Ollendick & J. S. March (Eds.), *Phobic and anxiety disorders in children and adolescents* (pp. 61–91). New York: Oxford University Press.

Courchesne, E. (2004). Brain development in autism: Early overgrowth followed by premature arrest of growth. *Mental Retardation and Developmental Disabilities Research Reviews, 10*(2), 106–111.

Couturier, J., & Lock, J. (2007). A review of medication use for children and adolescents with eating disorders. *Journal of the Canadian Academy of Child and Adolescent Psychiatry, 16*(4), 173–176.

Craft, M., Ismail, I. A., Krishnamurti, D., Mathews, J., Regan, A., Seth, R. V., et al. (1987). Lithium in the treatment of aggression in mentally handicapped patients: A double-blind trial. *British Journal of Psychiatry, 150,* 685–689.

Craney, J., & Geller, B. (2003). Clinical implications of antidepressant and stimulant use on switching from depression to mania in children. *Journal of Child and Adolescent Psychopharmacology, 13*(2), 201–204.

Crisp, A. H. (1980). *Let me be.* London: Academic Press.

Crisp, A. H., & Bhat, A. V. (1982). "Personality" and anorexia nervosa—the phobic avoidance stance: Its origins and its symptomatology. *Psychotherapy and Psychosomatics, 38*(1), 178–200.

Csikszentmihalyi, M. (1991). *Flow, the psychology of optimal experience.* New York: Harper & Row.

Curry, J. F. (2001). Specific psychotherapies for childhood and adolescent depression. *Biological Psychiatry, 49*(12), 1091–1100.

Daban, C., Vieta, E., Mackin, P., & Young, A. H. (2005). Hypothalamic-pituitary-adrenal axis and bipolar disorder. *Psychiatric Clinics of North America, 28*(2), 469–480.

Dahl, R. E., Kaufman, J., Ryan, N. D., Perel, J., Al-Shabbout, M., Birmaher, B., et al. (1992). The Dexamethasone Suppression Test in children and adolescents: A review and a controlled study. *Biological Psychiatry, 32*(2), 109–126.

Dalton, K. M., Nacewicz, B. M., Alexander, A. L., & Davidson, R. J. (2007). Gaze-fixation, brain activation, and amygdala volume in unaffected siblings of individuals with autism. *Biological Psychiatry, 61*(4), 512–520.

Dalton, K. M., Nacewicz, B. M., Johnstone, T., Schaefer, H. S., Gernsbacher, M. A., Goldsmith, H. H., et al. (2005). Gaze fixation and the neural circuitry of face processing in autism. *Nature Neuroscience, 8*(4), 519–526.

Davalos, D. B., Compagnon, N., Heinlein, S., & Ross, R. G. (2003). Neuropsychological deficits in children associated with increased familial risk for schizophrenia. *Schizophrenia Research, 67*(2–3), 123–130.

Davanzo, P., Gunderson, B., Belin, T., Mintz, J., Pataki, C., Ott, D., et al. (2003). Mood stabilizers in hospitalized children with bipolar disorder: A retrospective review. *Psychiatry and Clinical Neurosciences, 57*(5), 504–510.

David-Ferdon, C., & Kaslow, N. J. (2008). Evidence-based psychosocial treatments for child and adolescent depression. *Journal of Clinical Child and Adolescent Psychology, 37*(1), 62–104.

Davies, L., Stern, J. S., Agrawal, N., & Robertson, M. M. (2006). A case series of patients with Tourette's syndrome in the United Kingdom treated with aripiprazole. *Human Psychopharmacology, 21*(7), 447–453.

Daviss, W. B., Bentivoglio, P., Racusin, R., Brown, K. M., Bostic, J. Q., & Wiley, L. (2001). Bupropion sustained release in adolescents with comorbid attention deficit/hyperactivity disorder and depression. *Journal of the American Academy of Child and Adolescent Psychiatry, 40*(3), 307–314.

Dawson, G., Webb, S., Schellenberg, G. D., Dager, S., Friedman, S., Aylward, E., et al. (2002). Defining the broader phenotype of autism: Genetic, brain, and behavioral perspectives. *Development and Psychopathology, 14*(3), 581–611.

de Groot, C. M., Bornstein, R. A., Spetie, L., & Burriss, B. (1994). The course of tics in Tourette syndrome: A 5-year follow-up study. *Annals of Clinical Psychiatry, 6*(4), 227–233.

Deas, D. (2008). Evidence-based treatments for alcohol use disorders in adolescents. *Pediatrics, 121*(4), S348–S354.

DelBello, M. P., Findling, R. L., Earley, W. R., Stankowski, J., & Acevedo, L. D. (2007, October). *Efficacy of quetiapine in children and adolescents with bipolar mania.* Poster presented at the annual meeting of the American Academy of Child and Adolescent Psychiatry, Boston, Massachusetts.

DelBello, M. P., Findling, R. L., Wang, P. P., Gundapaneni, B., & Versael, M. (2008, May). *Safety and efficacy of ziprasidone in pediatric bipolar disorder.* Poster presented at the annual meeting of the Society of Biological Psychiatry, Washington, DC.

DelBello, M. P., Hanseman, D., Adler, C. M., Fleck, D. E., & Strakowski, S. M. (2007). Twelve-month outcome of adolescents with bipolar disorder following first hospitalization for a manic or mixed episode. *American Journal of Psychiatry, 164*(4), 582–590.

DelBello, M. P., Kowatch, R. A., Adler, C. M., Stanford, K. E., Welge, J. A., Barzman, D. H., et al. (2006). A double-blind randomized pilot study comparing quetiapine and divalproex for adolescent mania. *Journal of the American Academy of Child and Adolescent Psychiatry, 45*(3), 305–313.

DeLong, G. R., & Nieman, G. W. (1983). Lithium-induced behavior changes in children with symptoms suggesting manic-depressive illness. *Psychopharmacology Bulletin, 19*(2), 258–265.

DeLong, G. R., Ritch, C. R., & Burch, S. (2002). Fluoxetine response in children with autistic spectrum disorders: Correlation with familial major affective disorder and intellectual achievement. *Developmental Medicine and Child Neurology, 44*(10), 652–659.

DeVeaugh-Geiss, J., Moroz, G., Biederman, J., Cantwell, D., Fontaine, R., Greist, J. H., et al. (1992). Clomipramine hydrochloride in childhood and adolescent obsessive-compulsive disorder: A multicenter trial. *Journal of the American Academy of Child and Adolescent Psychiatry, 31*(1), 45–49.

Deykin, E. Y., & MacMahon, B. (1979). The incidence of seizures among children with autistic symptoms. *American Journal of Psychiatry, 136*(10), 1310–1312.

Díaz-Marsá, M., Carrasco, J. L., Basurte, E., Sáiz, J., López-Ibor, J. J., & Hollander, E. (2008). Enhanced cortisol suppression in eating disorders with impulsive personality features. *Psychiatry Research, 158*(1), 93–97.

Diefenbach, G. J., Reitman, D., & Williamson, D. A. (2000). Trichotillomania: A challenge to research and practice. *Clinical Psychology Review, 20*(3), 289–309.

Diller, L. H. (2002). Lessons from three year olds. *Journal of Developmental and Behavioral Pediatrics, 23*(1), S10–S12.

Dinan, T. G. (1998). Psychoneuroendocrinology of depression: Growth hormone. *Psychiatric Clinics of North America, 21*(2), 325–339.

Dodge, K. A., Pettit, G. S., Bates, J. E., & Valente, E. (1995). Social information processing patterns partially mediate the effect of early physical abuse on later conduct problems. *Journal of Abnormal Psychology, 104,* 632–643.

Donfrancesco, R., & Ferrante, L. (2007). Ginkgo biloba in dyslexia: A pilot study. *Phytomedicine, 14*(6), 367–370.

Donner, S., Pirkola, K., Silander, L., Kananen, J., Terwilliger, J., Lönnqvist, L., et al. (2008). An association analysis of murine anxiety genes in humans implicates novel candidate genes for anxiety disorders. *Biological Psychiatry, 64*(8), 672–680.

Donovan, S. J., Stewart, J. W., Nunes, E. V., Quitkin, F. M., Parides, M., Daniel, W., et al. (2000). Divalproex treatment for youth with explosive temper and mood lability: A double-blind, placebo-controlled crossover design. *American Journal of Psychiatry, 157,* 818–820.

Duffy, A. (2007). Does bipolar disorder exist in children? A selected review. *Canadian Journal of Psychiatry, 52*(7), 409–417.

Duffy, E. (1957). The psychological significance of the concept of "arousal" or "activation." *Psychological Review, 64,* 265–275.

Dusenbury, L., Khuri, E., & Millman, R. B. (1992). Adolescent substance abuse: A sociodevelopmental perspective. In J. H. Lowinson, P. Ruiz, & R. B. Milman (Eds.), *Substance abuse, a comprehensive textbook* (2nd ed.) (pp. 832–842). Baltimore: Williams & Wilkins.

Dykens, E. M., Hodapp, R. M., & Finucane, B. M. (2000). *Genetics and mental retardation syndromes: A new look at behavior and interventions.* Baltimore: Paul H. Brookes.

Edwards, M. (1984). Speech disability in children: Some general considerations. *International Rehabilitation Medicine, 6*(3), 114–116.

Egeland, J. A., Hostetter, A. M., Pauls, D. L., & Sussex, J. N. (2000). Prodromal symptoms before onset of manic-depressive disorder suggested by first hospital admission histories. *Journal of the American Academy of Child and Adolescent Psychiatry, 39*(10), 1245–1252.

Eisler, I., Dare, C., Russell, G. F. M., Szmukler, G., Le Grange, D., & Dodge, E. (1997). Family and individual therapy in anorexia nervosa: A 5-year follow-up. *Archives of General Psychiatry, 54,* 1025–1030.

Elder, J. H., Shankar, M., Shuster, J., Theriaque, D., Burns, S., & Sherrill, L. (2006). The gluten-free, casein-free diet in autism: Results of a preliminary double blind clinical trial. *Journal of Autism and Developmental Disorders, 36*(3), 413–420.

Eley, T. C., & Stevenson, J. (1999). Using genetic analyses to clarify the distinction between depressive and anxious symptoms in children. *Journal of Abnormal Child Psychology, 27*(2), 105–114.

Elia, J., Borcherding, B. G., Rapoport, J. L., & Keysor, C. S. (1991). Methylphenidate and dextroamphetamine treatments of hyperactivity: Are there true non-responders? *Psychiatry Research, 36*(2), 141–155.

Elliott, G. R., & Smiga, S. (2003). Depression in the child and adolescent. *Pediatric Clinics of North America, 50*(5), 1093–1106.

Emerson, E. (2003). Prevalence of psychiatric disorders in children and adolescents with and without intellectual disability. *Journal of Intellectual Disability Research, 47,* 51–58.

Emslie, G. J., Findling, R. L., Yeung, P. P., Kunz, N. R., & Li, Y. (2007). Venlafaxine ER for the treatment of pediatric subjects with depression: Results of two placebo-controlled trials. *Journal of the American Academy of Child and Adolescent Psychiatry, 46*(4), 479–488.

Emslie, G. J., Heiligenstein, J. H., Wagner, K. D., Hoog, S. L., Ernest, D. E, Brown, E., et al. (2002). Fluoxetine for acute treatment of depression in children and adolescents: A placebo-controlled, randomized clinical trial. *Journal of the American Academy of Child and Adolescent Psychiatry, 41*(10), 1205–1215.

Emslie, G. J., Rush, A. J., Weinberg, W. A., Kowatch, R. A., Hughes, C. W., Carmody, T., et al. (1997). A double-blind, randomized, placebo-controlled trial of fluoxetine in children and adolescents with depression. *Archives of General Psychiatry, 54*(11), 1031–1037.

Emslie, G. J., Rush, A. J., Weinberg, W. A., Rintelmann, J. W., & Roffwarg, H. P. (1990). Children with major depression show reduced rapid eye movement latencies. *Archives of General Psychiatry, 47*(2), 119–124.

Emslie, G. J., Wagner, K. D., Kutcher, S., Krulewicz, S., Fong, R., Carpenter, D. J., et al. (2006). Paroxetine treatment in children and adolescents with major depressive disorder: A randomized, multicenter, double-blind, placebo-controlled trial. *Journal of the American Academy of Child and Adolescent Psychiatry, 45*(6), 709–719.

Enderby, P., & Emerson, J. (1996). Speech and language therapy: Does it work? *British Medical Journal, 312*, 1655–1658.

Engleman, H., & Joffe, D. (1999). Neuropsychological function in obstructive sleep apnea. *Sleep Medicine Reviews, 3*(1), 59.

Erenberg, G. (2005). The relationship between Tourette syndrome, attention deficit hyperactivity disorder, and stimulant medication: A critical review. *Seminars in Pediatric Neurology, 12*(4), 217–221.

Erikson, E. H., & Erikson, J. M. (1997). *The life cycle completed.* New York: Norton.

Ersu, R., Arman, A. R., Save, D., Karadag, B., Karakoc, F., Berkem, M., et al. (2004). Prevalence of snoring and symptoms of sleep-disordered breathing in primary school children in Istanbul. *Chest Journal, 126*, 1.

Essen, J., & Peckham, C. (1976). Nocturnal enuresis in childhood. *Developmental Medicine and Child Neurology, 18*(5), 577–589.

Fairburn, C. G., Marcus, M., & Wilson, G. (1993). Cognitive-behavioral therapy for binge eating and bulimia nervosa: A comprehensive treatment manual. In C. G. Fairburn & G. T. Wilson (Eds.), *Binge eating: Nature, assessment and treatment* (pp. 361–404). New York: Guilford Press.

Fallone, G., Acebo, C., Arnedt, T. A., Seifer, R., & Carskadon, M. A. (2001). Effects of acute sleep restriction on behavior, sustained attention, and response inhibition in children. *Perceptual & Motor Skills, 93*(1), 213.

Fan, A. H., & Hassell, J. (2008). Bipolar disorder and comorbid personality psychopathology: A review of the literature. *Journal of Clinical Psychiatry, pii,* ej08r04175.

Faraone, S. V. (2000). Genetics of childhood disorders: XX. ADHD, part 4: Is ADHD genetically heterogeneous? *Journal of the American Academy of Child and Adolescent Psychiatry, 39*(11), 1455–1457.

Faraone, S. V., Biederman, J., Jetton, J. G., & Tsuang, M. T. (1997). Attention deficit disorder and conduct disorder: Longitudinal evidence for a familial subtype. *Psychological Medicine, 27*(2), 291–300.

Faraone, S. V., Biederman, J., Wozniak, J., Mundy, E., Mennin, D., & O'Donnell, D. (1997). Is comorbidity with ADHD a marker for juvenile-onset mania?

Journal of the American Academy of Child and Adolescent Psychiatry, 36(8), 1046–1055.

Faridi, K., & Suchowersky, O. (2003). Gilles de la Tourette's syndrome. *Canadian Journal of Neurological Sciences, 30*(1), S64–S71.

Feeham, M., McGee, R., Stanton, W., & Silva, P. A. (1990). A 6-year follow-up of childhood enuresis: Prevalence in adolescence and consequences for mental health. *Journal of Paediatrics and Child Health, 26,* 75–79.

Feeny, N. C., Danielson, C. K., Schwartz, L., Youngstrom, E. A., & Findling, R. L. (2006). Cognitive-behavioral therapy for bipolar disorders in adolescents: A pilot study. *Bipolar Disorders, 8*(5), 508–515.

Fergusson, D. M., & Boden, J. M. (2008). Cannabis use and later life outcomes. *Addiction, 103,* 969–976.

Fergusson, D. M., & Horwood, L. J. (1994). Nocturnal enuresis and behavioral problems in adolescence: A 15-year longitudinal survey. *Pediatrics, 94,* 662–668.

Fichter, M. M., Leibl, K., Rief, W., Brunner, E., Schmidt-Auberger, S., & Engel, R. R. (1991). Fluoxetine versus placebo: A double-blind study with bulimic inpatients undergoing intensive psychotherapy. *Pharmacopsychiatry, 24*(1), 1–7.

Filipek, P. A., Accardo, P. J., Ashwal, S., Baranek, G. T., Cook, E. H., Dawson, G., et al. (2000). Practice parameter: Screening and diagnosis of autism. *Report of the Quality Standards Subcommittee of the American Academy of Neurology and the Child Neurology Society, 55,* 468–479.

Findling, R. L., Frazier, J. A., Kafantaris, V., Kowatch, R., McClellan, J., Pavuluri, M., et al. (2008). The Collaborative Lithium Trials (CoLT): Specific aims, methods, and implementation. *Child and Adolescent Psychiatry and Mental Health, 2*(1), 21.

Findling, R. L., Greenhill, L. L., McNamara, N. K., Demeter, C. A., Kotler, L. A., O'Riordan, M. A., et al. (2007). Venlafaxine in the treatment of children and adolescents with attention-deficit/hyperactivity disorder. *Journal of Child and Adolescent Psychopharmacology, 17*(4), 433–445.

Findling, R. L., McNamara, N. K., Youngstrom, E. A., Stansbrey, R., Gracious, B. L., Reed, M. D., et al. (2005). Double-blind 18-month trial of lithium versus divalproex maintenance treatment in pediatric bipolar disorder. *Journal of the American Academy of Child and Adolescent Psychiatry, 44*(5), 409–417.

Findling, R. L., Preskorn, S. H., Marcus, R. N., Magnus, R. D., D'Amico, F., Marathe, P., et al. (2000). Nefazodone pharmacokinetics in depressed children and adolescents. *Journal of the American Academy of Child and Adolescent Psychiatry, 39*(8), 1008–1016.

Findling, R. L., Reed, M. D., O'Riordan, M. A., Demeter, C. A., Stansbrey, R. J., & McNamara, N. K. (2007). A 26-week open-label study of quetiapine in children with conduct disorder. *Journal of Child and Adolescent Psychopharmacology, 17,* 1–9.

Findling, R. L., Reed, M. D., O'Riordan, M. A., Demeter, C. A., Stansbrey, R. J., & McNamara, N. K. (2006). Effectiveness, safety, and pharmacokinetics of quetiapine in aggressive children with conduct disorder. *Journal of the American Academy of Child and Adolescent Psychiatry, 45,* 792–800.

Fisher, M. (2003). The course and outcome of eating disorders in adults and in adolescents: A review. *Archives of Pediatrics and Adolescent Medicine, 14*(1), 149–158.

Fisher, S. (1959). *Child research in psychopharmacology.* Springfield, IL: Charles C Thomas.

Flament, M. F., Rapoport, J. L., Berg, C. J., Sceery, W., Kilts, C., Mellström, B., et al. (1985). Clomipramine treatment of childhood obsessive-compulsive disorder. A double-blind controlled study. *Archives of General Psychiatry, 42*(10), 977–983.

Flavell, J. H. (1963). *Developmental psychology of Jean Piaget.* Princeton, NJ: D. Van Nostrand.

Fleischhaker, C., Munz, M., Böhme, R., Sixt, B., & Schulz, E. (2006). Dialectical behaviour therapy for adolescents (DBT-A): A pilot study on the therapy of suicidal, parasuicidal, and self-injurious behaviour in female patients with a borderline disorder. *Zeitschrift fur Kinder- und Jugendpsychiatrie und Psychotherapie, 34*(1), 15–25.

Fleming, J. E., & Offord, D. R. (1990). Epidemiology of childhood depressive disorders: A critical review. *Journal of the American Academy of Child and Adolescent Psychiatry, 29*(4), 571–580.

Fluoxetine Bulimia Nervosa Collaborative Study Group. (1992). Fluoxetine in the treatment of bulimia nervosa. A multicenter, placebo-controlled, double-blind trial. *Archives of General Psychiatry, 49*(2), 139–147.

Food and Drug Administration. (2006, February). *Drug safety and risk management advisory committee meeting, table of contents.* Retrieved January 26, 2009, from http://www.fda.gov/ohrms/dockets/ac/06/briefing/2006–4202_00_TOC.htm

Fountoulakis, K. N., & Vieta, E. (2008). Treatment of bipolar disorder: A systematic review of available data and clinical perspectives. *International Journal of Neuropsychopharmacology, 11*(7), 999–1029.

Foxx, R. M. (2008). Applied behavior analysis treatment of autism: The state of the art. *Child and Adolescent Psychiatric Clinics of North America, 17*(4), 821–834.

Frankhauser, M. P., Karumanchi, V. C., German, M. L., Yates, A., & Karumanchi, S. D. (1991). A double-blind, placebo-controlled study of the efficacy of transdermal clonidine in autism. *Journal of Clinical Psychiatry, 53*, 77–82.

Frazier, J. A., Chiu, S., Breeze, J. L., Makris, N., Lange, N., Kennedy, D. N., et al. (2005). Structural brain magnetic resonance imaging of limbic and thalamic volumes in pediatric bipolar disorder. *American Journal of Psychiatry, 162*(7), 1256–1265.

Fristad, M. A., Goldberg-Arnold, J. S., & Gavazzi, S. M. (2003). Multi-family psychoeducation groups in the treatment of children with mood disorders. *Journal of Marital and Family Therapy, 29*(4), 491–504.

Fruntes, V., & Limosin, F. (2008). Schizophrenia and viral infection during neurodevelopment: A pathogenesis model? *Medical Science Monitor, 14*(6), 71–77.

Gadow, K. D., Sverd, J., Sprafkin, J., Nolan, E. E., & Ezor, S. N. (1995). Efficacy of methylphenidate for attention-deficit hyperactivity disorder in children with tic disorder. *Archives of General Psychiatry, 52*(6), 444–455.

Gagiano, C., Read, S., Thorpe, L., Eerdekens, M., & Van Hove, I. (2005). Short- and long-term efficacy and safety of risperidone in adults with disruptive behavior disorders. *Psychopharmacology, 179,* 629–636.

Galaburda, A. M., Sherman, G. F., Rosen, G. D., Aboitiz, F., & Geschwind, N. (1985). Developmental dyslexia: Four consecutive patients with cortical anomalies. *Annals of Neurology, 18,* 222–233.

Galanter, C. A., Carlson, G. A., Jensen, P. S., Greenhill, L. L., Davies, M., Li, W., et al. (2003). Response to methylphenidate in children with attention deficit hyperactivity disorder and manic symptoms in the multimodal treatment study of children with attention deficit hyperactivity disorder titration trial. *Journal of Child and Adolescent Psychopharmacology, 13*(2), 123–136.

Garber, K. B., Visootsak, J., & Warren, S. T. (2008). Fragile X syndrome. *European Journal of Human Genetics, 16,* 666–672.

Garrison, C. Z., Addy, C. L., Jackson, K. L., McKeown, R. E., & Waller, J. L. (1992). Major depressive disorder and dysthymia in young adolescents. *American Journal of Epidemiology, 135*(7), 792–802.

Garstang, J., & Wallis, M. (2006). Randomized controlled trial of melatonin for children with autistic spectrum disorders and sleep problems. *Child: Care, Health and Development, 32*(5), 585–589.

Gauthier, I., Skudlarski, P., Gore, J. C., & Anderson, A. W. (2000). Expertise for cars and birds recruits brain areas involved in face recognition. *Nature Neuroscience, 3*(2), 191–197.

Geist, R. A. (1985). Therapeutic dilemmas in the treatment of anorexia nervosa: A self psychological perspective. In S. W. Emmett (Ed.), *Theory and treatment of anorexia nervosa and bulimia* (pp. 268–288). New York: Brunner/ Mazel.

Geller, B., Cooper, T. B., Sun, K., Zimerman, B., Frazier, J., Williams, M., et al. (1998). Double-blind and placebo-controlled study of lithium for adolescent bipolar disorders with secondary substance dependency. *Journal of the American Academy of Child and Adolescent Psychiatry, 37*(2), 171–178.

Geller, B., & Luby, J. (1997). Child and adolescent bipolar disorder: A review of the past 10 years. *Journal of the American Academy of Child and Adolescent Psychiatry, 36*(9), 1168–1176.

Geller, B., Tillman, R., & Bolhofner, K. (2007). Proposed definitions of bipolar I disorder episodes and daily rapid cycling phenomena in preschoolers, school-aged children, adolescents, and adults. *Journal of Child and Adolescent Psychopharmacology, 17*(2), 217–222.

Geller, B., Tillman, R., Bolhofner, K., Zimerman, B., Strauss, N. A., & Kaufmann, P. (2006). Controlled, blindly rated, direct-interview family study of a prepubertal and early-adolescent bipolar I disorder phenotype: Morbid risk, age at onset, and comorbidity. *Archives of General Psychiatry, 63*(10), 1130–1138.

Geller, B., Williams, M., Zimerman, B., Frazier, J., Beringer, L., & Warner, K. L. (1998). Prepubertal and early adolescent bipolarity differentiate from ADHD by manic symptoms, grandiose delusions, ultra-rapid or ultradian cycling. *Journal of Affective Disorders, 51*(2), 81–91.

Geller, B., Zimerman, B., Williams, M., Bolhofner, K., Craney, J. L., Delbello, M. P., et al. (2000). Six-month stability and outcome of a prepubertal and early adolescent bipolar disorder phenotype. *Journal of Child and Adolescent Psychopharmacology, 10*(3), 165–173.

Geller, B., Zimerman, B., Williams, M., DelBello, M. P., Bolhofner, K., Craney, J. L., et al. (2002). DSM-IV mania symptoms in a prepubertal and early adolescent bipolar phenotype compared to attention deficit hyperactive and normal controls. *Journal of Child and Adolescent Psychopharmacology, 12*, 11–25.

Geller, B., Zimerman, B., Williams, M., DelBello, M. P., Frazier, J., & Beringer, L. (2002). Phenomenology of prepubertal and early adolescent bipolar disorder: Examples of elated mood, grandiose behaviors, decreased need for sleep, racing thoughts and hypersexuality. *Journal of Child and Adolescent Psychopharmacology, 12*(1), 3–9.

Geller, D. A., Biederman, J., Stewart, S. E., Mullin, B., Farrell, C., Wagner, K. D., et al. (2003). Impact of comorbidity on treatment response to paroxetine in pediatric obsessive-compulsive disorder: Is the use of exclusion criteria empirically supported in randomized clinical trials? *Journal of Child and Adolescent Psychopharmacology, 13*, S19–S29.

Geller, D. A., Hoog, S. L., Heiligenstein, J. H., Ricardi, R. K., Tamura, R., Kluszynski, S., et al. (2001). Fluoxetine treatment for obsessive–compulsive disorder in children and adolescents: A placebo-controlled clinical trial. *Journal of the American Academy of Child and Adolescent Psychiatry, 40*, 773–779.

Geller, D. A., Wagner, K. D., Emslie, G., Murphy, T., Carpenter, D. J., Wetherhold, E., et al. (2004). Paroxetine treatment in children and adolescents with obsessive–compulsive disorder: A randomized, multicenter, double-blind, placebo-controlled trial. *Journal of the American Academy of Child and Adolescent Psychiatry, 43*, 1387–1396.

Gershon, E. S., Hamovit, J., Guroff, J. J., Dibble, E., Leckman, J. F., Sceery, W., et al. (1982). A family study of schizoaffective, bipolar I, bipolar II, unipolar, and normal control probands. *Archives of General Psychiatry, 39*, 1157–1167.

Gfroerer, J. C., Wu, L. T., & Penne, M. A. (2002). *Initiation of marijuana use: Trends, patterns, and implications.* Rockville, MD: Substance Abuse and Mental Health Services Administration, Office of Applied Studies.

Ghaziuddin, N., Kutcher, S. P., Knapp, P., Bernet, W., Arnold, V., Beitchman, J., et al. (2004). Practice parameter for use of electroconvulsive therapy with adolescents. *Journal of the American Academy of Child and Adolescent Psychiatry, 43*(12), 1521–1539.

Gibbons, R. D., Brown, C. H., Hur, K., Marcus, S. M., Bhaumik, D. K., Erkens, J. A., et al. (2007). Early evidence on the effects of regulators' suicidality warnings on SSRI prescriptions and suicide in children and adolescents. *American Journal of Psychiatry, 164*(9), 1356–1363.

Gibson, A. P., Bettinger, T. L., Patel, N. C., & Crismon, M. L. (2006). Atomoxetine versus stimulants for treatment of attention deficit/hyperactivity disorder. *Annals of Pharmacotherapy, 40*(6), 1134–1142.

Giddan, J. J. (1991). School children with emotional problems and communication deficits: Implications for speech-language pathologists. *Language, Speech, and Hearing Services in Schools, 22,* 291–295.

Gilbert, D. L., Dure, L., Sethuraman, G., Raab, D., Lane, J., & Sallee, F. R. (2003). Tic reduction with pergolide in a randomized controlled trial in children. *Neurology, 60*(4), 606–611.

Gilbert, D. L., Sethuraman, G., Sine, L., Peters, S., & Sallee, F. R. (2000). Tourette's syndrome improvement with pergolide in a randomized, double-blind, crossover trial. *Neurology, 54*(6), 1310–1315.

Gill, M., Daly, G., Heron, S., Hawi, Z., & Fitzgerald, M. (1997). Confirmation of association between attention deficit hyperactivity disorder and a dopamine transporter polymorphism. *Molecular Psychiatry, 2*(4), 311–313.

Gillberg, C., & Steffenburg, S. (1987). Outcome and prognostic factors in infantile autism and similar conditions: A population-based study of 46 cases followed through puberty. *Journal of Autism and Developmental Disorders, 17*(2), 273–287.

Gittelman-Klein, R., & Klein, D. F. (1973). School phobia: Diagnostic considerations in the light of imipramine effects. *Journal of Nervous and Mental Diseases, 156*(3), 199–215.

Glazener, C. M., & Evans, J. H. (2002). Simple behavioural and physical interventions for nocturnal enuresis in children. *Cochrane Database of Systematic Reviews, 2,* CD003637.

Glowinski, A. L., Madden, P. A., Bucholz, K. K., Lynskey, M. T., & Heath, A. C. (2003). Genetic epidemiology of self-reported lifetime DSM-IV major depressive disorder in a population-based twin sample of female adolescents. *Journal of Child Psychology and Psychiatry, 44*(7), 988–996.

Goetz, R. R., Goetz, D. M., Hanlon, C., Davies, M., Weitzman, E. D., & Puig-Antich, J. (1983). Spindle characteristics in prepubertal major depressives during an episode and after sustained recovery: A controlled study. *Sleep, 6*(4), 369–375.

Goetz, R. R., Puig-Antich, J., Ryan, N., Rabinovich, H., Ambrosini, P. J., Nelson, B., et al. (1987). Electroencephalographic sleep of adolescents with major depression and normal controls. *Archives of General Psychiatry, 44*(1), 61–68.

Goldberg, J. F., & Ernst, C. L. (2002). Features associated with the delayed initiation of mood stabilizers at illness onset in bipolar disorder. *Journal of Clinical Psychiatry, 63*(11), 985–991.

Goldman, L. S., Genel, M., Bezman, R. J., & Slanetz, P. J. (1998). Diagnosis and treatment of attention-deficit/hyperactivity disorder in children and adolescents. *Journal of the American Medical Association, 279*(14), 1100–1107.

Goldstein, B. I., Strober, M. A., Birmaher, B., Axelson, D. A., Esposito-Smythers, C., Goldstein, T. R., et al. (2008). Substance use disorders among adolescents with bipolar spectrum disorders. *Bipolar Disorder, 10*(4), 469–478.

Goldstein, D. J., Wilson, M. G., Ascroft, R. C., & al-Banna, M. (1999). Effectiveness of fluoxetine therapy in bulimia nervosa regardless of comorbid depression. *International Journal of Eating Disorders, 25*(1), 19–27.

Goldstein, M. J. (1989). Psychosocial treatment of schizophrenia. In S. C. Schultz & C. A. Tamminga (Eds.), *Schizophrenia: Scientific progress* (pp. 318–324). New York: Oxford University Press.

Goldstein, T. R., Axelson, D. A., Birmaher, B., & Brent, D. A. (2007). Dialectical behavior therapy for adolescents with bipolar disorder: A 1-year open trial. *Journal of the American Academy of Child and Adolescent Psychiatry, 46*(7), 820–830.

Goldstein, T. R., Birmaher, B., Axelson, D., Goldstein, B. I., Gill, M. K., Esposito Smythers, C., et al. (2008). Psychosocial functioning among bipolar youth. *Journal of Affective Disorders, 91*(2–3), 181–188.

Goldstein, T. R., Birmaher, B., Axelson, D., Ryan, N. D., Strober, M. A., Gill, M. K., et al. (2005). History of suicide attempts in pediatric bipolar disorder: Factors associated with increased risk. *Bipolar Disorder, 7*(6), 525–535.

Goodwin, F. K., & Jamison, K. R. (1990). *Manic-depressive illness.* New York: Oxford University Press.

Goodwin, R., Gould, M. S., Blanco, C., & Olfson, M. (2001). Prescription of psychotropic medications to youths in office-based practice. *Psychiatric Services, 52*(8), 1081–1087.

Gordon, R. A. (2000). *Eating disorders: Anatomy of a social epidemic.* (2nd ed). Malden, MA: Blackwell.

Gorwood, P., Leboyer, M., Jay, M., Payan, C., & Feingold, J. (1995). Gender and age at onset in schizophrenia: Impact of family history. *American Journal of Psychiatry, 152*(2), 208–212.

Gozal, D. (1998). Sleep-disordered breathing and school performance in children. *Pediatrics, 102,* 616–620.

Gozal, D., O'Brien, L., & Row, B. W. (2004). Consequences of snoring and sleep disordered breathing in children. *Pediatric Pulmonology Supplement, 26,* 166.

Gracious, B. L., Youngstrom, E. A., Findling, R. L., & Calabrese, J. R. (2002). Discriminative validity of a parent version of the Young Mania Rating Scale. *Journal of the American Academy of Child and Adolescent Psychiatry, 41*(11), 1350–1359.

Greenberg, B. S., Siemicji, M., & Dorfman, S. (1993). Sex content in R-rated films viewed by adolescents. In B. S. Greenberg, J. D. Brown, & N. Buerkel-Rothfuss, (Eds.), *Media, Sex and the Adolescent.* Cresskill, NJ: Hampton Press.

Greenberg, B. S., Siemicki, M., Dorfman, S., Heeter, C., Stanley, C., Soderman, A., et al. (2004). Effectiveness of collaborative problem solving in affectively dysregulated children with oppositional-defiant disorder: Initial findings. *Journal of Consulting and Clinical Psychology, 72*(6), 1157–1164.

Greenhill, L. L., Solomon, M., Pleak, R., & Ambrosini, P. (1985). Molindone hydrochloride treatment of hospitalized children with conduct disorder. *Journal of Clinical Psychiatry, 46*(8), 20–25.

Greenhill, L. L., Swanson, J. M., Vitiello, B., Davies, M., Clevenger, W., Wu, M., et al. (2001). Impairment and deportment responses to different methylphenidate doses in children with ADHD: The MTA titration trial. *Journal of the American Academy of Child and Adolescent Psychiatry, 40,* 180–187.

Grigorenko, E. L. (2006). Learning disabilities in juvenile offenders. *Child and Adolescent Psychiatric Clinics of North America, 15,* 353–371.

Griswold, K. S., Aronoff, H., Kernan, J. B., & Kahn, L. S. (2008). Adolescent substance use and abuse: Recognition and management. *American Family Physician, 77*(3), 331–336.

Guilleminault, C., Moscovitch, A., & Leger, D. (1995). Forensic sleep medicine: Nocturnal wandering and violence. *Sleep, 18*(9), 740–748.

Guttmacher, L. B., & Cretella, H. (1988). Electroconvulsive therapy in one child and three adolescents. *Journal of Clinical Psychiatry, 49*(1), 20–23.

Haapasalo-Pesu, K. M., Vuola, T., Lahelma, L., & Marttunen, M. (2004). Mirtazapine in the treatment of adolescents with major depression: An open-label, multicenter pilot study. *Journal of Child and Adolescent Psychopharmacology, 14*(2), 175–184.

Halbower, A. C., & Marcus, C. L. (2003). Sleep disorders in children. *Current Opinion in Pulmonary Medicine, 9*(6), 471–476.

Hammad, T. A., Laughren, T., & Racoosin, J. (2006). Suicidality in pediatric patients treated with antidepressant drugs. *Archives of General Psychiatry, 63*(3), 332–339.

Handen, B. L., & Gilchrist, R. (2006). Practitioner review: Psychopharmacology in children and adolescents with mental retardation. *Journal of Child Psychology and Psychiatry, 47*(9), 871–882.

Handen, B. L., & Hardan, A. Y. (2006). Open-label, prospective trial of olanzapine in adolescents with subaverage intelligence and disruptive behavioral disorders. *Journal of the American Academy of Child and Adolescent Psychiatry, 45,* 928–935.

Hannesdottir, D. K., & Ollendick, T. H. (2007). The role of emotion regulation in the treatment of child anxiety disorders. *Clinical Child and Family Psychology Review, 10*(3), 275–293.

Hardan, A., Birmahera, B., Williamsona, D. E., Dahla, R. E., Ambrosinib, P., Rabinovich, H., et al. (1999). Secretion in depressed children. *Biological Psychiatry, 46*(4), 506–511.

Harley, R., Sprich, S., Safren, S., Jacobo, M., & Fava, M. (2008). Adaptation of dialectical behavior therapy skills training group for treatment-resistant depression. *Journal of Nervous and Mental Disease, 196*(2), 136–143.

Harrington, R., Rutter, M., Weissman, M., Fudge, H., Groothues, C., Bredenkamp, D., et al. (1997). Psychiatric disorders in the relatives of depressed probands. Comparison of prepubertal, adolescent and early adult onset cases. *Journal of Affect Disorders, 42*(1), 9–22.

Harrington, R., Whittaker, J., & Shoebridge, P. (1998). Psychological treatment of depression in children and adolescents. A review of treatment research. *British Journal of Psychiatry, 173,* 291–298.

Hauser, P., Zametkin, A. J., Martinez, P., Vitiello, B., Matochik, J. A., Mixson, A. J., et al. (1993). Attention deficit-hyperactivity disorder in people with generalized resistance to thyroid hormone. *New England Journal of Medicine, 328*(14), 997–1001.

Hawkins, C., & Williams, T. I. (1992). Nightmares, life events and behaviour problems in preschool children. *Child: Care, Health and Development, 18*(2), 117–128.

Hazan, A. R., Lipton, H. L., & Glantz, S. A. (1994). Popular films do not reflect current tobacco use. *American Journal of Public Health, 84*, 998–1000.

Hazell, P. L., & Stuart, J. E. (2003). A randomized controlled trial of clonidine added to psychostimulant medication for hyperactive and aggressive children. *Journal of the American Academy of Child and Adolescent Psychiatry, 42*(8), 886–894.

Hazell, P., O'Connell, D., Heathcote, D., Robertson, J., & Henry, D. (1995). Efficacy of tricyclic drugs in treating child and adolescent depression: A meta-analysis. *British Medical Journal, 310*(6984), 897–901.

Hecker, E. (1871). Die hebephrenie. *Archiv Pathologie Anatomie Physiologie Klinik Medizi, 52*, 394.

Hedley, A. A., Ogden, C. L., Johnson, C. L., Carroll, M. D., Curtin, L. R., & Flegal, K. M. (2004). Prevalence of overweight and obesity among US children, adolescents, and adults, 1999–2002. *Journal of the American Medical Association, 291*, 2847–2850.

Heiervang, E., Hugdahl, K., Steinmetz, H., Smievoll, A. I., Stevenson, J., Lund, A., et al. (2000). Planum temporale, planum parietale and dichotic listening in dyslexia. *Neuropsychologia, 38*(13), 1704–1713.

Heinicke, C. M., & Ramsey-Klee, D. M. (1986). Outcome of child psychotherapy as a function of frequency of session. *Journal of the American Academy of Child and Adolescent Psychiatry, 25*(2), 247–253.

Hellings, J. A., Kelley, L. A., Gabrielli, W. F., Kilgore, E., & Shah, P. (1996). Sertraline response in adults with mental retardation and autistic disorder. *Journal of Clinical Psychiatry, 57*, 333–336.

Hellström, A. L., Hanson, E., Hansson, S., Hjalmas, K., & Jodal, U. (1990). Micturition habits and incontinence in 7-year-old Swedish school entrants. *European Journal of Pediatrics, 149*, 434–437.

Hemminki, K., & Mutanen, P. (2001). Genetic epidemiology of multistage carcinogenesis. *Mutation Research, 473*(1), 11–21.

Henggeler, S. W., & Lee, T. (2003). Multisystemic treatment of serious clinical problems. In A. E. Kazdin & J. R. Weisz (Eds.), *Evidence-based psychotherapies for children and adolescents* (pp. 301–322). New York: Guilford Press.

Hepworth, J. (1999). *The social construction of anorexia nervosa.* Thousand Oaks, CA: Sage.

Herpertz-Dahlmann, B. (2009). Adolescent eating disorders: Definitions, symptomatology, epidemiology and comorbidity. *Child and Adolescent Psychiatry Clinics of North America, 18*(1), 31–47.

Herpertz-Dahlmann, B., & Salbach-Andrae, H. (2009). Overview of treatment modalities in adolescent anorexia nervosa. *Child and Adolescent Psychiatry Clinics of North America, 18*(1), 131–145.

Herschell, A., Calzada, E., Eyberg, S. M., & McNeil, C. B. (2002). Parent-child interaction therapy: New directions in research. *Cognitive and Behavioral Practice, 9*, 9–16.

Hettema, J. M., Neale, M. C., & Kendler, K. S. (2001). A review and meta-analysis of the genetic epidemiology of anxiety disorders. *American Journal of Psychiatry, 158*, 1568–1578.

Heywood, L. (1996). *Dedicated to hunger: The anorexic aesthetic in modern culture*. Berkeley: University of California Press.

Hirshfeld, D. R., Rosenbaum, J. F., Biederman, J., Bolduc, E. A., Faraone, S. V., Snidman, N., et al. (1992). Stable behavioral inhibition and its association with anxiety disorder. *Journal of the American Academy of Child and Adolescent Psychiatry, 31*(1), 103–111.

Ho, B., & Andreasen, N. C. (2001). Long delays in seeking treatment for schizophrenia. *Lancet, 357*(9260), 898–900.

Hollander, E., Anagnostou, W., Chaplin, K., Esposito, M., Haznedar, E., Licalzi, S., et al. (2005). Striatal volume on magnetic resonance imaging and repetitive behaviors in autism. *Biological Psychiatry, 58*(3), 226–232.

Hollander, E., Phillips, A., Chaplin, W., Zagursky, K., Novotny, S., Wasserman, S., et al. (2005). A placebo-controlled crossover trail of liquid fluoxetine on repetitive behaviors in childhood and adolescent autism. *Neuropsychopharmacology, 30*, 582–589.

Holma, K. M., Melartin, T. K., Holma, I. A., & Isometsä, E. T. (2008). Predictors for switch from unipolar major depressive disorder to bipolar disorder type I or II: A 5-year prospective study. *Journal of Clinical Psychiatry, 69*(8), 1267–1275.

Honda, H., Shimizu, Y., & Rutter, M. (2005). No effect of MMR withdrawal on the incidence of autism: A total population study. *Journal of Child Psychology and Psychiatry, 46*(6), 572–579.

Howlin, P., Goode, S., Hutton, J., & Rutter, M. (2004). Adult outcome for children with autism. *Journal of Child Psychology and Psychiatry, 45*, 212–229.

Howlin, P., Gordon, R. K., Pasco, G., Wade, A., & Charman, T. (2007). Picture exchange communication system (PECS). *Journal of Child Psychology and Psychiatry, 48*(5), 473–481.

Hoyert, D. L., Mathews, T. J., Menacker, F., Strobino, D. M., & Guyer, B. (2006). Annual summary of vital statistics: 2004. *Pediatrics, 117*(1), 168–183.

Hunter, L. C., O'Hare, A., Herron, W. J., Fisher, L. A., & Jones, G. E. (2003). Opioid peptides and dipeptidyl peptidase in autism. *Developmental Medicine and Child Neurology, 45*, 121–128.

Ialongo, N., Edelsohn, G., Werthamer-Larsson, L., Crockett, L., & Kellam, S. (1995). The significance of self-reported anxious symptoms in first grade children: Prediction to anxious symptoms and adaptive functioning in fifth grade. *Journal of Child Psychology and Psychiatry, 36*(3), 427–437.

Indig, D., Copeland, J., & Conigrave, K. M. (2008). Young people who attend specialist alcohol treatment: Who are they and do they need special treatment? *Australian and New Zealand Journal of Public Health, 32*(4), 336–340.

Institute of Medicine of the National Academies. (2004). *Immunization safety review: Vaccines and autism.*

Itard, J. (1825). Mémoire sur quelques fonctions involontaires des appareils de la locomotion, de la préhension et de la voix. *Archives Générales de Médecine, 8,* 405.

Ivanenko, A., Barnes, M. E., Crabtree, V. M., & Gozal, D. (2005). Psychiatric symptoms in children with insomnia referred to a pediatric sleep medicine center. *Sleep Medicine, 5*(3), 253.

Ivanenko, A., Crabtree, V. M., & Gozal, D. (2004). Sleep in children with psychiatric disorders. *Pediatric Clinics of North America, 51*(1), 51.

Ivanenko, A., Crabtree, V. M., & Gozal, D. (2005). Sleep and depression in children and adolescents. *Sleep Medicine Reviews, 9*(2), 115–129.

Jacobsen, L. K., Hamburger, S. D., Van Horn, J. D., Vaituzis, A. C., McKenna, K., Frazier, J. A., et al. (1997). Cerebral glucose metabolism in childhood onset schizophrenia. *Psychiatry Research, 75*(3), 131–144.

James, A., Soler, A., & Weatherall, R. (2005). Cognitive behavioural therapy for anxiety disorders in children and adolescents. *Cochrane Database Systematic Reviews, 19*(4), CD004690.

Janowsky, D. S., Kraus, J. E., Barnhill, J., Elamir, B., & Davis, J. M. (2003). Effects of topiramate on aggressive, self-injurious, and disruptive/destructive behaviors in the intellectually disabled: An open-label retrospective study. *Journal of Clinical Psychopharmacology, 23,* 500–504.

Janowsky, D. S., Shetty, M., Barnhill, J., Elamir, B., & Davis, J. M. (2005). Serotonergic antidepressant effects on aggressive, self-injurious and destructive/disruptive behaviors in intellectually disabled adults: A retrospective open naturalistic trial. *International Journal of Neuropsychopharmacology, 8,* 37–48.

Johnson, K. P., & Malow, B. A. (2008). Sleep in children with autism spectrum disorders. *Current Treatment Options in Neurology, 10*(5), 350–359.

Johnston, L. D., O'Malley, P. M., Bachman, J. G., & Schulenberg, J. E. (2005). *Monitoring the future national survey results on drug use.* Retrieved www .monitoringthefuture.org

Jolin, E. M., Weller, E. B., & Weller, R. A. (2008). Anxiety symptoms and syndromes in bipolar children and adolescents. *Current Psychiatry Reports, 10*(2), 123–129.

Jones, E. A. (2008). Establishing response and stimulus classes for initiating joint attention in children with autism. *Research in Autism Spectrum Disorders.* Received August 11, 2008; accepted August 15, 2008. Available online October 11, 2008, Elsevier Ltd.

Jones, K. L. (1997). *Smith's recognizable patterns of human malformation* (5th ed.). Philadelphia: W. B. Saunders.

Kadesjö, B., & Gillberg, C. (2000). Tourette's disorder: Epidemiology and comorbidity in primary school children. *Journal of the American Academy of Child and Adolescent Psychiatry, 39*(5), 548–555.

Kafantaris, V., Coletti, D. J., Dicker, R., Padula, G., Pleak, R. R., & Alvir, J. M. (2004). Lithium treatment of acute mania in adolescents: A placebo-controlled discontinuation study. *Journal of the American Academy of Child and Adolescent Psychiatry, 43*(8), 984–993.

Kagan, J., Reznick, J. S., & Snidman, N. (1988). Biological bases of childhood shyness. *Science, 240*(4849), 167–171.

Kagan, J., & Snidman, N. (1999). Early childhood predictors of adult anxiety disorders. *Biological Psychiatry, 46*(11), 1536–1541.

Kalanithi, P. S., Zheng, W., Kataoka, Y., DiFiglia, M., Grantz, H., Saper, C. B., et al. (2005). Altered parvalbumin-positive neuron distribution in basal ganglia of individuals with Tourette syndrome. *Proceedings of the National Academy of Sciences (US), 102*(37), 13307–13312.

Kalo, B. B., & Bella, H. (1986). Enuresis: Prevalence and associated factors among primary school children in Saudi Arabia. *Acta Paediatrica, 85,* 1217–1222.

Kane, J. M. (2006). Tardive dyskinesia circa 2006. *American Journal of Psychiatry, 163,* 1316–1318.

Kanner, L. (1965). Infantile autism and the schizophrenias. *Behavioral Science, 10*(4), 412–420.

Kaplan, H. I., & Sadock, B. J. (2007). *Kaplan and Sadock's synopsis of psychiatry: Behavioral sciences, clinical psychiatry* (10th ed.) New York: Lippincott Williams & Wilkins.

Kaplan, H. I., Sadock, B. J., & Greb, J. A. (1994a). *Kaplan and Sadock's synopsis of psychiatry.* (7th ed., pp. 689–698). New York: Williams & Wilkins.

Kaplan, H. I., Sadock, B. J., & Greb, J. A. (1994b). *Kaplan and Sadock's synopsis of psychiatry* (7th ed., p. 700). Baltimore: Williams & Wilkins.

Kashani, J. H., Barbero, G. J., & Bolander, F. D. (1981). Depression in hospitalized pediatric patients. *Journal of the American Academy of Child Psychiatry, 20*(1), 123–134.

Kashani, J. H., & Carlson, G. A. (1987). Seriously depressed preschoolers. *American Journal of Psychiatry, 144*(3), 348–350.

Kashani, J. H., Carlson, G. A., Beck, N. C., Hoeper, E. W., Corcoran, C. M., McAllister, J. A., et al. (1987). Depression, depressive symptoms, and depressed mood among a community sample of adolescents. *American Journal of Psychiatry, 144*(7), 931–934.

Kashani, J. H., Sherman, D. D., Parker, J. R., & Reid, J. C. (1990). Utility of the Beck Depression Inventory with clinic-referred adolescents. *Journal of the American Academy of Child and Adolescent Psychiatry, 29*(2), 278–282.

Kauffman, J. M. (1997). *Characteristics of emotional and behavioral disorders of children and youth* (6th ed.). Englewood Cliffs, NJ: Prentice Hall.

Kavale, K. A., & Forness, S. R. (1995). *The nature of learning disabilities: Critical elements of diagnosis and classification.* Mahwah, NJ: Lawrence Erlbaum.

Kaye, W. H., Klump, L., Frank, G. K. W., & Strober, M. (2000). Anorexia and bulimia nervosa. *Annual Review of Medicine, 51,* 299–313.

Kaye, W. H., Nagata, T., Weltzin, T. E., Hsu, L. K., Sokol, M. S., McConaha, C., et al. (2001). Double-blind placebo-controlled administration of fluoxetine in restricting- and restricting-purging-type anorexia nervosa. *Biological Psychiatry, 49*(7), 644–652.

Kazdin, A. E. (1997). Parent management training: Evidence, outcomes, and issues. *Journal of the American Academy of Child and Adolescent Psychiatry, 36*(10), 1349–1356.

Kazdin, A. E. (2003). Problem-solving skills training and parent management training for conduct disorder. In A. E. Kazdin & J. R. Weisz (Eds.), *Evidence-based psychotherapies for children and adolescents* (pp. 241–262). New York: Guilford Press.

Kazdin, A. E. (2005). *Parent management training.* New York: Oxford University Press.

Keller, M. B., Ryan, N. D., Strober, M., Klein, R. G., Kutcher, S. P., Birmaher, B., et al. (2001). Efficacy of paroxetine in the treatment of adolescent major depression: A randomized, controlled trial. *Journal of the American Academy of Child and Adolescent Psychiatry, 40*(7), 762–772.

Kemner, C., Willemsen-Swinkels, S. N., deJonge, M., Tuynman-Qua, H., & van Engeland, H. (2002). Open-label study of olanzapine in children with pervasive developmental disorder. *Journal of Clinical Psychopharmacology, 22,* 455–460.

Kendall, P. C., Safford, S., Flannery-Schroeder, E., & Webb, A. (2004). Child anxiety treatment: Outcomes in adolescence and impact on substance use and depression at 7.4-year follow-up. *Journal of Consulting and Clinical Psychology, 72*(2), 276–287.

Kendler, K. S. (2001). Twin studies of psychiatric illness: An update. *Archives of General Psychiatry, 58,* 1005–1014.

Kenny, M. C., & Faust, J. (1997). Mother-child agreement on self-report of anxiety in abused children. *Journal of Anxiety Disorders, 11*(5), 463–472.

Kerr, S., & Jowett, S. (1994). Sleep problems in pre-school children: A review of the literature. *Child: Care, Health and Development, 20*(6), 379–391.

Kessler, R. C., Berglund, P., Demler, O., Jin, R., Merikangas, K. R., & Walters, E. E. (2005a). Lifetime prevalence and age-of-onset distributions of DSM-IV disorders in the National Comorbidity Survey Replication. *Archives of General Psychiatry, 62*(6), 593–602.

Kessler, R. C., Chiu, W. T., Demler, O., Merikangas, K. R., & Walters, E. E. (2005b). Prevalence, severity, and comorbidity of 12-month DSM-IV disorders in the National Comorbidity Survey Replication. *Archives of General Psychiatry, 62*(6), 617–627.

Kessler, R. C., Nelson, C., McGonagle, K., Edlund, M., Frank, R., & Leaf, P. (1996). The epidemiology of co-occurring addictive and mental disorders: Implications for prevention and service utilization. *American Journal of Orthopsychiatry, 66,* 17–31.

Kessler, R. C., & Walters, E. E. (1998). Epidemiology of DSM-III-R major depression and minor depression among adolescents and young adults in the National Comorbidity Survey. *Depression and Anxiety, 7*(1), 3–14.

Kessler, R. J. (2004). Electroconvulsive therapy for affective disorders in persons with mental retardation. *Psychiatric Quarterly, 75*(1), 99–104.

Keverne, E. B. (2004). Understanding well-being in the evolutionary context of brain development. *Philosophical Transactions of the Royal Society of London, 359*(1449), 1349–1358.

Kieseppä, T., Partonen, T., Haukka, J., Kaprio, J., & Lönnqvist, J. (2004). High concordance of bipolar I disorder in a nationwide sample of twins. *American Journal of Psychiatry, 161*(10), 1814–1821.

Kim, W. J. (2003). Child and adolescent psychiatry workforce: A critical shortage and national challenge; the American Academy of Child and Adolescent Psychiatry Task Force on Workforce Needs. *Academic Psychiatry, 27*(4), 277–282.

King, B. H., State, M. W., Shah, B., Davanzo, P., & Dykens, E. (1997). Mental retardation: A review of the past 10 years. Part I. *Journal of the American Academy of Child and Adolescent Psychiatry, 36*(12), 1656–1663.

King, R. A., Scahill, L., Findley, D., & Cohen, D. J. (1999). Psychosocial and behavioral treatments. In J. F. Leckman & D. J. Cohen (Eds.), *Tourette syndrome—tics, obsessions, compulsions: Developmental psychopathology and clinical care* (pp. 338–359). New York: Wiley.

Klackenberg, G. (1981). Nocturnal enuresis in a longitudinal perspective. *Acta Paediatrica, 70*, 453–457.

Klein, N. J. (2001). Management of primary nocturnal enuresis. *Urologic Nursing, 21*(2), 71–76.

Klein, R. G., Koplewicz, H. S., & Kanner, A. (1992). Imipramine treatment of children with separation anxiety disorder. *Journal of the American Academy of Child and Adolescent Psychiatry, 31*(1), 21–28.

Klin, A., Jones, W., Schultz, R., Volkmar, F., & Cohen, D. (2002). Defining and quantifying the social phenotype in autism. *American Journal of Psychiatry, 159*(6), 895–908.

Klin, A., Volkmar, F. R., & Sparrow, S. S. (2000). *Asperger sydrome.* New York: Guilford Press.

Knable, M. B., Kleinman, J. E., & Weinberger, D. R. (1998). Neurobiology of schizophrenia. In A. F. Schatzberg & C. B. Nemeroff (Eds.), *Textbook of psychopharmacology* (2nd ed., pp. 589–607). Washington, DC: American Psychiatric Press.

Knutson, J. F, & Sullivan, P. M. (1993). Communication disorders as a risk factor in abuse. *Topics in Language Disorders, 13*(4), 1–14.

Kopelowicz, A., Liberman, R. P., & Wallace, C. J. (2003). Psychiatric rehabilitation for schizophrenia. *International Journal of Psychology and Psychological Therapy, 3*(2), 283–298.

Kotagal, S. (2008). Narcolepsy and idiopathic hypersomnia in childhood. In A. Ivanenko (Ed.), *Sleep and psychiatric disorders in children and adolescents* (pp. 163–171). London: Informa Health Care.

Kotler, L. A., Devlin, M. J., Davies, M., & Walsh, B. T. (2003). An open trial of fluoxetine for adolescents with bulimia nervosa. *Journal of Child and Adolescent Psychopharmacology, 13*(3), 329–335.

Kovacs, M. (1985). The Children's Depression Inventory (CDI). *Psychopharmacology Bulletin, 21*(4), 995–998.

Kovacs, M., Devlin, B., Pollock, M., Richards, C., & Mukerji, P. (1997). A controlled family history study of childhood-onset depressive disorder. *Archives of General Psychiatry, 54*(7), 613–623.

Kovacs, M., & Pollock, M. (1995). Bipolar disorder and comorbid conduct disorder in childhood and adolescence. *Journal of the American Academy of Child and Adolescent Psychiatry, 34*(6), 715–723.

Kowatch, R. A., Findling, R. L., Scheffer, R. E., & Stanford, K. E. (2007, October). *Placebo-controlled trial of divalproex versus lithium for bipolar disorder.* Poster presented at the annual meeting of the American Academy of Child and Adolescent Psychiatry, Boston, Massachusetts.

Kowatch, R. A., Fristad, M., Birmaher, B., Wagner, K. D., Findling, R. L., & Hellander, M. (2005). Treatment guidelines for children and adolescents with bipolar disorder. *Journal of the American Academy of Child and Adolescent Psychiatry, 44,* 213–235.

Kowatch, R. A., Suppes, T., Carmody, T. J., Bucci, J. P., Hume, J. H., Kromelis, M., et al. (2000). Effect size of lithium, divalproex sodium, and carbamazepine in children and adolescents with bipolar disorder. *Journal of the American Academy of Child and Adolescent Psychiatry, 39*(6), 713–720.

Krous, H. F., Beckwith, J. B., Byard, R. W., Rognum, T. O., Bajanowski, T., Corey, T., et al. (2004). Sudden infant death syndrome and unclassified sudden infant deaths: A definitional and diagnostic approach. *Pediatrics, 114*(1), 234–238.

Kulig, J. W. (2005). Tobacco, alcohol, and other drugs: The role of the pediatrician in prevention, identification, and management of substance abuse. *Pediatrics, 115*(3), 816–821.

Kulman, G., Lissoni, P., Rovelli, F., Roselli, M. G., Brivio, F., & Sequeri, P. (2000). Evidence of pineal endocrine hypofunction in autistic children. *Neuroendocrinology Letters, 21*(1), 31–34.

Kurlan, R. (2003). Tourette's syndrome: Are stimulants safe? *Current Neurology and Neuroscience Reports, 3*(4), 285–288.

Kushner, H. I. (1995). Medical fictions: The case of the cursing marquise and the (re)construction of Gilles de la Tourette's syndrome. *Bulletin of the History of Medicine, 69*(2), 224.

Kutcher, S., & Robertson, H. A. (1995). Electroconvulsive therapy in treatment-resistant bipolar youth. *Journal of Child and Adolescent Psychopharmacology, 5,* 167–175.

Lahey, B. B., Loeber, R., Hart, E. L., Applegate, B., Zhang, Q., Green, S. M., et al. (1995). Four-year longitudinal study of conduct disorder in boys: Patterns and predictors of persistence. *Journal of Abnormal Psychology, 104,* 83–93.

La Malfa, G., Bertelli, M., & Conte, M. (2001). Fluvoxamine and aggression in mental retardation. *Psychiatric Services, 52,* 1105.

Landon, T. M., & Barlow, D. H. (2004). Cognitive-behavioral treatment for panic disorder: Current status. *Journal of Psychiatric Practice, 10*(4), 211–226.

Langberg, J. M., Epstein, J. N., & Graham, A. J. (2008). Organizational-skills interventions in the treatment of ADHD. *Expert Reviews of Neurotherapeutics, 8*(10), 1549–1561.

Larson, J. C., Mostofsky, S. H., Goldberg, M. C., Cutting, L. E., Denckla, M. B., & Mahone, E. M. (2007). Effects of gender and age on motor exam in typically developing children. *Developmental Neuropsychology, 32*(1), 543–562.

Last, C. G., Hersen, M., Kazdin, A. E., Finkelstein, R., & Strauss, C. C. (1993). Comparison of DSM-III separation anxiety and overanxious disorders:

Demographic characteristics and patterns of comorbidity. *Harvard Review of Psychiatry, 1*(1), 2–16.

Last, C. G., Perrin, S., Hersen, M., & Kazdin, A. E. (1996). A prospective study of childhood anxiety disorders. *Journal of the American Academy of Child and Adolescent Psychiatry, 35*(11), 1502–1510.

Laugeson, E. A., Frankel, F., Mogil, C., & Dillon, A. R. (2008). Parent-assisted social skills training to improve friendships in teens with autism spectrum disorders. *Journal of Autism and Developmental Disorders, 18.*

Leach, C. E., Blair, P. S., Fleming, P. J., Smith, I. J., Platt, M. W., Berry, P. J., et al. (1999). Epidemiology of SIDS and explained sudden infant deaths. CESDI SUDI Research Group. *Pediatrics, 104*(4), e43.

LeBlanc, J. C., Binder, C. E., Armenteros, J. L., Aman, M. G., Wang, J. S., Hew, H., et al. (2005). Risperidone reduces aggression in boys with a disruptive behaviour disorder and below average intelligence quotient: Analysis of two placebo-controlled randomized trials. *International Clinical Psychopharmacology, 20,* 275–283.

Leckman, J. F. (2003). Phenomenology of tics and natural history of tic disorders. *Brain and Development, 25*(1), S24–S28.

Leckman, J. F., & Cohen, D. J. (1996). Tic disorders. In M. Lewis (Ed.), *Child and adolescent psychiatry, a comprehensive textbook* (2nd ed.). Baltimore: Williams & Wilkins.

Leckman, J. F., Goodman, W. K., North, W. G., Chappell, P. B., Price, L. H., Pauls, D. L., et al. (1994). Elevated cerebrospinal fluid levels of oxytocin in obsessive-compulsive disorder. Comparison with Tourette's syndrome and healthy controls. *Archives of General Psychiatry, 51*(10), 782–792.

Leckman, J. F., Walker, D. E., & Cohen, D. J. (1993). Premonitory urges in Tourette's syndrome. *American Journal of Psychiatry, 150*(1), 98–102.

Leckman, J. F., Zhang, H., Vitale, A., Lahnin, F., Lynch, K., Bondi, C., et al. (1998). Course of tic severity in Tourette syndrome: The first two decades. *Pediatrics, 102*(1), 14–19.

Lecomte, T., Leclerc, C., Corbière, M., Wykes, T., Wallace, C. J., & Spidel, A. (2008). Group cognitive behavior therapy or social skills training for individuals with a recent onset of psychosis? Results of a randomized controlled trial. *Journal of Nervous and Mental Disease, 196*(12), 866–875.

le Grange, D., & Eisler, I. (2009). Family interventions in adolescent anorexia nervosa. *Child and Adolescent Psychiatry Clinics of North America, 18*(1), 159–173.

Leibson, C. L., Katusic, S. K., Barbaresi, W. J., Ransom, J., & O'Brien, P. C. (2001). Use and costs of medical care for children and adolescents with and without attention deficit/hyperactivity disorder. *Journal of the American Medical Association, 285*(1), 60–66.

Leonard, H. L., Swedo, S. E., Rapoport, J. L., Koby, E. V., Lenane, M. C., Cheslow, D. L., et al. (1989). Treatment of obsessive–compulsive disorder with clomipramine and desipramine in children and adolescents. A double-blind crossover comparison. *Archives of General Psychiatry, 46,* 1088–1092.

Leonard, H. L., Topol, D., Bukstein, O., Hindmarsh, D., Allen, A. J., & Swedo, S. (1994). Case study: Clonazepam as an augmenting agent in the treatment of childhood-onset obsessive-compulsive disorder. *Journal of the American Academy of Child and Adolescent Psychiatry, 33,* 792–794.

Levin, H. S., & Hanten, G. (2005). Executive functions after traumatic brain injury in children. *Pediatric Neurology, 33*(2), 79–93.

Lewinsohn, P. M., Clarke, G. N., Seeley, J. R., & Rohde, P. (1994). Major depression in community adolescents: Age at onset, episode duration, and time to recurrence. *Journal of the American Academy of Child and Adolescent Psychiatry, 33*(6), 809–818.

Lewinsohn, P. M., Hops, H., Roberts, R. E., Seeley, J. R., & Andrews, J. A. (1993). Adolescent psychopathology: Prevalence and incidence of depression and other DSM-III-R disorders in high school students. *Journal of Abnormal Psychology, 102*(1), 133–144.

Lewinsohn, P. M., Klein, D. N., & Seeley, J. R. (1995). Bipolar disorders in a community sample of older adolescents: Prevalence, phenomenology, comorbidity, and course. *Journal of the American Academy of Child and Adolescent Psychiatry, 34*(4), 454–463.

Lewis, M. H., Bodfish, J. W., Powell, S. B., & Golden, R. N. (1995). Clomipramine treatment for stereotype and related repetitive movement disorders associated with mental retardation. *American Journal of Mental Retardation, 100,* 299–312.

Lewis, M. H., Bodfish, J. W., Powell, S. B., Parker, D. E., & Golden, R. N. (1996). Clomipramine treatment for self-injurious behavior of individuals with mental retardation: A double-blind comparison with placebo. *American Journal of Mental Retardation, 100*(6), 654–665.

Licinio, J., & Wong, M. L. (2005). Depression, antidepressants and suicidality: A critical appraisal. *Nature Reviews Drug Discovery, 4*(2), 165–171.

Liddle, H. A., Rowe, C. L., Dakof, G. A., Henderson, C. E., & Greenbaum, P. E. (2009). Multidimensional family therapy for young adolescent substance abuse: Twelve-month outcomes of a randomized controlled trial. *Journal of Consulting and Clinical Psychology, 77*(1), 12–25.

Lieberman, J. A., Stroup, T. S., McEvoy, J. P., Swartz, M. S., Rosenheck, R. A., Perkins, D. O., et al. (2005). Effectiveness of antipsychotic drugs in patients with chronic schizophrenia. *New England Journal of Medicine, 353*(12), 1209–1223.

Liebowitz, M. R., Turner, S. M., Piacentini, J., Beidel, D. C., Clarvit, S. R., Davies, S. O., et al. (2002). Fluoxetine in children and adolescents with OCD: A placebo-controlled trial. *Journal of the American Academy of Child and Adolescent Psychiatry, 41,* 1431–1438.

Lindenmayer, L. P., & Kotsaftis, A. (2000). Use of sodium valproate in violent and aggressive behaviors: A critical review. *Journal of Clinical Psychiatry, 61,* 123–128.

Linehan, M. M. (1993). *Cognitive-behavioral treatment of borderline personality disorder.* New York: Guilford Press.

Ling, W., Oftedal, G., & Weinberg, W. (1970). Depressive illness in childhood presenting as severe headache. *American Journal of Diseases of Children, 120*(2), 122–124.

Lish, J. D., Dime-Meenan, S., Whybrow, P. C., Price, R. A., & Hirschfeld, R. M. (1994). The National Depressive and Manic-depressive Association (DMDA) survey of bipolar members. *Journal of Affective Disorders, 31*(4), 281–294.

Liu, X., Buysse, D. J., Gentzler, A. L., Kiss, E., Mayer, L., Kapornai, K., et al. (2007). Insomnia and hypersomnia associated with depressive phenomenology and comorbidity in childhood depression. *Sleep, 30*(1), 83–90.

Loeber, R., Burke, J. D., Lahey, B. B., Winters, A., & Zera, M. (2000). Oppositional defiant and conduct disorder: A review of the past 10 years, part I. *Journal of the American Academy of Child and Adolescent Psychiatry, 39*(12), 1468–1484.

Luby, J., Mrakotsky, C., Stalets, M. M., Belden, A., Heffelfinger, A., Williams, M., et al. (2006). Risperidone in preschool children with autistic spectrum disorders: An investigation of safety and efficacy. *Journal of Child and Adolescent Psychopharmacology, 16*(5), 575–587.

Luiselli, J. K., Blew, P., & Thibadeau, S. (2001). Therapeutic effects and long-term efficacy of antidepressant medication for persons with developmental disabilities. Behavioral assessment in two cases of treatment-resistant aggression and self-injury. *Behavior Modification, 25*, 62–78.

Määttä, T., Tervo-Määttä, T., Taanila, A., Kaski, M., & Iivanainen, M. (2006). Mental health, behavior and intellectual abilities of people with Down syndrome. *Down Syndrome Research and Practice, 11*(1), 37–43.

Madsen, K. M., Hviid, A., Vestergaard, M., Schendel, D., Wohlfahrt, J., Thorsen, P., et al. (2002). A population-based study of measles, mumps, and rubella vaccination and autism. *New England Journal of Medicine, 347*(19), 1477–1482.

Mahowald, M. W., & Rosen, G. M. (1990). Parasomnias in children. *Pediatrician, 17*(1), 21–31.

Mahowald, M. W., & Schenck, C. H. (1996). NREM sleep parasomnias. *Neurologic Clinics, 14*(4), 675–696.

Makris, N., Biederman, J., Valera, E. M., Bush, G., Kaiser, J., Kennedy, D. N., et al. (2007). Cortical thinning of the attention and executive function networks in adults with attention-deficit/hyperactivity disorder. *Cerebral Cortex, 17*(6), 1364–1375.

Manassis, K., & Monga, S. (2001). A therapeutic approach to children and adolescents with anxiety disorders and associated comorbid conditions. *Journal of the American Academy of Child and Adolescent Psychiatry, 40*(1), 115–117.

Mandoki, M. W., Tapia, M. R., Tapia, M. A., Sumner, G. S., & Parker, J. L. (1997). Venlafaxine in the treatment of children and adolescents with major depression. *Psychopharmacology Bulletin, 33*(1), 149–154.

Mann, J. J., Oquendo, M., Underwood, M. D., & Arango, V. (1999). The neurobiology of suicide risk: A review for the clinician. *Journal of Clinical Psychiatry, 60*(2), 7–11, 18–20, 113–116.

Manni, R., Ratti, M. F., Marchioni, E., Castelnovo, G., Murelli, R., Sartori, I., et al. (1997). Poor sleep in adolescents: A study of 869 17-year-old Italian secondary school students. *Journal of Sleep Research, 6*, 44–49.

Mano, M. J., Tom-Revzon, C., Bukstein, O. G., & Crismon, M. L. (2007). Changes and challenges: Managing ADHD in a fast-paced world. *Journal of Managed Care Pharmacy Supplement, 9*(13), S-b.

March, J. S., Biederman, J., Wolkow, R., Safferman, A., Mardekian, J., Cook, E. H., et al. (1998). Sertraline in children and adolescents with obsessive–compulsive disorder: A multicenter randomized controlled trial. *Journal of the American Medical Association, 280*, 1752–1756.

March, J. S., Entusah, A. R., Rynn, M., Albano, A. M., & Tourian, K. A. (2007). A randomized controlled trial of venlafaxine ER versus placebo in pediatric social anxiety disorder. *Biological Psychiatry, 62*(10), 1149–1154.

March, J., Silva, S., Petrycki, S., Curry, J., Wells, K., Fairbank, J., et al. (2004). Fluoxetine, cognitive behavioral therapy, and their combination for adolescents with depression: Treatment for Adolescents with Depression Study (TADS) randomized controlled trial. *Journal of the American Medical Association, 292*(7), 807–820.

March, J. S., Silva, S., Petrycki, S., Curry, J., Wells, K., Fairbank, J., et al. (2007). The Treatment for Adolescents with Depression Study (TADS): Long-term effectiveness and safety outcomes. *Archives of General Psychiatry, 64*(10), 1132–1143.

Marder, S. R. (1998). Antipsychotic medications. In A. F. Schatzberg & C. B. Nemeroff (Eds.), *Textbook of psychopharmacology* (2nd ed., pp. 309–321). Washington, DC: American Psychiatric Press.

Marshall, M., Lewis, S., Lockwood, A., Drake, R., Jones, P., & Croudace, T. (2005). Association between duration of untreated psychosis and outcome in cohorts of first-episode patients: A systematic review. *Archives of General Psychiatry, 62*(9), 975–983.

Martin, A., Koenig, K., Anderson, G., & Scahill, L. (2003). Low-dose fluvoxamine treatment of children and adolescents with pervasive developmental disorders: A prospective, open-label study. *Journal of Autism and Developmental Disorders, 33*(1), 77–85.

Mash, E. S., & Wolfe, D. A. (2005). *Abnormal child psychology*. Belmont, CA: Thomson Wadsworth.

Masi, G., Marcheschi, M., & Pfanner, P. (1997). Paroxetine in depressed adolescents with intellectual disability: An open label study. *Journal of Intellectual Disability Research, 41*, 268–272.

Masi, G., Milone, A., Canepa, G., Millepiedi, S., Mucci, M., & Muratori, F. (2006). Olanzapine treatment in adolescents with severe conduct disorder. *European Psychiatry, 21*, 51–57.

Masi, G., Perugi, G., Toni, C., Millepiedi, S., Mucci, M., Bertini, N., et al. (2004). Predictors of treatment nonresponse in bipolar children and adolescents with manic or mixed episodes. *Journal of Child and Adolescent Psychopharmacology, 14*(3), 395–404.

Masserman, J. H. (1941). Psychodynamics in anorexia nervosa and neurotic vomiting. *Psychoanalytic Quarterly, 10*, 211–242.

Mazza, M., Di Nicola, M., Della Marca, G., Janiri, L., Bria, P., & Mazza, S. (2007). Bipolar disorder and epilepsy: A bidirectional relation? Neurobiological underpinnings, current hypotheses, and future research directions. *Neuroscientist, 13*(4), 392–404.

McClellan, J., Kowatch, R., & Findling, R. L. (2007). Practice parameter for the assessment and treatment of children and adolescents with bipolar disorder. *Journal of the American Academy of Child and Adolescent Psychiatry, 46*(1), 107–125.

McClellan, J., & Werry, J. (1997). Practice parameters for the assessment and treatment of children and adolescents with schizophrenia. *Journal of the American Academy of Child and Adolescent Psychiatry, 36*(10), 177S–193S.

McCracken, J. T., McGough, J., Shah, B., Cronin, P., Hong, D., Aman, M. G., et al. (2002). Risperidone in children with autism and serious behavioral problems. *New England Journal of Medicine, 347*(5), 314–321.

McCracken, J. T., Suddath, R., Chang, S., Thakur, S., & Piacentini, J. (2008). Effectiveness and tolerability of open label olanzapine in children and adolescents with Tourette syndrome. *Journal of Child and Adolescent Psychopharmacology, 18*(5), 501–508.

McDonald, C., Marshall, N., Sham, P. C., Bullmore, E. T., Schulze, K., Chapple, B., et al. (2006). Regional brain morphometry in patients with schizophrenia or bipolar disorder and their unaffected relatives. *American Journal of Psychiatry, 163*(3), 478–487.

McDougle, C. J., Kresch, L. E., & Posey, D. J. (2000). Repetitive thoughts and behavior in pervasive developmental disorders: Treatment with serotonin reuptake inhibitors. *Journal of Autism and Developmental Disorders, 30*(5), 427–435.

McDougle, C. J., Naylor, S. T., Cohen, D. J., Volkmar, F. R., Heninger, G. R., & Price, L. H. (1996). A double-blind, placebo-controlled study of fluvoxamine in adults with autistic disorder. *Archives of General Psychiatry, 53,* 1001–1008.

McGlashan, T. H. (2006). Is active psychosis neurotoxic? *Schizophrenia Bulletin, 32*(4), 609–613.

McIntosh, W. D., Bazzini, D. G., Smith, S. M., & Wayne, S. M. (1998). Who smokes in Hollywood? Characteristics of smokers in popular films from 1940 to 1989. *Addictive Behaviors, 23,* 395–398.

McLaren, J., & Bryson, S. E. (1987). Review of recent epidemiological studies of mental retardation: Prevalence, associated disorders, and etiology. *American Journal of Mental Retardation, 92,* 243–254.

McLoyd, V. C. (1998). Socioeconomic disadvantage and child development. *American Psychologist, 53,* 185–204.

Mereu, G., Lilliu, V., Vargiu, P., Muntoni, A. L., Diana, M., & Gessa, G. L. (1995). Depolarization inactivation of dopamine neurons: An artifact? *Journal of Neuroscience, 15,* 1144–1149.

Messias, E., & Kirkpatrick, B. (2001). Summer birth and deficit schizophrenia in the epidemiological catchment area study. *Journal of Nervous and Mental Disease, 189,* 608–612.

Meyer, S. E., Carlson, G. A., Youngstrom, E., Ronsaville, D. S., Martinez, P. E., Gold, P. W., et al. (2009). Long-term outcomes of youth who manifested the CBCL-pediatric bipolar disorder phenotype during childhood and/or adolescence. *Journal of Affective Disorders, 113*(3), 227–235.

Meyer, V. (1966). Modification of expectations in cases with obsessional rituals. *Behaviour Research and Therapy, 4,* 273–280.

Miklowitz, D. J., Axelson, D. A., Birmaher, B., George, E. L., Taylor, D. O., Schneck, C. D., et al. (2008). Family-focused treatment for adolescents with bipolar disorder: Results of a 2-year randomized trial. *Archives of General Psychiatry, 65*(9), 1053–1061.

Miklowitz, D. J., George, E. L., Axelson, D. A., Kim, E. Y., Birmaher, B., Schneck, C., et al. (2004). Family-focused treatment for adolescents with bipolar disorder. *Journal of Affective Disorders, 82*(1), S113–S128.

Milberger, S., Biederman, J., Faraone, S. V., Murphy, J., & Tsuang, M. T. (1995). Attention deficit hyperactivity disorder and comorbid disorders: Issues of overlapping symptoms. *American Journal of Psychiatry, 152*(12), 1793–1799.

Miller, A. L., Rathus, J. H., & Linehan, M. M. (2006). *Dialectical behavior therapy with suicidal adolescents.* New York: Guilford Press.

Miller, L., Gur, M., Shanok, A., & Weissman, M. (2008). Interpersonal psychotherapy with pregnant adolescents: Two pilot studies. *Journal of Child Psychology and Psychiatry, 49*(7), 733–742.

Millward, C., Ferriter, M., Calver, S., & Connell-Jones, G. (2008). Gluten- and casein-free diets for autistic spectrum disorder. *Cochrane Database of Systematic Reviews, 16*(2), CD003498.

Minuchin, S., Rosman, B. L., & Baker, L. (1978). *Psychosomatic families: Anorexia nervosa in context.* Cambridge, MA: Harvard University Press.

Mitchell, J., McCauley, E., Burke, P. M., & Moss, S. J. (1988). Phenomenology of depression in children and adolescents. *Journal of the American Academy of Child and Adolescent Psychiatry, 27*(1), 12–20.

Moehler, E., Kagan, J., Oelkers-Ax, R., Brunner, R., Poustka, L., Haffner, J., et al. (2008). Infant predictors of behavioural inhibition. *British Journal of Developmental Psychology, 26*(1), 145–150.

Molitch, M., & Eccles, A. K. (1937). The effect of benzedrine sulphate on the intelligence scores of children. *American Journal of Psychiatry, 94,* 587, 590.

Molitch, M., & Poliakoff, S. (1937). The effect of benzedrine sulfate on enuresis. *Archives of Pediatrics and Adolescent Medicine, 54,* 499–501.

Molitch, M., & Sullivan, J. P. (1937). The effect of benzedrine sulphate on children taking the new Stanford Achievement Tests. *American Journal of Orthopsychiatry, 7,* 519–522.

Mondraty, N., Birmingham, C. L., Touyz, S., Sundakov, V., Chapman, L., & Beumont, P. (2005). Randomized controlled trial of olanzapine in the treatment of cognitions in anorexia nervosa. *Australas Psychiatry, 13*(1), 72–75.

Monteleone, P., Castaldo, E., & Maj, M. (2008). Neuroendocrine dysregulation of food intake in eating disorders. *Regulatory Peptides, 149*(1–3), 39–50.

Montgomery, P., Bjornstad, G., & Dennis, J. (2006). Media-based behavioural treatments for behavioural problems in children. *Cochrane Database of Systematic Reviews, 1,* CD002206.

Morgan, D., Grant, K. A., Gage, H. D., Mach, R. H., Kaplan, J. R., Prioleau, O., et al. (2005). Social dominance in monkeys: Dopamine D2 receptors and cocaine self-administration. *Nature Neuroscience, 5*(2), 169–174.

Morral, A. R., McCaffrey, D. F., & Ridgeway, G. (2004). Effectiveness of community-based treatment for substance-abusing adolescents: 12-month outcomes of youths entering Phoenix Academy or alternative probation dispositions. *Psychology of Addictive Behaviors, 18*(3), 257–268.

MTA Cooperative Group. (1999). A 14-month randomized clinical trial of treatment strategies for attention-deficit/hyperactivity disorder. *Archives of General Psychiatry, 56,* 1073–1086.

Mufson, L., Weissman, M. M., Moreau, D., & Garfinkel, R. (1999). Efficacy of interpersonal psychotherapy for depressed adolescents. *Archives of General Psychiatry, 56*(6), 573–579.

Mukaddes, N. M., & Abali, O. (2003). Quetiapine treatment of children and adolescents with Tourette's disorder. *Journal of Child and Adolescent Psychopharmacology, 13*(3), 295–299.

Müller, T. D., Föcker, M., Holtkamp, K., Herpertz-Dahlmann, B., & Hebebrand, J. (2009). Leptin-mediated neuroendocrine alterations in anorexia nervosa: Somatic and behavioral implications. *Child and Adolescent Psychiatry Clinics of North America, 18*(1), 117–129.

Muñoz-Solomando, A., Kendall, T., & Whittington, C. J. (2008). Cognitive behavioural therapy for children and adolescents. *Current Opinion in Psychiatry, 21*(4), 332–337.

Munson, J., Dawson, G., Abbott, R., Faja, S., Webb, S. J., Friedman, S. D., et al. (2006). Amygdalar volume and behavioral development in autism. *Archives of General Psychiatry, 63*(6), 686–693.

Murialdo, G., Barreca, A., Nobili, F., Rollero, A., Timossi, G., Gianelli, M. V., et al. (2000). Dexamethasone effects on cortisol secretion in Alzheimer's disease: Some clinical and hormonal features in suppressor and nonsuppressor patients. *Journal of Endocrinology Investment, 23*(3), 178–186.

Muris, P., Merckelbach, H., Gadet, B., & Moulaert, V. (2000). Fears, worries, and scary dreams in 4- to 12-year-old children: Their content, developmental pattern, and origins. *Journal of Clinical Child Psychology, 29*(1), 43.

Murray, C. J. L., & Lopez, A. D. (1996). *The global burden of disease.* (Published on behalf of the World Health Organization and the World Bank.) Cambridge, MA: Harvard School of Public Health.

Nacewicz, B. M., Dalton, K. M., Johnstone, T., Long, M. T., McAuliff, E. M., Oakes, T. R., et al. (2006). Amygdala volume and nonverbal social impairment in adolescent and adult males with autism. *Archives of General Psychiatry, 63*(12), 1417–1428.

Nagaraj, R., Singhi, P., & Malhi, P. (2006). Risperidone in children with autism: Randomized, placebo-controlled, double-blind study. *Journal of Child Neurology, 21*(6), 450–455.

Nasrallah, H. A. (2006). Focus on lower risk of tardive dyskinesia with atypical antipsychotics. *Annals of Clinical Psychiatry, 18*(1), 57–62.

National Institute for Clinical Excellence. (2004). *Eating disorders: Core interventions in the treatment and management of anorexia nervosa, bulimia nervosa and related eating disorders.* London: National Institute for Clinical Excellence.

National Institute of Mental Health research roundtable on prepubertal bipolar disorder. *Journal of the American Academy of Child & Adolescent Psychiatry, 40*(8), 871–878.

National Institute on Drug Abuse (NIDA). (2008). *Preventing drug abuse among children and adolescents.* Retrieved January 30, 2009, from http://www.nida .nih.gov/Prevention/risk.html

National Institutes of Health. (2000). The practical guide: Identification, evaluation, and treatment of overweight and obesity in adults. *NIH Publication Number 00–4084.*

Nelson, J. C. (2007). Augmentation strategies in the treatment of major depressive disorder. Recent findings and current status of augmentation strategies. *CNS Spectrums, 12*(22), 6–9.

Newman-Toker, J. (2000). Risperidone in anorexia nervosa. *Journal of the American Academy of Child and Adolescent Psychiatry, 39*(8), 941–942.

Newschaffer, C. J., Croen, L. A., Daniels, J., Giarelli, E., Grether, J. K., Levy, S. E., et al. (2007). The epidemiology of autism spectrum disorders. *Annual Review of Public Health, 28*, 235–258.

Newschaffer, C. J., Falb, M. D., & Gurney, J. G. (2005). National autism prevalence trends from US special education data. *Pediatrics, 115*, 277–282.

Niendam, T. A., Bearden, C. E., Rosso, I. M., Sanchez, L. E., Hadley, T., Nuechterlein, K. H., et al. (2003). A prospective study of childhood neurocognitive functioning in schizophrenic patients and their siblings. *American Journal of Psychiatry, 160*(11), 2060–2062.

Nigg, J. T., & Casey, B. J. (2005). An integrative theory of attention-deficit/hyperactivity disorder based on the cognitive and affective neurosciences. *Development and Psychopathology, 17*(3), 785–806.

Nigg, J. T., Stavro, G., Ettenhofer, M., Hambrick, D. Z., Miller, T., & Henderson, J. M. (2005). Executive functions and ADHD in adults: Evidence for selective effects on ADHD symptom domains. *Journal of Abnormal Psychology, 114*(4), 706–717.

Nir, I., Meir, D., Zilber, N., Knobler, H., Hadjez, J., & Lerner, Y. (1995). Brief report: Circadian melatonin, thyroid-stimulating hormone, prolactin, and cortisol levels in serum of young adults with autism. *Journal of Autism and Developmental Disorders, 25*(6), 641–654.

Norton, K. I. (1996). Ken and Barbie at life size. *Sex Roles, 34*(3–4), 287–294.

Novak Sarotar, B., Pesek, M. B., Agius, M., & Kocmur, M. (2008). Duration of untreated psychosis and its effect on the symptomatic recovery in schizophrenia: Preliminary results. *Neuroendocrinology Letters, 29*(6).

Nuño-Gutiérrez, B. L., Rodriguez-Cerda, O., & Alvarez-Nemegyei, J. (2006). Why do adolescents use drugs? A common sense explanatory model from the social actor's perspective. *Adolescence, 41*(164), 649–665.

Nybäck, H., Wiesel, F. A., Berggren, B. M., & Hindmarsh, T. (1982). Computed tomography of the brain in patients with acute psychosis and in healthy volunteers. *Acta Psychiatrica Scandinavica, 65*(6), 403–414.

Oberman, L. M., Hubbard, E. M., McCleery, J. P., Altschuler, E. L., Ramachandran, V. S., & Pineda, J. A. (2005). EEG evidence for mirror neuron dysfunction in autism spectrum disorders. *Cognitive Brain Research, 24*, 190–198.

O'Brien, L. M., & Gozal, D. (2004). Neurocognitive dysfunction and sleep in children: From human to rodent. *Pediatric Clinics of North America, 51*(1), 187.

Offord, D. R., Boyle, M. H., Racine, Y. A., Fleming, J. E., Cadman, D. R., Blum, H. M., et al. (1992). Outcome, prognosis, and risk in a longitudinal follow-up study. *Journal of the American Academy of Child and Adolescent Psychiatry, 31*, 916–922.

Ogden, C. L., Carroll, M. D., Curtin, L. R., McDowell, M. A., Tabak, C. J., & Flegal, K. M. (2006). The prevalence of overweight and obesity in the United States, 1999–2004. *Journal of the American Medical Association, 295*, 1549–1555.

Okie, S. (2006). ADHD in adults. *New England Journal of Medicine, 354*(25), 2637–2641.

Olfson, M., Blanco, C., Liu, L., Moreno, C., & Laje, G. (2006). National trends in the outpatient treatment of children and adolescents with antipsychotic drugs. *Archives of General Psychiatry, 63*(6), 679–685.

Ollendick, T. H. (1998). Panic disorder in children and adolescents: New developments, new directions. *Journal of Clinical Child Psychology, 27*(3), 234–245.

Olsson, I., Steffenburg, S., & Gillberg, C. (1988). Epilepsy in autism and autisticlike conditions: A population-based study. *Archives of Neurology, 45*(6), 666–668.

O'Malley, P. M., & Johnston, L. D. (2007). Drugs and driving by American high school seniors, 2001–2006. *Journal of Studies on Alcohol and Drugs, 68*(6), 834–842.

Oslejskova, H., Kontrová, I., Foralová, R., Dusek, L., & Némethová, D. (2007). The course of diagnosis in autistic patients: The delay between recognition of the first symptoms by parents and correct diagnosis. *Neuroendocrinology Letters, 28*(6), 895–900.

Ospina, M. B., Krebs Seida, J., Clark, B., Karkhaneh, M., Hartling, L., Tjosvold, L., et al. (2008). Behavioral and developmental interventions for autism spectrum disorder: A clinical systematic review. *PLoS ONE, 3*(11), e3755.

Othmer, E., Desouza, C. M., Penick, E. C., Nickel, E. J., Hunter, E. E., Othmer, S. C., et al. (2007). Indicators of mania in depressed outpatients: A retrospective analysis of data from the Kansas 1500 study. *Journal of Clinical Psychiatry, 68*(1), 47–51.

Owens, J. A., & Witmans, M. (2004). Sleep problems. *Current Problems Pediatric and Adolescent Health Care, 34*(4), 154–179.

Palmer, L. J., Knuiman, M. W., Divitini, M. L., Burton, P. R., James, A. L., Bartholomew, H. C., et al. (2001). Familial aggregation and heritability of adult lung function: Results from the Busselton Health Study. *European Respiratory Journal, 17*(4), 696–702.

Pandina, G. J., Aman, M. G., & Findling, R. L. (2006). Risperidone in the management of disruptive behavior disorders. *Journal of Child and Adolescent Psychopharmacology, 16*(4), 379–392.

Pandina, G. J., DelBello, M. P., Kushner, S., et al. (2007, October). *Risperidone for the treatment of acute mania in bipolar youth.* Poster presented at the annual meeting of the American Academy of Child and Adolescent Psychiatry, Boston, Massachusetts.

Papatheodorou, G., Kutcher, S. P., Katic, M., & Szalai, J. P. (1995). The efficacy and safety of divalproex sodium in the treatment of acute mania in adolescents and young adults: An open clinical trial. *Journal of Clinical Psychopharmacology, 15*(2), 110–116.

Papolos, D., Hennen, J., & Cockerham, M. S. (2005). Factors associated with parent reported suicide threats by children and adolescents with community-diagnosed bipolar disorder. *Journal of Affective Disorders, 86*(2–3), 267–275.

Pappadopulos, E., Macintyre II, J. C., Crismon, M. L., Findling, R. L., Malone, R. P., Derivan, A., et al. (2003). Treatment recommendations for the use of antipsychotics for aggressive youth (TRAAY), part II. *Journal of the American Academy of Child and Adolescent Psychiatry, 42*(2), 132–144.

Parmeggiani, A., Posar, A., Antolini, C., Scaduto, M. C., Santucci, M., & Giovanardi-Rossi, P. (2007). Epilepsy in patients with pervasive developmental disorder not otherwise specified. *Journal of Child Neurology, 22*(10), 1198–1203.

Patel, N. C., DelBello, M. P., Cecil, K. M., Adler, C. M., Bryan, H. S., Stanford, K. E., et al. (2006). Lithium treatment effects on Myo-inositol in adolescents with bipolar depression. *Biological Psychiatry, 60*(9), 998–1004.

Patten, C. A., Choi, W. S., Gillin, J. C., & Pierce, J. P. (2000). Depressive symptoms and cigarette smoking predict development and persistence of sleep problems in US adolescents. *Pediatrics, 106*(2), E23.

Patterson, G. R., DeBarshe, B. D., & Ramsey, E. (1989). A developmental perspective on antisocial behavior. *American Psychologist, 44*(2), 329–335.

Patzold, L. M., Richdale, A. L., & Tonge, B. J. (1998). An investigation into sleep characteristics of children with autism and Asperger's disorder. *Journal of Paediatrics and Child Health, 34*(6), 528–533.

Paul, R. (2008). Interventions to improve communication in autism. *Child and Adolescent Psychiatric Clinics of North America, 17*(4), 832–856.

Pavuluri, M. N., Graczyk, P. A., Henry, D. B., Carbray, J. A., Heidenreich, J., & Miklowitz, D. J. (2004). Child- and family-focused cognitive-behavioral therapy for pediatric bipolar disorder: Development and preliminary results. *Journal of the American Academy of Child and Adolescent Psychiatry, 43*(5), 528–537.

Pavuluri, M. N., Henry, D. B., Carbray, J. A., Sampson, G., Naylor, M. W., & Janicak, P. G. (2004). Open-label prospective trial of risperidone in combination with lithium or divalproex sodium in pediatric mania. *Journal of Affective Disorders, 82*(1), S103–S111.

Pavuluri, M. N., Henry, D. B., Carbray, J. A., Sampson, G. A., Naylor, M. W., & Janicak, P. G. (2006). A one-year open-label trial of risperidone augmentation in lithium nonresponder youth with preschool-onset bipolar disorder. *Journal of Child and Adolescent Psychopharmacology, 16*(3), 336–350.

Pavuluri, M. N., Henry, D. B., Devineni, B., Carbray, J. A., & Birmaher, B. (2006). Child mania rating scale: Development, reliability, and validity. *Journal of the American Academy of Child and Adolescent Psychiatry, 45*(5), 550–560.

Pediatric OCD Treatment Study (POTS) Team. (2004). Cognitive behavior therapy, sertraline, and their combination for children and adolescents with obsessive compulsive disorder: The Pediatric OCD Treatment Study (POTS) randomized controlled trial. *Journal of the American Medical Association, 292*, 1969–1976.

Perry, B. D. (1998). Anxiety disorders. In C. E. Coffey & R. A. Brumback (Eds.), *Textbook of pediatric neuropsychiatry* (pp. 579–595). Washington, DC: American Psychiatric Press.

Peterson, B. S., Pine, D. S., Cohen, P., & Brook, J. S. (2001). Prospective, longitudinal study of tic, obsessive-compulsive, and attention deficit/hyperactivity disorders in an epidemiological sample. *Journal of the American Academy of Child and Adolescent Psychiatry, 40*(6), 685–695.

Peterson, B. S., Thomas, P., Kane, M. J., Scahill, L., Zhang, H., Bronen, R., et al. (2003). Basal ganglia volumes in patients with Gilles de la Tourette syndrome. *Archives of General Psychiatry, 60*(4), 215–224.

Petraitis, J., Flay, B. R., Miller, T. Q., Torpy, E. J., & Greiner, B. (1998). Illicit substance use among adolescents: A matrix of prospective predictors. *Substance Use and Misuse, 33*(13), 2561–2604.

Petropoulos, H., Friedman, S. D., Shaw, D. W. W., Artru, A. A., Dawson, G., & Dager, S. R. (2006). Gray matter abnormalities in autism spectrum disorder revealed by T2 relaxation. *Neurology, 67*, 632–636.

Petti, T. A. (1978). Depression in hospitalized child psychiatry patients. Approaches to measuring depression. *Journal of the American Academy of Child Psychiatry, 17*(1), 49–59.

Philip, N. S., Carpenter, L. L., Tyrka, A. R., & Price, L. H. (2008). Augmentation of antidepressants with atypical antipsychotics: A review of the current literature. *Journal of Psychiatric Practice, 14*(1), 34–44.

Piacentini, J. C., & Chang, S. W. (2006). Behavioral treatments for tic suppression: Habit reversal training. *Advances in Neurology, 99*, 227–233.

Piazza, C. C., Hagopian, L. P., Hughes, C. R., & Fisher, W. W. (1998). Using chronotherapy to treat severe sleep problems: A case study. *American Journal of Mental Retardation, 102*(4), 358–366.

Pilkington, H. (2007). Beyond "peer pressure": Rethinking drug use and "youth culture." *International Journal of Drug Policy, 18*(3), 213–224.

Pine, D. S., Cohen, P., Gurley, D., Brook, J., & Ma, Y. (1998). The risk for early adulthood anxiety and depressive disorders in adolescents with anxiety and depressive disorders. *Archives of General Psychiatry, 55*(1), 56–64.

Pinna, G., Costa, E., & Guidotti, A. (2006). Fluoxetine and norfluoxetine stereospecifically and selectively increase brain neurosteroid content at doses that are inactive on 5-HT reuptake. *Psychopharmacology, 186*(3), 362–372.

Pirke, K. M. (1996). Central and peripheral noradrenalin regulation in eating disorders. *Psychiatry Research, 62*(1), 43–49.

Platt, J. E., Campbell, M., Green, W. H., Perry, R., & Cohen, I. L. (1981). Effects of lithium carbonate and haloperidol on cognition in aggressive hospitalized school-age children. *Journal of Clinical Psychopharmacology, 1*, 8–13.

Pliszka, S. R., McCracken, J. T., & Maas, J. W. (1996). Catecholamines in attention deficit hyperactivity disorder: Current perspectives. *Journal of the American Academy of Child and Adolescent Psychiatry, 35*(3), 264–272.

Posey, D. J., Erickson, C. A., Stigler, K. A., & McDougle, C. J. (2006). The use of selective serotonin reuptake inhibitors in autism and related disorders. *Journal of Child and Adolescent Psychopharmacology, 16*(1–2), 181–186.

Posey, D. J., Puntney, J. I., Sasher, T. M., Kem, D. L., & McDougle, C. J. (2004). Guanfacine treatment of hyperactivity and inattention in pervasive developmental disorders: A retrospective analysis of 80 cases. *Journal of Child and Adolescent Psychopharmacology, 14*(2), 233–241.

Posey, D. J., Stigler, K. A., Erickson, C. A., & McDougle, C. J. (2008). Antipsychotics in the treatment of autism. *Journal of Clinical Investigation, 118*(1), 6–14.

Post, R. M. (2007). Kindling and sensitization as models for affective episode recurrence, cyclicity, and tolerance phenomena. *Neuroscience and Biobehavioral Reviews, 31*(6), 858–873.

Preskorn, S. H., Weller, E. B., Hughes, C. W., Weller, R. A., & Bolte, K. (1987). Depression in prepubertal children: Dexamethasone nonsuppression predicts differential response to imipramine vs. placebo. *Psychopharmacology Bulletin, 23*(1), 128–133.

Preti, A., Cardascia, L., Zen, T., Marchetti, M., Favaretto, G., & Miotto, P. (2000). Risk for obstetric complications and schizophrenia. *Psychiatry Research, 96*, 127.

Price, R. A., Kidd, K. K., Cohen, D. J., Pauls, D. L., & Leckman, J. F. (1985). A twin study of Tourette syndrome. *Archives of General Psychiatry, 42*(8), 815–820.

Primack, B. A., Dalton, M. A., Carroll, M. V., Agarwal, A. A., & Fine, M. J. (2008). Content analysis of tobacco, alcohol, and other drugs in popular music. *Archives of Pediatrics and Adolescent Medicine, 162*(2), 169–175.

Pringsheim, T., Davenport, W. J., & Lang, A. (2003). Tics. *Current Opinion in Neurology, 16*(4), 523–527.

Prizant, B. M., & Meyer, E. C. (1993). Socioemotional aspects of language and social-communication disorders in young children and their families. *American Journal of Speech-Language Pathology, 2*, 56–71.

Puig-Antich, J., Goetz, R., Hanlon, C., Davies, M., Thompson, J., Chambers, W. J., et al. (1982). Sleep architecture and REM sleep measures in prepubertal children with major depression: A controlled study. *Archives of General Psychiatry, 39*(8), 932–939.

Rahim, S. I., & Cederblad, M. (1986). Epidemiology of nocturnal enuresis in a part of Khartoum, Sudan: The extensive study. *Acta Paediatrica, 75*, 1017–1020.

Randazzo, A. C., Muehlbach, M. J., Schweitzer, P. K., & Walsh, J. K. (1998). Cognitive function following acute sleep restriction in children ages 10–14. *Sleep, 21*(8), 861.

Rapin, I., & Katzman, R. (1998). Neurobiology of autism. *Annals of Neurology, 43*(1), 7–14.

Rapport, M. D., & Denney, M. A. (1997). Titrating methylphenidate in children with attention-deficit/hyperactivity disorder: Is body mass predictive of clinical response? *Journal of the American Academy of Child and Adolescent Psychiatry, 36*, 523–530.

Rasmussen, S. A. (1984). Lithium and tryptophan augmentation in clomipramine resistant obsessive-compulsive disorder. *American Journal of Psychiatry, 141*, 1283–1285.

Rasmussen, S. A., & Tsuang, M. T. (1986). Clinical characteristics and family history in DSM-III obsessive-compulsive disorder. *American Journal of Psychiatry, 143,* 317–322.

Reber, A. S. (1985). *The Penguin dictionary of psychology.* New York: Penguin Books.

Reddy, L. A., & Pfeiffer, S. I. (1997). Effectiveness of treatment foster care with children and adolescents: A review of outcome studies. *Journal of the American Academy of Child and Adolescent Psychiatry, 36,* 581–588.

Regier, D. A., Farmer, M. E., Rae, D. S., Locke, B. Z., Keith, S. J., Judd, L. L., et al. (1990). Comorbidity of mental disorders with alcohol and other drug abuse: Results from the Epidemiologic Catchment Area (ECA) study. *Journal of the American Medical Association, 264,* 2511–2518.

Research Units for Pediatric Psychopharmacology (RUPP) Anxiety Study Group. (2001). Fluvoxamine for the treatment of anxiety disorders in children and adolescents. *New England Journal of Medicine, 344,* 1279–1285.

Reveley, A. M., Reveley, M. A., Clifford, C. A., & Murray, R. M. (1982). Cerebral ventricular size in twins discordant for schizophrenia. *Lancet, 1*(8271), 540–541.

Rey, J. M., & Walter, G. (1997). Half a century of ECT use in young people. *American Journal of Psychiatry, 154,* 595–602.

Richdale, A. L., & Prior, M. R. (1995). The sleep/wake rhythm in children with autism. *European Child and Adolescent Psychiatry, 4*(3), 175–186.

Riddle, M. A., Bernstein, G. A., Cook, E. H., Leonard, H. L., March, J. S., & Swanson, J. M. (1999). Anxiolytics, adrenergic agents, and naltrexone. *Journal of the American Academy of Child and Adolescent Psychiatry, 38*(5), 546–556.

Riddle, M. A., Reeve, E. A., Yaryura-Tobias, J. A., Yang, H. M., Claghorn, J. L., Gaffney, G., et al. (2001). Fluvoxamine for children and adolescents with obsessive–compulsive disorder: A randomized, controlled, multicenter trial. *Journal of the American Academy of Child and Adolescent Psychiatry, 40,* 222–229.

Riddle, M. A., Scahill, L., King, R. A., Hardin, M. T., Anderson, G. M., Ort, S. I., et al. (1992). Double-blind, crossover trial of fluoxetine and placebo in children and adolescents with obsessive-compulsive disorder. *Journal of the American Academy of Child and Adolescent Psychiatry, 31,* 1062–1069.

Ritvo, E. R., Freeman, B. J., Mason-Brothers, A., Mo, A., & Ritvo, A. M. (1985). Concordance for the syndrome of autism in 40 pairs of afflicted twins. *American Journal of Psychiatry, 142,* 74–77.

Rizzo, C. J., Esposito-Smythers, C., Swenson, L., Birmaher, B., Ryan, N., Strober, M., et al. (2007). Factors associated with mental health service utilization among bipolar youth. *Bipolar Disorders, 9*(8), 839–850.

Roane, B. M., & Taylor, D. J. (2008). Adolescent insomnia as a risk factor for early adult depression and substance abuse. *Sleep, 31*(10), 1351–1356.

Robbins, D. R., Alessi, N. E., Cook, S. C., Poznanski, E. O., & Yanchyshyn, G. W. (1982). The use of the Research Diagnostic Criteria (RDC) for depression in adolescent psychiatric inpatients. *Journal of the American Academy of Child Psychiatry, 21*(3), 251–255.

Roberts, D. F., Henriksen, L., & Christenson, P. G. (1999). *Substance use in popular movies and music.* Washington, DC: Office of National Drug Control Policy and the Department of Health and Human Services.

Robins, D., Fein, D., Barton, M., & Green, J. (2001). The Modified-Checklist for Autism in Toddlers (M-CHAT): An initial investigation in the early detection of autism and pervasive developmental disorders. *Journal of Autism and Developmental Disorders, 31*(2), 131–144.

Robson, L. M., & Leung, A. K. (2002). Urotherapy recommendations for bedwetting. *Journal of the National Medical Association, 94*(7), 577–580.

Rogers, S. J. (1996). Brief report: Early intervention in autism. *Journal of Autism and Developmental Disorders, 26*(2), 243–246.

Romero, S., Birmaher, B., Axelson, D., Goldstein, T., Goldstein, B. I., Gill, M. K., et al. (2009). Prevalence and correlates of physical and sexual abuse in children and adolescents with bipolar disorder. *Journal of Affective Disorders, 112*(1–3), 144–150.

Ronan, K. R., & Kendall, P. C. (1990). Non-self-controlled adolescents: Applications of cognitive-behavioral therapy. *Adolescent Psychiatry, 17,* 479–505.

Ropers, H. H., & Hamel, B. C. J. (2005). X-linked mental retardation. *Nature Reviews, Genetics, 6,* 46–57.

Rosenbaum, J. F., Biederman, J., Bolduc-Murphy, E. A., Faraone, S. V., Chaloff, J., Hirshfeld, D. R., et al. (1993). Behavioral inhibition in childhood: A risk factor for anxiety disorders. *Harvard Review of Psychiatry, 1*(1), 2–16.

Ross, D. P., Shillington, E. R., & Lockhead, C. (1994). *The Canadian fact book on poverty—1994.* Ottawa, Ontario, Canada: Canadian Council on Social Development.

Rosselló, J., & Bernal, G. (1999). The efficacy of cognitive-behavioral and interpersonal treatments for depression in Puerto Rican adolescents. *Journal of Consulting and Clinical Psychology, 67*(5), 734–745.

Rosselló, J., Bernal, G., & Rivera-Medina, C. (2008). Individual and group CBT and IPT for Puerto Rican adolescents with depressive symptoms. *Cultural Diversity and Ethnic Minority Psychology, 14*(3), 234–245.

Rowe, C., Liddle, H., Caruso, J., & Dakof, G. (2004). Clinical variations of adolescent substance abuse: An empirically based typology. *Journal of Child and Adolescent Substance Abuse, 14*(2), 19–40.

Rumpold, G., Klingseis, M., Dornauer, K., Kopp, M., Doering, S., Höfer, S., et al. (2006). Psychotropic substance abuse among adolescents: A structural equation model on risk and protective factors. *Substance Use and Misuse, 41*(8), 1155–1169.

Russell, A. T., & Tanguay, P. E. (1996). Mental retardation. In M. Lewis (Ed.), *Child and adolescent psychiatry: A comprehensive textbook.* (2nd ed., pp. XXX–XXX). Baltimore: Williams & Wilkins.

Russell, G. (1979). Bulimia nervosa: An ominous variant of anorexia nervosa. *Psychological Medicine, 9,* 429–448.

Rutter, M. (2000). Genetic studies of autism: From the 1970s into the millennium. *Journal of Abnormal Child Psychology, 28*(1), 3–14.

Ryan, N. D., Meyer, V., Dachille, S., Mazzie, D., & Puig-Antich, J. (1988). Lithium antidepressant augmentation in TCA-refractory depression in adolescents. *Journal of the American Academy of Child and Adolescent Psychiatry, 27*(3), 371–376.

Ryan, N. D., Puig-Antich, J., Ambrosini, P., Rabinovich, H., Robinson, D., Nelson, B., et al. (1987). The clinical picture of major depression in children and adolescents. *Archives of General Psychiatry, 44*(10), 854–861.

Ryan, N. D., Puig-Antich, J., Rabinovich, H., Fried, J., Ambrosini, P., Meyer, V., et al. (1988). MAOIs in adolescent major depression unresponsive to tricyclic antidepressants. *Journal of the American Academy of Child and Adolescent Psychiatry, 27*, 755–758.

Rynn, M. A., Riddle, M. A., Yeung, P. P., & Kunz, N. R. (2007). Efficacy and safety of extended-release venlafaxine in the treatment of generalized anxiety disorder in children and adolescents: Two placebo-controlled trials. *American Journal of Psychiatry, 164*(2), 290–300.

Rynn, M. A., Siqueland, L., & Rickels, K. (2001). Placebo-controlled trial of sertraline in the treatment of children with generalized anxiety disorder. *American Journal of Psychiatry, 158*, 2008–2014.

Saarenpää-Heikkilä, O., Laippala, P., & Koivikko, M. (2001). Subjective daytime sleepiness and its predictors in Finnish adolescents in an interview study. *Acta Paediatrica, 90*(5), 552–557.

Sagud, M., Mihaljevi-Peles, A., Pivac, N., Muck-Seler, D., Simunovi, I., & Jakovljevi, M. (2008). Genetics of schizophrenia in the context of integrative psychiatry. *Psychiatria Danubina, 20*(3), 364–368.

Sallee, F. R., Kurlan, R., Goetz, C. G., Singer, H., Scahill, L., Law, G., et al. (2000). Ziprasidone treatment of children and adolescents with Tourette's syndrome: A pilot study. *Journal of the American Academy of Child and Adolescent Psychiatry, 39*(3), 292–299.

Sallee, F., McGough, J., Wigal, T., Donahue, J., Lyne, A., & Biederman, J. (2008). Guanfacine extended release in children and adolescents with attention deficit/hyperactivity disorder: A placebo-controlled trial. *Journal of the American Academy of Child and Adolescent Psychiatry, 48*(2), 155–165.

Sandler, A., Glesne, C., & Geller, G. (2008). Children's and parents' perspectives on open-label use of placebos in the treatment of ADHD. *Child: Care, Health and Development, 34*(1), 111–120.

Sanson, A., & Prior, M. (1999). Temperament and behavioral precursors to oppositional defiant disorder and conduct disorder. In H. C. Quay & A. E. Hogan (Eds.), *Handbook of disruptive behavior disorders* (pp. 397–417). New York: Kluwer Academic/Plenum.

Santisteban, D. A., Suarez-Morales, L., Robbins, M. S., & Szapocznik, J. (2006). Brief strategic family therapy: Lessons learned in efficacy research and challenges to blending research and practice. *Family Process, 45*(2), 259–271.

Sawyer Radloff, L. (1991). The use of the Center for Epidemiologic Studies Depression Scale in adolescents and young adults. *Journal of Youth and Adolescence, 20*(2), 149–166.

Saxena, K., Howe, M., Simeonova, D., Steiner, H., & Chang, K. (2006). Divalproex sodium reduces overall aggression in youth at high risk for bipolar disorder. *Journal of Child and Adolescent Psychopharmacology, 16*(3), 252–259.

Schaeffer, J. L., & Ross, R. G. (2002). Childhood-onset schizophrenia: Premorbid and prodromal diagnostic and treatment histories. *Journal of the American Academy of Child and Adolescent Psychiatry, 41*(5), 538–545.

Schapiro, N. A. (2002). "Dude, you don't have Tourette's": Tourette's syndrome, beyond the tics. *Pediatric Nursing, 22*(3), 243–246.

Schechter, R., & Grether, J. K. (2008). Continuing increases in autism reported to California's developmental services system: Mercury in retrograde. *Archives of General Psychiatry, 65*(1), 19–24.

Scheffler, R. M., Hinshaw, S. P., Modrek, S., & Levine, P. (2007). The global market for ADHD medications. *Health Affairs, 26*(2), 450–457.

Schmidt, U. (2009). Cognitive behavioral approaches in adolescent anorexia and bulimia nervosa. *Child and Adolescent Psychiatry Clinics of North America, 18*(1), 147–158.

Schneider, K. (1959). *Clinical psychopathology.* New York: Grune & Stratton.

Schultz, R. T., Gauthier, I., Klin, A., Fulbright, R. K., Anderson, A. W., Volkmar, F., et al. (2000). Abnormal ventral temporal cortical activity during face discrimination among individuals with autism and Asperger syndrome. *Archives of General Psychiatry, 57,* 331–340.

Schulz, H. (2008). Rethinking sleep analysis. Comment on the AASM manual for the scoring of sleep and associated events. *Journal of Clinical Sleep Medicine, 4*(2), 99–103.

Schumann, C. M., Hamstra, J., Goodlin-Jones, B. L., Lotspeich, L. J., Kwon, H., Buonocore, M. H., et al. (2004). The amygdala is enlarged in children but not adolescents with autism; the hippocampus is enlarged at all ages. *Journal of Neuroscience, 24,* 6392–6401.

Schur, S. B., Sikich, L., Findling, R. L., Malone, R. P., Crismon, M. L., Derivan, A., et al. (2003). Treatment recommendations for the use of antipsychotics for aggressive youth (TRAAY), part I. *Journal of the American Academy of Child and Adolescent Psychiatry, 42*(2), 145–161.

Sears, L. L., Vest, C., Mohamed, S., Bailey, J., Ranson, B. J., & Piven, J. (1999). An MRI study of the basal ganglia in autism. *Progress in Neuro-Psychopharmacology and Biological Psychiatry, 23*(4), 613–624.

Sebat, J., Lakshmi, B., Malhotra, D., Troge, J., Lese-Martin, C., Walsh, T., et al. (2007). Strong association of de novo copy number mutations with autism. *Science, 316*(5823), 445–449.

Seo, W. S., Sung, H. M., Sea, H. S., & Bai, D. S. (2008). Aripiprazole treatment of children and adolescents with Tourette disorder or chronic tic disorder. *Journal of Child and Adolescent Psychopharmacology, 18*(2), 197–205.

Shaffer, D., Fisher, P., Dulcan, M. K., Davies, M., Piacentini, J., Schwab-Stone, M. E., et al. (1996). The NIMH Diagnostic Interview Schedule for Children Version 2.3 (DISC-2.3): Description, acceptability, prevalence rates, and performance in the MECA Study. Methods for the Epidemiology of Child and

Adolescent Mental Disorders Study. *Journal of the American Academy of Child and Adolescent Psychiatry, 35*, 865–877.

Shakespeare, W. (1936). *Hamlet.* In W. A. Wright (Ed.). *The complete works of William Shakespeare* (pp. 65–68). Garden City, NY: Garden City Books.

Shatkin, J. P. (2004). Atomoxetine for the treatment of pediatric nocturnal enuresis. *Journal of Child and Adolescent Psychopharmacology, 14*(3), 443–447.

Shatkin, J. P., Feinfeld, K., & Strober, M. (2002). The misinterpretation of a non-REM sleep parasomnia as suicidal behavior in an adolescent. *Sleep and Breathing, 6*(4), 175–179.

Shaw, P., Lerch, J., Greenstein, D., Sharp, W., Clasen, L., Evans, A., et al. (2006). Longitudinal mapping of cortical thickness and clinical outcome in children and adolescents with attention deficit/hyperactivity disorder. *Archives of General Psychiatry, 63*, 540–549.

Shaywitz, S. E., Shaywitz, B. A., Pugh, K. R., Fulbright, R. K., Constable, R. T., Mencl, W. E., et al. (1998). Functional disruption in the organization of the brain for reading in dyslexia. *Neurobiology, 95*, 2636–2641.

Shea, S., Turgay, A., Carroll, A., Schulz, M., Orlik, H., Smith, I., et al. (2004). Risperidone in the treatment of disruptive behavioral symptoms in children with autistic and other pervasive developmental disorders. *Pediatrics, 114*(5), 634–641.

Shelton, R. C., & Weinberger, D. R. (1986). X-ray computerized tomography studies in schizophrenia: A review and synthesis. In H. A. Nasrallah & D. R. Weinberg (Eds.), *Handbook of schizophrenia, vol. I: The neurology of schizophrenia* (pp. 207–250). Amsterdam: Elsevier.

Sher, L. (1997). Autistic disorder and the endogenous opioid system. *Medical Hypotheses, 48*(5), 413–414.

Sher, L. (2006). Combined dexamethasone suppression-corticotropin-releasing hormone stimulation test in studies of depression, alcoholism, and suicidal behavior. *Scientific World Journal, 6*, 1398–1404.

Shriberg, L. D., & Kwiatkowski J. (1988). A follow-up study of children with phonologic disorders of unknown origin. *Journal of Speech and Hearing Disorders, 53*, 144–155.

Siegel, D. J. (1999). *The developing mind.* New York: Guilford Press.

Sikich, L., Frazier, J. A., McClellan, J., Findling, R. L., Vitiello, B., Ritz, L., et al. (2008). Double-blind comparison of first- and second-generation antipsychotics in early-onset schizophrenia and schizo affective disorder: Findings from the treatment of early-onset schizophrenia spectrum disorders (TEOSS) study. *American Journal of Psychiatry, 165*(11), 1420–1431.

Silani, G., Frith, U., Demonet, J. F., Fazio, F., Perani, D., Price, C., et al. (2005). Brain abnormalities underlying altered activation in dyslexia: A voxel based morphometry study. *Brain, 128*(10), 2453–2461.

Simonoff, E., Pickles, A., Charman, T., Chandler, S., Loucas, T., & Baird, G. (2008). Psychiatric disorders in children with autism spectrum disorders: Prevalence, comorbidity, and associated factors in a population-derived sample. *Journal of the American Academy of Child and Adolescent Psychiatry, 47*(8), 921–929.

Singh, N., Ellis, C., & Wechsler, H. (1997). Psychopharmacoepidemiology of mental retardation: 1966 to 1995. *Journal of Child and Adolescent Psychopharmacology, 7*, 255–266.

Smedje, H., Broman, J. E., & Hetta, J. (2001). Short-term prospective study of sleep disturbances in 5–8-year-old children. *Acta Paediatrica, 90*(12), 1456–1463.

Smoller, J. W., Yamaki, L. H., Fagerness, J. A., Biederman, J., Racette, S., Laird, N. M., et al. (2005). The corticotrophin releasing hormone gene and behavioral inhibition in children at risk for panic disorder. *Biological Psychiatry, 57*(12), 1485–1492.

Snyder, R., Turgay, A., Aman, M., Binder, C., Fisman, S., & Carroll, A. (2002). Effects of risperidone on conduct and disruptive behavior disorders in children with subaverage IQs. *Journal of the American Academy of Child and Adolescent Psychiatry, 41*, 1026–1036.

Sowell, E. R., Levitt, J., Thompson, P. M., Holmes, C. J., Blanton, R. E., Kornsand, D. S., et al. (2000). Brain abnormalities in early-onset schizophrenia spectrum disorder observed with statistical parametric mapping of structural magnetic resonance images. *American Journal of Psychiatry, 157*(9), 1475–1484.

Spear, L. P. (2000). The adolescent brain and age-related behavioral manifestations. *Neuroscience and Biobehavioral Reviews, 24*, 417–463.

Spencer, T., Biederman, J., Coffey, B., Geller, D., Crawford, M., Bearman, S. K., et al. (2002). A double-blind comparison of desipramine and placebo in children and adolescents with chronic tic disorder and comorbid attention-deficit/hyperactivity disorder. *Archives of General Psychiatry, 59*(7), 649–656.

Spencer, T. J., Biederman, J., Harding, M., O'Donnell, D., Faraone, S. V., & Wilens, T. E. (1996). Growth deficits in ADHD children revisited: Evidence for disorder associated growth delays? *Journal of the American Academy of Child and Adolescent Psychiatry, 35*(11), 1460–1469.

Spencer, T., Biederman, J., & Wilens, T. (1999). Attention-deficit/hyperactivity disorder and comorbidity. *Pediatric Clinics of North America, 46*(5), 915–927.

Spencer, T., Biederman, J., & Wilens, T. (2000). Pharmacotherapy of attention deficit hyperactivity disorder. *Child and Adolescent Psychiatric Clinics of North America, 9*(1), 77–97.

Spivak, H., & Prothrow-Stith, D. (2001). The need to address bullying: An important component of violence prevention. *Journal of the American Medical Association, 285*, 2131–2132.

Stahl, S. M. (2002). *Essential psychopharmacology of antipsychotics and mood stabilizers*. Cambridge, UK: Cambridge University Press.

Stanley, B., Brodsky, B., Nelson, J. D., & Dulit, R. (2007). Brief dialectical behavior therapy (DBT-B) for suicidal behavior and non-suicidal self injury. *Archives of Suicide Research, 11*(4), 337–341.

State, M. W., King, B. H., & Dykens, E. (1997). Mental retardation: A review of the past 10 years. Part II. *Journal of the American Academy of Child and Adolescent Psychiatry, 36*(12), 1664–1671.

Statistics Canada. (2006). *Persons in low income before tax*. Retrieved from www.statcan.ca/english/pgdb/famil41a.htm

Staton, D., Volness, L. J., & Beatty, W. W. (2008). Diagnosis and classification of pediatric bipolar disorder. *Journal of Affective Disorders, 105*(1–3), 205–212.

Steffenburg, S., Gillberg, C., Hellgren, L., Andersson, L., Gillberg, I. C., Jakobsson, G., et al. (1989). A twin study of autism in Denmark, Finland, Iceland, Norway and Sweden. *Journal of Child Psychology and Psychiatry, 30*(3), 405–416.

Stehr-Green, P., Tull, P., Stellfeld, M., Mortenson, P. B., & Simpson, D. (2003). Autism and thimerosal-containing vaccines: Lack of consistent evidence for an association. *American Journal of Preventive Medicine, 25*(2), 101–106.

Stein, D., & Laakso, W. (1988). Bulimia: A historical perspective. *International Journal of Eating Disorders, 7*(2), 201–210.

Stein, M. A., Mendelson, J., Obermeyer, W. H., Amronin, J., & Benca, R. (2001). Sleep and behavior problems in school-aged children. *Pediatrics, 107*(4), E60.

Steiner, H., Petersen, M. L., Saxena, K., Ford, S., & Matthews, Z. (2003). Divalproex sodium for the treatment of conduct disorder: A randomized controlled clinical trial. *Journal of Clinical Psychiatry, 64*, 1183–1191.

Steiner, H., Remsing, L., & the AACAP Work Group on Quality Issues. (2007). Practice parameter for the assessment and treatment of children and adolescents with oppositional defiant disorder. *Journal of the American Academy of Child and Adolescent Psychiatry, 46*(1), 126–141.

Steiner-Adair, C. (1986). The body politic: Normal female adolescent development and the development of eating disorders. *Journal of the American Academy of Psychoanalysis and Dynamic Psychiatry, 14*(1), 95–114.

Steingard, R. J., Zimnitzky, B., DeMaso, D. R., Bauman, M. L., & Bucci, J. P. (1997). Sertraline treatment of transition-associated anxiety and agitation in children with autistic disorder. *Journal of Child and Adolescent Psychopharmacology, 7*(1), 9–15.

Steinhausen, H. C. (2009). Outcome of eating disorders. *Child and Adolescent Psychiatry Clinics of North America, 18*(1), 225–242.

Stephens, C. E. (2008). Spontaneous imitation by children with autism during a repetitive musical play routine. *Autism, 12*(6), 645–671.

Stephens, R. J., Bassel, C., & Sandor, P. (2004). Olanzapine in the treatment of aggression and tics in children with Tourette's syndrome: A pilot study. *Journal of Child and Adolescent Psychopharmacology, 14*(2), 255–266.

Sterling, L., Dawson, G., Webb, S., Murias, M., Munson, J., Panagiotides, H., et al. (2008). The role of face familiarity in eye tracking of faces by individuals with autism spectrum disorders. *Journal of Autism and Developmental Disorders, 38*(9), 1666–1675.

Stewart, S. E., Geller, D. A., Jenike, M., Pauls, D., Shaw, D., Mullin, B., et al. (2004). Long-term outcome of pediatric obsessive-compulsive disorder: A meta-analysis and qualitative review of the literature. *Acta Psychiatrica Scandinavica, 110*(1), 4–13.

Stouthamer-Loeber, M., Loeber, R., Wei, E., Farrington, D. P., & Wikström, P. O. H. (2002). Risk and promotive effects in the explanation of persistent serious delinquency in boys. *Journal of Consulting and Clinical Psychology, 70*, 111–123.

Stowell, R. J. A., & Estroff, T. W. (1992). Psychiatric disorders in substance-abusing adolescent inpatients: A pilot study. *Journal of the American Academy of Child and Adolescent Psychiatry, 31*, 1036–1040.

Stringaris, A., & Goodman, R. (2008). Mood lability and psychopathology in youth. *Psychological Medicine, 11*, 1–9.

Strober, M., Birmaher, B., Ryan, N., Axelson, D., Valeri, S., Leonard, H., et al. (2006). Pediatric bipolar disease: Current and future perspectives for study of its long-term course and treatment. *Bipolar Disorders, 8*(4), 311–321.

Strober, M., Freeman, R., Lampert, C., Diamond, J., & Kaye, W. (2000). Controlled family study of anorexia nervosa and bulimia nervosa: Evidence of shared liability and transmission of partial syndromes. *American Journal of Psychiatry, 157*(3), 393–401.

Strober, M., Freeman, R., Rigali, J., Schmidt, S., & Diamond, R. (1992). The pharmacotherapy of depressive illness in adolescence: Effects of lithium augmentation in nonresponders to imipramine. *Journal of the American Academy of Child and Adolescent Psychiatry, 31*(1), 16–20.

Strober, M., Morrell, W., Lampert, C., & Burroughs, J. (1990). Relapse following discontinuation of lithium maintenance therapy in adolescents with bipolar I illness: A naturalistic study. *American Journal of Psychiatry, 147*(4), 457–461.

Strober, M., Schmidt-Lackner, S., Freeman, R., Bower, S., Lampert, C., & DeAntonio, M. (1995). Recovery and relapse in adolescents with bipolar affective illness: A five-year naturalistic, prospective follow-up. *Journal of the American Academy of Child and Adolescent Psychiatry, 34*(6), 724–731.

Strober, M., & Schneider, M. (2005). *Just a little too thin: How to pull your child back from the brink of an eating disorder.* Cambridge, MA: Da Capo Press.

Stromme, P., & Diseth, T. H. (2000). Prevalence of psychiatric diagnoses in children with mental retardation: Data from a population-based study. *Developmental Medicine and Child Neurology, 42*, 266–270.

Substance Abuse and Mental Health Services Administration (SAMHSA). (2001). *The DASIS report—coerced treatment among youths: 1993 to 1998.* Washington, DC: Author.

Substance Abuse and Mental Health Services Administration (SAMHSA). (2003). *The National Household Survey on Drug Abuse Report.* Rockville, MD: Author.

Substance Abuse and Mental Health Services Administration (SAMHSA). (2007). *2006 national survey on drug use and health.* Rockville, MD: Author.

Substance Abuse and Mental Health Services Administration (SAMHSA). (2008a). *The NSDUH report: Misuse of over-the-counter cough and old medications among persons aged 12 to 25.* Retrieved from http://www.oas.samhsa.gov/2k8/cough/cough.cfm

Substance Abuse and Mental Health Services Administration (SAMHSA). (2008b). *Results from the 2007 national survey on drug use and health: National findings.* Rockville, MD: Author.

Sumi, S., Taniai, H., Miyachi, T., & Tanemura, M. (2006). Sibling risk of pervasive developmental disorder estimated by means of an epidemiologic survey in Nagoya, Japan. *Journal of Human Genetics, 51*(6), 518–522.

Sumner, C. R., Schuh, K. J., Sutton, V. K., Lipetz, R., & Kelsey, D. K. (2006). Placebo controlled study of the effects of atomoxetine on bladder control in children with nocturnal enuresis. *Journal of Child and Adolescent Psychopharmacology, 16*(6), 699–711.

Sung, V., Hiscock, H., Sciberras, E., & Efron, D. (2008). Sleep problems in children with attention-deficit/hyperactivity disorder: Prevalence and the effect on the child and family. *Archives of Pediatrics and Adolescent Medicine, 162*(4), 336–342.

Susser, E. S., & Lin, S. P. (1992). Schizophrenia after prenatal exposure to the Dutch hunger winter of 1944–1945. *Archives of General Psychiatry, 49*(12), 983–988.

Swain, J. E., Scahill, L., Lombroso, P. J., King, R. A., & Leckman, J. F. (2007). Tourette syndrome and tic disorders: A decade of progress. *Journal of the American Academy of Child and Adolescent Psychiatry, 46*(8), 947–968.

Swanson, J., Gupta, S., Lam, A., Shoulson, I., Lerner, M., Modi, N., et al. (2003). Development of a new once-a-day formulation of methylphenidate for the treatment of attention-deficit/hyperactivity disorder: Proof-of-concept and proof-of-product studies. *Archives of General Psychiatry, 60*(2), 204–211.

Swanson, J. M., Lerner, M., & Williams, L. (1995). More frequent diagnosis of attention deficit-hyperactivity disorder. *New England Journal of Medicine, 333*(14), 944.

Swanson, J. M., Sunohara, G. A., Kennedy, J. L., Regino, R., Fineberg, E., Wigal, T., et al. (1998). Association of the dopamine receptor D4 (DRD4) gene with a refined phenotype of attention deficit hyperactivity disorder (ADHD): A family-based approach. *Molecular Psychiatry, 3*(1), 38–41.

Swedo, S. E., Garvey, M., Snider, L., Hamilton, C., & Leonard, H. L. (2001). The PANDAS subgroup: Recognition and treatment. *CNS Spectrums, 6*(5), 419–422, 425–426.

Swedo, S. E., Leonard, H. L., Garvey, M., Mittleman, B., Allen, A. J., Perlmutter, S., et al. (1998). Pediatric autoimmune neuropsychiatric disorders associated with streptococcal infections: Clinical description of the first 50 cases. *American Journal of Psychiatry, 155*(2), 264–271.

Szatmari, P., Brysin, S. E., Streiner, D. L., Wilson, F., Archer, L., & Ryerse, C. (2000). Two-year outcome of preschool children with autism or Asperger's syndrome. *American Journal of Psychiatry, 157*(12), 1980–1987.

Tani, P., Lindberg, N., Nieminen-von Wendt, T., von Wendt, L., Alanko, L., Appelberg, B., et al. (2003). Insomnia is a frequent finding in adults with Asperger syndrome. *BMC Psychiatry, 3*, 12.

Tannock, R., Schachar, R., & Logan, G. (1995). Methylphenidate and cognitive flexibility: Dissociated dose effects in hyperactive children. *Journal of Abnormal Child Psychology, 23*(2), 235–266.

Target, M., & Fonagy, P. (1994). Efficacy of psychoanalysis for children with emotional disorders. *Journal of the American Academy of Child and Adolescent Psychiatry, 33*(3), 361–371.

Tauber, E. S., & Glovinsky, P. B. (1987). New views on the function of REM sleep in the evolution of mammals. *Contemporary Psychoanalysis, 23*, 438–445.

Temple, E. (2002). Brain mechanisms in normal and dyslexic readers. *Current Opinion in Neurobiology, 12*(2), 178–183.

Temple, E., Deutsch, G. K., Poldrack, R. A., Miller, S. L., Tallal, P., Merzenich, et al. (2003). Neural deficits in children with dyslexia ameliorated by behavioral remediation: Evidence from functional MRI. *Source Proceedings of the National Academy of Sciences of the United States of America, 100*(5), 2860–2865.

Teri, L. (1982). The use of the beck depression inventory with adolescents. *Journal of Abnormal Child Psychology, 10*(2), 277–284.

Thiedke, C. C. (2003). Nocturnal enuresis. *American Family Physician, 67*(7), 1499–1506.

Thomas, A., Chess, S., & Birch, H. G. (1968). *Temperament and behavior disorders in children.* New York: New York University Press.

Thomas, C. R., & Holzer, C. E. (2006). The continuing shortage of child and adolescent psychiatrists. *Journal of the American Academy of Child and Adolescent Psychiatry, 45*(9), 1023–1031.

Thompson, J. W., & Blaine, J. D. (1987). Use of ECT in the United States in 1975 and 1980. *American Journal of Psychiatry, 144*(5), 557–562.

Thompson, K. M., & Yokota, F. (2001). Depiction of alcohol, tobacco, and other substances in G-rated animated feature films. *Pediatrics, 107*(6), 1369–1374.

Thompson, P. M., Vidal, C., Giedd, J. N., Gochman, P., Blumenthal, J., Nicolson, R., et al. (2001). Mapping adolescent brain change reveals dynamic wave of accelerated gray matter loss in very early-onset schizophrenia. *Proceedings of the National Academy of Science, 98*(20), 11650–11655.

Thunström, M. (2002). Severe sleep problems in infancy associated with subsequent development of attention-deficit/hyperactivity disorder at 5.5 years of age. *Acta Paediatrica, 91*(5), 584–592.

Tiegerman, E., & Primavera, L. (1981). Object manipulation: An interactional strategy with autistic children. *Journal of Autism and Developmental Disorders, 11*(4), 427–438.

Tohen, M., Kryzhanovskaya, L., Carlson, G., Delbello, M., Wozniak, J., Kowatch, R., et al. (2007). Olanzapine versus placebo in the treatment of adolescents with bipolar mania. *American Journal of Psychiatry, 164*(10), 1547–1556.

Tolstoy, L. (2004). *Anna Karenina.* London: Penguin Classics.

Tomasi, P. A., Siracusano, S., Monni, A. M., Mela, G., & Delitala, G. (2001). Decreased nocturnal urinary antidiuretic hormone excretion in enuresis is increased by imipramine. *British Journal of Urology, 88*(9), 932–937.

Tourette's Syndrome Study Group. (2002). Treatment of ADHD in children with tics: A randomized controlled trial. *Neurology, 58*(4), 527–536.

Towbin, K. E., & Riddle, M. A. (1993). Attention deficit hyperactivity disorder. In R. Hurla (Ed.). *Handbook of Tourette's syndrome and related tic and behavioral disorders.* New York: Marcel Dekker.

Towbin, K. E., & Riddle, M. A. (1996). Obsessive-compulsive disorder. In M. Lewis (Ed.), *Child and adolescent psychiatry: A comprehensive textbook* (2nd ed., pp. 684–693). Baltimore: Williams & Wilkins.

Tremblay, R., Pihl, R. O., Vitaro, F., & Dobkin, P. L. (1994). Predicting early onset of male antisocial behavior from preschool behavior. *Archives of General Psychiatry, 51,* 732–739.

Trimble, M. R. (1996). *Biological psychiatry* (2nd ed.). Hoboken, NJ: Wiley.

Trócme, N., & Wolfe, D. A. (2001). Child maltreatment in Canada: Selected results from the Canadian Incidence Study of Reported Child Abuse and Neglect. Ottowa, ON: Minister of Public Works and Government Services, Canada. Retrieved from www.hc-sc.gc.ca/ppub-dgspsp/publicat/cissr-ecirc/index.html

Tyrer, S. P., Walsh, A., Edwards, D. E., Berney, T. P., & Stephens, D. A. (1984). Factors associated with good response to lithium in aggressive mentally handicapped students. *Progress in Neuro-Psychopharmacology and Biological Psychiatry, 8,* 751–755.

U.S. Bureau of the Census. (2005). *Small area income and poverty estimates program.* Retrieved from www.census.gov/hhes/www/saipe.html

U.S. Department of Health and Human Services. (1999). *Mental health: A report of the Surgeon General.* Rockville, MD: U.S. Department of Health and Human Services, Substance Abuse and Mental Health Services Administration, Center for Mental Health Services, National Institutes of Health, National Institute of Mental Health.

U.S. Department of Health and Human Services. (2003). *Child maltreatment 2001.* Washington, DC: U.S. Government Printing Office.

U.S. Drug Enforcement Agency. (2000). Retrieved January 26, 2009, from http://www.usdoj.gov/dea/pubs/cngrtest/ct051600.htm

U.S. Food and Drug Administration. (2004). *Relationship between psychotropic drugs and pediatric suicidality: Review and evaluation of clinical data.* Retrieved February 1, 2009, from http://www.fda.gov/ohrms/dockets/ac/04/briefing/2004-4065b1-10-TAB08-Hammads-Review.pdf

U.S. Surgeon General. (2005). *Surgeon general's advisory on alcohol use in pregnancy.* Retrieved November 17, 2008, from http://www.cdc.gov/ncbddd/fas/documents/Released%20Advisory.pdf

University of Michigan. (2008). *Monitoring the future.* Retrieved January 31, 2009, from http://www.monitoringthefuture.org/data/08data.html#2008data-drugs

Valicenti-McDermott, M. R., & Demb, H. (2006). Clinical effects and adverse reactions of off-label use of aripiprazole in children and adolescents with developmental disabilities. *Journal of Child and Adolescent Psychopharmacology, 16*(5), 549–560.

Van Ameringen, M., Mancini, C., & Oakman, J. M. (1998). The relationship of behavioral inhibition and shyness to anxiety disorder. *Journal of Nervous and Mental Disease, 186*(7), 425–431.

Van den Eynde, F., Naudts, K. H., De Saedeleer, S., van Heeringen, C., & Audenaert, K. (2005). Olanzapine in Gilles de la Tourette syndrome: Beyond tics. *Acta Neurologica Belgica, 105*(4), 206–211.

Van Kampen, M., Bogaert, G., Feys, H., Baert, L., De Raeymaeker, I., & De Weerdt, W. (2002). High initial efficacy of full-spectrum therapy for nocturnal enuresis in children and adolescents. *British Journal of Urology,* *90*(1), 84–87.

Van Riper, C. (1973). *The treatment of stuttering.* Englewood Cliffs, NJ: Prentice Hall.

Varanka, T. M., Weller, R. A., Weller, E. B., & Fristad, M. A. (1988). Lithium treatment of manic episodes with psychotic features in prepubertal children. *American Journal of Psychiatry, 145*(12), 1557–1559.

Varley, C. K. (2001). Sudden death related to selected tricyclic antidepressants in children: Epidemiology, mechanisms and clinical implications. *Pediatric Drugs, 3*(8), 613–627.

Verhoeven, W. M., Veendrik-Meekes, M. J., Jacobs, G. A., van den Berg, Y. W. M. M., & Tuinier, S. (2001). Citalopram in mentally retarded patients with depression: A long-term clinical investigation. *European Psychiatry, 16*, 104–108.

Vetter, V. L., Elia, J., Erickson, C., Berger, S., Blum, N., Uzark, K., et al. (2008). Cardiovascular monitoring of children and adolescents with heart disease receiving medications for attention deficit/hyperactivity disorder. *Circulation, 117*, 2407–2423.

Volkmar, F. R. (1996a). Childhood and adolescent psychosis: A review of the past 10 years. *Journal of the American Academy of Child and Adolescent Psychiatry, 35*(7), 843–851.

Volkmar, F. R. (1996b). Childhood schizophrenia. In M. Lewis (Ed.), *Child and adolescent psychiatry: A comprehensive textbook* (2nd ed., pp. 629–635). Baltimore: Williams & Wilkins.

Volkmar, F. R., & Klin, A. (2000). Diagnostic issues. In A. Klin & F. R. Volkmar (Eds.), *Asperger sydrome.* New York: Guilford Press.

Volkow, N. D. (2004). Imaging the addicted brain: From molecules to behavior. *Journal of Nuclear Medicine, 45*(11), 13N–16N, 19N–20N.

von Knorring, A. L., Olsson, G. I., Thomsen, P. H., Lemming, O. M., & Hultén, A. (2006). A randomized, double-blind, placebo-controlled study of citalopram in adolescents with major depressive disorder. *Journal of Clinical Psychopharmacology, 26*(3), 311–315.

Wachsmuth, D., & Dolce, G. (1980). Visual and computerized analysis of EEG during transcendental meditation and sleep. *EEG EMG Zeitschrift fur Elektroenzephalograhie, Elektromyographir und Verwandte Gebiete, 11*(4), 183–188.

Wagner, K. D., Ambrosini, P., Rynn, M., Wohlberg, C., Yang, R., Greenbaum, M. S., et al. (2003). Efficacy of sertraline in the treatment of children and adolescents with major depressive disorder: Two randomized controlled trials. *Journal of the American Medical Association, 290*(8), 1033–1041.

Wagner, K. D., Berard, R., Stein, M. B., Wetherhold, E., Carpenter, D. J., Perera, P., et al. (2004). A multicenter, randomized, double-blind, placebo-controlled trial of paroxetine in children and adolescents with social anxiety disorder. *Archives of General Psychiatry, 61*, 1153–1162.

Wagner, K. D., Jonas, J., Findling, R. L., Ventura, D., & Saikali, K. (2006). A double blind, randomized, placebo-controlled trial of escitalopram in the treatment of pediatric depression. *Journal of the American Academy of Child and Adolescent Psychiatry, 45*(3), 280–288.

Wagner, K. D., Kowatch, R. A., Emslie, G. J., Findling, R. L., Wilens, T. E., McCague, K., et al. (2006). A double-blind, randomized, placebo-controlled trial of oxcarbazepine in the treatment of bipolar disorder in children and adolescents. *American Journal of Psychiatry, 163*(7), 1179–1186.

Wagner, K. D., Nyilas, M., & Johnson, B. (2007). *Long-term efficacy of aripiprazole in children (10–17 years old) with mania.* Poster presented at the annual meeting of the American Academy of Child and Adolescent Psychiatry, Boston, Massachusetts.

Wagner, K. D., Robb, A. S., Findling, R. L., Jin, J., Gutierrez, M. M., & Heydorn, W. E. (2004). A randomized, placebo-controlled trial of citalopram for the treatment of major depression in children and adolescents. *American Journal of Psychiatry, 161*(6), 1079–1083.

Wagner, K. D., Weller, E. B., Carlson, G. A., Sachs, G., Biederman, J., Frazier, J. A., et al. (2002). An open-label trial of divalproex in children and adolescents with bipolar disorder. *Journal of the American Academy of Child and Adolescent Psychiatry, 41*(10), 1224–1230.

Wakefield, A., Murch, S., Anthony, A., Linnell, J., Casson, D., Malik, M., et al. (1998). Ileal-lymphoid-nodular hyperplasia, non-specific colitis, and pervasive developmental disorder in children. *Lancet, 351*(9103), 637–641.

Walkup, J. T., Albano, A. M., Piacentini, J., Birmaher, B., Compton, S. N., Sherrill, J. T., et al. (2008). Cognitive behavioral therapy, sertraline, or a combination in childhood anxiety. *New England Journal of Medicine, 359,* 2753–2766.

Wals, M., van Os, J., Reichart, C. G., Hillegers, M. H., Ormel, J., Verhulst, F. C., et al. (2004). Multiple dimensions of familial psychopathology affect risk of mood disorder in children of bipolar parents. *American Journal of Medical Genetics Part B: Neuropsychiatric Genetics, 127B*(1), 35–41.

Walsh, B. T., Kaplan, A. S., Attia, E., Olmsted, M., Parides, M., Carter, J. C., et al. (2006). Fluoxetine after weight restoration in anorexia nervosa: A randomized controlled trial. *Journal of the American Medical Association, 295*(22), 2605–2612.

Walter, G., Lyndon, B., & Kubb, R. (1998). Lithium augmentation of venlafaxine in adolescent major depression. *Australian and New Zealand Journal of Psychiatry, 32*(3), 457–459.

Walters, E. E., & Kendler, K. S. (1995). Anorexia nervosa and anorexic-like syndromes in a population-based female twin sample. *American Journal of Psychiatry, 152*(1), 64–71.

Webster-Stratton, C., & Reid, M. J. (2003). The incredible years parents, teachers, and children training series: A multifaceted treatment approach for young children with conduct problems. In A. E. Kazdin & J. R. Weisz (Eds.), *Evidence-based psychotherapies for children and adolescents* (pp. 224–249). New York: Guilford Press.

Weinberg, N. Z., Rahdert, E., Colliver, J. D., & Glantz, M. D. (1998). Adolescent substance abuse: A review of the past 10 years. *Journal of the American Academy of Child and Adolescent Psychiatry, 37*(3), 252–261.

Weisbrod, B. (1983). A guide to benefit-cost analysis, as seen through a controlled experiment in treating the mentally ill. *Journal of Health Politics, Policy and Law, 4*, 808–845.

Weiss, M. D., Wasdell, M. B., Bomben, M. M., Rea, K. J., & Freeman, R. D. (2006). Sleep hygiene and melatonin treatment for children and adolescents with ADHD and initial insomnia. *Journal of the American Academy of Child and Adolescent Psychiatry, 45*(5), 512–519.

Weissman, M. M., Pilowsky, D. J., Wickramaratne, P. J., Talati, A., Wisniewski, S. R., Fava, M., et al. (2006). Remissions in maternal depression and child psychopathology: A STAR*D-child report. *Journal of the American Medical Association, 295*(12), 1389–1398.

Weissman, M. M., Warner, V., Wickramaratne, P., Moreau, D., & Olfson, M. (1997). Offspring of depressed parents. 10 years later. *Archives of General Psychiatry, 54*(10), 932–940.

Weissman, M. M., Warner, V., Wickramaratne, P., & Prusoff, B. A. (1988). Early-onset major depression in parents and their children. *Journal of Affective Disorders, 15*(3), 269–277.

Weissman, M. M., Wickramaratne, P., Nomura, Y., Warner, V., Pilowsky, D., & Verdeli, H. (2006b). Offspring of depressed parents: 20 years later. *American Journal of Psychiatry, 163*(6), 1001–1008.

Werner, E. E. (1995). Resilience in development. *Current Directions in Psychological Science, 4*, 81–85.

West, S. A., McElroy, S. L., Strakowski, S. M., Keck, P. E., & McConville, B. J. (1995). Attention deficit hyperactivity disorder in adolescent mania. *American Journal of Psychiatry, 152*(2), 271–273.

Whitaker, A., Johnson, J., Shaffer, D., Rapoport, J. L., Kalikow, K., Walsh, B. T., et al. (1990). Uncommon troubles in young people: Prevalence estimates of selected psychiatric disorders in a nonreferred adolescent population. *Archives of General Psychiatry, 47*(5), 487–496.

Wickramaratne, P. J., Greenwald, S., & Weissman, M. M. (2000). Psychiatric disorders in the relatives of probands with prepubertal-onset or adolescent-onset major depression. *Journal of the American Academy of Child and Adolescent Psychiatry, 39*(11), 1396–1405.

Wiggins, L. D., Baio, J., & Rice, C. (2006). Examination of the time between first evaluation and first autism spectrum diagnosis in a population-based sample. *Journal of Developmental and Behavioral Pediatrics, 27*(2), S79–S87.

Wiggs, L., & Stores, G. (1996). Severe sleep disturbance and daytime challenging behaviour in children with severe learning disabilities. *Journal of Intellectual Disability Research, 40*(6), 518–528.

Wiggs, L., & Stores, G. (1998). Behavioural treatment for sleep problems in children with severe learning disabilities and challenging daytime behaviour: Effect on sleep patterns of mother and child. *Journal of Sleep Research, 7*(2), 119–126.

Wilens, T. E., & Spencer, T. J. (1998). Pharmacology of amphetamines. In R. E. Tarter, R. T. Ammerman, & P. J. Ott (Eds.), *Handbook of substance abuse: Neurobehavioral pharmacology* (pp. 501–513). New York: Plenum Press.

Wilens, T. E., Adamson, J., Monuteaux, M. C., Faraone, S. V., Schillinger, M., Westerberg, D., et al. (2008). Effect of prior stimulant treatment for attention-deficit/hyperactivity disorder on subsequent risk for cigarette smoking and alcohol and drug use disorders in adolescents. *Archives of Pediatrics and Adolescent Medicine, 162*(10), 916–921.

Wilens, T. E., Spencer, T. J., Biederman, J., & Schleifer, D. (1997). Case study: Nefazodone for juvenile mood disorders. *Journal of the American Academy of Child and Adolescent Psychiatry, 36*(4), 481–485.

Williams, R. J., & Chang, S. Y. (2000). Comprehensive and comparative review of adolescent substance abuse treatment outcome. *Clinical Psychology: Science and Practice, 7*(2), 138–166.

Winters, K. C., Stinchfield, R. D., Opland, E., Weller, C., & Latimer, W. W. (2000). The effectiveness of the Minnesota Model approach in the treatment of adolescent drug abusers. *Addiction, 95*(4), 601–612.

Trocmé, N. & Wolfe, D. A. (2001). *Child maltreatment in Canada: Selected results from the Canadian incidence study of reported child abuse and neglect*. Ottawa, Ontario, Canada: Minister of Public Works and Government Services Canada. Retrieved from www.hc-sc.gc.ca/pphb-dgspsp/publicat/cissr-ecirc/index.html

World Health Organization. (1993). *The ICD-10 classification of mental and behavioral disorders: Diagnostic criteria for research*. Geneva, Switzerland: Author.

Yakovlev, P. I., & Lecours, A. R. (1967). The myelogenetic cycles of regional maturation of the brain. In A. Minkowski (Ed.), *Regional development of the brain in early life* (pp. 3–70). Oxford: Blackwell.

Yeganeh, R., Beidel, D. C., Turner, S. M., Pina, A. A., & Silverman, W. K. (2003). Clinical distinctions between selective mutism and social phobia: An investigation of childhood psychopathology. *Journal of the American Academy of Child and Adolescent Psychiatry, 42*(9), 1069–1075.

Yeh, C., Wu, C., Tsung, H., Chen, C., Shyu, J., & Leckman, J. F. (2006). Antineural antibody in patients with Tourette's syndrome and their family members. *Journal of Biomedical Science, 13*, 101–112.

Yerkes, R. M., & Dodson, J. D. (1908). The relation of strength of stimulus to rapidity of habit-formation. *Journal of Comparative Neurology and Psychology, 18*, 459–482.

Yeung, C. K. (2003). Nocturnal enuresis (bedwetting). *Current Opinion in Urology, 13*(4), 337–343.

Zahn, T. P., Jacobsen, L. K., Gordon, C. T., McKenna, K., Frazier, J. A., & Rapoport, J. L. (1997). Autonomic nervous system markers of psychopathology in childhood onset schizophrenia. *Archives of General Psychiatry, 54*(10), 904–912.

Zarcone, J. R., Hellings, J. A., Crandall, K., Reese, R. M., Marguis, J., Fleming, K., et al. (2001). Effects of risperidone on aberrant behavior of persons with developmental disabilities: A double-blind crossover study using multiple measures. *American Journal of Mental Retardation, 106*, 525–538.

Zareba, W., & Lin, D. A. (2003). Antipsychotic drugs and QT interval prolongation. *Psychiatric Quarterly, 74*(3), 291–306.

Zemrak, W. R., & Kenna, G. A. (2008). Association of antipsychotic and antidepressant drugs with Q-T interval prolongation. *American Journal of Health-System Pharmacy, 65*(11), 1029–1038.

Zohar, A. H., Apter, A., King, R. A., Pauls, D. L., Leckman, J. F., & Cohen, D. J. (1999). Epidemiological studies. In J. F. Leckman and D. J. Cohen (Eds.), *Tourette's syndrome—tics, obsessions, compulsions: Developmental psychopathology and clinical care* (pp. 177–192). New York: Wiley.

Zucker, R. A. (1996). Longitudinal research on alcohol problems: The flow of risk, problems, and disorder over time. *Alcohol: Clinical and Experimental Research, 20*(8), 93A–95A.

Index